Emerging Automation Techniques for the Future Internet

Mohamed Boucadair
Orange, France

Christian Jacquenet
Orange, France

A volume in the Advances in Wireless
Technologies and Telecommunication (AWTT)
Book Series

Published in the United States of America by
    IGI Global
    Information Science Reference (an imprint of IGI Global)
    701 E. Chocolate Avenue
    Hershey PA, USA 17033
    Tel: 717-533-8845
    Fax: 717-533-8661
    E-mail: cust@igi-global.com
    Web site: http://www.igi-global.com

Library of Congress Cataloging-in-Publication Data

Names: Boucadair, Mohamed, editor. | Jacquenet, Christian, editor.
Title: Emerging automation techniques for the future internet / Mohamed
    Boucadair and Christian Jacquenet, editors.
Description: Hershey, PA : Information Science Reference, an imprint of IGI
    Global, [2019] | Includes bibliographical references and index.
Identifiers: LCCN 2018017252| ISBN 9781522571469 (hardcover) | ISBN
    9781522571476 (ebook)
Subjects: LCSH: Internet. | Internetworking (Telecommunication) | Computer
    networks--Technological innovations.
Classification: LCC TK5105.875.I57 E466 2019 | DDC 629.8/954678--dc23 LC record available at https://lccn.loc.
gov/2018017252

This book is published in the IGI Global book series Advances in Wireless Technologies and Telecommunication (AWTT) (ISSN: 2327-3305; eISSN: 2327-3313)

British Cataloguing in Publication Data
A Cataloguing in Publication record for this book is available from the British Library.

For electronic access to this publication, please contact: eresources@igi-global.com.

Advances in Wireless Technologies and Telecommunication (AWTT) Book Series

Xiaoge Xu
Xiamen University Malaysia, Malaysia

ISSN:2327-3305
EISSN:2327-3313

MISSION

The wireless computing industry is constantly evolving, redesigning the ways in which individuals share information. Wireless technology and telecommunication remain one of the most important technologies in business organizations. The utilization of these technologies has enhanced business efficiency by enabling dynamic resources in all aspects of society.

The **Advances in Wireless Technologies and Telecommunication Book Series** aims to provide researchers and academic communities with quality research on the concepts and developments in the wireless technology fields. Developers, engineers, students, research strategists, and IT managers will find this series useful to gain insight into next generation wireless technologies and telecommunication.

COVERAGE

- Mobile Web Services
- Network Management
- Radio Communication
- Broadcasting
- Global Telecommunications
- Cellular Networks
- Digital Communication
- Mobile Technology
- Mobile Communications
- Wireless Technologies

IGI Global is currently accepting manuscripts for publication within this series. To submit a proposal for a volume in this series, please contact our Acquisition Editors at Acquisitions@igi-global.com or visit: http://www.igi-global.com/publish/.

The Advances in Wireless Technologies and Telecommunication (AWTT) Book Series (ISSN 2327-3305) is published by IGI Global, 701 E. Chocolate Avenue, Hershey, PA 17033-1240, USA, www.igi-global.com. This series is composed of titles available for purchase individually; each title is edited to be contextually exclusive from any other title within the series. For pricing and ordering information please visit http://www.igi-global.com/book-series/advances-wireless-technologies-telecommunication/73684. Postmaster: Send all address changes to above address. Copyright © 2019 IGI Global. All rights, including translation in other languages reserved by the publisher. No part of this series may be reproduced or used in any form or by any means – graphics, electronic, or mechanical, including photocopying, recording, taping, or information and retrieval systems – without written permission from the publisher, except for non commercial, educational use, including classroom teaching purposes. The views expressed in this series are those of the authors, but not necessarily of IGI Global.

Titles in this Series

For a list of additional titles in this series, please visit: www.igi-global.com/book-series

Mobile Applications and Solutions for Social Inclusion
Sara Paiva (Instituto Politécnico de Viana do Castelo, Portugal)
Information Science Reference • copyright 2018 • 354pp • H/C (ISBN: 9781522552703) • US $195.00 (our price)

Optimizing E-Participation Initiatives Through Social Media
Laura Alcaide-Muñoz (University of Granada, Spain) and Francisco José Alcaraz-Quiles (University of Granada, Spain)
Information Science Reference • copyright 2018 • 307pp • H/C (ISBN: 9781522553267) • US $195.00 (our price)

Centrality Metrics for Complex Network Analysis Emerging Research and Opportunities
Natarajan Meghanathan (Jackson State University, USA)
Information Science Reference • copyright 2018 • 183pp • H/C (ISBN: 9781522538028) • US $175.00 (our price)

Mobile Technologies and Socio-Economic Development in Emerging Nations
Fredrick Japhet Mtenzi (Dublin Institute of Technology, Ireland & Aga Khan University, Tanzania) George S. Oreku (Open University of Tanzania (OUT), Tanzania) Dennis M. Lupiana (Institute of Finance Management, Tanzania) and Jim James Yonazi (Tanzania Standard (Newspapers) Limited, Tanzania)
Information Science Reference • copyright 2018 • 366pp • H/C (ISBN: 9781522540298) • US $195.00 (our price)

Affordability Issues Surrounding the Use of ICT for Development and Poverty Reduction
Sam Takavarasha Jr. (University of Fort Hare, South Africa & University of Zimbabwe, Zimbabwe) and Carl Adams (University of Portsmouth, UK)
Information Science Reference • copyright 2018 • 319pp • H/C (ISBN: 9781522531791) • US $195.00 (our price)

Handbook of Research on Environmental Policies for Emergency Management and Public Safety
Augustine Nduka Eneanya (University of Lagos, Nigeria)
Engineering Science Reference • copyright 2018 • 393pp • H/C (ISBN: 9781522531944) • US $295.00 (our price)

Positioning and Navigation in Complex Environments
Kegen Yu (Wuhan University, China)
Information Science Reference • copyright 2018 • 577pp • H/C (ISBN: 9781522535287) • US $195.00 (our price)

Examining Cloud Computing Technologies Through the Internet of Things
Pradeep Tomar (Gautam Buddha University, India) and Gurjit Kaur (Gautam Buddha University, India)
Information Science Reference • copyright 2018 • 311pp • H/C (ISBN: 9781522534457) • US $215.00 (our price)

701 East Chocolate Avenue, Hershey, PA 17033, USA
Tel: 717-533-8845 x100 • Fax: 717-533-8661
E-Mail: cust@igi-global.com • www.igi-global.com

Table of Contents

Section 1
The Automation Journey: A Vision, a Framework, and Lots of Cognition

Section 2
Advanced Techniques for the Future Internet

Section 3
Sample Service Automation Deployments

Chapter 12

Detailed Table of Contents

Section 1
The Automation Journey: A Vision, a Framework, and Lots of Cognition

Chapter 1

  Patrick Moore, Itential, LLC, USA

As networks have evolved, there has been an evolution in how they are managed as well. This evolution has seen a move from manual configuration via command line interface (CLI) to script-based automation and eventually to a template-based approach with workflow to coordinate multiple templates and scripts. The next step in this evolution is the introduction of models to provide a more dynamic capability than is in place today. This chapter will discuss three major layers of modelling that should be considered during implementation of this approach: device models focused on the configuration of the hardware itself; service models focused on the customer or network facing services that leverage the hardware level configuration; and operational models focused on people, processes, and tools involved in application of device and service models. This includes the orchestration of activities with other tools, such as operational support systems (OSS) and business support systems (BSS).

Chapter 2

  Kireeti Kompella, Juniper Networks, USA

This chapter presents a new vision of network operations, the self-driving network, that takes automation to the next level. This is not a description of existing work; rather, it is a challenge to dramatically rethink how we manage networks (or rather, how we do not manage networks). It draws upon an analogy with the development of self-driving cars and presents motivations for this effort. It then describes the technologies needed to implement this and an overall architecture of the system. As this endeavor will cause a major shift in network management, the chapter offers an evolutionary path to the end goal. Some of the consequences and human impacts of such a system are touched upon. The chapter concludes with some research topics and a final message. Key takeaways are that machine learning and feedback loops are fundamental to the solution; a key outcome is to build systems that are adaptive and predictive, for the benefit of users.

Chapter 3

Laurent Ciavaglia, Nokia Bell Labs, France
Pierre Peloso, Nokia Bell Labs, France

The increased use of software-driven and virtualization techniques enables more versatile network infrastructures. Realizing the full potential of such large and dynamic systems requires advanced automation and adaptation capabilities. In this chapter, the authors review recent development of so-called self-driving networks combining cognitive techniques and autonomic behaviors. In particular, the authors provide insights on a set of core mechanisms for the operation of self-driving networks: (1) a governance function to help operators deploy, pilot, control, and track run-time behaviors and performance of self-driving functions; (2) a coordination function to ensure stability and performance when several self-driving functions are running together; (3) a knowledge function to share relevant information to empowering their actions; and (4) common workflows, lifecycles, and APIs to enable deployment and interoperability of autonomic functions. The analysis connects with reference work in scientific literature and the most recent developments in standards (e.g., IETF/IRTF and ETSI).

Chapter 4

Toerless Eckert, Huawei, USA

This chapter presents the work of the Autonomic Networking Integrated Model and Approach (ANIMA) working group of the Internet Engineering Task Force (IETF). It was formed to standardize protocols and procedures for an ANIMA autonomic network (AN) and first chartered to define the ANIMA secure autonomic network infrastructure (ANI). This chapter describes the technical history and goals leading to this working group. It then describes how the ANIMA approach provides an evolutionary approach to securing and automating networks and to provide a common infrastructure to evolve into future autonomic networks. Finally, this chapter compares this approach to adjacent standards technologies and discusses interesting next steps.

Chapter 5

Imen Grida Ben Yahia, Orange Labs, France
Jaafar Bendriss, Orange Labs, France
Teodora Sandra Buda, IBM, Ireland
Haytham Assem, IBM, Ireland

Artificial intelligence (AI) and in particular machine learning are seen as cornerstones to automate and rethink network management operations in the context of network softwarization (i.e., SDN, NFV, and Cloud). In this regard, operators and service providers target the creation of service offerings, the customization of network solutions, and the fast adaptation to rapidly changing market demands. This translates into requirements for increased flexibility, modularity, and scalability in network management operations. This chapter presents a detailed specification of a cognitive (AI-based) network management framework applicable for existing and future (software-defined) networks. The framework is built upon the combined state-of-the-art on autonomic, policy-based management and big data. It is exemplified with two detailed use cases: the urban mobility awareness for today's mobile networks and SLA (service level agreement) enforcement in the context of NFV and cloud.

Section 2
Advanced Techniques for the Future Internet

Chapter 6

Luis Contreras, Telefonica, Spain

The advent of 5G introduces the concept of network slicing which is meant to permit network service providers to overcome the great challenge of forthcoming 5G services: how to support and operate different kinds of services with very distinct needs onto the same infrastructure. Deploying altogether on the same network makes it quite difficult to define a common architecture capable of keeping the diverse requirements of all of them. The network slicing concept foresees a number of logically independent slices, each comprising different network nodes and service functions, which are interconnected and are involved in the delivery and the operation of a specific service. By instantiating network slices, the network will be able to provide completely different services in a dynamic way over the same infrastructure. This chapter overviews the challenges raised by the implementation of the network slicing concept and which will be faced by the network operators.

Chapter 7

Nancy Perrot, Orange Labs, France
Amal Benhamiche, Orange Labs, France
Yannick Carlinet, Orange Labs, France
Eric Gourdin, Orange Labs, France

This chapter gives an insight into some challenging combinatorial optimization problems that have to be tackled to deliver efficient and appropriate decision algorithms to manage future networks. The first part of the chapter is dedicated to variants of routing optimization problems in future IP networks, and the second part is dedicated to two optimization problems related to network virtualization and 5G network slicing, the virtual network embedding problem and the service function chaining problem. Each of these optimization problems is described along with the main challenges to overcome, and a recent and extensive related state of the art is given, so as to highlight the most recent and promising approaches to solve them.

Chapter 8

Zoran Despotovic, Huawei, Germany
Xun Xiao, Huawei, Germany
Ramin Khalili, Huawei, Germany
Maja Curic, Huawei, Germany
Artur Hecker, Huawei, Germany

The authors see problems with current network control models. Their control networks (i.e., control channels, necessary for control operation) are not thought of as part of the control model itself. Current network control is not transactional. Network updates are neither atomic nor isolated, and the application is not aware of the details of an update outcome. This chapter presents an alternative design in which the control channel is an integral part of the network control model. Its key part is a robust, in-band resource connectivity layer that interconnects all available network elements, including the controller(s). The control is also transactional. Applications can safely assume that their updates will not clash in the network, as well as that they will always affect the right, intended fraction of the network. Building on these two postulates, the authors see service scheduling as its third essential part of network control. The scheduling takes service requirements into account and assigns the services network resources that will meet their requirements.

Section 3
Sample Service Automation Deployments

Chapter 9

Myo Zarny, vArmour Networks, USA
Meng Xu, vArmour Networks, USA
Yi Sun, vArmour Networks, USA

Network security policy automation enables enterprise security teams to keep pace with increasingly dynamic changes in on-premises and public/hybrid cloud environments. This chapter discusses the most common use cases for policy automation in the enterprise, and new automation methodologies to address them by taking the reader step-by-step through sample use cases. It also looks into how emerging automation solutions are using big data, artificial intelligence, and machine learning technologies to further accelerate network security policy automation and improve application and network security in the process.

Chapter 10

Jun Bi, Tsinghua University, China
Chongfeng Xie, China Telecom, China
Chen Li, China Telecom, China
Qiong Sun, China Telecom, China

The increase in number, diversity, and complexity of modern network devices and services creates unprecedented challenges for the currently prevailing approach of manual IP address management. Manually maintaining IP addresses could always be sub-optimal for IP resource utilization. Besides, it requires heavy human effort from network operators. To achieve high utilization and flexible scheduling of IP network addresses, it is necessary to automate the address scheduling process in the Internet of the future. Based on analysis of the gap between existing address management methods and emerging requirements of the IP network, this chapter illustrates CASM, a new approach for IP address scheduling, including its background, use cases, requirements, general framework, system architecture, interface, and workflow. A prototype system is developed and evaluated based on data from real-world networks and users in two Chinese provinces. Experimental results demonstrate that our system can largely improve the address utilization efficiency and reduce the workload of network resource maintenance.

Service level agreements (SLAs) allow networked services established between providers and their customers to operate according to the conditions defined in the SLA. Measurement mechanisms can be used to support SLA monitoring. However, these mechanisms are expensive in terms of resource consumption. In addition, if the number of SLA violations at any given time is greater than the available measurement sessions, some violations will likely be missed. The current best practice is to observe just a subset of network destinations based upon the expertise of a few human administrators. Such observation mode is error prone, reactive, and scales poorly. Such practice can lead to SLA violations being missed, which hampers the reliability of the SLA monitoring process. In this context, the use of autonomic network features can improve such processes, especially when these features are deployed in a decentralized manner. The use of these autonomic features is described in RFC 8316. The authors expect that such a document can lead to better SLA monitoring tools and methods.

Open source communities have had and continue to have a major influence on the evolution of the Internet. By their nature, such communities involve people with diverse coding cultures and skills. Automation has consequently been of major interest to open source software developers for a long time, and many open source tools have been developed to address code variability and sustainability challenges. This chapter discusses why open source communities must automate and the challenges they will face. Solutions and current examples of automation in open source projects are provided as a guide to what is achievable. OpenShift, OpenStack, and OPNFV communities are used to illustrate different approaches and best practices. Two recently initiated automation initiatives are detailed: "Cross Community Continuous Integration" (XCI) and "Cross Testing" (Xtesting). Finally, some recommendations are provided for new projects as a guide to ease adoption of appropriate tools and methods.

Preface

DO ANDROIDS DREAM OF TRUE AUTOMATION?

The Internet has become the federative network that supports a wide range of service offerings. As these services not only grow in variety but also in complexity, their design, delivery, and operation have become a complex alchemy that often requires various levels of expertise. This situation is further aggravated by the wide variety of (network) protocols and tools, as well as recent Any Time Any-Where Any Device (ATAWAD)-driven convergence trends that are meant to make sure an end-user can access the whole range of services he/she has subscribed to, whatever the access and device technologies, wherever the end-user is connected to the network, and whether this end-user is in motion or not.

Yet, most of these services have been deployed for the past two decades primarily based on often static service production procedures that are more and more exposed to the risk of malformed configuration commands. In addition, most of these services do not assume any specific parameter negotiation between the customer and the provider or between providers besides the typical financial terms. Multi-service, multi-protocol, multi-technology convergent, and dynamically-adaptive networking environments have therefore become one of the major challenges faced by providers.

The diversity and the complexity of these services have been raising technical challenges for many years, from both design and operational perspectives. The emergence of Software-Defined Networking (SDN) techniques such as dynamic resource allocation schemes, as well as Network Function Virtualization (NFV) techniques has often been the opportunity to make debatable promises about their so-called 'flexibility' or their intrinsic ability to facilitate the automation of service delivery procedures.

Reality Is Much Different

Claimed automation is currently mostly restricted to elaboration and the execution of configuration scripts, which reflect the application of decision-making procedures that remain "manually declarative": the data that are used to drive the execution of configuration tasks are statically declared.

In addition, this rather embryonic automation mostly deals with tasks that remain local to a device to the detriment of a global and systemic view of the whole network (including its topology and components) that would be able to guarantee the global consistency of the set of actions taken to deliver a service.

Automation Is Actually Far More Protean

From the dynamic exposure and negotiation of service parameters to feedback mechanisms that are meant to assess that what has been allocated or delivered complies with what has been negotiated, the automation of service delivery procedures relies upon a set of functional blocks (dynamic discovery of network resources (including active service functions) and network topology, service and network capability exposure, dynamic negotiation techniques, dynamic resource allocation and policy enforcement schemes, autonomous back-up mechanisms, etc.) coupled with control loops that interact in a deterministic and sometimes autonomic fashion.

AUTOMATION FRAMEWORK AND CHALLENGES

Automation is primarily meant to significantly improve the time it takes to deliver a service but also to provide guarantees about the expected, possibly negotiated, quality, and robustness of such services.

The completion of the service ordering and the order handling phases provides an input to the (SDN-based) computation logic of the automation system. Thus, the corresponding service will then be structured accordingly, i.e., according to the service-specific policy provisioning information that will be derived from the outcome of the said service ordering.

Typically, this policy-provisioning information will then be translated into network- and device-specific configuration information and actions. Such policy provisioning information can either be service or customer-specific. Upon completion of these configuration tasks, the service is delivered to the customer in a completely deterministic fashion.

Automated Network Production and Operation Must Be Deterministic by Design

In physics, determinism refers to the principle that the values of a system's variables at a given time completely determine the values of the said variables at any later time. Within the context of automated networking, determinism is a key feature: it is indeed expected that the resources that will be allocated and the policies that will be enforced to deliver and operate any given service will be derived from the service parameters captured during the ordering phase and that may have been dynamically negotiated between a customer and a provider.

Indeed, the behavior of systems deployed into operational networks should be predictable and always remain under control. Outputs and states of those systems should be deterministic and, ideally, no unexpected behavior should be experienced.

From a deterministic standpoint, a high degree of automation can be introduced inside a system only if such automation relies upon well-known, carefully-designed procedures. The latter can be decomposed into state machines, policies, etc., which will reflect the different behaviors of the system under various conditions. This means that how the service/network will behave within certain circumstances, with particular entries, is known in advance and the expected result of such behavior is therefore predictable.

Automating Network Production and Operation Starts With Proper Bootstrapping Procedures

The design, delivery, and operation of connectivity services can be facilitated by SDN architectures. These architectures assume a computation logic that makes various decisions such as resource allocation, including policy enforcement, to accommodate service requirements, operator's guidelines, available resources, underlying functional capabilities, and other considerations that include network-originated notifications.

The proper operation of the SDN decision-making process therefore assumes an up-to-date, global view of the resources and their status. Such information needs to be dynamically acquired and maintained over time.

Feeding the SDN computation logic with a comprehensive description of all the resources that may be solicited for service delivery purposes is thus critical. Also, the computation logic needs to dynamically acquire information about the nature of service functions (e.g., a network address translator, an IP route computation engine, a TCP optimizer, etc.), their location and status (e.g., idle, available, faulty, etc.).

An SDN controller therefore needs to dynamically acquire the information that pertains to the network, its topology, its functional capabilities, inputs from other controllers (if present), and the service functions they support, as well as the status of such functions upon bootstrap.

Express Your Intent and Automation Will Do the Rest

The current 5G specification effort conducted by 3GPP adopts the notion of network slicing that is meant to provide multiple logical networks on top of a shared infrastructure. Slices are composed or various resources (network, CPU, storage) and service functions, such as traffic marking and conditioning, firewall, control functions, etc.

The automated production of network slices can start from the expression of intent by a slice tenant, yielding the notion of Intent-Based Networking (IBN). Intent-Based Networking techniques have been introduced a few years ago to facilitate the expression of high-level requirements and constraints that will be eventually derived into a set of low-level instructions. The basic concept of IBN corresponds to the vision of *Don't tell me what to do! Tell me what you want.*

The IBN concept aims at better accommodating the ever-increasing technological heterogeneity and diversity of the functions supported by networking infrastructures. Therefore, the overarching motivation of IBN is to not require users or network administrators to issue concrete configuration commands, but rather to express the needs for the delivery of a service.

IBN relies upon declarative expressions ("what I need is a 100 Mbit/s access to the corporate headquarters") as opposed to prescriptive policies that are enforced to process the said expressions. IBN is perceived as an important step towards fully automated service delivery procedures, where new levels of abstractions (by means of APIs, languages, *etc.*) are combined with Artificial Intelligence (AI) techniques to hopefully execute efficient, rapid, and trustworthy management operations.

Artificial Intelligence Can Help

AI can be defined as a set of cognitive capabilities that contribute to a decision-making procedure. AI techniques may have many applications in operators' environments. For example, AI techniques can help transform the network into a protective infrastructure that can anticipate and prevent any kind of attack (Distributed Denial-of-Service (DDoS), man-in-the-middle, spoofing, etc.) before it even reaches its targets. Such anticipation and prevention capabilities rely upon predictive analysis techniques coupled with machine learning algorithms and behavioral models.

Concretely, smart agents are distributed in the network (e.g., embedded in network devices or hosted in specific virtual machines). These agents are meant to monitor traffic and compare in real time the patterns they observe with the behavioral models they maintain. Whenever a discrepancy arises, smart agents dynamically signal what may look like a suspicious traffic to their peers but also to the computation logic that then makes appropriate decision such as the dynamic enforcement of corrective traffic filtering policies or the automated activation of traffic wells. Behavioral models are then updated accordingly.

This is not science fiction, albeit current implementations remain prototypical. For example, the DDoS Open Threat Signaling (DOTS) architecture defines a signaling mechanism used by the aforementioned smart agents (called DOTS clients) to report about the detection of a DDoS attack and to ask for mitigation. An SDN controller may be typically responsible for managing these smart agents, processing their notifications and making decisions accordingly (traffic redirection, source tracking, etc.).

Automation Remains a Risky Business

The path towards full network automation is paved with numerous challenges and requirements. In particular, a critical requirement is to make sure automation is well implemented so as to facilitate testing (including validation checks) and troubleshooting. This suggests the need for emulation tools that accurately assess the impact of introducing a high level of automation in the overall service delivery procedure, so as to avoid a typical "mad robot" syndrome whose consequences can be severe, from a control and QoS standpoints, among others.

An example of the "mad robot" effect is the outage experienced by some Google services in 2014. Indeed, on January 24, 2014, most Google users who subscribed to logged-in services like Gmail, Google+, Calendar, and Documents were unable to access those services for approximately 25 minutes. For about 10 percent of users, the problem persisted for as much as 30 minutes longer.

The flaw came from an internal system that generates information that tells other systems how to behave. This system encountered a software bug and generated an incorrect configuration. The incorrect configuration was then sent to live services over the next 15 minutes, causing users' requests for their data to be ignored, and those services, in turn generated errors.

This event further emphasizes the need for a network automation system that relies upon deterministic behaviors that can be monitored during service operation cycles. Normal behaviors under normal operation conditions should be defined as inputs to such automation system (so as to assess whether a service is up and running as expected, in particular). The automation system must also integrate feedback loops to assess whether policies are properly enforced, and that the set of policies is consistent with the service objectives. The automation system can be pre-wired to indicate how it will react whenever a problem occurs. This deterministic assessment capability can also be implemented inside the supervision system in order to improve the efficiency of fault detection mechanisms.

Humans Still Matter

The Google misadventure is a lesson that should not be forgotten by those who claim that service flexibility and agility come at no cost and no risk: automation is where the complexity resides, and no so-called service orchestration intelligence should be solicited regardless of the nature and the number of services to be delivered without an accurate modeling of predictable behaviors and without monitoring the results of executing automated actions on network components. We all know that software is never bug-free and humans are required more than ever to quickly detect and correct any unexpected behavior.

As such, the introduction of a high level of automation in the overall service delivery procedures strongly advocate for the maintenance and the development of human expertise, for optimized troubleshooting and diagnostic. This is one of the reasons why carefully designed information and data models are of paramount importance.

SO, WHAT IS THIS BOOK ABOUT?

This book sketches a vision for network automation, explores some of the emerging techniques that can benefit to automated network production and operation, and details some deployment cases to illustrate the automation benefits.

The first section of the book is dedicated to the description of the automation journey (Chapter 1, "Model-Centric Fulfillment Operations and Maintenance Automation"), the presentation of a vision towards networks designed, deployed, and operated with high level of automation and autonomy (Chapter 2, "Self-Driving Networks") together with a framework that relies upon the required functional blocks and interfaces to achieve such vision (Chapter 3, "A Unifying Framework Design for the Management of Autonomic Network Functions"), the introduction of protocols that have been recently specified to help the adoption and the deployment of the aforementioned vision and framework (Chapter 4, "ANIMA: Secure Autonomic Network Infrastructure"). Finally, a zoom on recent advances in cognitive management networking infrastructures (Chapter 5, "Automating Network Management with Artificial Intelligence: In Software Networks and Beyond") completes this first section.

The second section of the book is devoted to the description of automation techniques that serve a specific purpose (network slicing, resource placement, dynamic structuring and automated operation of Service Function Chains, etc.). Particularly, this section covers:

- Network slicing and the inherent challenges for deploying and endorsing such novel techniques by providers (Chapter 6, "Slicing Challenges for Operators").
- Algorithms used to optimize the placement of the resources (network, CPU, storage) that will be involved in the delivery and the operation of services (Chapter 7, "Future Networks: Panorama of Optimization Problems in Decision-Making Procedures").
- A novel transactional control model, including service scheduling matters (Chapter 8, "Dynamic and Scalable Control as Foundation for Future Networks").

The third section of the book is dedicated to sample automation deployment use cases. The following use cases are covered:

- Dynamic security policy enforcement schemes (Chapter 9, "Network Security Policy Automation: Enterprise Use Cases and Methodologies").
- Automated address management procedures and how they can foster the delivery of connectivity services supported by various access networking infrastructures, in particular (Chapter 10, "Automatic Address Scheduling and Management for Broadband IP Networks").
- The optimization of QoS policy enforcement schemes by means of automated SLA (Service Level Agreement) detection means and adequate probing techniques (Chapter 11, "A Perspective on the Standardization of Autonomic Detection of Service Level Agreements Violations").
- Test automation and the corresponding effort conducted by various Open Source communities and projects (Chapter 12, "The Open Source Community Choice: Automate or Die!").

What This Book Brings: A Better Understanding of the Challenges Raised and Techniques Used by Automated Network Production and Operation

Given the amount of emerging ideas and proposals, an in-depth understanding and analysis of the emerging automation techniques should be conducted so as to help Internet players in making appropriate, robust, and reliable design choices.

We believe this book can be useful to students, network engineers, and technical strategists who want to get a picture of what automation can bring to networks. It discusses some of the most attractive automation techniques that are currently being debated in the industry and various standardization bodies.

This book provides a rather comprehensive description of these advanced, sometimes revolutionary techniques that are very likely to (positively) affect how networks will be soon designed, produced, and operated in a fully automated manner. This book has been written by some of the key experts of the domain who deserve our deepest gratitude for their invaluable contribution.

We hope you will enjoy this fascinating journey as much as we did.

Acknowledgment

Many thanks to the following reviewers who provided thoughtful insights:

Alex Galis, Carl Moberg, Carlos Jesús Bernardos Cano, Carmen Guerrero, Catalin Meirosu, Dhruv Dhody, Diego R. Lopez, Filip Idzikowski, Gert Grammel, Hannu Flinck, Hassnaa Moustafa, Jordi Palet Martinez, Kostas Pentikousis, Liang Geng, Matsushima Satoru, Mikael Abrahamsson, Mithun Mukherjee, Nik Teague, Ning Wang, Prashanth Patil, Qian Duan, Qiang Li, Rajiv Asati, Seungik Lee, Shunsuke Homma, Stefano Secci, Stéphane Litkowski, Tianran Zhou, Tirumaleswar Reddy, and Tom Petch.

Thanks also to the following individuals for their availability:

Andrew Mortensen, Daniele Ceccarelli, Ethan Grossman, Lee young, Leo Liubing, Sheng Jiang, and Uma Chunduri.

Section 1

The Automation Journey:
A Vision, a Framework, and Lots of Cognition

Chapter 1
Model–Centric Fulfillment Operations and Maintenance Automation

Patrick Moore
Itential, LLC, USA

ABSTRACT

As networks have evolved, there has been an evolution in how they are managed as well. This evolution has seen a move from manual configuration via command line interface (CLI) to script-based automation and eventually to a template-based approach with workflow to coordinate multiple templates and scripts. The next step in this evolution is the introduction of models to provide a more dynamic capability than is in place today. This chapter will discuss three major layers of modelling that should be considered during implementation of this approach: device models focused on the configuration of the hardware itself; service models focused on the customer or network facing services that leverage the hardware level configuration; and operational models focused on people, processes, and tools involved in application of device and service models. This includes the orchestration of activities with other tools, such as operational support systems (OSS) and business support systems (BSS).

INTRODUCTION

As networks have become more complex, the ability of traditional management tools to scale has decreased. With the introduction of more dynamic networks, enabled by Software Defined Networking (SDN) and Network Function Virtualization (NFV) technologies, performance will only get worse. Legacy tools for managing the network have struggled to maintain accurate data about the current, mostly static networks. As such, there is little to support the ability to manage the more dynamic networks of the future.

Much like the network itself, these management tools were designed to be static. As a result, it has been a challenge to maintain the synchronization of Operational Support Systems (OSS) inventory with network reality, even with infrequent changes taking place. The author's experience is that the accuracy of data in OSS inventory when audited against what is configured in the network falls into the 65-75%

DOI: 10.4018/978-1-5225-7146-9.ch001

range. A change to the network can often involve more time and effort to update the OSS than it takes to execute the change itself.

With the virtualization of some network functions, new tools are being introduced. The resulting divergence of management between physical and virtual networks has created an "Operations Gap." This gap will continue to grow as operations teams are required to optimize the maintenance of these new infrastructure types, while continuing to support existing ones.

There has been a natural evolution in network management, as networks have themselves evolved. There has been a move from manual configuration via Command Line Interface (CLI), to script-based automation, to a template-based approach that involves workflow to coordinate multiple templates and scripts to accomplish highly repeatable actions. The next step in this evolution is the application of models to replace the script and template-based management in place today.

This chapter discusses closing the "Operations Gap". Three primary levels of modelling are discussed:

- **Device Models:** These are primarily the configuration options involved in the hardware itself, how it functions and provides a platform for services to traverse. This includes modelling virtual hardware.
- **Service Models:** These are the internal or customer-facing services that exist in the network, which provide functionality that leverages the Device level configurations. Internal services are technology specific, such as Carrier Grade NAT (CGN), while customer-facing services are technology-agnostic and traverse the devices and internal services defined to supply functionality to the customer.
- **Operational Models:** These are the combination of what is required to be completed at the Device layer, Service Layer, and any workflow and orchestration actions required.

There are many paths forward to solve the problem, and this chapter focuses on solutions within the installation and configuration management domains, with less emphasis on fault and performance management. Additionally, these techniques are most applicable to the service provider space, though each is directly applicable to an Enterprise network as well.

The traditional OSS vendors champion an approach to retrofitting these new technologies into their existing OSS solution. There is some value to this due to the very large investment service providers have in these tools. It seems to make sense to leverage this investment and not start from scratch. The issue is SDN/NFV concepts being introduced to network management do not play well together.

Other vendors espouse a total model-based approach that takes the NFV approach and extends it to the entire network. This would be valid if the average network did not have devices, or whole segments, not capable of being managed in this manner. Too many networks still have legacy devices that, at best, can only be scripted.

The middle ground approach is also put forth by some of the newer vendors on the scene. These vendors recognize that there is the legacy network to deal with, and that it will not be going away in the near term. They also recognize that network operators are going to be reluctant to throw away their significant investment in the current toolchain and will be introducing the new SDN/NFV model-based applications in conjunction. The resulting approach is to federate the data, capabilities, and functions of these various application domains using an automation platform to provide a unified automation tool. There are a few variations in how these vendors propose for this to work, but conceptually they align on this approach.

BACKGROUND

Programmability of networks creates a higher dynamic in configuring networks, so they have become difficult to be managed using traditional command line interfaces. The network should be modelled in such a way that changes to the model can easily be applied to the network itself. One of the most popular ways this is done today (2018) is to model using YANG language (Bjorklund, 2016) and to utilize tools that translate this to NETCONF, RFC6241 (Enns, Bjorklund, Schoenwaelder, & Bierman, **A**, 2011) commands to be applied to the network. There have been some past efforts in the policy arena using COPS, RFC2748, (Durham, 2000) and COPS-PR, RFC3084, (Durham, 2001). In this chapter the focus is on a NETCONF/YANG based approach.

In software development, the concept of DevOps is one of continuous integration (CI) and deployment (CD) into production. CI/CD is a dynamic approach to change management that embraces constant update versus a static environment. The application of a model-based approach allows the network to be managed similarly, a necessity for managing a network that is becoming more dynamic with time.

This chapter focuses on the application of this concept for improved network operations within the domains of installation and configuration management and, specifically, the maintenance activities required to ensure that the network continues to function properly (that is, as expected).

The Operations Gap

There are specific issues created by the evolution of the network as virtual and programmable elements are introduced. Primarily, this involves multiple technologies being integrated into a common network architecture, each with its own software architecture and techniques for management. This section covers both, where service provider network management has been traditionally, and where it must go in the future to prevent this from reaching critical mass and overburdening the continued growth of networks to the point it becomes prohibitively expensive in terms of cost and effort to maintain.

Past Approaches to Network Management

Network management has traditionally relied heavily on the use of Command Line Interfaces (CLI) to access the individual elements for all configuration activities. This provided a very effective way for humans to interact with the operation of very complex devices that abstract much of the internal workings of the operating system components. This has supported for the growth of the network over time.

A very important evolution of the CLI method of managing the network was the introduction of primitive automation by using scripts, which strung together multiple CLI commands into a file that could be executed and repeated on demand. As changes to the network became more and more frequent, this became not just a convenience but a necessity. Scripts allowed a single engineer to execute multiple changes to the network simultaneously. Another challenge soon became apparent.

The scripts that engineers use are very static entities. A script that works for one vendor's device will not work for another's. A script that performs one specific action for one type of device will almost always not suffice when another action is required to be performed for a different device, even if both devices are from the same vendor. This has led to an exponential growth in the number of scripts maintained by the typical network engineering team. The number of vendors multiplied by the number of device types multiplied by the number of specific activities to be automated can easily add up to hundreds, and sometimes thousands, of scripts. The burden on the engineering staff is unsupportable.

Within this scenario of exponential growth in the number of scripts is the introduction of new network architectures and technologies, such as NFV and SDN. By simply adding new vendors, device types, interfaces, management tools, and management techniques into existing structures, silos would be created around technologies, vendors, devices, and tools. This would result in widening the "Operations Gap" between the business-as-usual operations of the existing network and these new domains.

The Journey to Effective Network Automation

Traditional network management practices in the area of provisioning and configuration management have largely been a manual activity with scripting introducing some level of automation. Moving toward full automation is not a destination, but a journey. This is because of the continuous introduction of new tools, technologies, and ways of leveraging those to produce new and more complex services for the end users of the network. In this journey, there will be segments of the network that will remain on the current manual/scripted path, those that will take that are introduced over time.

Figure 1 illustrates the path that this journey will take. Over the course of time, the industry has been striving to automate everything possible via the scripted approach, and there is a large segment of the current network that will continue to maintain this path. Among the reasons for this are:

- Many network devices are aging and nearing the end of their service life within the network. The cost to automate these soon-to-be-decommissioned elements does not justify itself based on the likely return.
- There are also segments of the network that are extremely static in nature. These may be devices that are largely passive in the roles they play, and, therefore, require very little configuration management. These may also include devices that are static enough that the current techniques are sufficient to maintain them into the future. In both cases, just as with the aging devices mentioned above, the return expected cannot justify the cost of automation.
- Furthermore, there are devices that, for one reason or another, can only provide modest improvement to the bottom line of the network operator.

It is critical to have an approach to managing the network that is both dynamic and flexible. A vital aspect of this path relies on modelling techniques that have emerged in the last decade or so to address these very challenges. Key to this will also be the ability to discover and be able to manage devices that appear within the network in a very dynamic manner.

As the network, particularly at layer 3, becomes more and more programmable through the introduction of controllers and orchestrators it also becomes more able to be managed in a "software-like" manner by leveraging APIs to devices and applications. This allows the inclusion of DevOps style automation within the network. DevOps techniques, along with the flexibility introduced with models, significantly accelerates the ability to automate. It also aligns with the management tools and techniques being introduced by the new technologies, such as SD-WAN (Softwire-Defined Wide Area Network), data center overlay, vCPE (virtual CPE), vPE (virtual Provide Edge), vFW (virtual firewall), and other applications of NFV and SDN. This alignment will firmly place an operator on the path to converged operations mentioned above.

Figure 1. The network operations journey

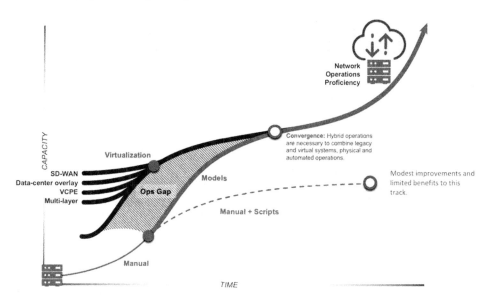

An important note for the future here is that the model-based approach is also key to readying the network and its management structure for both Intent-Based Networking (IBN) and for the application of Artificial Intelligence (AI) for networks. In the next section, the topic of modelling will be detailed to introduce the three levels of modelling the author believes are required for success on this path.

SOLUTIONS AND RECOMMENDATIONS

In this section, the focus is on the models required to move from a typical CLI/script-based network operation on the path laid out at a high level in the previous section. In addition to the model-specific items, there will also be information on how to leverage the scripts that exist today in parallel with the introduction of models to accelerate the automation of the network in parallel with introducing new data models.

Historically, device management has looked at the full configuration on a device, both device setup and the configuration related to services that traverse that device. One of the first changes that need to take place is the idea of devices and services levels as separate entities. As shown in Figure 2, there is a specific set of lifecycle functions involved for the devices and for the services offered that should be managed separately.

At the device level, the three main concepts to focus on are:

1. Device Lifecycle
2. Config Drift
3. Compliance

Figure 2. Network templates and models for automation

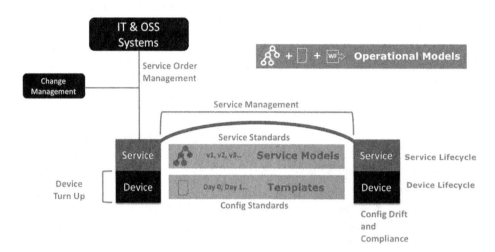

Device Lifecycle involves all of the activities from installation and configuration of physical and virtual devices on day one, through management of the configuration changes that occur over the useable life of that device in the network.

Config Drift involves the management of untracked changes to the device configuration. As long as engineering and operations staff has CLI access to the devices, there will be untracked changes to those configurations over time. Tooling must be put into place to recognize this drift, which has the ability to correct it to bring the device back within standards that have been defined.

Compliance involves the auditing the network against a defined network configuration standard and flagging those devices found not to conform to it. The primary challenge to this activity is the definition of standards that are flexible enough to accommodate all of the variations required in a complex network, or understanding the variations well enough to define exceptions to the standards that apply to specific use cases.

At the device level, it is possible to apply a templated approach, as these configurations are relatively static when compared to services. It is the author's recommendation that models are applied even at this level to better integrate with the higher levels, but this is not strictly required for success. More details on this will follow as each model layer is discussed.

At the service level, things become significantly more complicated. Services usually traverse multiple devices, over multiple network segments, and may involve interactions with multiple, defined standards and device types. This complexity is hard to manage with a template-based approach.

Services also have a lifecycle management component that includes the equivalent activities mentioned above for devices. Services should also have defined standards that allow for compliance and configuration drift monitoring. However, there are many more opportunities for there to be an exception to a standard in the services domain. This is especially so in the services that providers supply to businesses, where the businesses may have unique requirements to allow proper integration of their internal network.

The top level is not one that is frequently included in the discussion of network automation. The services listed above are very important and are prerequisites to being able to manage an end-to-end automation activity, however there are many manual tasks that occur in the process of a maintenance window that also should be considered. This end-to-end view of the device model, service model, and workflow processes is referred to in this chapter as the Operational Model. Lack of proper attention to the operational level will result in automation projects that appear to meet all of the stated goals, but never seem to produce the desired results.

In order to further illustrate the options available, and importance of all three of levels working together, the following sections will discuss each in detail.

Device Models

Device models focus on the configuration aspects of network elements. These models can take a couple of forms, templates, or models. The application of YANG for modelling the device configurations allows for a more dynamic and flexible approach. In this section, both approaches are discussed.

Regardless of the approach chosen, it is important to establish a "Golden Configuration" standard for each device type that also considers the various roles those devices may play in the network. The creation of a standard allows for compliance auditing and remediation to be automated.

The template-based approach is closely aligned with the way configuration management is done in most networks today. The standard is literally a text file that is stored in a repository and live configurations are pulled from the network and compared to the text filed-based standard as illustrated in Figure 3.

These text file-based standards can easily be applied to devices using scripts, tools like Ansible, or more advanced tools, such as orchestrators or controllers. The shortcomings of this approach come when variations in the standard are required. In this scenario, a separate text file is required for each variation, much like the problem with scripts discussed in a previous section. This can quickly become a management issue, which is where the next approach comes in.

A model-based approach is expected to bring much more flexibility and intelligence into the networks. According to RFC 7950, YANG is used "to model configuration data, state data, RPC calls, and notifications related to network management protocols" (Bjorklund, 2016). The YANG standard defines

Figure 3. Template-based configuration difference example

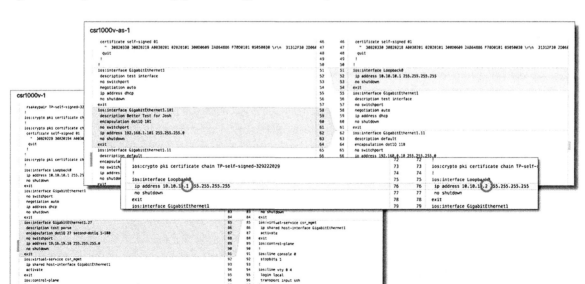

the ability to embed intelligence in the model to set allowable values, and to set decision points based on data entered into certain key/value pairs, among many others. This enables a single model to account for a wide range of scenarios, such as the role a device is playing in the network.

The use of models still allows for the "config diff" view illustrated in Figure 3, while introducing the flexibility and intelligence mentioned above. A key improvement to this approach is the decrease in the number of entities to be managed. Whereas the template-based approach could easily result in hundreds of templates to manage, the model-based approach reduces this significantly. Even in a complex network, the number of models should remain in the sub-100 range.

Service Models

At the service level, the suggested method is implementing a model-based approach. A good reference for beginning to use service models is IETF RFC 8309, Service Models Explained (Wu, Liu, & Farrel, A, 2018). Based on the type of service being modelled there are choices in how to model. For cloud-based services Topology and Orchestration Specification for Cloud Applications (TOSCA) is a common modelling language to use (OASIS, 2018). TOSCA maps very closely align to the ETSI NFV standard for management and orchestration, making it an ideal candidate for this type of service.

The most common service modelling language currently is YANG. YANG is based on IETF RFC 6020 (Bjorklund, 2010), version 1 of the YANG standard, and version 1.1 defined in RFC 7950 (Bjorklund, 2016). Most vendor implementations have used the more recent standard, but per RFC 7950, "Note that this document does not obsolete RFC 6020". The flexibility and intelligence mentioned in the last section is crucial to properly managing services.

An excerpt of a YANG service model for VLANs from the OpenConfig repository (OpenConfig Community, 2018) for VLANs is illustrated here:

```
...
// grouping statements
  grouping vlan-config {
    description "VLAN configuration container.";
    leaf vlan-id {
      type oc-vlan-types:vlan-id;
      description "Interface VLAN id.";
    }
    leaf name {
      type string;
      description "Interface VLAN name.";
    }
    leaf status {
      type enumeration {
        enum ACTIVE {
          description "VLAN is active";
        }
        enum SUSPENDED {
          description "VLAN is inactive / suspended";
```

```
          }
      }
      default ACTIVE;
      description "Admin state of the VLAN";
   }
}
grouping vlan-state {
  description "State variables for VLANs";
  // placeholder
}
grouping vlan-tpid-config {
  description
    "TPID configuration for dot1q-enabled interfaces";
  leaf tpid {
    type identityref {
      base oc-vlan-types:TPID_TYPES;
    }
    default oc-vlan-types:TPID_0X8100;
    description
      "Optionally set the tag protocol identifier field (TPID) that
      is accepted on the VLAN";
  }
}
grouping vlan-tpid-state {
  description
    "TPID opstate for dot1q-enabled interfaces";
  // placeholder
}
grouping vlan-members-state {
  description
    "List of interfaces / subinterfaces belonging to the VLAN.";
  container members {
    description
      "Enclosing container for list of member interfaces";
    list member {
      config false;
      description
        "List of references to interfaces / subinterfaces
        associated with the VLAN.";
      uses oc-if:base-interface-ref-state;
    }
  }
}
grouping vlan-switched-config {
```

```
description
  "VLAN related configuration that is part of the physical
  Ethernet interface.";
leaf interface-mode {
  type oc-vlan-types:vlan-mode-type;
  description
    "Set the interface to access or trunk mode for
    VLANs";
}
leaf native-vlan {
  when "interface-mode = 'TRUNK'" {
    description
      "Native VLAN is valid for trunk mode interfaces";
  }
  type oc-vlan-types:vlan-id;
  description
    "Set the native VLAN id for untagged frames arriving on
    a trunk interface.  Tagged frames sent on an interface
    configured with a native VLAN should have their tags
    stripped prior to transmission. This configuration is only
    valid on a trunk interface.";
}
leaf access-vlan {
  when "interface-mode = 'ACCESS'" {
    description
      "Access VLAN assigned to the interfaces";
  }
  type oc-vlan-types:vlan-id;
  description
    "Assign the access vlan to the access port.";
}
leaf-list trunk-vlans {
  when "interface-mode = 'TRUNK'" {
    description
      "Allowed VLANs may be specified for trunk mode
      interfaces.";
  }
  type union {
    type oc-vlan-types:vlan-id;
    type oc-vlan-types:vlan-range;
  }
  description
    "Specify VLANs, or ranges thereof, that the interface may
    carry when in trunk mode. If not specified, all VLANs are
```

```
        allowed on the interface. Ranges are specified in the form
        x..y, where x<y - ranges are assumed to be inclusive (such
        that the VLAN range is x <= range <= y.";
    }
}
grouping vlan-switched-state {
  description
    "VLAN related operational state that is part of Ethernet
    interface state data";
  //TODO: placeholder for operational state related to VLANs
  //on the physical interface
}
...
```

This excerpt illustrates some important concepts, such as the hierarchical nature of the model, the specification of default values, and the intelligence offered by "when" statements to indicate rules that are applied to certain attributes when specific conditions are met. Additional capabilities are described in RFC 7950 (Bjorklund, 2016).

In practical implementations of YANG service models with an orchestrator there are three key pieces involved:

- The YANG service model
- The device model/template
- The mapping between the previous two items

The device model/template provides a software-based representation of the network elements the service will traverse. These network elements have a degree of dynamic capability to them as new functionality is introduced by software upgrades, but this is minimal when compared to the changes that occur frequently with services.

The service model provides the same software-based representation for the service itself. Then there is a mapping of the service attributes to the configuration capabilities of the network element. This is often done in either Java or Python, with Python quickly becoming the preferred language due to its popularity in other network automation areas. This popularity stems largely from Python being much easier to learn by the non-software engineers than Java.

When these three components are combined within the environment of an orchestrator it becomes possible to instantiate service by executing the service model, supplying the correct data, and have that data be translated to the device in the proper commands to provision the service in an automated fashion.

Operational Models

The levels explained in the previous two sections enable a great deal of capability with regard to automation of the network. However, it is the author's opinion that these alone do not supply the full capability required to realize the potential cost-savings and productivity improvements.

Tasks at this layer leverage the lower two levels, as well as integration with other systems in the OSS/BSS domain (as required), to do things such as OS upgrades, service provisioning, issue resolution, grooming activities in coordination with the physical work required, etc.

In a typical maintenance activity there is a significant amount of time involved in the pre and post work of executing the required activity. In many cases, a maintenance task that may take 20-30 minutes to manually execute all of the commands automated by the application of device and service models will have up to an hour of pre-check tasks. These pre-checks have the intent of recording the state of the device(s) involved in the maintenance and are repeated after the changes are applied in order to allow a comparison. The 1-2 hours of work here, and an additional 1-2 hours of manually comparing the pre and post results is where the real potential for gain exists. This is one of the major pitfalls commonly seen in automation projects. All of the budget and effort is applied to automate the 20-30 minutes and not the 2-4 hours that make up the full process.

On account of this, it is necessary to take a view one level up from the device and service. This is the operational level. At this level, the model is composed of the device model, the service model, the process itself, and analytic rules that can take the pre-check data and automatically compare it to the post-check data to ensure that the maintenance was a success or failure.

Success criteria should be defined as part of the analytic rules. It is important to note to include in these rules is the fact that the maintenance may not return the network to the exact state it was in prior to completion. A common mistake in this area is to assume identical state case and oversimplify the analytics. It is not sufficient to merely check that the pre and post results are equal. For example, if part of the maintenance is to turn up three new interfaces on a device, then it is not a success if the number of interfaces on the device in pre-check equals the number in post-check. In this example it would be necessary to define, in the analytics rules, the ability to check that the number of interfaces equals pre-check quantity plus three.

Implementation considerations at this level involve putting into place a higher level "coordinator" than can work across multiple orchestrators, controllers, and with various model types (e.g., YANG and TOSCA). In the author's experience, this has been best met by a platform that can consume the APIs of southbound tools and present a unified experience that supplies:

- A single user interface that exposes data from all southbound orchestrators and controllers.
- A workflow engine that exposes the capabilities of all southbound orchestrators and controllers to the engineers using the platform and its applications.
- An analytics capability that allows for automated pre/post checks and comparison of those results based on defined success criteria.
- Exposure of all APIs northbound for a single integration point for other systems, such as OSS/BSS.
- The ability to develop custom applications leveraging all of the above, in addition to out-of-the-box applications for the most common activities such as:
  - Golden Configuration Standards Definition
  - Standards Compliance auditing and reporting
  - Workflow Definition for maintenance processes
  - Analytics Templating for definition of pre, post, and comparison rules
  - Policy Management

Within this architecture (depicted in Figure 4) there are:

- Devices that exist in the network that are interconnected, as indicated by the solid lines between devices.
- Services that traverse these devices, as indicated by the dotted arcs overlaying the devices below.
- A mix of Controllers, Orchestrators, and other systems that each control a portion of the underlying network. The matching shading between this layer and the network below indicate a relationship between system and device(s) controlled.
- Each of those controllers, orchestrators, or other components expose a northbound API that is consumed by the broker component of the network automation platform of choice, based on the approach suggested in this chapter. The models discussed exist in, and are owned by, the following:
    ○ Device and Service Models are owned by the controller, orchestrator, and other system level, but are federated to the network automation platform for use in operational models.
    ○ Operational Models are owned by the network automation platform, and are exposed to human users via the unified GUI and to external systems via the APIs northbound of the automation platform.

The Methodology to Network Automation

The next component of implementation is less about the technical pieces and more about a methodology that will allow taking full advantage of the model-based approach. In the author's experience, this

Figure 4. Architecture to Support an Operational Model-Based Solution

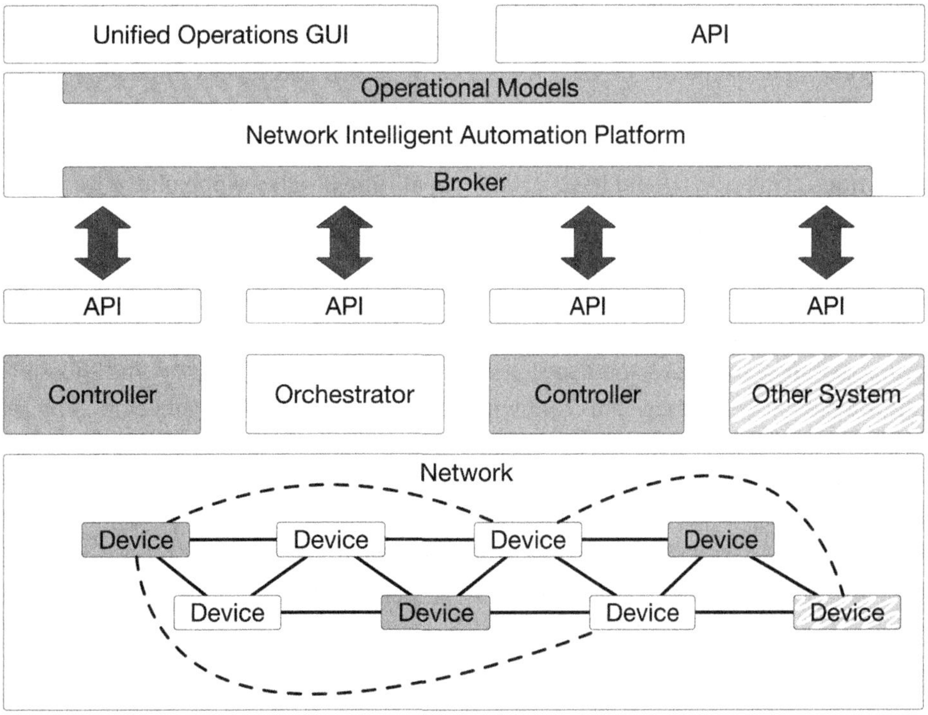

should be executed using methodologies that have been common in the software world for years, but with an adjustment to accommodate some of the network specific requirements.

This section on what is involved from a methodology perspective touches upon three major areas: people, process, and tools. Based on the author's many years of experience in consulting, this has proven to be the most effective way to describe an implementation of this sort.

People

The first section does not focus on people-related items, such as organization charts, but instead will discuss the roles required to put into place an effective network automation program. These roles are:

- Architect
- Automation Designer
- Software Engineer
- Operator
- Subject Matter Experts

The role of Architect manages the overall program and ensures that proper requirements are gathered for each automation request. The Architect role must be filled by someone that is proficient in project/program management, is in a position to influence decisions on the finances required to continue the operation of the program, and who has a high-level understanding of the technology involved. It is not a requirement that this position be highly knowledgeable about the details behind how the technology works.

The role of Automation Designer is the technical lead on the project. In many cases, if an organization is small enough, this role is filled by the same person that acts as Architect. The more complex the network, and the more activities there are to automate, and the more likely this position will need to be a dedicated resource. The Automation Designer is responsible for low-level design of the automation solutions and should understand the process for building device and service models. It is not required, but in smaller organizations, this role may also be responsible for some of the development work.

The Software Engineer is the role that will assist the Automation Designer in the creation of the automation solutions. This role should have similar capabilities as described above for the Automation Designer, but can be a less senior resource that takes direction on day-to-day activities from the Automation Designer. Primary responsibilities include: workflow creation, device model creation, service model creation, integration work with other systems, such as orchestrators and controllers (or northbound to OSS/BSS), and testing of the completed solution.

The Operator is the customer of the above listed roles. This is the group or individual that will be using the solution once it is in place. This role will execute the automations developed by the Software Engineer, as well as administer the system on a day-to-day basis. It is common that this role also has the ability to create workflows that utilize pre-built capabilities and integrations, but do not require development work.

The Subject Matter Experts (SMEs) are pulled in as needed to assist in the definition of requirements and to conduct acceptance testing as solutions are deployed.

Process

From a methodology perspective, there are two primary domains in the process category: Gating and Development. An important concept to keep in mind as these are put into place is that automation of the network is not a single project effort. The network will continuously change as new technologies are introduced, and that means there will be a long-term need to manage the automation of each of these technologies as they are implemented. In order to accommodate this long-term need, the author suggests the use of an agile approach with a backlog of requests that are continuously growing and being evaluated for approval. This is where the gating process comes into play.

A Gating process needs to be put in place to enable the entry of automation requests and the analysis of each request. This can be incorporated into the requirements management tool that is mentioned in the next section, whereby requestors enter Epics (high level requirements) directly into the system for consideration. These requests should then undergo a vetting process that considers value in a few key areas:

- **Customer Experience Impact:** Cycle time of overall process, error rates and/or trouble tickets.
- **Operational Impact:** Headcount, regulatory gaps and/or visibility.
- **Process Impact:** Cycle time and/or error rates.
- **Financial Impact:** Cost reduction and/or revenue increase.

The above four areas should each have an objective scoring system that generates a benefit score for each new request. This will prioritize the backlog and enable moving only the most impactful items into an active status.

Just as the process for recording a backlog of requests must be agile and flexible, so must be the process for executing on each automation project. In the software world there are essentially two high-level choices when it comes to methodology, waterfall or agile. Within each of these are many different disciplines to choose from, but the author suggests an Agile Scrum approach which is summarized well by the Scrum Reference Card (James, 2017).

There are many reasons to choose agile over waterfall-based methods, but among the most important with regard to network automation are:

- Waterfall tends to spend a long period of time defining requirements, which can cause issues in a dynamic, constantly changing environment. This methodology also tends to be slower due to this approach, which can mean delivery of an automation only to find that the network has changed, and the models/processes must be modified immediately to accommodate the new network state.
- Related to the previous point is the fact that agile is very accommodating to change. The idea is to deliver smaller benefits more often. This is accomplished in short bursts of work called sprints, and each sprint involves constant verification and demo of the upcoming functionality with the stakeholders. This prevents long periods of time from passing with required modifications being unknown until after deployment.

Figure 5 illustrates a typical Agile Scrum-based process.

Figure 5. Agile/Scrum based methodology

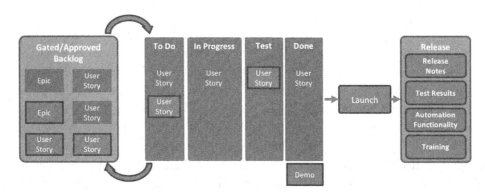

Platform/Tools

The purpose of the tools in this section is specifically in regard to supporting the Gating and Development processes mentioned above. These tools should be readily available without the need for large investment, and likely are in use at most companies currently. The required tools include:

- **Project/Program Management:** This involves some way to track the resource and budgeting aspects of the program.
- **Requirements:** This involves the ability to capture the requirements involved in each automation request. To align with the Agile/DevOps approach described above, it is important that these tools allow for the idea of Epics, User Stories, Test Cases, etc. Commonly found tools for this include JIRA, Rally, and the Rational Suite of products.
- **Development:** This involves the ability to manage the development, testing, and deployment of automation solutions. Common tools for this include Github, Bitbucket, GitLab, and others. With these, it is possible to put into place a pipeline to facilitate continuous development and deployment of the automation capabilities as they are completed.

FUTURE RESEARCH DIRECTIONS

Future expansion of research in this area will look at Intent-Based Networking, in which the end user is no longer required to define any of the configuration attributes. In an Intent-based approach, the models will become sophisticated enough that, for example, a user will be able to request a video connection from point A to point B, and the model will understand the technical requirements underpinning that request with no need for the user to know anything about them.

Another area that will exist further down the journey mentioned in this chapter is the application of Artificial Intelligence (AI) to enable a self-provisioning and self-healing network. In this approach, there is the possibility of utilizing big data concepts to feed information to an AI system and allowing that system to make decisions about how the network should be reconfigured to best utilize resources available. This self-managing network will also have the capability of reconfiguring itself around outages and other network issues.

CONCLUSION

This chapter has discussed many individual components. It has laid out the need for a model-based technical approach to managing network device and services configuration. Layered on top of this is an operational model that defines the details of how the models, processes, and businesses need to inter-operate to achieve the required automation.

It has also described a recommended methodology for managing requests for new network automation, one which includes how to accept new requests, evaluate those requests to determine the most beneficial automations to approve, and finally how to implement the requested automation.

A term that the author has taken to using for this overall process is that of an "automation factory." This involves the need to put into place a dedicated group, even if it is 3-5 people only, who are focused on the process of automating the network. This team should have a combination of network engineering and software development skills, which in the near term will be a challenge for organizations to find in any one person.

The concept is one of a continuously running assembly line that creates the raw materials of models, workflows, and integrations, and produces out the back end fully functioning network automation solutions that consider the full end-to-end process, not just the commands run against network devices alone.

There are operational tasks that make sense to not automate any more than they currently are. This can range from activities on network devices that are on the roadmap to being decommissioned, or activities that are already sufficiently automated to an extent that no return on the investment of changing how they are automated is possible.

In the past, only repetitive tasks could be automated, but with the flexibility of model-based automation, more complex activities can now be included. This brings into play issues such as the automation of business services that are frequently one-off configurations, but almost always fall within the definition of what a single model can accommodate. This also enables maintenance tasks to be automated that may be repetitive for short periods of time only, such as a software upgrade across 500 devices.

REFERENCES

Bjorklund, M. (2016). *The YANG 1.1 modeling language*. Internet Engineering Task Force, RFC7950. Retrieved from https://tools.ietf.org/html/rfc7950

Bjorklund, M. (2016). *YANG – A data modeling language for the network configuration protocol (NET-CONF)*. Internet Engineering Task Force, RFC6020. Retrieved from https://tools.ietf.org/html/rfc6020

Bjorklund, M. (2016). *The YANG 1.1 modeling Language*. Internet Engineering Task Force, RFC7950. Retrieved from https://tools.ietf.org/html/rfc7950

Durham, D. (2000). *The COPS (Common Open Policy Service) Protocol*. Internet Engineering Task Force, RFC2748. Retrieved from https://tools.ietf.org/html/rfc2748

Durham, D. (2001). *COPS for Policy Provisioning (COPS-PR)*. Internet Engineering Task Force, RFC3084. Retrieved from https://tools.ietf.org/html/rfc3084

Enns, R., Bjorklund, M., Schoenwaelder, J., & Bierman, A. (2011). *Network Configuration Protocol (NETCONF)*. Internet Engineering Task Force, RFC6241. Retrieved from https://tools.ietf.org/html/rfc6241

James, M. (2017). *Scrum Reference Card*. Retrieved from https://www.collab.net/sites/default/files/uploads/CollabNet_scrumreferencecard.pdf

OASIS Topology & the Orchestration Specification for Cloud Applications Technical Committee. (2016). *TOSCA Simple Profile in YAML Version 1.1*. Retrieved from http://docs.oasis-open.org/tosca/TOSCA-Simple-Profile-YAML/v1.1/os/TOSCA-Simple-Profile-YAML-v1.1-os.html

OpenConfig Community. (2018). *Public release models VLAN*. Retrieved from https://github.com/openconfig/public/blob/master/release/models/vlan/openconfig-vlan.yang

Wu, Q., Liu, W., & Farrel, A. (2018). *Service Models Explained*. Internet Engineering Task Force, RFC8309. Retrieved from https://datatracker.ietf.org/doc/rfc8309/

ADDITIONAL READING

Bierman, A. (2011). *Guidelines for authors and reviewers of YANG data model documents*. Internet Engineering Task Force, RFC6087. https://tools.ietf.org/html/rfc6087

Chatras, B. (2017). *Network functions virtualisation (NFV) release 2: Management and orchestration. Network Service Templates Specification*. Retrieved from http://www.etsi.org/deliver/etsi_gs/NFV-IFA/001_099/014/02.01.01_60/gs_NFV-IFA014v020101p.pdf

Flauw, M. (2017). *Network functions virtualisation (NFV) release 2: Information modeling*. Retrieved from *UML Modeling Guidelines*. http://www.etsi.org/deliver/etsi_gr/NFV-IFA/001_099/017/02.01.01_60/gr_NFV-IFA017v020101p.pdf

Flauw, M. (2017). *Network functions virtualisation (NFV) release 2: Management and orchestration. Os-Ma-Nfvo reference point - Interface and Information Model Specification*. Retrieved from http://www.etsi.org/deliver/etsi_gs/NFV-IFA/001_099/013/02.03.01_60/gs_nfv-ifa013v020301p.pdf

Flauw, M., & Worndle, P. (2017). *Network functions virtualisation (NFV) release 2: Management and orchestration. Report on NFV Information Model*. Retrieved from http://www.etsi.org/deliver/etsi_gr/NFV-IFA/001_099/015/02.03.01_60/gr_nfv-ifa015v020301p.pdf

Jong-Hwa, Yi. (2017). *Network functions virtualisation (NFV) release 2: Protocols and data models*. Retrieved from http://www.etsi.org/deliver/etsi_gs/NFV-SOL/001_099/002/02.03.01_60/gs_NFV-SOL002v020301p.pdf

Matsumoto, C. (2017). *NFV, SDN, big data – It's all about automation*. Retrieved from https://www.lightreading.com/automation/nfv-sdn-big-data-andndash-its-all-about-automation/a/d-id/734797

Moore, P. (2017). *Network automation and programmability: Reality versus vendor hype*. Retrieved from https://www.youtube.com/watch?v=N5wbYncUS9o

Moore, P. (2018). *Network automation: Do i need expensive tools to do meaningful automation?* Retrieved from https://www.youtube.com/watch?v=r-TdsK3RKvo&t=24s

Purdy, C. (2015). *Orchestrator of orchestrators: Streamlining NFV complexity.* Retrieved from https://www.sdxcentral.com/articles/contributed/orchestrators-streamlining-nfv-complexity-chris-purdy/2015/09/

Schoenwaelder, J. (2010). Common *YANG data types.* Internet Engineering Task Force, RFC6021. https://tools.ietf.org/html/rfc6021

Shafer, P. (2011). *An architecture for network management using NETCONF and YANG.* Internet Engineering Task Force, RFC6244. https://trac.tools.ietf.org/html/rfc6244

Wade, C. (2017). *The road ahead – Facing the reality of the network operations journey to automation.* Retrieved from https://www.vanillaplus.com/2017/06/08/27856-road-ahead-facing-reality-network-operations-journey-automation/

Zhipeng, H. (2017). *Network functions virtualisation (NFV) release 2: Management and orchestration. Or-Vi reference point - Interface and Information Model Specification.* Retrieved from http://www.etsi.org/deliver/etsi_gs/NFV-IFA/001_099/004/02.03.01_60/gs_nfv-ifa004v020301p.pdf

KEY TERMS AND DEFINITIONS

Artificial Intelligence for Networks: Tools and techniques that extend AI practices into the network management domain. These include the integration of Big Data concepts to receive a constant feed of information and make decisions on the configuration of the network with no human intervention, and automatically applying those changes.

CI/CD: Continuous integration/continuous deployment. This is the concept that development of a solution, in this case a network automation solution, is an on-going process. Small incremental changes are constantly being coded, and then tested and deployed into product on a continuous, automated basis. This approach is central to DevOps as a methodology.

Controller: Typically associated with software-defined networking. The controller is the functional component that manages the control plane of the network and can be utilized to apply some level of configuration management to devices and how those devices interact with one another.

DevOps: Develop operations, or DevOps, is an agile methodology that merges the functions of software development and operations in the enterprise software development domain. This approach has been adopted in the networking world to facilitate a programmable approach to network operations. Often when applied to networking the term is changed to NetOps.

Intent-Based Networking: This is the application of models and intelligent network automation to present a simplified way of requesting network services. Instead of the traditional manner of entering relevant configuration data, a request will communicate the "intent" and rely on the intelligence built into the models to define the technical details required to provision the service. For example, a request for video connection between two locations will give no more detail than that. That request will then rely on the models involved to define details, such as circuit type, bandwidth, QoS, etc.

Model: A model is an intelligent representation of a device or service that indicates the available configuration attributes, default values, required values, decision points based on values entered, and the ability to be translated into network device understandable language to deploy the configuration. Common modelling languages include YANG and TOSCA.

Network Function Virtualization (NFV): This is the decomposition of network devices into the specific network functions they each provide, and the virtualization of those network functions in the cloud. These virtual network functions (VNFs) can then be "chained" together to replicate the capabilities of physical devices, or to provide a single source of a combined network service that no single physical device can offer. NFV features a management layer referred to as management and orchestration, or MANO.

Orchestrator: An orchestrator defines and manages policies and service levels by utilizing automated workflows and change management. Orchestrators are typically purpose built for a specific domain, such as the NFV Orchestrators defined by the ETSI NFV MANO standard. Network orchestrators provide a communication layer with the network devices that is vendor agnostic and exposes that communication northbound to other systems via APIs.

Software-Defined Networking: Is the separation of the data and control planes of the network. Often associated with OpenFlow, the purpose of SDN is to enable the network to be programmed in a similar manner to software applications.

TOSCA: Stands for topology and orchestration specification for cloud applications. TOSCA is a cloud services specific modelling language.

YANG: Stands for yet another next generation. YANG is a data modelling language developed for use with the NETCONF protocol for speaking to network devices. YANG has been adopted for use beyond NETCONF, such as use by some NFV orchestrators for cloud-based services.

Chapter 2
Self–Driving Networks

Kireeti Kompella
Juniper Networks, USA

ABSTRACT

This chapter presents a new vision of network operations, the self-driving network, that takes automation to the next level. This is not a description of existing work; rather, it is a challenge to dramatically rethink how we manage networks (or rather, how we do not manage networks). It draws upon an analogy with the development of self-driving cars and presents motivations for this effort. It then describes the technologies needed to implement this and an overall architecture of the system. As this endeavor will cause a major shift in network management, the chapter offers an evolutionary path to the end goal. Some of the consequences and human impacts of such a system are touched upon. The chapter concludes with some research topics and a final message. Key takeaways are that machine learning and feedback loops are fundamental to the solution; a key outcome is to build systems that are adaptive and predictive, for the benefit of users.

PROBLEM STATEMENT

Network operations, from configuration to service provisioning and management to capacity planning and other activities, tend to be fairly manual, with some automation scripts thrown in to take care of common situations such as upgrading devices, and some robots to detect service degradation. Increasingly, though, there are attempts to increase automation in networks – for example, event-driven automation, where the appropriate responses to a number of foreseen network events are captured in scripts that "fire" when an event is observed. There are also areas (e.g., Self-Organizing Networks, Autonomic Networks, and Zero-Touch Provisioning) where the goal is to eliminate the need for human operation. However, these are limited to a small set of functions in specific areas of networking. Nonetheless, interest in these and similar efforts is the genesis of this book; moreover, they are a necessary step in the evolution towards "self-driving" networks.

One may think that incremental progress in automation is a fine path forward. The author feels otherwise. Consider the development of automobiles. The invention of the automobile, and especially its mass manufacture, was a complete disruption in transportation. Since then, automation has been in-

DOI: 10.4018/978-1-5225-7146-9.ch002

creasingly deployed, to the great benefit of drivers and passengers – increased safety and convenience, and a wider cross-section of drivers. But that was all incremental. Fast forward to today, where we stand on the brink of another revolution: self-driving cars. The impact of this is still being explored. Over the next five years, expect major upheavals in legislation, urban planning, and insurance. Automation was an absolute necessity for self-driving cars, but it was far from sufficient; the fundamental advance is the elimination of the human element from driving. We took a bold leap in driving; we need a similarly bold leap in networking.

The problem statement before us is the similar complete elimination of humans from all aspects of network operation, in all areas of networking. The motivations for doing so are described below. In the author's opinion, humans are needed at the front end of any change, in specifying what the change should accomplish as a very high-level, declarative statement of intent; and at the back end, conducting post-mortems of the actual (machine-led) operation, with a view towards improvement. Everything in between should (and eventually will) be done by machines equipped with the necessary intelligence to do so. In this chapter, the author shows how. Once Self-Driving Networks are realized, one may be able to remove humans both from the front end and back end of changes: infer required changes, implement the changes and ensure that the intended result was indeed accomplished.

INTRODUCTION

Advances in autonomous systems[1] are all around us. As processors become more powerful and more energy efficient; as data becomes more ubiquitous and purposeful; and as software gets more sophisticated; our ability to hand over control to machines increases. In a very real sense, this is the logical conclusion of automation, the progression being: do things manually; find (sub-)tasks that are repetitive and automate them; and eventually, give the whole job over to a machine. This process requires considerable technological progress, as well as human considerations. Both of these will be explored in this chapter. A useful intermediate stage between automation and full autonomy is "augmentation," where man and machine cooperatively operate a system; this will be discussed as well.

The very visible face of autonomous systems today is the self-driving car. Here again, we have gone from a very manual approach, where humans control every aspect of driving, to automating various driving functions; and from this, to creating fully autonomous vehicles. Efforts to automate driving functions have been sprinkled throughout the car's 130-year history; efforts to build self-driving cars are much more recent. A significant trigger in the latter came from the Defense Advanced Research Projects Agency's Grand Challenge to build an autonomous ground vehicle, held in 2004. Fifteen teams participated, albeit unsuccessfully; the following year, though, 5 teams were successful. This journey since has been long, but finally appears quite near technological success; now, human considerations dominate. The author will draw on this analogy in the discussion of self-driving networks; there are valuable lessons to learn in so doing, while bearing in mind that no analogy is perfect.

Of course, the autonomous system the author focuses on in this chapter is a network, what he likes to call a "self-driving network[2]" (and abbreviated as SDN2). Here, "network" refers to both the connectivity infrastructure (Layer 1 to Layer 4) as well as the service infrastructure (VPN, VoIP, BNG, IPTV, etc.). This is not a description of an existing technology, but rather, a description of a vision of what network operations could (and should!) look like in the future. The author first looks at the motivations for building (or transitioning to) such networks and then the technology needed for SDN2. He next offers some thoughts on the evolution of SDN2 and discusses some of the consequences of self-driving networks. Finally, he touches on human considerations in this journey and suggests topics for further study.

MOTIVATIONS

There are many reasons for pursuing the ideal of self-driving networks:

1. **Effective Personnel:** The ratio of total Operational Expenditure (of which personnel costs are a big component) to total Capital Expenditure in service provider networks is high and growing, from 4.04 in 2007 to 4.35 in 2017 (IHS Markit, 2018). Thus, these personnel must be effectively used. Furthermore, the acquisition of appropriately skilled personnel gets harder from year to year; as evidenced by the following comment by Thierry Bonhomme, the former CEO of Orange Business Services: "The main challenge is competencies." In other words, Orange Business Services is finding it hard to recruit enough people with the right skills: "We are running out of competent staff" (Bonhomme, 2017). However, the use of SDN2 may need new skills (detailed in a later section), as well as the need to maintain current competencies in case SDN2 cannot cope with certain situations.

2. **Efficient Use of Assets:** There are two high-level approaches to managing network capacity: "sweat your assets with traffic engineering" or "throw bandwidth at the problem." SDN2 cuts through this Gordian knot by ambitioning reduce the cost of managing resources, and furthermore, by predicting future needs more accurately. In effect, resources can be used optimally without the concomitant cost of humans micromanaging the network.

3. **Prompt, Accurate Responses to Security Incidents:** The number of security incidents is growing; worse, the fraction of "false positives" is high (Barker, 2018)—draining valuable time and resources from security analysts. A "self-defending network," using much the same techniques as SDN2, can dramatically improve the accuracy and speed both of identifying the real threats and of providing fast, automated responses. (This also contributes to personnel being more effective.) This will be vital typically for the Internet of Things, where the sheer scale of the network (and the dumbness of the vast majority of the devices) points to a looming security nightmare.

4. **Error-Free Operation:** (Koley, 2016) states that in the Google network, "70% of network failures occur when a management operation is in progress" (p. 21). The statistics for other service providers is no better. Such outages increase cost and have an impact on branding. A subtler effect is to make operations more risk-averse and slower, thereby impacting agility. Automation – and eventually, autonomous operation – should reduce these outages to nearly zero. Of course, scenarios where SDN2 is inadequate or incapable of handling, as well as possible bugs in the software can still lead to errors which may at times be catastrophic (the "mad robot" syndrome), amplified because of SDN2's scope is larger than systems today.

5. **Proactive Rather than Reactive Service Handling:** Service assurance and fulfillment are crucial aspects of providing network services, whether as a telco or an enterprise. However, all too often, the network operations center is unaware of service degradation until it happens – or worse, until the subscriber calls in angry. SDN2 can monitor, detect and autonomously remediate service degradations and outages; moreover, it can predict potential failures and avoid impact. Finally, it can learn the subscriber's pattern of network use, and in advance, prepare the network for that. For example, if a subscriber uploads data to the cloud at 4 AM every day, SDN2 can set up adequate

bandwidth and Quality of Service (QoS) to accommodate that behavior, without an explicit request from the subscriber. If successful, this may well be SDN2's greatest contribution.

To summarize, SDN2 is about running your network more efficiently—with higher accuracy, security, and customer satisfaction. To achieve this, SDN2 has to be adaptive (defined here as giving a different output for the same input, based on history and context) and predictive/deterministic. Note that these goals primarily appeal to the network operator's Chief Financial Officer (1, 2 and 4); the Chief Human Resources Officer (1); Chief Information Security Officer (3); and the Chief Customer Officer (5), rather than to the Chief Technology Officer. SDN2 does not look for technological outcomes per se (although it needs significant technology advances); rather, it aims at business outcomes. The ultimate goal is autonomous operation of the network.

PREVIOUS WORK

There have been several previous attempts to reduce human involvement in network operations. Discussed here are: Automation, Self-Organizing Networks (SON), Zero-Touch Provisioning (ZTP), Autonomous Networks (AN), and Zero-Touch Networks (ZTN).

Automation

Automation frameworks have long been used in server complexes. Some that come to mind are Chef, Puppet, Ansible and SaltStack (Chef Docs, 2018; Puppet, 2018; Ansible, 2018; SaltStack, 2018). Alternatively, one can use scripting languages such as Python. These tools simplify configuration, allowing for uniformity across a number of devices. They also make repetitive tasks (such as massive rollouts and software upgrades) easier to manage. They can also be a component of rule-based event-driven utilities (Event-driven programming, 2018) designed to automatically handle common eventualities. These tools have now come to the field of networking. While the goal is to use them across the network, their use tends to be limited to islands of devices from a single equipment vendor, mostly because each vendor's equipment integrates with these tools differently.

SON

Self-Organizing Networks is an effort designed to make the planning and deployment of mobile radio networks simpler and faster; the behavior and functionality has been specified by 3GPP and NGMN (Self-Organizing Networks, 2016). SON has also been proposed for adaptive and scalable network services (Nakano & Suda, 2005). The primary goal is the automatic management of radios, especially the setting of parameters such as power and antenna tilt and their dynamic adjustment; as subscribers and towers come online or go offline. Sub-functions include configuration, optimization, self-healing and self-protection. SON was the focus of some European Union projects (such as SOCRATES (SOCRATES, 2011)); however, there doesn't seem to be much active work going on any longer.

ZTP

Zero-touch provisioning (Watsen, 2018) is the ability to identify and automatically download initial configuration profiles and software to a device (typically on-premise equipment). Once this is done, the device is securely accessible and can be managed remotely or via a web portal. ZTP greatly reduces installation costs and time, as well as errors. The use of reverse ssh (Watsen, RFC 8071, 2017) improves security. ZTP usually only applies on initialization of the device; on-going management is done in a more traditional manner. ZTP is generally offered by the equipment vendor; while there are some standards used in ZTP, most of the implementation is proprietary.

AN

Autonomic networks are the focus of an IETF Working Group (ANIMA WG, 2018) and an IRTF Research Group (NMRG, 2018). This work is primarily focused on network node level autonomy: making nodes self-managing, self-configuring, self-healing, and self-protecting; these are aspects that SDN2 also addresses. This effort is more fully described in Chapters *A Unifying Framework Design for the Management of Autonomic Network Functions* and *ANIMA: Secure Autonomic Network Infrastructure*, so this topic will not be discussed further here.

ZTN

Zero-touch networking is the idea of reducing errors while making changes in the network. The basic idea is to specify the changes at a high-level via "intent". Once this specification is made, the ZTN system uses its current knowledge of the network topology, activities, and statistics to figure out what configuration changes need to be made to what devices, then begins the process of moving from current state to the desired state. These changes are done in a controlled fashion; and at any point, the system can roll back to the original state – if proceeding along the current path is considered risky.

This Work

Of the previous work, ZTN comes closest to SDN2. However, in the author's opinion SDN2 incorporates ideas from automation, autonomous networks, ZTP, ZTN, and goes well beyond. Ideally, network changes are not *driven* by intent, but rather are *guided* by intent. The subtle distinction between "driven" and "guided" lies in whether intent is expressed as an abstract, high-level directive, in which case it retains an imperative nature, or intent captures a desired goal or purpose, in which case intent is purely declarative. In ZTN, intent is a short-lived statement whereby a human specifies the change he/she wants to happen (albeit as an abstract, high-level directive rather than as CLI commands), and the ZTN mechanisms go into action. In SDN2, intent is long-lived: a statement of how the network should be, i.e., the desired state of the network. If the network departs from that, changes in the network happen "on their own" (rather than being triggered by a human) to make the network again satisfy the intent.

Say SLA1 means "less than 40ms site-to-site latency". In ZTN, one might say "Change the network so that customer A's service meets SLA1." The ZTN system would then effect this change. In SDN2, one might instead specify that "all gold customers' service must meet SLA1." Provisioning a new gold customer would trigger changes to meet SLA1. If network conditions change in a way that SLA1 is violated (say, a link fails), changes are automatically made to bring network conditions back in line with the intent (traffic is rerouted); if these attempts fail, a human operator is informed that the intent can no longer be met. More than that, if there is reason to believe that SLA1 may be violated (say a link experiences increasing bit error rates, and that this behavior has historically foreshadowed a link failure; and further, say that this link's failure would violate SLA1), automatic action should be taken to maintain the intent – even though SLA1 has yet to fail. Thus, we progress from intent dictating an action (in ZTN), to intent guiding a reactive response (SDN2 phase 1), to intent guiding a proactive response (SDN2 phase 2). In the future, SDN2 may be able to deduce local intent from network usage patterns or other indicators, but the global goal of the network will still have to be provided by a human (the CFO?).

To use an analogy with cars, ZTN is like using automatic transmission, where the driver (still in charge) expresses their intent (give me more power) and the car takes over the mundane task of managing the clutch and changing gears. On the other hand, SDN2 is analogous to a self-driving car, where the passenger (much less directly in charge) says, "I have a plane to catch" or "I would like to be at the airport"—and the car handles everything from choosing a route to staying within lanes, avoiding obstacles and managing gearing.

Can such networks be built? The author believes so, and hence he proposes the following Networking Grand Challenge (one analogous to the DARPA Grand Challenge in 2004):

Build a system that will handle the full lifecycle of network services – from discovering topology, to identifying customers[3], to provisioning their services, to managing the underlay, to predicting and/or responding to degradation and faults – all without human intervention.

TECHNOLOGY

The SDN2 system is visualized as comprising two subsystems:

- One that, based on real-time data from the network, makes predictions about the network; and
- The other that, given the specification of intent, the real-time data, and the predictions, takes action in the network.

This works in a continuous closed loop.
There are five components needed to make this happen:

1. **Intent:** This consists of a declarative statement about the desired state of the network, what should it optimize for, and what should it avoid. Ideally, this is the only aspect directly controlled by a human.
2. **Streaming Real-Time Telemetry:** This consists of all types of network data, from routing information and topology to statistics about ports, paths, packets and flows, to event notifications.
3. **Prediction:** Given the past and current state of the network, this module makes an informed guess about what is likely to happen.
4. **Evaluation:** This module appraises how well is the intent being met based on the measured state of the network.

5.   **Decision-Making:** Given 1-4, this module makes a systematic choice of actions to take to meet intent.

The following sections will go into each of these in some detail. As a guide, Figure 1 shows how these components interact with the network. Some of them may be partially or fully embedded in network devices.

Intent

Intent is a very high-level specification of the desired state of the network; this desired state will offer SDN2 guidance on how to manage the network. Contrast this with how networks are run today, where operating a network often means logging in to a router, firing up the CLI, and typing commands. This is an imperative approach to operations, where the operator gives direct commands to a device. This is a very device-dependent, narrow view – a service consists of a number of configuration snippets spread across a number of devices—making it hard to provision, understand, update, and troubleshoot. NMS and OSS systems address this by making the commands somewhat more abstract and task-oriented and less device-dependent. One may say, "create a VRF[4] with these 10 endpoints," or "add a new endpoint to this VRF." This approach makes provisioning easier to carry out, to understand and to update, as well as to troubleshoot. However, this is still imperative. ZTN takes this a step further: "transform my network to this new topology" – even more abstract, but still imperative.

On the other hand, a declarative approach says what the desired end state is, without saying how to get there. Telling a self-driving car "take me to the airport" is a very high-level, very abstract statement – but it is still imperative. Telling the car, "I feel like having a richly marbled Wagyu" and having the car take you to your favorite high-end steakhouse is the Holy Grail sought by many AI systems today. This is a truly declarative approach.

However, even though telling a network "Run well" or "Cost less" may be truly declarative, expecting meaningful results with such statements is perhaps a bit too futuristic; too Panglossian. For now, a pragmatic approach is to give the SDN2 system an objective function to optimize, with constraints de-

Figure 1. Network View

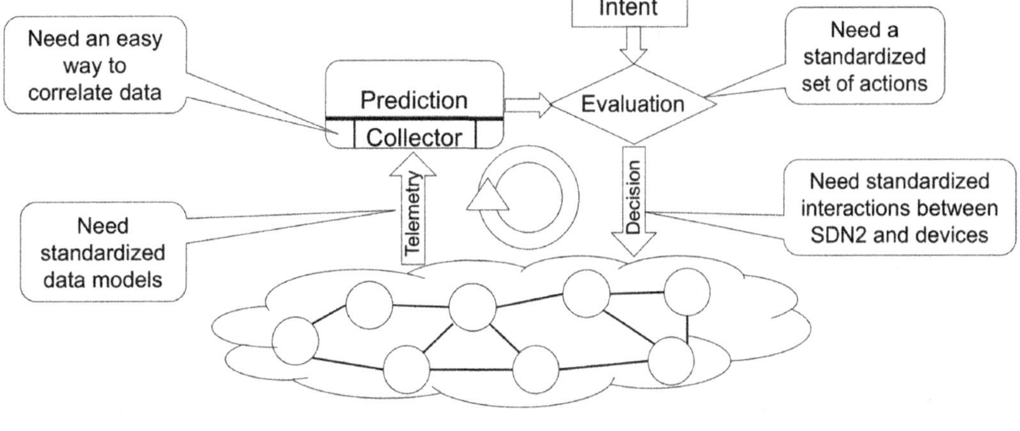

fined by the current network resources. Many (if not all) of the resource constraints can be automatically generated from the network topology, device inventory, and service catalog; so enumerating constraints need not be burdensome. This is a declarative but eminently actionable approach and seems a constructive way forward. This approach is also well-suited for specifying business outcomes, such as customer satisfaction or profitability.

However, most of our interactions with machines are imperative. A statement like "Take appropriate corrective measures if you see unusual traffic patterns for this customer" blurs the boundary between imperative (it is indeed a command) and declarative (it doesn't say much on how to accomplish it). Thus, in addition to the declarative approach, one will need very high-level imperative commands. These imperative commands start by being prescriptive – but over time, the parameters will allow more and more leeway to the SDN2 system as to how to implement the commands. As this happens, the SDN2 system will have more autonomy, and its operation will be less predictable and possibly less deterministic. Of all the technologies mentioned here, the author believes that research into specifying intent – determining the primitives that balance between actionable and abstract; imperative and declarative – is the most open-ended and the most promising approach.

Real-Time Telemetry

The power of "big data" and modern analytics starts with lots of useful, usable data. Such data should be accurate, complete, consistent, relevant, uniform, and timely. Multimodal data should be easy to correlate; this will allow better validation and the extraction of wider and deeper insights.

Network operators collect lots of data. Unfortunately, much of this data is gathered using archaic pull-based methods like SNMP—and then often just put into storage – or, at best, displayed in some graphs. Unless the data is stress-tested, its usefulness is in doubt. Unless one attempts to put the data to use, one has no idea if there is value to be mined. A systematic pursuit of high-quality network data is fundamental to better decision-making. Pull-based telemetry collection tends to be heavy-weight, so the pulling frequency is lower; a bidirectional interaction for each datum is an overkill. The author therefore advocates push-based, streaming, real-time telemetry using standardized data models (Clemm, 2108; Streaming Telemetry, 2018). This means that devices are told: emit such-and-such data (e.g., port statistics) with this accuracy, at this frequency, and in the format defined by this data model. From that point on, the data is streamed from the device to the collector. This collection methodology ensures a much higher quality of data, better timeliness, better uniformity across device types, and easier "correlatability". Before the data is first used, it should be subject to "cleaning"; then, collection rules and validity tests should be put in place to ensure ongoing data hygiene.

By the term 'network data,' the author means: packet and byte statistics bound to ports, paths, flows, applications and services; packet metadata (e.g., source and destination IP addresses, source and destination ports) and contents; syslog data; events and traps; routing and topology updates; time-stamped DHCP and DNS information; timing information, including latency and jitter; transponder power levels and FIB fill levels; mundane items like fan speed and dust levels, and a host of other data. The goal should be to collect every possible type of data as accurately and as often as may be reasonable. However, the "big data" idea of collecting everything all the time from every device is infeasible; just transporting and storing the data may prove too costly. Instead, it is advocated to set reasonable default collection parameters that can be changed dynamically in real time to collect more or less, as needed. For example, packet sampling may pick up one in every 10,000 packets from a port; if something looks suspicious (perhaps via an "smart agent" with behavioral analytics embedded in the device), this may be dialed up to every 100th packet. If deeper analysis indicates this is benign, one can go back to 1:10,000; otherwise, every packet may need to be examined until a decision can be made. This ability to "zoom in" and "zoom out" dynamically as needed balances reasonable data collection with the precision occasionally needed. Furthermore, a hierarchical system that aggregates data at each level makes for a more scalable data collection infrastructure.

Given the multimodal nature of network telemetry, correlation is both a requirement and a feature. For example, one can obtain a packet's metadata by sampling a flow; this contains the source and destination IP addresses. However, these mean little without the time-stamped DHCP information to map the source IP (say) to the subscriber, or without the routing information needed to map the destination IP to the path through the network and the exit peer. One could further correlate this to syslog information related to a transit port's spike in bit error rate and determine that that port's hiccup led to packet loss for this subscriber (see Figure 2). All of this would be enhanced and made simpler if all network elements were to stream telemetry using common data models. This train of thought leads to the next section: putting data to work. The IETF (Clemm, 2108) and OpenConfig (Streaming Telemetry, 2018) have made a start on defining data models for telemetry, although much work remains; companies like Packet Design and Kentik do data correlation.

Prediction

Prediction refers to the ability to go from data to insight – to glean information that may not be obvious at first glance from the data. To do this, one must have high-quality data, as detailed in the previous section. This data must be accurate, timely, and easily correlatable. The insights gleaned may be finding unexpected relations in the data, identifying anomalies, clustering related data points, detecting trends, or forecasting the future. (Agrawal, Gans, & Goldfarb, 2018) consider all of these as being aspects of prediction; prediction is, as they put it, "the ability to take information you have and generate information you didn't previously have," with the ultimate goal of making decisions in the face of uncertainty.

Figure 2. Correlation

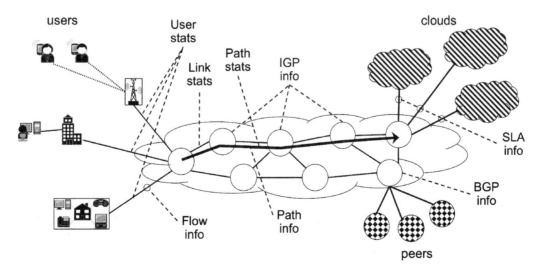

Broadly speaking, there are two approaches to obtain insights: human expertise, encapsulated in rule-based systems and machine learning (ML) systems. The former consists of a set of rules, usually of the form "if this, then that" – basically, if such-and-such an event occurs, take the corresponding action. This requires subject matter experts to define the rules, usually drawing on their extensive experience to define the event-action pairs. While conceptually simple and easy to fine-tune, these rules can quickly become cumbersome; there may be lots of special cases and exceptions, and often prioritization among rules can make it hard to say which rules will fire under a given set of circumstances.

ML takes a different approach: give the machine a large set of training data and allow it to find patterns, classify the data and discover the insights. The emphasis moves from programming rules to curating data. There are three broad classes of ML algorithms: supervised (or semi-supervised) learning, unsupervised learning, and reinforcement learning. Supervised learning requires "labeled data," where for each piece of training data, there is a desired response which is what the ML algorithm is supposed to learn. Obtaining large amounts of labeled data is difficult; manually labeling a given data set is often prohibitive. However, supervised learning has proven very effective and is the basis for great advances in image recognition, speech understanding, and machine translation. Unsupervised learning consists of sorting the training data into clusters of related objects. This does not require the costly labeling process that supervised learning needs; however, the outcomes are less compelling. Reinforcement learning consists of allowing a machine to take action in order to maximize a reward. The trial-and-error nature of this method may dissuade some, but it is a hot topic of research among machine learning experts.

There are many different ML methods; the choice among them depends on the type and quantity of data one has, the insights one wishes, and the desired accuracy. For example, to process log files, one would use one of the methods for "natural language processing," albeit with a specialized vocabulary. To forecast continuous data, one would use one of the time-series analysis methods. There are the so-called "online" methods where one can produce a general model using data from a generic network (say, from all enterprise networks) and then refine that model for a specific network (say a particular financial sector network). Today, much of the process of choosing an ML method, refining it, picking the "hyperparameters" (such as the number of layers in deep learning and the number of neurons in each layer), and tuning the algorithms for highest accuracy without overfitting the data is a black art. Nonetheless, the power and capability of ML methods make them prime candidates for the prediction module. A significant reason for choosing to use ML is that an ML-based system is naturally adaptive—with a different history or context, the same input can give rise to a different (better!) output.

In the final analysis, SDN2 systems will probably use a combination of rule-based and ML systems— much the same way that self-driving cars did (Bilger, 2013), and for much the same reasons. To this end, the development of ML algorithms specialized for networking would be an essential prerequisite.

Evaluation

Networking operations is an ongoing 24/7/365 effort. There are events that stand out, like the introduction of a new device, the provisioning of a new subscriber, or the provisioning of a software upgrade for a set of devices; but most of the activity goes to the "care and feeding" of the network. In SDN2, this is reflected in the continual monitoring of telemetry, comparing the current state to the desired state, and taking actions to bring the network back in line with the intent. This continual evaluation is key to good operations.

Evaluation can be straightforward: Are packets flowing as expected? Is the SLA being met? However, evaluation can draw on predictions: What do these symptoms mean to the effective operation of the network? How does the traffic to a peer compare to the usual baseline traffic? What is the root cause of this failure, and what does that mean for a service? A large part of evaluation is isolating the root cause, so that one treats not just the symptoms but their cause as well.

Evaluation – especially when it determines that network operation is sub-optimal – leads to the next component: decision-making.

Decision-Making

Decisions, and their consequence, actions, may seem like the main focus of network operations. However, they constitute just one part of the overall workflow. Nevertheless, accurate and timely decision-making can be the difference between a quiet, behind-the-scenes aversion of a major outage and a messy public emergency action to rectify a disaster.

Decision-making consists of reading early signs of trouble ahead or a departure from a baseline, isolating the cause, and understanding how best to address the issue. Much of this lies in people's heads, in the form of intuition, instinct, and experience—and isn't written down or codified. In many cases, there is no adequate explanation for why an action is taken, apart from recognition of the fact that "it works!" This makes it harder to pass on the knowledge – whether to the next cadre of operations folks, or to an automation script. But it is vital to codify this, so that the decision is reliably repeatable; the consequences are understood; and errors are minimized. This brings us to another aspect of decision-making: how to operationalize the decision.

Since networks are (by their nature) interconnected systems, it is important, when making a change, to know what the "blast radius" is – the possible side effects and their range of influence – and to find ways to limit this. It is also important (as far as possible) to have contingency plans to revert the change in case there are unforeseen repercussions. Finally, there may be simultaneous changes in other parts of the network whose interactions with the current change are unknown. For all these reasons, changes are first tried out in a safe zone (such as a lab); are planned carefully as a sequence of steps, each of which can be reversed; and are generally done in a "maintenance window" when network usage is at a low (often from 1 AM to 4 AM). However, such a cautious approach means that network upgrades (of both software and hardware) and new service offerings are rolled out slowly. Automation can significantly speed this up. Increasingly, the available network downtime is shrinking as network usage spans all 24 hours of a day and every day of the week.

Even with automation, a similar cautious approach is recommended. But the speed with which each step is carried out, and the accuracy of evaluating whether the step is successful before moving on to the next step can be much higher. With experience and some learning, each step can be customized in real-time to the situation at hand—thereby reducing the likelihood of having to roll it back. The net result is that one can carry out upgrades of the network and of services much more confidently, and thus more frequently. In a later section, this increased confidence in automation will be seen to culminate in the notion of "Service Motion."

Architecture

The five components detailed above work together to form an SDN2 system, as described in Figure 3. The SDN2 systems take two inputs:

- The real-time telemetry from the network, and;
- The intent defined by the network operator. and produces a single output:
- Actions that change network state.

The SDN2 system includes a Prediction subsystem (shown here as being a single ML unit, but which would in practice consist of multiple ML units and rules engines – plus, for the foreseeable future, human input). The Prediction subsystem needs trained ML models. These are the output of the ML Model Creation (MLMC) subsystem whose input is training data. The Prediction subsystem's output (the model) is fed into the Evaluation subsystem, which (in turn) feeds into the Decision subsystem, which takes the needed actions to bring the network in line with the operator's intent.

This is, of course, an idealistic view. In practice, there will be several SDN2 systems, each in charge of a part of the network. These systems may be divided on an administrative basis, a geographical basis, and/or a functional basis. These will interact with each other for the overall management of the network. Again, this is analogous with self-driving cars, where there is a subsystem for managing the gears, and another for lane control, and yet another for obstacle detection and avoidance; furthermore, there are four sets of sensors, one for each tire. The overall self-driving experience is the sum total of all of these subsystems working together. Of course, the interaction of these SDN2 subsystems must be harmonized, and that can often be a challenge. Some more details on hierarchical/functional decomposition will be forthcoming in the next section (in Figure 5).

Figure 3. Architecture of SDN2

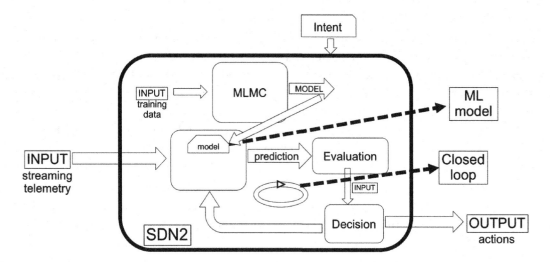

EVOLUTION

One may look at this vision and say, "Nice, perhaps – but this is a faraway, futuristic dream." It's likely that the same attitude was evoked twenty years ago whenever the notion of a fully autonomous car was discussed. The author believes that achieving SDN2 is well within our capabilities; he sees SDN2 evolving in a series of stages outlined in Figure 4.

SAE issued a taxonomy of "automated driving systems" (SAE International, 2016) identifying six levels of driving automation from 0 ("no automation") to 5 ("full automation"). Here, a similar classification of automation is proposed for networks, from 0 ("manual") to 5 ("fully autonomous"). This taxonomy serves multiple purposes:

- It presents a feasible roadmap for getting from where most networks are today to SDN2. Without this, SDN2 may appear as a faraway, futuristic dream. These stages ground the vision in a concrete reality—each stage of which is attainable, and the benchmark of progress towards which is tangible and beneficial.
- It offers an objective means whereby operators can evaluate where they are on the journey to SDN2. It also allows them to determine the skills, capabilities and functional blocks they need to advance to the next stage.
- It allows equipment vendors to [A] set a roadmap to achieve these objectives and [B] build the functional blocks needed by operators in a purposeful manner.

The SDN2 system will have to be developed, debugged, optimized, and customized. All this will take time; however, equally important is the process whereby humans adapt to the new technology, learn how to work with it, and eventually come to trust it. The author sees the following evolution:

Manual → Automation → Motorization → Analytics → Augmentation → Autonomy.

Figure 4. Six stages of SDN2

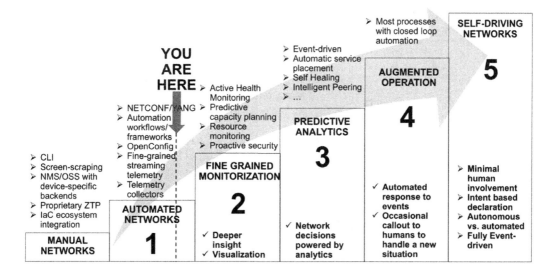

Most networks are between Manual and Automation, whereas the goal is full autonomy. However, in between is an interesting and viable step: man and machine working together for the most responsive, optimal operation of the network. This is a feasible, realistic stage in the quest for full autonomy, where the machine

- **Takes in Enormous Amounts of Data:** In real-time from everywhere in the network,
- **Crunches Them Down:** To a relative small set of urgent and important triggers, and
- **Presents These to the Human:** Whose intuition, experience, and creativity may suggest the right course of action.

Thereupon, the machine may learn and throw up fewer and fewer "exceptions" for the human to handle; and at some point, the human may step back and allow the machine full reign over the network.

Another aspect of SDN2 is the closed loop automation that lies at the heart of the system. This is another vehicle for building systems that are adaptive and predictive. Constructing a closed loop with the required properties may appear daunting at first. Divide-and-conquer helps ground it in reality. A closed loop is implemented as a set of constituent, closed sub-loops, each with a particular function; but which, as a whole, is carrying out the tasks of the main loop (see Figure 5).

In this diagram, the main loop monitors a service end-to-end. To do this, the loop relies on sub-loops that manage aspects of the service:

- Service placement;
- Health monitoring;
- SLA monitoring, and;
- Underlay management.

Figure 5. Sub-loops of the main loop

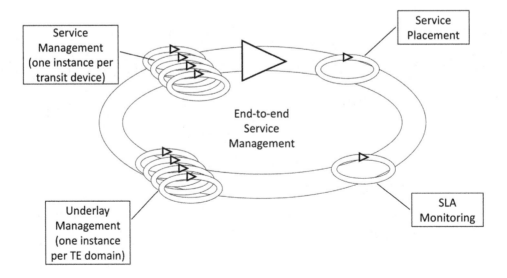

Each of these sub-loops is itself a closed loop that may further be decomposed into constituent parts. To see how these sub-loops interact, suppose service placement configures a service on a given line card. The health monitor kicks in to monitor the line card; SLA monitoring watches how the end-to-end service is working. The health monitor may indicate that a line card essential to the delivery of the service is about to fail. This triggers root cause analysis to attempt to find where the problem lies and remediate the problem. If this is successful, the problem has been averted. If remediation is unsuccessful, the health monitor may alert the service management loop of the impending failure. The service management loop may in turn call upon the underlay management sub-loop to find an alternative path that bypasses the failing line card. If that proves successful, the problem has again been averted. If not, the alert –along with the status of the SLA monitor to indicate how urgent the problem is – may be propagated to a person so that a human can handle the problem.

Note that it is perfectly valid to implement each loop/sub-loop in the manner most suitable to its function. For example, the Service Management sub-loop may be implemented as a rule-based event-driven script. For instance:

1. If the FIB is over 90% full, a script may trigger garbage collection and redownload the FIB.
2. If queue lengths exceed latency limits, a script may activate more aggressive RED.
3. If local remediation fails, a script may trigger the Service Placement sub-loop to handle the problem.

On the other hand, the Underlay Manager may rely on predictive, time series-based analysis to manage paths. If the bandwidth on a link in a given path exceeds a threshold learnt from past behavior, the underlay manager may trigger a path change to proactively avoid congestion.

The goal here is to build each sub-loop in the most pragmatic way possible—and then to consider how they interact to implement the overall loop. Furthermore, each sub-loop may be implemented regionally, by administrative domain, or by device. Thus, the relationships between loops may be hierarchical and/or distributed.

CONSEQUENCES

As progress is made towards the goal of building functional Self-Driving Networks, attention should be paid in parallel to some of the consequences of this technology. This section will look at some of these consequences; but the bigger picture is to be aware of, and to prepare for, the tremendous impact SDN2 will have on how we build, operate, and even conceive networks.

Fundamentally, the thesis that machine learning has dramatically reduced the cost of making predictions and increased their accuracy (Agrawal, Gans, & Goldfarb, 2018) – and will continue to do so – has far-reaching implications. Capacity planning – which today often uses outdated assumptions, inexact forecasting, and gross generalizations – can be much more targeted, more precise and quantifiable, and more sensitive in future to "weak signals" that today would be dismissed as a rounding error. This would result in better use of CAPEX and deployed infrastructure and better planned upgrade cycles. At a finer granularity, prediction allows operators to have some idea of when and where to expect traffic surges; the need for specific network services; or an early indication of a security breach. As operators get more comfortable with predictive methods in networking, there is increased scope to incorporate external influences such as weather conditions, social media, current or planned events, and disasters.

Why does this matter? As has been mentioned, the effective use of prediction changes the philosophy of network operations from a reactive to a proactive approach. Truly understanding this has a huge impact on operational strategy, marketing, customer retention, and competitiveness. To illustrate one possibility, the author offers the notion of "Service Motion" (analogous to virtual machine motion in compute orchestration).

Service Placement and Motion

Figure 6 This shows how services are deployed in a compute environment (on the left-hand side of Figure 6) and in a service provider network environment (on the right), both in a pre-orchestration world. The compute servers are dedicated, single-function devices—each running one application (for example, a database). The servers are generally very similar – there may be some differences in peripherals. For example, the web server may have more network links; and the database server may have greater storage. Each server is directly connected to the storage it needs. On the right-hand side of Figure 6, there are "network servers" – i.e., edge routers that provide VPN, peering, and broadband services. These again are dedicated, single-function devices directly attached to the access circuits that connect them to their customers or peers.

In this environment, the database administrator "owns" the database server and dictates when the server hardware and software is upgraded; schedules downtime for maintenance; etc. However, this freedom came at the cost of server inefficiency. More than that, an irreparable crash meant days of downtime while a replacement server was obtained. Capacity expansion meant weeks or months of delays while the servers were ordered, received, racked, and ready to run – basically, the laws of physics ruled. Virtualization coupled with orchestration provided a solution and has upended how apps are deployed over the past decade—and, in a very real way, this combination has freed us from the chains of physics.

In the post-orchestration picture, a physical server runs multiple virtual machines (VMs) (and nowadays, containers). Each VM replaces the dedicated server of old. When an app needs to run, a server is found to host the app's VM. This placement is driven both by the app's needs (CPU; memory; storage; networking) and by the current state of the data center. To allow the placer freedom of action, storage is network-attached, so that every server is a viable candidate for hosting the app. After placement, the app is started. While it is running, telemetry is sent to the orchestrator, which is monitoring how the app's service levels. If the app is not doing well (say, if the CPU is insufficient, or if network connectivity is poor), the orchestrator can move the app to another physical server. This process is called "VM motion."

Figure 6. Pre-orchestration service deployment

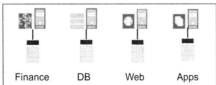

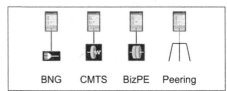

Figure 7. Post-orchestration/SDN2 service deployment

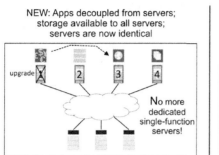
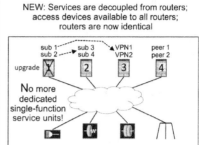

How can a similar system be used to deploy network services? Do we need virtualization as pursued by the Network Function Virtualization effort (ETSI NFV, 2012)? No. All edge routers can support multiple network services. The missing piece is the orchestration, which is a self-driving mini-loop responsible for service placement and service motion. Here is how it would work:

- To start with, every edge router must have connectivity to a reasonable set of access equipment.
- When a new subscriber tries to connect, a service orchestrator authenticates her and gets her service profile. Then, the mini-loop kicks in: using telemetry from candidate edge routers, it evaluates which one is best suited to offer the subscriber her service, a decision is made and the provisioning carried out, and the subscriber is connected.
- The mini-loop continues monitoring the subscriber's service levels as well as telemetry from the serving router; if the service isn't doing well, she is moved to another router using the same process.

Freedom from physics!

Note that doing service motion manually would lead to the (legitimate) fear of service disruption due to operator error. Doing it via an automation script initiated by a human operator monitoring and evaluating service levels would be both too labor-intensive and too slow. The best way to do this would be via a self-driving mini-loop as described above. Note that service motion may not be hitless; it is a trade-off between a quick disconnection and a lengthy period of poor service.

Managing and Securing at Scale

Another consequence of SDN2 is that operators will be much better prepared to deal with the scale of, for example, the Internet of Things (IoT) than they are today. While much has been said of the benefits of IoT, the applications it will enable, and the scale that it will drive, not enough has been said about how to manage IoT at scale, or indeed how to secure IoT at scale. Experts expect that IoT will add tens of billions of end points to the Internet over the next few years. Managing these devices – and managing the network connecting them to the "cloud" (where their application services live) – will be non-trivial tasks. IoT devices will use the network in extremely diverse ways, from thermostats sending a few bytes every few minutes to security cameras streaming 4K video; from services that are life-critical or mission-critical to those that are frivolous entertainment.

To meet these challenges, automation is critical but is insufficient in and of itself. The ability to autonomously adjust the network to the needs of IoT devices will be crucial, especially when a change is multiplied 10,000-fold. Fortunately, large sets of IoT devices will behave similarly enough that they can be treated as a "flock of birds" (Kohalmi, 2018) that move roughly in synchrony. ML can detect these patterns and nudge the flock as needed; ML can also detect individual devices with anomalous behavior and flag them for further inspection. Mini-loops that autonomously oversee similar flocks of IoT devices make the task of managing them much more tractable than managing the devices individually.

Skills Requirement

The current interest in open source software, Software Defined Networking, and "netops" has led network operators to focus on hiring or developing personnel with software or scripting skills in addition to expertise on network protocols and services, and various network operating systems. However, as SDN2 receives more attention, there will be a need for personnel who understand how ML works and who know how to guide and regulate its behavior. There will additionally be a need for understanding control loops and how to manage them and ensure their safe operation. New techniques for debugging ML and control loops will have to be learned; there may be new scripting languages or primitives to create new mini-loops for managing some aspect of the network.

Another direction for skills development is service creation. As operators are freed up from the mundane tasks of managing the network, they can focus on the more creative aspects of network management. This may involve service "mash-ups"—putting together existing service modules to devise new services, monitoring their uptake, and evaluating what aspects attract and hold customers. Of course, for this to work out, deploying new services must be easy and cheap; and existing service constructs must be modular and simple to plug together. SDN2 guarantees that deploying services will be easy and cheap – but making them modular is the responsibility of the humans designing them. This presents an opportunity for new skills: creating new pluggable service modules from scratch. Other possibilities for creativity include finding new ways to monitor and monetize services. Another area is guiding SDN2 how to adapt to changing customer interests so as to reduce "churn," especially in mobile networks.

This is not to say that current skills, in knowing how networking works, how protocols run, or how devices interoperate; certification programs in vendor operating systems and their CLI; expertise in designing networks for new applications; or experience in debugging and troubleshooting faults will lose their value overnight. These will still be in high demand (and today, they are often in short supply); but they will need to be augmented with other skills described above. For example, if a statement of peering intent leads to a certain BGP policy that is expressed the CLI of a given networking OS, someone will have to parse the CLI command, see if it matches the BGP policy requirement, and see if that (in turn) is a reasonable implementation of the intent. This requires familiarity with both the CLI and the BGP policy. If the intent is not properly implemented, though, this will further require either restating the intent to achieve the desired goal or tweaking the SDN2 system to produce the desired result. Thus, BGP and CLI know-how will have to be enhanced with proficiency in the intent language and in the SDN2 system.

HUMAN CONSIDERATIONS

In this section, some of the human impacts of SDN2 will be considered. Much of this chapter has focused on the benefits of SDN2; here, some of the challenges that SDN2 will bring are examined.

Building an autonomous system is not simply an act of creation. It is also an avenue of transfer of control from human to machine. For example, automatic transmission takes over the choice of which gear to drive in from the human driver. Self-driving cars take over from humans the entire task of driving the car. To rephrase William Lamb, "With autonomy comes great responsibility." So, in both of these cases, who takes responsibility if something goes wrong? This problem has come to the fore with recent fatal incidents involving autonomous cars. Is the machine at fault? The designer? The manufacturer? Does the driver retain some responsibility? There are those who say that focusing on this issue dampens enthusiasm for autonomous cars—which will eventually surpass humans' ability to drive safely. While it is true that self-driving cars will eventually be safer than humans, it does not necessarily follow that one must avoid a discussion of who bears responsibility. Similarly, for SDN2, one should discuss what happens if an SDN2 system misbehaves and disrupts service to a wide swath of customers – or if it fails to detect a security breach – even as one works to realize SDN2 and make it successful.

In this description, SDN2 may appear to be a neat, organized sequence of steps; in practice, it will not be so. Events are asynchronous; an action taken will lead to changes that may in turn require a new action; some decisions will take longer than others, meaning that the responses may be out of sync. Thus, the operation of SDN2 will often seem chaotic and incomprehensible. Moreover, SDN2 will likely start off as a rule-based system, but over time will move to a more dynamic ML basis so as to adapt more readily to changing circumstances. Thus, SDN2 may appear non-deterministic: the same event in different contexts may provoke different responses at different times.

This situation is exacerbated with the current reality that while ML systems work amazingly well for certain problems, most experts have little idea how[5]. Debugging and fine-tuning ML is largely a black art today. As ML forms a significant component of SDN2, this is a big concern. To the SDN2 behavior described above, add the probably correct but rather opaque operation of the ML subsystem—and the problems multiply. It would behoove us to build introspection and self-monitoring into SDN2.

Furthermore, the control loop subsystem of SDN2 is another area which needs attention from the point of view of correctness and the ability to troubleshoot. Careful consideration must be given to how actions are sequenced, whether they can be reversed individually or in aggregate, and how many autonomous decisions are taken without human oversight. Another aspect is the relationship between SDN2 systems; as has been mentioned, practical SDN2 systems will be structured hierarchically and distributed geographically. If each system makes autonomous decisions and runs its control loop independently, even if each individual decision is good in the context where it was made, the overall result may not be desirable.

Security is another concern. Centralized systems invite attack; subverting a single device is less exciting than taking control of a regional network or an entire data center. Besides the usual security breaches, deep neural nets are vulnerable to "adversarial attacks" (Eykholt, 2018) that, while easily thwarted by humans, can utterly confuse ML systems.

Ultimately, what is needed to hand over control is a strong measure of trust. When humans are in charge, one is aware that they may err, sometimes even spectacularly; but one generally trusts that their experience and "common sense" will prevent catastrophic mistakes. (This trust is occasionally unwarranted; but nonetheless, it exists.) However, there is not an equal trust in machines, either that they won't err, or that they will recognize and ignore unreasonable requests (whether accidental or deliberate). This trust will have to be earned; any misstep along the way will result in a disproportionate loss of confidence. A failsafe system where a human can take over if needed is a must until we have enough confidence in SDN2.

Fortunately, there is a good solution to this issue of trust: the "augmentation" mode of operation, whereby man and machine work together. This is one case where the analogy between self-driving cars and self-driving networks breaks down. The augmented mode of autonomous driving (Level 3 or 4) means that the car will mostly drive itself, but will occasionally alert the human driver to take over. This can have adverse results: expecting a human driver to switch contexts from whatever they were doing (texting/snoozing) to driving and to make a sub-second life-or-death decision is unreasonable. However, with network operations, this mode can work really well. In a fully autonomous mode, the SDN2 system takes in tons of data and outputs what it determines to be the best response. In augmented mode, the SDN2 system takes in the same data, but outputs instead what it considers to be (say) the five most influential determinants of action, and the top three choices of response—and lets the human pick between them. Typically, a network action isn't life-or-death or urgent, so this mode works well. Augmented systems build trust, as the human in the loop can inject experience and "common sense" into the algorithmic response; further, one can tally how often SDN2 comes up with the right determinants and responses, and thereby have a quantitative measure of the system's trustworthiness. This process is not unlike an expert mentoring an apprentice.

On an orthogonal note, SDN2 is driven almost entirely on data. This data can be general telemetry about the network; it can also be deeply personal data on subscribers: when and how they use the network, what websites they visit, their network behavior patterns. This data can be sensitive and may intrude on the subscriber's privacy; it can also be used to mount a security attack on the subscriber. This applies equally to business customers: Data on when and how they talk to other corporations and to their own customers; traffic patterns; and so on can be confidential—revealing relationships that the business would prefer to remain private; or providing an avenue for a security breach. As we are seeing with the current debate on social media, there is a careful balance to be maintained between gathering highly individualized data and providing well-targeted services (or ads) – and the privacy of the subscriber. It would serve us well to keep this in mind when building SDN2, rather than trying to retrofit this after the fact (as the social media giants are doing).

Finally, one must consider what impact SDN2 would have on jobs. In the past, automation has led to short-term job loss, but longer-term job gains, both in the number and quality of jobs. The disruption and pain from the short-term job loss is real and not to be discounted; however, the jobs lost have almost always been replaced with better-paying and more fulfilling jobs. It is not clear that that trend will continue, however; (Ford, 2015) offers a bleaker view of the future. In the Skills Requirement in the last section, the author outlines some new jobs and new skills that can replace the mundane tasks that SDN2 will take over. The question is really about numbers: how many jobs will be lost, and how many new ones will be created. Technological progress is ineluctable, and even if SDN2 (and automation in general, the theme of this book) is not pursued simply to save personnel costs but rather for the other benefits (as well as to remain competitive), this "side effect" has to be pondered and prepared for.

Each of the above topics has corresponding implications for legislation, many of which parallel those for self-driving cars: who is responsible for failures; how are decisions monitored, defended and certified; how is the safety of a sequence of autonomous actions guaranteed; what constitutes responsible use of data; and finally, should there be laws regarding what jobs can and should be given over to autonomous systems?

RESEARCH TOPICS

The foremost of the research topics is an intent language in which one can specify at a high-level what one desires the network to do, and yet is concrete enough to be realizable. As was mentioned, one possibility is to express intent as an optimization problem. This only captures some types of intent; other approaches are needed, including those that are imperative. The SDN2 system posits the use of ML; some of these are fairly straightforward (natural language processing for textual data; time series analysis for continuous data), but other applications may require either new techniques or a novel combination of existing techniques. It would be useful to superpose inferences on a topology. For example, doing root cause analysis of IGP failures is enhanced when events and actions of IGP neighbors can be incorporated. Similarly, one can use a Layer 1 topology to diagnose optical faults, or one can use the BGP topology to diagnose BGP problems.

Research into how best to achieve the "zoom in, zoom out" approach to telemetry that would allow the efficient gathering of network data is of interest. The exploration of how anonymized or aggregated data can be used be used to make good predictions is also of interest. As we use telemetry data to make predictions, new sensors and new sensor technologies may suggest themselves. On the standardization front, good data models for network telemetry of every kind are necessary; these would have to have effective means of correlation to improve our ability to reason about the data.

Feedback loops form a critical part of autonomous systems. There is an extensive theory of control loops. However, in the context of SDN2, it would be necessary to understand how to regulate these loops (analogously, what would be the required number of "cadmium rods" to prevent meltdown?), how to assess the effect of interacting control loops, and how to evaluate the potential "blast radius" of their actions.

CONCLUSION

A vision for the future of network operations – the Self-Driving Network – has been presented here. It is a vision that the author believes is feasible, necessary, and in some sense inevitable. Many of the technologies needed to implement this vision are available today; some avenues for research are given above. The overall task is huge, but a viable sequence of stages has been presented whereby the end goal can be achieved. While the ultimate goal is full autonomy, the author argues for a stage where man and machine work together for the best of both worlds: the machine's ability to crunch large amounts of data, to tirelessly monitor systems, and to flawlessly execute instructions – coupled with a human's intuition, experience and "common sense" – is a pragmatic approach to improving agility, reducing error, and enhancing the speed and accuracy of network operations.

Ultimately, the goal is to build networks that adapt and meaningfully respond to changes in network usage, that predict the user needs and proactively prepare for them, and that understand baseline behavior and flag anomalies. These changes would make networks much more user-friendly and would result in higher customer satisfaction. The author proposes that machine learning and closed feedback loops are key elements to building such networks.

While much works remains to be done, the good news is that we can make significant progress with the tools we have today – telemetry, data models, intent-based configuration and automation. As we proceed along the stages of SDN2, we will discover new applications of SDN2; new ways to construct networks; new benefits to this work; and new research topics to explore. The main thing is to start the journey.

ACKNOWLEDGMENT

Many thanks to the many people who contributed to the discussion and helped crystallize my thoughts and refine my ideas. Those who stand out especially are Javier Antich, Mark Seery, Raghu Subramanian, and Ahmed Guetari. In particular, I would like to thank Javier for the initial inspiration for Figure 4: Six stages of SDN2. There are indeed many more who helped refine my thinking and evangelize this vision – too many to mention for fear of leaving someone out. Thank you, all – you know who you are!

REFERENCES

Agrawal, A., Gans, J., & Goldfarb, A. (2018). *Prediction Machines: The Simple Economics of Artificial Intelligence*. Harvard Business Press.

ANIMA WG. (2018, March). Retrieved April 2018, from IETF: https://datatracker.ietf.org/wg/anima/about/

Ansible. (2018, June 1). Retrieved from Ansible: https://www.ansible.com

Barker, I. (2018, February). *Security service providers suffer from false positive alert overload*. Retrieved April 2018, from Beta news: https://betanews.com/2018/02/12/false-positive-alert-overload/

Bilger, B. (2013, November 25). Auto Correct. *The New Yorker*.

Bonhomme, T. (2017, March/April). *Global Telecoms Business*.

Chef Docs. (2018). Retrieved April 2018, from https://docs.chef.io/chef_overview.html

Clemm, A. E. (2108, May 31). *YANG Datastore Subscription*. Retrieved from IETF: https://datatracker.ietf.org/doc/draft-ietf-netconf-yang-push/

ETSI NFV. (2012). Retrieved April 2018, from ETSI: http://www.etsi.org/technologies-clusters/technologies/nfv

Event-driven programming. (2018, June 1). Retrieved from Wikipedia: https://en.wikipedia.org/wiki/Event-driven_programming

Eykholt, K. E. (2018, April 10). *Robust Physical-World Attacks on Deep Learning Models*. Retrieved April 2018, from arxiv: https://arxiv.org/abs/1707.08945

Ford, M. (2015). *Rise of the Robots: Technology and the Threat of a Jobless Future*. Basic Books.

IBM Knowledge Center. (2018, June 1). *Rule-based event-driven solutions*. Retrieved from IBM: https://www.ibm.com/support/knowledgecenter/en/SSQP76_8.9.0/com.ibm.odm.itoa.overview/topics/con_how_to_develop_solution.html

SAE International. (2016). *Taxonomy and definitions for terms related to driving automation systems for on-road motor vehicles*. Standard J3016.

Kohalmi, S. (2018, April). *AINet 2018, Day 3*. Retrieved April 2018, from Upperside Conferences: https://www.uppersideconferences.com/ainet/ainet_2018_agenda_day_3.html

Koley, B. (2016). *Twelfth International Conference on Network and Servce Management*. Montreal: IFIP; https://edas.info/web/cnsm2016/index.html

IHS Markit. (2018). *Service Provider Capex, Opex, Revenue and Subscribers Database*. Author.

Nakano, T., & Suda, T. (2005). Self-Organizing Network Services and Evolutionary Adaptation. *IEEE Transactions on Neural Networks*, 6(5), 1269–1278. doi:10.1109/TNN.2005.853421 PMID:16252832

NMRG. (2018, April). Retrieved April 2018, from IRTF: https://datatracker.ietf.org/rg/nmrg/about/

Puppet. (2018). Retrieved April 2018, from https://puppet.com

SaltStack. (2018). Retrieved April 2018, from https://saltstack.com

Self-Organizing Networks. (2016, December 7). Retrieved April 2018, from Wikipedia: https://en.wikipedia.org/wiki/Self-organizing_network

SOCRATES. (2011, February 22). Retrieved from fp7: http://www.fp7-socrates.eu

Streaming telemetry. (2018, June 1). Retrieved from OpenConfig: http://openconfig.net/projects/telemetry/

Watsen, K. (2017, February). *RFC 8071*. Retrieved from IETF: https://tools.ietf.org/html/rfc8071

Watsen, K. (2018, March 5). *Zero Touch Provisioning for Networking Devices*. Retrieved from IETF: https://tools.ietf.org/html/draft-ietf-netconf-zerotouch-21

KEY TERMS AND DEFINITIONS

Augmentation: A system where man and machine work together, leveraging each partner's strengths and compensating for the other's weaknesses, to achieve a certain goal.

Autonomous System: A system in charge of some entity (such as a network) that monitors conditions, evaluates them in the light of some goal, and makes decisions to achieve the goal, without the help of a human.

Intent: An abstract, declarative statement of a desired state or action.

Machine Learning: A field of computer science that uses statistical techniques to give computer systems the ability to "learn" (e.g., progressively improve performance on a specific task) with data, without being explicitly programmed.

Prediction: The act of taking information one has and generating information one didn't previously have.

Proactive Management: Action in anticipation of an event or condition that may affect a system, based on a prediction that the event will occur, or the condition will arise.

Service Motion: The live migration of a network service from a port on a network device to a different port on the same or a different network device.

Telemetry: the measurement and transmission of the readings of a sensor to a collector where the information is stored and catalogued.

ENDNOTES

[1] Not to be confused with BGP Autonomous Systems! Here, the term refers to systems that operate without the need for human control or management. An autonomous system may use automation, but that is not necessary.

[2] The author believes that he is the first to coin this term, which he presented at an Upperside conference in Paris in March 2016. Since then, the term has proved popular, e.g., for a Stanford University Computer Science Project in November 2017; for a workshop on Self-Driving Networks at the SIGCOMM, August 2018; and in various collateral corporate settings.

[3] This challenge is limited to customers already known to the network; recruiting and bringing on board new customers is best left to another system (not SDN2), which may be run by a human or machine.

[4] Virtual Routing and Forwarding (a type of IP layer Virtual Private Network).

[5] Often, humans cannot say why they took a certain action; this is explained away as "instinct" or "intuition." That latitude is not given to machines.

Chapter 3
A Unifying Framework Design for the Management of Autonomic Network Functions

Laurent Ciavaglia
Nokia Bell Labs, France

Pierre Peloso
Nokia Bell Labs, France

ABSTRACT

The increased use of software-driven and virtualization techniques enables more versatile network infrastructures. Realizing the full potential of such large and dynamic systems requires advanced automation and adaptation capabilities. In this chapter, the authors review recent development of so-called self-driving networks combining cognitive techniques and autonomic behaviors. In particular, the authors provide insights on a set of core mechanisms for the operation of self-driving networks: (1) a governance function to help operators deploy, pilot, control, and track run-time behaviors and performance of self-driving functions; (2) a coordination function to ensure stability and performance when several self-driving functions are running together; (3) a knowledge function to share relevant information to empowering their actions; and (4) common workflows, lifecycles, and APIs to enable deployment and interoperability of autonomic functions. The analysis connects with reference work in scientific literature and the most recent developments in standards (e.g., IETF/IRTF and ETSI).

INTRODUCTION

Networks evolve constantly because of recurring factors such as the steady increase in the traffic volume, number of devices and their interactions (e.g., machine-to-machine type communications). In parallel other characteristics of networks endure: technology heterogeneity, and silos (technological and administrative) despite the continuous progress in techniques, computing, and storage capacity.

DOI: 10.4018/978-1-5225-7146-9.ch003

The above combination impacts negatively the complexity of distributed systems and their control and management; the scalability, speed, and human–dependency of their operations; and contributes to network capabilities under-utilization. As a result, networks operate in worst-case or over-provisioning scenarios, advanced features are not used because of lack of knowledge how to configure them properly or by fear to make the network unstable.

Furthermore, network operations are typically human-driven and thus time-consuming, expensive, and error-prone. Complexity and costs hinder network innovation and the deployment of new enriched service.

The ultimate goal of self-managing networks is to overcome these limits by providing intelligent, adaptive, modular, and automated carrier-grade control functions for seamless, end-to-end, and cross-technology interworking. This overarching goal can be derived into the following objectives:

Objective 1: Multi-facet unification, consisting in the federation of existing architectures and unification management principles across multiple technologies.

Objective 2: Network empowerment, consisting in the embedding of network intelligence to achieve true self-managing networks.

Objective 3: Industry readiness, consisting in the demonstration of deployability and developing migration strategies for large adoption by the industry.

Objective 4: Trust and confidence, consisting in demonstrating the reliability of every autonomic solution and developing standard testing and certification procedures.

Coping With Network Ecosystem Diversity

As illustrated in Figure 1, the network ecosystem is composed of multiple types of autonomic functions (AFs) using diverse technologies, and generating multiple roles, interactions, and relationships.

Figure 1. Diversity of autonomic functions in the network ecosystem

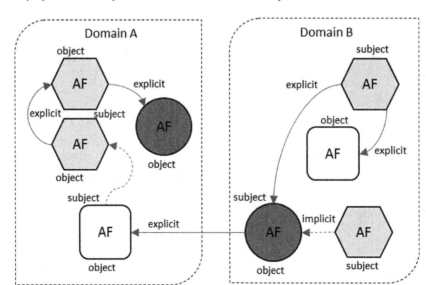

In this context an autonomic function can be defined as: designed and deployed for a specific purpose, An AF uses a relevant method to solve an operational problem with a given performance objective, within a specific network (or service) technology domain and controls network resources. For example, an autonomic function performing load balancing in core IP/MPLS network is described in (Fotenios, Tsagkaris, Peloso, Ciavaglia, & Demestichas, 2014).

There can be as many autonomic functions as they are problems to solve and variations of autonomic functions as designers to implement them. Therefore, to cope with the natural diversity of the networks' ecosystem and potentially large amount of autonomic function versions, certain levels of commonalities should be defined. Two primary levels of such commonalities emerge (Figure 2): a common model for autonomic functions and common framework for the management of those autonomic functions.

Both levels aim at providing: (1) uniform representation of the respective entities and; (2) uniform operation and control means.

The AF Application Programming Interface (API) consists in a unified abstraction of the AF external behavior, exposed via a set of interfaces to connect and interact with functions of the management framework, other AFs, and AF-controlled resources (e.g., network elements). As such, the AF API is an important element of AF standardization.

Towards a Unified Management Framework

Proposing a clean-slate management framework architecture faces deep scepticism from network operators, who are reluctant to give complete control of their networks to some novel autonomic processes without strong guarantees. Moreover, such clean-slate approaches run the risk of being unrelated to real network operation and management issues. Thus, an evolutionary approach to the problem is usually preferred.

First, a general framework and its functional planes should be defined for autonomic networking.

Figure 2. Autonomic functions (AFs) and their management framework (MF)

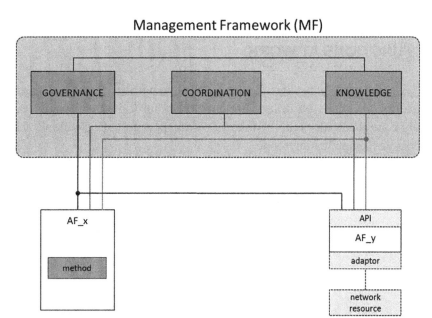

Services spanning over multiple technological boundaries necessitate advances in network management and transform consequently the operational models. From this evolution emerges the need for a unified and extensible framework realizing a cross-technology and common operational substrate for autonomic mechanisms and their related management processes. Such a Management Framework (MF) enables deploying AFs at scale, and following common operational principles (Galani, Tsagkaris, Demestichas, Nguengang, BenYahia, Stamatelatos,... & Ciavaglia, 2012; Stamatelatos, Yahia, Peloso, Fuentes, Tsagkaris, & Kaloxylos, 2013).

An AF encapsulates the code of the "autonomic function fulfilled", i.e., a closed control loop mechanism, and interacts with other AFs. The main objective of the MF is thus to enable a trustworthy interworking through coordination and cooperation among AFs and ensure their seamless deployment (technology-agnostic plug-and-play capability) within an operator's management ecosystem. The successful deployment of multiple AFs relies on the ability to govern based on the principles of policy continuum, to orchestrate AF operations, and to enable the unified exchange of information among involved entities. These three essential building blocks constitute the MF core functions and unified interfaces: Governance, Coordination, and Knowledge, as depicted in Figure 3:

- The MF provides a unified hierarchy with reliable operation at the autonomic function level, trustworthy interworking at the inter-autonomic function level, and seamless deployment at the management framework level. The MF uses three main functions and unified interfaces to interact with the AFs: Governance, which provides tools for the operators to deploy, pilot, control, and track progress of AFs in a unified way.
- Coordination, which provides tools to identify/avoid conflicts and ensure stability, and performance when several AFs are concurrently working.
- Knowledge, which provides tools to make AFs find, formulate and share relevant information to enable or improve their operation.

At the AF level, the AF API enables "plug & play" deployment, interoperability, and control.

AUTONOMIC FUNCTIONS AT WORK

While autonomic functions may be pre-installed and integrated with the network elements they manage, this is not a mandatory condition. Allowing autonomic functions to be first dynamically installed and second to remotely control resources are by themselves the keys to both enable versatile deployment approaches and enlarge the application scope.

The analysis of autonomic functions deployment schemes through the different steps allows defining a generic lifecycle and identifying required features for AFs. These will become the specifications of AFs, or more precisely of constraints on AF design and on their API.

Figure 3. Same interfaces and hierarchy unifying network empowerment functions

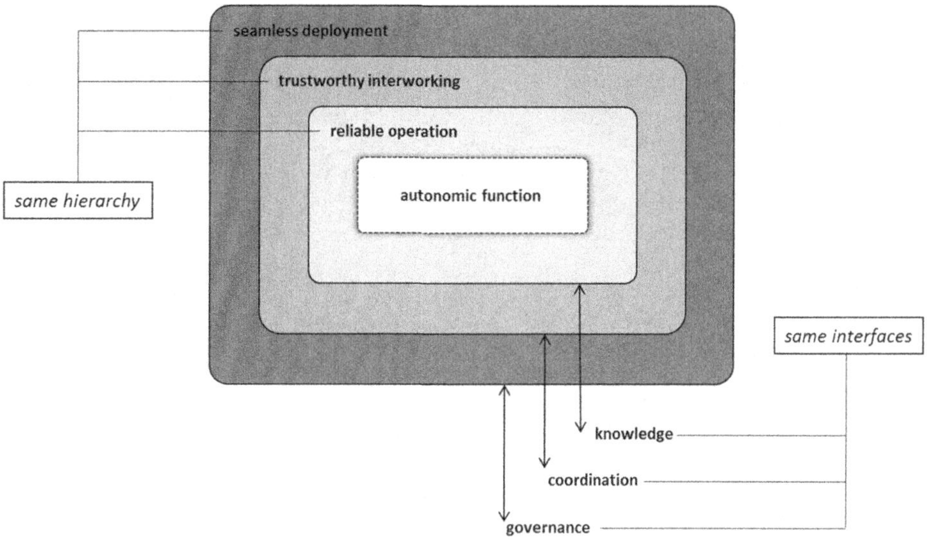

FOREWORD ON DEPLOYMENT OF AUTONOMIC FUNCTIONS

Scope of Responsibilities

Deployment of autonomic functions is too rarely tackled, though this topic is of importance, mainly because of the very nature of networks: namely their being numerous network nodes and interconnecting links, of different technologies, organized in areas, offering different services. On such diversity, the operator's expectations are not homogeneously spread, so are the objectives and hence scope of autonomic functions and for the sake of simple management the operator is likely to rely on multiple instances of autonomic functions (Figure 4).

Autonomic functions control resources of one or multiple network elements. An AF may be instantiated by one or more agents. An AF agent is a piece of software; thus, it needs first to be installed and to execute on a host machine before controlling the network elements resources.

Conditions Influencing Deployment

The multiplicity of criteria and conditions creates very numerous cases of AFs deployment.

Networking nodes may be of different models (or having different software versions), of different equipment vendors, of different technologies (e.g., IP routers, Ethernet switches). Also, AFs may:

- Have different objectives such as traffic load optimization energy consumption optimization;
- Be composed of a single agent (e.g., because of single node control, or centralized implementation);
- Be composed by a set of agents in charge of a set of nodes. The agents' organization might result from an embedded self-organization mechanism or from the network operator guidance (e.g., through intents/policies), and;

Figure 4. Autonomic functions having different scope of responsibilities

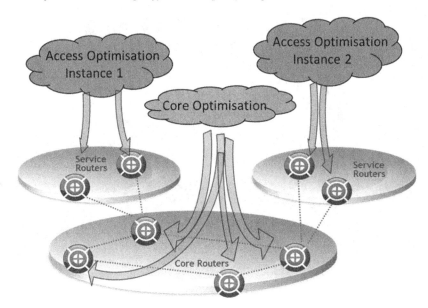

- Work internally in a peer-to-peer fashion (where every agent has the same prerogatives) or in a hierarchical fashion (where some agents have some prerogatives over others).

The AF agents can be pieces of software, which is:

- Embedded inside the node OS;
- Running in a machine different than the node (this could be a node controller or any other host or virtual machine). The agent would then likely require external credentials to interact with the node;
- Directly monitoring and configuring the equipment (likely requires the agent to be embedded) or through a device management interface, e.g., SNMP described in RFC 3411 by Harrington, Presuhn, and Wijnen (2002), or OpenFlow as illustrated by McKeown et al. (2008);
- Either activated by default at start-up or as the result of a management action, and;
- Provided by the same vendor as the equipment it manages or by a third.

Exploring an Operator Scenario of AF Deployment

The following example describes the operator's intent with regards to deployments of autonomic functions over its infrastructure. The autonomic function involved is a load balancing function, which uses monitoring information of links load to autonomously modify the links metrics to balance the load over the network:

Step 1: The network is composed of five domains, a core transport network and four metropolitan networks, each interconnected through the core network. The operator manages its network and benefits from the autonomic function on the nodes which have the installed autonomic function agents.

Step 2: The operator specifies to the autonomic function an objective to minimize network-wide link load variation.

Step 3: The operator sets a different objective to the autonomic functions for each of the five domains.

Step 4: The operator decides to install an additional autonomic function in each metropolitan domain. The new AF learns traffic demands to predict traffic variations. The operator instructs the load balancing AF to augment its monitored input with the traffic predictions of the new AF.

Step 5: As the algorithm of the load balancing AF is relying on interactions between AF agents, the operator expects the interactions to happen in-between AF agents of each domain, hence the load will be balanced inside each of the domains, while previously it would have been balanced over the whole network.

Step 6: Finally, the operator upgrades the load balancing AF with a more powerful algorithm. For trial sake, this upgraded load balancing AF is installed in only one of the metropolitan domains.

This example illustrates variations of deployment scenarios. From these scenarios, it is possible to derive AF management requirements, e.g.:

- Setting a scope of work for each AF.
- Monitoring the AF actions and their effects (i.e., KPIs (Key Performance Indicators)).
- Suspending the execution of a given AF (either because the AF instance is untrusted, or because an operation on the network is to be conducted without interference from autonomic functions, etc.).
- Configuring AFs by adjusting its parameters.

A Lifecycle for Autonomic Functions

Figure 5 illustrates the successive state transitions of an AF, which is a simplified variant of what Stamatelatos et al. (2013) detail in their information model:

- **Code Available:** AF is a piece of software available on a code repository, and the network operator and the MF can access the AF Class Manifest (which describes in a generic way how the AF works).
- **Installed:** AF agents or deployment interfaces are available on one (or multiple) host(s). In this state, the AF is waiting for an AF Instance Mandate, to determine which resources it manages.
- **Instantiated:** The AF instance knows which resources it should manage. The AF agents, running on one (or multiple) host(s), are organized. The AF instance is waiting for a "Set Up" message to start executing its control loop. The AF instance can now share an Instance Manifest (which describes how the AF instance is going to work).
- **Operational:** AF instances are executing their control loop, acting on the network, by modifying resources parameters. A "Set Down" message will put the instance back in an Instantiated state and hence stop the AF from acting.

Figure 5. Lifecycle of autonomic functions

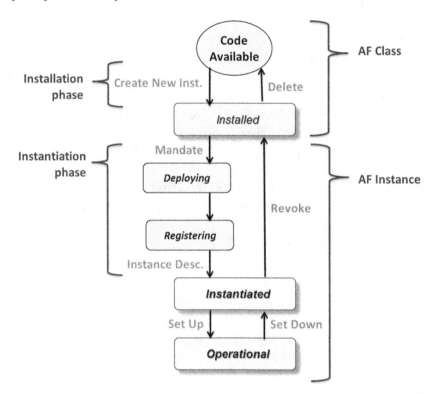

Installation Phase

During the installation phase the code is made available to hosts, this phase finishes when the code has been successfully installed, and AF agents can be started. From the conclusion of this phase the MF knows an end-point to which it can send an instance mandate.

Before being able to instantiate and run autonomic functions, the operator must first provision the infrastructure with the pieces of software corresponding to its needs and objectives. The provisioning of the infrastructure is realized in the installation phase and consists in installing (or checking the availability of) the pieces of software of the different AF Classes in a set of installation hosts.

Instantiation Phase

This phase is the one during which an autonomic function instance handles a mandate, deploys itself, and concludes with registration with the MF.

Once the AF codes are installed on the appropriate hosts in the network, corresponding agents may start to operate. From the operator's viewpoint, an operating autonomic function means the function manages the corresponding network resources as per the objectives given. Note that an AF is said to be "operating" when it executes its control loop/algorithm.

But right before that, there are two aspects to take into consideration. First, there is a difference between: (1) having a piece of code available to run on a host and; (2) having an agent based on this piece of code running within the host. Second, in a coupled case, determining which resources are controlled by an agent is straightforward (the determination is embedded), in a decoupled mode determining this is a bit more complex (hence a starting agent will have to either discover or be explicitly informed of such resources by means of configuration, for example).

The instantiation phase of an autonomic function covers both aspects: starting the agent piece of code (when the latter does not start automatically) and determining which resources must be controlled (when this is not made obvious by the embedding of the autonomic function inside the resource).

MESSAGES CONSOLIDATING THE LIFECYCLE

Autonomic Function Class Manifest

An AF Class designates the piece(s) of software that contain(s) the computer program that will be executed by AF instances. An AF instance is the running agent(s) of an AF Class.

To install and instantiate appropriately an autonomic function in the network, the operator needs to know which are the characteristics of this AF Class. Those characteristics are described by the AF Class Manifest.

This section describes a format for such a Class Manifest (see Table 1), which is a machine-readable description of both the autonomic function and the piece of code that executes the function.

Autonomic Function Mandate

To turn the installed pieces of software into a running agent pursuing a self-management goal, the operator would specify to such AF instances what they are supposed to do: which resources to manage and which objective to reach.

This is achieved through an AF Mandate (see the format in Table 2), which is a machine-readable set of instructions sent to create autonomic functions instances out of installed autonomic function agent(s).

Autonomic Function Instance Manifest

Once the AF is properly instantiated (through its agents which are started and organized), it will register to its managing entity. The registration, which contains all relevant information about the newly deployed instances of every AF, will be used by the operator (if the operator wants to track its system) and before all, by the Management Framework which needs to know which are the detailed characteristics of this autonomic function.

This section details how AF instances register by sharing their Instance Manifests (see the format in Table 3), which is a machine-readable description summarizing which are the resources managed by the function, for which purposes, which are the actions it may perform and which are the inputs used. In fine, one of the main roles of this manifest is to describe the control loop instantiated by this autonomic function. There are multiple usages of this description of the control loop. They are mainly addressing the purposes of collaboration between various classes of autonomic functions.

Table 1. Format for the manifest of an AF Class

Field Name	Type	Description
ID	Struct	Provides a unique identifier of the AF Class (would contain name of the AF Class, provider name, code version, and code release date).
Description	Struct	Describes what is the feature achieved by the AF, meant to be read by the operator and provide links to more documentation.
Network Segment	List<NetworkSegment>	Lists the network segments on which the AF is applicable (e.g., IP backbone or Radio Access Network (RAN)).
Possible Hosts	List<OS>	Lists the OS on which the AF agents can be executed.
Manageable Entities	List<ManagedEntityDesc>	Lists the type of network devices or services that can be managed by the AF (e.g., different router technologies and platforms).
Functionality Family	List<Functionality>	Lists optimization targets of the AF.
Deployment Properties	Boolean triplet	Depicts whether the AF relies on a single agent or on an organized set of agents, whether the AF agents can be decoupled from the managed entities, and whether the AF is dynamically installable.
Acquired Inputs	List< MetricClassDesc>	Lists the nature of metrics acquired by the AF from the entities it will manage.
External Inputs	List< MetricClassDesc>	Lists the nature of metrics that the AF should or must receive from the MF knowledge function (directly or indirectly).
Available Outputs	List<MetricClassDesc>	Lists the nature of information that can be shared by the AF with MF Knowledge function.
Possible Actions	List<ParameterClassDesc>	Lists the nature of parameters that the AF can modify on the entities it will manage.
Configuration Options	Unexplicited	Lists the configuration options that can be applied to the AF. The specific policies must be depicted in this clause.

Table 2. Format of an AF Mandate

Field Name	Type	Description
AF Management	URI	The address/ID of the management entity in charge of the AF instance (to perform registration when being deployed).
Managed Resources	List<URI>	Listing all the elements/resources/services that the AF instance has to handle (i.e., monitor, optimize, etc.) when being deployed.
Configuration Options	List<Policy>	Listing chosen values for generic or specific options.

In Table 3, the attributes from "Acquired Inputs" to "Possible Actions" have the same names as those in Table 1, but the fields are different. In the AF Class Manifest, the "MetricDescriptor" indicates the nature of the metric (e.g., load of a link), while when the AF is being deployed, the AF Instance Manifest details the list of metrics (e.g., load of the link between interface 10.0.0.1 and 10.0.0.2, and load of the link between 10.0.1.1 and 10.0.1.2). The "MetricDescriptor" is therefore an instantiation of a "Metric-ClassDescriptor" (see Appendix 2).

Table 3. AF Instance Manifest

Field Name	Type	Description
Class ID	Struct	The identification of the AF Class
Instance ID	Identifier	The unique ID of this AF instance
Management Address	URI	The management address of AF instance (to be used by management)
Acquired Inputs	List<MetricDescriptor>	Lists of the metrics acquired by the AF itself
External Inputs	List<MetricDescriptor>	Lists of the metrics that the AF should or must receive from Knowledge (directly or indirectly)
Available Outputs	List<MetricDescriptor>	Lists of the metrics that can be shared by the AF to the framework and its elements.
Possible Actions	List<ParameterDescriptor>	Lists of the parameters that the AF can modify onto the managed entities

GOVERNING AUTONOMIC FUNCTIONS

While one of the goals of autonomic networking is self-management, a framework aiming to manage an autonomic network must include tools to facilitate the control and supervision of the network. Network operators and service providers should be driving their digital transformation. Human-to-network communication represents a central piece of the overall architecture for the control digital infrastructure, focusing on the business rather than technical aspects of the network which ought to self-manage thanks to autonomic techniques. Declarative policies take new relevance in this scenario. The perception brought to the operator by this approach is to focus on network governance while the tasks of network management are transferred to the autonomic functions.

Governance is a high-level construct which involves all functionalities necessary to address the gap between high-level specification of human operators' objectives and existing resource management infrastructures towards the achievement of global business goals. Governance also encompasses Human-to-Network communication and means to specify and apply policies and business goals to the network.

Governance Challenges

The operational weight of managing complexity motivates some operators to change their vision on current management approaches (López, Muñoz, & Morilla, 2007).

Future network infrastructures should be highly adaptive and autonomous, and involved resources operate with even more dynamic relationships. Some functions that were traditionally performed by management systems would no longer held by them, but autonomously carried out by the network itself.

Operators will be mostly settled about decision-oriented operational tasks for the different network elements. What these decision-oriented tasks are and how they impact the decision elements are the main issues. After introducing autonomic capabilities, there is a re-assignment of tasks carried out by human network managers, which will focus on the network operation and planning for the future, rather than continuously monitoring the behavior of individual components.

The building of a network governance framework also faces technical challenges in five main functional areas: business language, translation, reasoning, policies, and configuration enforcement.

Network governance is meant to provide a mechanism for the operator to adjust the features of the required service/infrastructure using a high-level language. In order to achieve this objective a business language may be required that will help the operator to express what is needed from the network (Open Networking Foundation, 2016). Such a business language may be modelled, for example, using ontology to add semantics and enable machine reasoning on the goals.

These high-level directives must be translated into low-level policy rules that can be enforceable to control behavior of self-managed resources whatever their type, either a single device or a set of devices that can group their self-* features (set of devices managed by one single autonomic function).

Reasoning is also an important challenge in the scope of network governance, as it can be exploited for the mediation and negotiation between separate federated domains. It is thus an important capability of the governance function to support multiple domain specific information models to allow interoperability between semantically equivalent, but differently instantiated models. This leads to the use of ontologies for semantic fusion and reasoning with knowledge extracted from the various sources of data and information.

Network governance is almost always interwoven with policies lying at the highest level of the so-called policy continuum (Davy, Jennings, & Strassner, 2007). Policies specify rules that should govern the behavior of the managed entities. In network governance, policies are required for the selection of the optimal configuration of a service and for the translation from business level entries to low-level policies.

Furthermore, configuration enforcement mechanisms are necessary to apply the decisions. First, it is required to identify concerned devices and request each of them to perform the appropriate configuration actions. Then, each of the targeted devices must translate and apply the decision. The term "configuration" implies self-configuration and includes reconfiguration and re-optimization actions. Such actions can be triggered to adjust the configuration parameters following the evolution of the network, the service, or customer conditions.

The challenge thus consists in designing and specifying a network governance functionality (Tsagkaris, Nguengang, Peloso, Fuentes, Mamatas, Georgoulas … & Smirnov, 2013) based on a high-level language, reasoning, policies and distribution capabilities) that can:

- Work with proper business rules and policies, while connecting high-level goals and network resources to provide the operator with an appropriate, human-friendly governance interface, simple enough to be used by non-highly specialized technicians.
- Guide infrastructure behaviors while offering a service view.
- Offer mechanisms that assist the operator to express goals, objectives, constraints, and rules to ensure the desired operation of its autonomic network.
- Help to convince the operators of the benefices of adopting autonomic approaches.

Governance Functional Blocks

Governance responds to the need for the human network operators to supervise the functioning and controlling the behavior not only of the underlying autonomic functions, but of the management system as well, i.e., of the MF core blocks.

Four main functions appear necessary for the proper governance of future networks and services (Figure 6):

Figure 6. Governance functional blocks

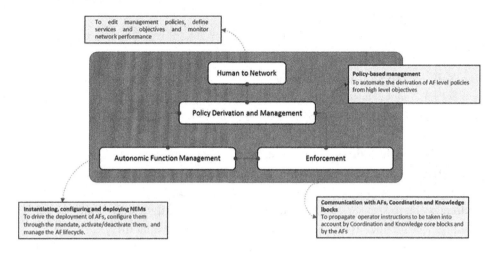

- The Human-to-Network function;
- The Policy Derivation and Management function;
- The AF Management function, and;
- The Enforcement function.

The Human-to-Network function provides methods allowing human network operators to manage the whole autonomic network, its services and the other components of the MF by editing and validating high-level objectives. A high-level objective can be defined as an overall target that the network must achieve. These objectives are expressed in a close-to-natural language and therefore need to be translated into a language that can be understood by targeted elements as detailed in ONF Technical Recommendation (Open Networking Forum, 2016). This translation process is implemented in the Policy Derivation and Management function, which produces low-level policies as outputs. The Enforcement function then transmits the low-level policies to the corresponding AF or MF components, while the AF Management function allows a fine-grained control of the AF lifecycle as described in Section "Autonomic functions at work".

Human to Network Function

The Human-to-Network function provides means for injecting input to the network through the definition of high-level objectives, and at the same time, for receiving information about the functioning of the network, services, and the MF. To reach these goals, the Human-to-Network interface can be decomposed into a set of methods: Service Definition, High Level Objectives Definition, and Supervision. The first two methods offer the programming functionality for the network, the services, and the MF, while the latter provides feedback about their current status.

Service Definition

Service Definition is about the creation and representation of service descriptions. This description is later on translated into terms that allow an AF to understand the requirements of individual services, such as QoS (Quality of Service), availability, or security. The definition of a service describes its invariant characteristics and their parameters (Table 4).

High Level Objectives Definition

The Human-to-Network function provides the definition of technology-agnostic management objectives using a high-level language. These objectives are used to tune the network behavior and the MF core blocks configuration. These high-level objectives correspond to:

- **Service Characteristic Values:** Service demands concern requests relevant to service provision, such as the delivery of a new service to a given customer with given service characteristics, the accommodation of new traffic in a specific geographical area and time period, or the modification of already active service quality conditions. Service configuration assigns values to already predefined service characteristics (e.g., redundancy level or availability).
- **Configuration of MF Core Blocks:** Tuning behavior of the Coordination and Knowledge functional blocks.

These high-level objectives need to be further propagated to the targeted elements (AFs or MF core components), which requires their prior transformation into lower level policies. This translation process is accomplished by the Policy Derivation and Management function. After the translation process, low-level policies will be generated that correspond to:

- **AF Configuration Options:** These are policies sent to the AF to set its configuration and its behavior. The different configuration options are specified in the AF Manifest of each AF Class.
- **Coordination Configuration Options Can Specify:**

Table 4. Service definition parameters

Field Name	Description
Name, ID and Description	Identification of the service and its Textual Description.
Resources	List of equipment types needed, with requirements for hardware, protocol and software.
AF Classes	List of AF Classes instantiated for the service deployment.
Location	Geographical area where the service will be available.
Characteristics	List of parameters describing the service, e.g., redundancy level or availability/
Characteristics Values	Matching values of the service characteristics.
Performance Parameters	KPIs used to measure the performance when the service is running (AFs will have to monitor and communicate these measurements to the Knowledge functional block).
Templates	A service template represents a type of Service Specification introduced for the purposes of fulfilment. It defines specific service values that can be dynamically referenced by multiple service instances during their lifecycle span. Several templates can be produced for the same service, corresponding to different levels (e.g., Gold, Silver and Bronze levels).
Level Objective	A set of quality goals for the service defined in terms of metrics, thresholds, and tolerances. Two types of parameters must be considered here: KPIs and KQIs (Key Quality Indicators). A KPI measures a specific aspect of the performance of a resource or a homogeneous group of resources. A KQI measures a specific aspect of the service performance of a service.

  ○ **Sensitivity, as a Value [0, 1]:** This configuration option defines how sensitive Coordination can be when identifying potential conflict situations, and how to assign mechanisms. This sensitivity affects the loop search algorithm in the identification of conflicts using conflict maps (see Identifying potential conflicts subsection), when the strength of a loop is too weak, it is not considered as a conflict to be addressed.

  ○ **Orientation:** To be used by Coordination to prioritize/weigh AFs according to the operator's performance objectives. It can be set on a per-segment basis and requires that AFs also include their orientation in their manifests. For instance, if AF A states "Energy" as orientation and another AF B "Load Balancing" as orientation, and Governance in general states that "Energy">>"Load Balancing", then the priority assigned by Coordination to AF B will be lower than the one assigned to AF A.

- **Knowledge Configuration Options:** Such as optimization goals to reduce the communication overhead, or the definition of a threshold for the detection of untrustworthy AFs.

Supervision

The previous sections describe the operations of the Human-to-Network function that facilitates the communication of human network operators with the MF core, network elements, and AFs. Conversely, the Human-to-Network function should provide information about the status of the abovementioned elements. This information refers to the configuration, status, contexts and alerts of networks, services, AFs, and MF core. The Supervision operation provides the human operator with a clear picture of current network and system conditions. Based on that, a human operator may decide to use the other operations to modify the behavior of the network or system, performing so called informed decision.

The process that decides which information must be shown to address human operators' requirements is very important. The minimal amount of information that any MF-based Governance implementation should provide are: Alerts AFs may reach a situation where they cannot fulfil the specified goals in their current context. When all the self-healing attempts have failed, the AF should escalate the problem. In some circumstances, the misbehavior of a set of coordinated AFs may be the origin of the problem, and therefore Coordination is informed in the first place. If all the feasibility checks of the coordination mechanisms fail, then the human network operator should be alerted.

The information attached to each alert should contain all the details needed for the human operator to take control over the situation:

- **Importance Factor and Priority:** An indication of the impact of this alert on the functioning of the network. Alerts should be prioritized, so those of the highest severity level should be processed first.
- **Originating System, Description, Category:** To better understand the nature of the alert.
- **Time Markers:** History of the alert and its changes.
- **Related Alerts and Affected Resources:** Link to related alerts and tells affected entities.
- **Status:** Indicates if the alert is active, closed or under investigation.
- **Root Cause:** To be filled when the problem that caused the alert is diagnosed.

The Policy Derivation and Management Function

Operators need to control the behavior of autonomic elements and to set technology-agnostic high-level objectives that must be properly achieved by the different elements. More importantly, operators need to customize the operation of their highly complex, heterogeneous, and decentralized network on the fly. This necessitates to orchestrate various entities behavior, which may belong to different segments and operational layers. Policies which will be used from Governance must span entities of different layers, administrative domains and network segments. The preservation of the relationships of policies between the respective different levels of abstraction, used and influenced by different entities/elements, requires policy continuum (Davy, Jennings, & Strassner, 2007). Briefly, the purpose of the Policy Continuum is to provide a semantic linkage between different types of policies that exist at different levels of abstraction. Each of the levels is optimized for a different type of user that needs and/or uses different information. For example, a business user may need SLA information. That user is not interested in how the network is programmed to deliver QoS, just that the network is in fact delivering the right type of QoS to the right people. Conversely, the network administrator may want to "translate" the QoS that is implied by different SLAs into sets of different CLI commands to program the appropriate devices. This is a completely different representation of the same policy.

Policy continuum enables policies with a high level of abstraction, written from the concepts, terminology and structure/syntax (namely, different policy model and policy language) of this level, to be transformed to policies of a lower level of abstraction, with different corresponding characteristics. Policy continuum, in essence, considers a policy as a potential continuum of many different policies with dependencies among them.

The proposed policy levels are the Business level, the Service level, and the AF level (Figure 7). The Business level corresponds to "Market, product & customer" layer of the highest conceptual view of eTOM (eTOM business process framework – Level 0 processes) (ITU-T, 2007). The Service level and AF level corresponds to the "Service" layer and the "Resource (Application, computing and network)" layer, respectively. More precisely, the Business level policies are related to Strategy, Infrastructure and Product and Operations processes (eTOM business process framework – Level 1 processes). The Service level policies are related to Service management and operations processes of Operations, and the AF level policies are related to Resource management and operations processes of Operations. This policy hierarchy enables the definition of new sub-levels in the future, based on the emerging network and service requirements. Furthermore, the specification of policy levels based on eTOM, which entails the usage of basic common terminology, facilitates the policy translation between the different levels, enabling policy continuum.

The Business level policies, which are administration-oriented and technology-independent policies based on the technology-agnostic business objectives and service requests, are transformed into service policies that are service-oriented and technology-independent, and correlate service characteristics to specific network parameters. The service level policies, in sequence, are transformed into AF policies, which are technology-specific configuration commands related to the required operation of resources in specific network segments. The AF policies that are imposed on the corresponding AFs trigger specific actions from AFs, leading to vendor-specific commands executed by specific managed network elements. Concisely, the main objective of Governance operation is the automatic transformation of business goals into AF's configuration.

Figure 7. Schematic representation of the business, service and AF policy levels

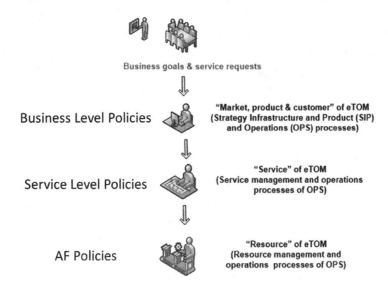

The Policy Derivation and Management function has been decomposed into the following operations:

- Build Business Policy
- Policy Repository Management: Create/Update/Retrieve/Delete Policy operations
- Validate Policy
- Detect Policy Conflicts
- Resolve Policy Conflicts
- Translate Policy
- Check Feasibility & Optimize
- Policy Efficiency

These operations must be applied at each of the levels of the Policy Continuum, with the exception of Build Business Policy operation that only applies to the business level of the continuum.

The AF Management Function

The AF Management function collects and stores in the AF Registry all the management information of the deployed AFs. It also manages the state transition (including the activation and deactivation of the autonomic control loops) of the AFs and defines the reporting strategy that meets the operator needs.

This gives the human network operator the possibility of governing the autonomic behavior of the network through the control of the operation of a particular AF or set of AFs. The AF Management function can be decomposed into the following operations:

- **AF Registry Management Operations:** The information related to each AF instance should be kept in an AF registry, and therefore operations must exist for its management: creation, update, deletion and retrieval of AF information.

- **AF Lifecycle Management Operations:** An AF from the moment it is installed until the moment it is uninstalled follows the lifecycle depicted in Section "Autonomic functions at work".
- **Reporting Strategy-Related Operations:** AF reporting strategy operations allow the human operator to define the frequency and level of detail of the information the AF must report to the MF core. This operation may be useful under specific circumstances when the behavior of an AF must be closely observed (e.g., when a malfunctioning has been detected, or when an event has been programmed that will increase the demand of services in a given area). In that case, the human network operator may wish to increase the frequency and the level of detail of the reported information.
- **Request Specific Behavior for AFs:** Request specific behavior for AFs is an operation which permits Governance to request specific control of AFs, in order to modify the mode of operation of a given AF or group of AFs. This feature allows for instance the network operator to set AFs into the so-called "under trial" mode, where AFs are not allowed to enforce actions on the network. The behavior of the AF can then be observed without risking the network operation.

There are two immediate usages for the "under trial" mode: observation of a misbehaving AF and certification activities. In the former case, when the online trust mechanisms find a deviation of the runtime behavior of an AF with respect to the specified behavior, the human network operator may decide, instead of stopping the AF, the deactivation of any kind of actions of the AF on the network and still observe its activity. Alternatively, instead of manually requesting the modification of the AF behavior, the human operator may use the Human-to-Network function to set thresholds when certain behaviors of the AF must be (de-)activated. When measured trust for a given AF drops below the threshold, the trust mechanism in the Knowledge block issues a notification to the Governance, which triggers the AF Management function in order to set the AF in the "under trial" state. Similar observational needs may appear when a new AF is deployed during a test process or at the early stages of deployment in production environments, allowing the examination of the AF activity and its process of decision making without allowing the actual execution of corrective or preventive actions on the network elements.

Given an AF in operational state runs under the control of the Coordination functional block, the communication between both blocks is fundamental in this case, so Coordination can take appropriate actions to guarantee the stability of the network. Take for instance the case when the AF to be set "under trial" is part of a group of AFs being orchestrated. Given that one of them will be set to the "under trial" state may affect the behavior of the group and therefore Coordination may need to send new control policies to those AFs. To ensure the proper coordination of the two blocks, Governance will not communicate directly with the AFs, but will request Coordination to control a given AF. This request will be in the form of policies, which will be realized by the Enforcement function. As part of these policies, Governance may request different options to Coordination. It may request a change in Coordination mechanism settings, in order to see the behavior of the AF as if it was acting and to assess the influence of this AF on the other AFs, or it may just wish to observe the AF working in isolation from the other AFs.

The Enforcement Function

Enforcement encapsulates the communication mechanism between Governance and AFs or other MF core components. It allows the other functions of the Governance block to be independent of the communication aspects for the interconnection with AFs and core blocks. In the case of AFs, the communication is mainly achieved through the Mandate object.

EXAMPLES OF GOVERNANCE MECHANISMS

Translation Mechanisms

The proposed policy translation method is based on a three-fold approach in order to maximize automation, retain low complexity and high precision, while being highly reusable. Firstly, the operator's High-Level Objectives are classified into categories (e.g., QoE (Quality of Experience), Energy Efficiency), while a set of KPIs are assigned to each category. Secondly, the translation process is not realized from scratch. In the proposed approach described in this chapter, the translation is led by a set of guidelines which are documented in a set of policy templates stored in a policy template pool. These templates have the form of XML documents with a predefined XML schema.

In the considered example, a set of high level objectives parameters (e.g., User Class, Availability) comprise the values of the predefined "Policy Variable" and "Policy Value" elements. Thirdly, the modelling of high level objectives and translation process is realized using ontologies (OWL, Web Ontology Language as detailed by Antoniou and Van Harmelen, 2009) and ontological rules. Ontologies constitute a means to capture information and organize information and knowledge representation in a reusable and machine-readable format. Consequently, ontologies enable the representation and communication of business, network and AF information, and the development of reasoning schemes. To this effect, the utilization of ontology-based policy translation is suitable for the relevant MF mechanisms. The formulation and realization of the ontology should be suitable to support taxonomy among the defined concepts and specification of relations in the form of Subject-Predicate-Object clauses. Furthermore, the designed ontology should ensure consistency of the included captured concepts and inferring of relations by assignment of meta-properties to existing properties, enabling deductive and inductive reasoning.

The translation process adopts the Policy Continuum approach as described in the previous subsection, and is accomplished at every policy level from the Policy Derivation and Management Function, through mapping of the policies' parameters to information parameters (and respective attributes) of the ontology. According to this approach, a set of three different levels / views are defined (Business Level, Service Level and AF Level), each of which constitutes a different representation of the initial business goal. The policies of all levels are described in OWL. The policies of the business level are modelled based on the ontology reflecting the business level, close to natural language, while the policies of other levels are modelled on the policy language that relies upon the SID (Shared Information and Data model standardized by the Telemenagement Forum, 2018) information model standardized. The ontologies of different levels are linked in OWL by means of interoperability relationships between classes, which express the interrelation between subsequent levels, while SWRL (Semantic Web Rule Language) rules are used for the translation of the policies.

The translation process is illustrated in Figure 8.

The translation process comprises the following steps:

Figure 8. Policy Translation

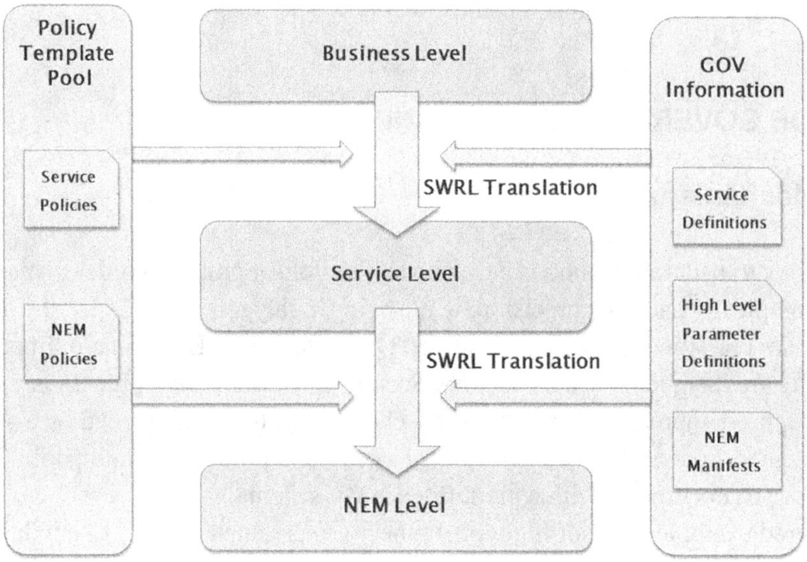

Step 1: The initial Policy Variables which constitute High Level Objectives for the operator, are classified into High Level Objectives' Categories (HLO Category) based on operator's selections. For instance, HLO "Availability" may be comprised of four categories (e.g., Excellent, Good, Normal, Critical). Through the use of Human-to-Network function, the operator has the possibility to introduce both High Level Objectives and their categories respectively.

Step 2: Based on High Level Objectives Definition, Build Business Policy operation expresses them in the form of business level policies.

Step 3: The initial translation from business policies to service policies is realized based on High Level Objectives' Category to KPI mapping, the selected combination of high level semantics and the mapping of available services to KPI values (e.g., KPIDelay < 50 msec). For each HLO Category a series of service policy templates are extracted from the policy template pool. The selection of the appropriate policy template is done based on the set of KPIs involved and the initial classification. Each policy template is a policy skeleton which contains the policy structure and the policy variables, while the values of variables are missing. During the translation process the missing values are filled and the instances of policies are generated.

Step 4: On the second level of translation each service level policy is further translated into a set of operational AF level policies. The translation is realized by using a set of AF templates, including KPI/parameter-related information filling them with KPI/parameter's values. In this step a mapping is realized between the involved KPIs/parameters and the available operations, inputs and outputs of the available AFs, which are described into the AF Manifest.

In its general form an AF policy is formed and described based on the SID policy model. Examples of some indicative policies are:

- **Energy Efficient Policy:** IF (time > 3:00 AND time < 8:00 AND NetworkUtilisation < 0.2 AND PercentageOfInactiveENodeBs < 0.1) THEN SET PercentageOfInactiveENodeBs = 0.1.

The AF policy implies that the AF that will receive the policy from Governance has the capabilities to monitor the network utilization (KPI) and control the percentage of inactive eNodeBs in the network.

- **QoS/QoE Policy:** ON SLAViolationAlarm IF SLAClass = Gold AND AdmissionControlThreshold > 0.9 THEN SET AdmissionControlThreshold = 0.9.

The above AF policy implies the specific AF can receive SLA violation alarms and control the threshold of admission control mechanisms of the access network.

Semantic-Based Approach for Policy Conflict Detection

The semantic-based approach for the conflict identification described concerns the identification of parameters and their assigned values in the event, conditions and action clauses that can lead to a conflict between policies. This implies the definition of the suitable classes, properties and axioms. A relevant taxonomy between concepts defined for conflict identification in OWL is illustrated by Figure 9. For example, an information piece can be correlated to:

- Parameter (observable and adjustable) comprising ComparableParameters (where predicates like isLessThan/isGreaterThan can be applied to their values) and NonComparableParameters (where there exists no natural ordering among their values, but isEqualTo/isNotEqualTo can still be applied),
- Value/ValueSet, comprising ComparableValueSet, (which has a lower and upper bound, either exclusive or inclusive) and NonComparableValueSet (which is a set of values, a union, or an intersection of sets), and
- ParameterType (which is the data type to be used for assigning actual values).

In the case of the action clauses, the identification of possible conflicts is transformed into the detection of the alteration of the targeted parameters from the policies. Then the focus is on the action of the active policies, namely the targeted control of specific parameters. For example,

policyA minimizes parameterX (Goal of policyA),

policyB maximizes (or maintains value of) parameterX (Goal of policyB),

These policies are identified as conflicted policies.

Figure 9. Taxonomy between concepts defined for conflict identification

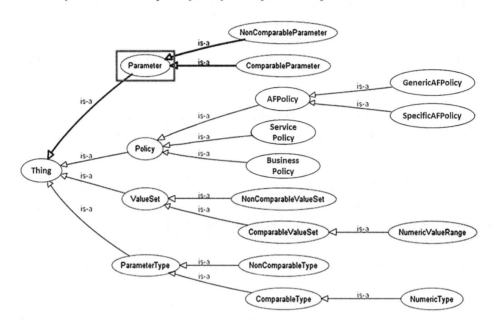

COORDINATING MULTIPLE AUTONOMIC FUNCTIONS

Within the network, autonomic functions are likely to compete with one another, either to control some network parameters or to influence different metrics. From far above, a self-driving network can be seen as an ecosystem of control loops, where chaos can emerge because of the independency of these loops.

The role of coordination when managing multiple AFs is primarily to protect the network from instabilities and effects due to the presence of multiple AFs running concurrently. It ensures the proper triggering sequence of AFs and guarantees their stable operation. To this end, the coordination block defines conditions/constraints under which AFs will be invoked (i.e., produce their output), taking into account operator service and network requirements.

Coordination aims at steering the network towards a better "operating" point, by avoiding/mitigating detrimental interactions between AFs that may lead to unstable and oscillatory behaviors, as illustrated in the prototype demonstrated by Koutsouris et al. (2013).

The first step of such a process is the identification of these interactions and their classification to determine which ones must be handled, i.e., conflicting interactions.

The second step clusters the identified interactions into groups that can be handled together while insuring the proper behavior of the network.

The third step is the instantiation of coordination mechanisms well suited to handle each group of interactions previously identified.

Identifying Potential Conflicts

The mathematical problem to solve is computationally hard and also complex in some matters. Computationally hard, because the number of interactions between AFs is big. It may become complex, because the nature of these interactions cannot always be predicted, and some knowledge may be lacking to identify all of them.

Radio Access Network (RAN) is one of the networking environment where autonomic functions have been deployed first (based upon the 3GPP Self Organizing Network - SON functions specification) (3GPP, 2011). Taking time to analyze the SON functions, looking at which are the classes of parameters modified by each of those, the classes of metric used as input (also named KPI in the RAN context), and when trying to build the graph of these relations, results in a highly meshed graph. This is the static conflict map drawn in Figure 10 (Ciavaglia, Ghamri-Doudane, Smirnov, Demestichas, Stavroulaki, Bantouna, & Sayrac, 2012).

A detailed description of this graph is provided in Appendix 1. From this interaction graph, one can deduce that SON function 4 is Mobility Robustness Optimization (MRO), which modifies the Handover selection from monitored inputs which are Handover errors, Number of Handovers and Ping-pong handovers, respectively.

This map shows for the controls (SON functions), which are the classes of parameters modified and which are the classes of metrics monitored, and finally which is the efficiency they aim at optimizing. Tables detailing the edges of the graph are available in Appendix 1.

This static map already looks complicated, though it only displays static interactions. In the static map, the graph vertices are AF classes, the 'MetricClassDescriptor', and the 'ParameterClassDescriptor'. A more accurate view of conflicts would consist in plotting the deployed graph with instantiated vertices (AF instance, 'MetricDescriptor' and 'ParameterDescriptor' – see Appendix 2). Taking the example of the MRO AF, when deployed over multiple eNodeBs, there would be a vertex of Handover error per eNodeB (respectively other metrics). A deployed conflict map means that:

Figure 10. Static conflicts map derived from 3GPP SONs definition

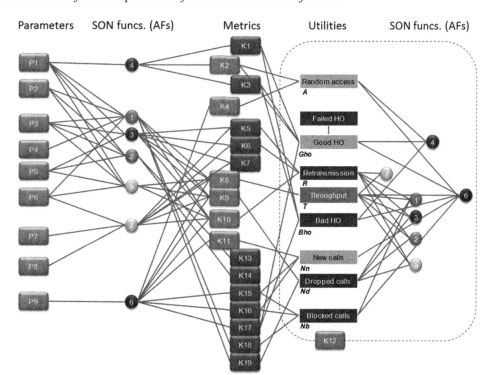

- For an AF that is deployed over multiple resources, the number of actual metrics monitored is multiplied by the number of resources hence multiplying the number of metric and parameters vertices and the number of edges between those;
- If the same AF Class is deployed multiple times (with multiple instances), each instance responsible for resources that are neighbors of resources of other instances, this will also multiply the number of atomic graphs interrelated by edges materializing the coupling between neighboring resources (or more exactly between vertices of neighboring resources);
- The graph shall also contain edges representing the coupling between different instances of the same metric class (the same parameter of neighboring resources) or even between instances of metrics having any other type of relation/dependency, and;
- Finally, the graph shall also contain edges representing influences between instances of parameters and instances of metrics (i.e., a parameter whose value influences the metric of another AF).

When the graph is plotted with the entire set of dependencies for the whole network, then the network operator ends-up with a very complicated graph. Additionally, deriving the coupling in-between metrics on one hand and the influences between parameters and metrics on the other hand is a complex task. It either requires an a priori extensive knowledge of the network and of its topology plus knowing the relations between metrics, but still there is a risk that the graph may not be exhaustive or, even worse, error-free.

Types of Conflicts

Conflicts between AFs come from various types of interactions between these autonomic functions.

The most obvious conflict appears when two competing AFs decide over the value of a same parameter. Of course, this conflict can occur only if the parameter in-between is the same, meaning the same instance of parameter, not limited to the class. Let's imagine the competition between a congestion avoidance AF and an energy efficiency AF, if they both manipulate the metrics of router links, they would obviously compete only when both AFs are deployed over the same router links. This kind of conflict

Figure 11. Conflict between two autonomic functions modifying the value of the same parameter

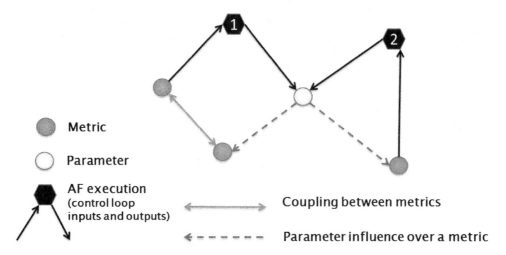

appears in the conflict map as shown in Figure 11. This figure displays two autonomic functions and the graph shows the conflict and the closed control loops of each AF.

Another type of conflict occurs when two AFs rely on metrics which are coupled the one with another (or have some degree of coupling, or are the same) (shown in Figure 12). Each AF will change network parameters to augment the value of their utility function. The risk appears when the relation between utility function of each AF has variation opposite the other one regarding the coupled metrics (expressed mathematically: the partial derivative utility function of AF#1 has an opposite sign as the one of AF#2).

Another type of conflict occurs when multiple AFs create a control loop that they close all together, as shown in Figure 13. This figure shows both the control loops of each individual AF and the broader control loop achieved by their interaction. Depending on the derivative of their utilities, this may lead to oscillation.

The types of conflict presented above can occur with more than two AFs (e.g., an interaction can involve three or more AFs), which makes the problem of identification all the more complicated.

Times of the Identification of Interactions Between AFs

The Coordination function manages AFs; hence its operation is related to the different states of AFs namely during their installation phase, their instantiation phase and when being in the operational state. Hence, the coordination function also presents a lifecycle consisting of these 3 different states, in which the coordination function behaves according to the following descriptions:

During the installation phase, a common description of the autonomic function attributes (metrics, parameters, actions, capabilities, etc.) leads to the construction of a "static interaction map" from the a priori knowledge that can be derived/inferred from the AFs control loop relationship. The static interaction map can be used as a first element by the operator (or mechanism) to (pre-)define policies and priorities as coordination strategies to manage the a priori conflicts that have been identified. There is an example of such an analysis focused on 3GPP Self Organizing functions in Figure 10.

Figure 12. Conflict between two autonomic functions using coupled metrics as input

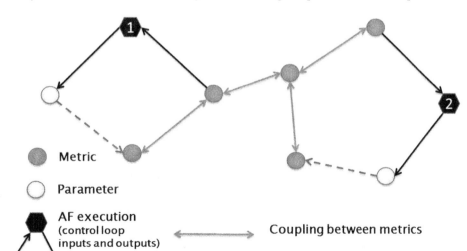

Figure 13. Conflict between two autonomic functions forming a closed control loop

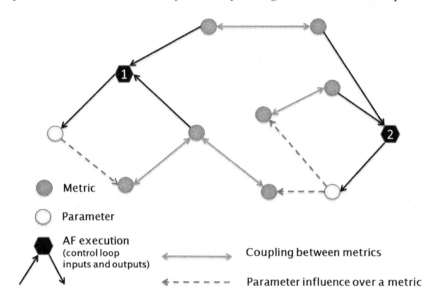

During the instantiation phase, autonomic functions are sequentially deployed then registered but are not acting on the network and its resources yet. At this stage, for each instance of AF and on a per resource basis, coordination is building an inventory of the metrics monitored, and of the actions performed. Augmenting this inventory with the relations between these metrics and these actions and their relationships can be realized, resulting in a "dynamic interaction map". The dynamic interaction map provides the basis to identify conflicts that will happen at run-time, categorize them and plan for the appropriate coordination strategies/mechanisms.

At runtime, conflicts may happen and arbitration is driven by the coordination strategies and available mechanisms. This is also the stage where new dependencies can be observed and inferred, ultimately resulting in updating the dynamic interaction map and possible adaptation of the coordination strategies and mechanisms.

Identifying Conflicts During Instantiation

This type of conflict identification is based on a priori knowledge of conflicting parameters that is captured by the Management Framework system (mostly offline) and is then exploited to identify conflicts at runtime. This type of conflict identification is triggered upon configuration changes in the network or in the MF (e.g., the assignment of a new mandate to an AF), in order to detect and prevent conflicting setups.

The main advantage of such identification is that it detects conflicts proactively (i.e., before they actually occur). The major disadvantage on the other hand, is that networking experts' knowledge must be carefully passed to the system through some manual, human-involving way, which is most often error-prone and time-consuming. In this respect, the Management Framework employs knowledge engineering techniques such as ontology, logic programming, and reasoning languages to empower static conflict identification and relax the requirements of a priori given knowledge.

The process of conflict detection contains multiple steps:

- Collect the instances manifest of all AFs, and build the conflict map. The instance's description lists for each AF the parameters they modify and the metrics they take as input. Then the graph contains these vertices and the edges provided by AF (the black ones as plotted in Figures 11, 12, and 13),
- Complete the conflict map, by coupling both in-between metrics and influences of parameter values over metrics (the other kind of edges plotted in Figures 11, 12, and 13). To do so, the Management Framework employs ontology describing relations in between metrics and influences of parameters and a reasoning engine to derive the graph edges. Actually, it is simpler to have an ontology describing such relations in a static way, and expand the graph when mapping it with network topology information (e.g., "1" (when the ontology tells that the link metric value influences the load of the link, it is easy to apply this on every link of the network) or "2" (when the ontology tells the load of a link is coupled with the load of adjacent links, using a topology information easily allows plotting such coupling in the instantiated conflict map)),
- Parse the conflict map to identify loops involving more than one AF, and pinpoint those as potential conflicts.

This implies quite a sufficient knowledge injected inside the ontology, as the more accurate the ontology and topology information, the more accurate the instantiated conflict map. Additionally, the ontology and the reasoning mechanisms have both to be able to infer additional knowledge (e.g., the facts that "parameter A affects metric B", and "metric B is coupled to metric C" constitute sufficient knowledge to infer that "parameter A affects metric C", provided that the semantics of "affects" and "is coupled" are properly captured during design time).

Identifying Conflicts During Runtime

The role of the dynamic conflict identification is to "catch" conflicts and problematic situations that may have been missed during the previous identification phase. To do so, the dynamic conflict identification method needs to collect regularly AFs metrics as a function of AF parameters.

As such, the AFs must regularly share both their metrics and the values set to parameters. From metrics and parameter values, Coordination can calculate the matrix A with elements A_{ij}, where A_{ij} is metric i as a function of parameter j. This means that variation of metrics against all parameters must be calculated. Once this is done the eigenvalues of matrix A are calculated. If all eigenvalues are negative then the set of AFs can be considered as stable; otherwise there is risk of instability and as such, the runtime conflict identification has to finely monitor the AF behavior to detect oscillations or untrusted behaviors, or even raise alarms.

Specifically, groups of AFs coordinated by a same instance of a coordination mechanism, can benefit from a dedicated runtime identification, as coordination can infer from that, whether AFs can keep operating in their current mode (and even relax gradually their constraints) or a new grouping under the available conflict managing mechanisms is needed.

Algorithms to Insure Coordination

The solutions to avoid conflicts between multiple control loops can rely on different categories of algorithms as detailed by Luo, Zeng, Su, Li, and Xiao (2012), or by Combes, Altman, and Altman (2013) or by Iacoboaiea, Sayrac, Ben Jemaa, and Bianchi (2014). In the context of a framework capable of handling any sort of autonomic functions not known a priori, algorithms specifically designed for a given interaction between control loop shall not be considered. The algorithms requiring little to no tailoring are better suited for the proposed framework. Hereafter is provided an overview of algorithm families capable of achieving coordination between autonomic functions, or at least to avoid conflicts:

- **Random Token:** Such algorithms insure that each autonomic function is executing its control-loop one after the other, the sequence is following a random pattern.
- **Hierarchical Coordination:** Such algorithms insure that each autonomic function is executing its control loop at different rates, e.g., for two functions: one is running fast enough to have time to converge in between two iterations of the slowest one (this algorithm requires proper settings with regards of the autonomic functions to coordinate).
- **Efficiency Bids:** In such algorithms, each autonomic function predicts which improvement its executing of its control loop would bring, and communicates this bid to the coordination algorithm, which then picks the autonomic function promising the "best" improvement, and grants it the right to execute. Then this process repeats itself.
- **Multi-Objective Optimization:** For such algorithms, the autonomic functions delegate the computation of their outcome to the coordination algorithm. They supposedly have communicated in advance their analytical utility to the coordination algorithm, which itself computes a multi-objective optimum, and returns back to the autonomic function the output the autonomic function would apply.

A Generic Mechanism of Random Token

This method for managing conflicts belongs to the separation in time strategies and is the simplest possible mechanism. It sets the baseline for all other conflict managing mechanisms. It can be viewed as the last resort when other mechanisms cannot be applied, due to AFs being unable to provide the needed information required by mechanisms offering better coordination.

In such cases, AFs identified as possibly conflicting are waiting for a token before executing their autonomic loop. During the initialization phase of this mechanism, coordination will instruct AFs that they should wait for the token to run. During runtime, upon receiving the token, the AF will run its optimization cycle only once and, once finished, it returns it to coordination.

A Generic Mechanism Based on Hierarchical Coordination

This method for managing conflicts is based on AF control loops that operate on different time scales according to the dynamics of the resources which they control. By enforcing different time scales at these AFs, one defines a hierarchical control system which is denoted as hierarchical optimization. After each control action (e.g., parameter modification) of a slow AF, faster AFs act rapidly and converge. Hence the slow AF is seen as quasi-static by the fast AFs. If the periodicity of the fast AF is denoted as

T_f and that of the slow AF as T_s, then convergence of the hierarchical system is guaranteed if $T_f/T_s \rightarrow 0$, or in practice, a small value. In Game Theory, the slow AF can be considered as a "leader", while the fast AF is considered as a "follower"; and the optimal point of operation is known as Stackelberg equilibrium.

For this method to be applicable, the AFs must be able to operate periodically. This mechanism does not require any runtime information from the network or from AFs themselves, it only requires that during initialization phase, coordination imposes to AFs the periodicities they should follow. From this time on, the AFs are in principle allowed to operate without any additional constraints.

A Generic Mechanism Based on Efficiency Bids

This method for conflict avoidance can be regarded as an extension of the random token mechanism, with the key following differences:

- AFs must be able to predict the outcome of their actions (predicted utility).
- AFs must have the same periodicity, or at least periodicity equals to multiples of the same base periodicity.
- AFs -ideally- should be able to tolerate the temporary suspension of their actions and still converge.

In such cases, AFs with the above characteristics can be coordinated by an efficiency bids mechanism. This mechanism does require the reception of predicted utilities from the controlled AFs. AFs report their predicted utilities only when their triggering conditions are met. Then the AF with the highest predicted utility is selected to complete its control loop IF the triggering conditions are still valid. If not, then the AF with the second highest predicted utility is selected, etc.

During the initialization phase, this mechanism will instruct AFs that they must report their predicted utility when asked, and not to execute their control loop, apart when granted a token.

During runtime, coordination will be requesting from AFs their predicted utilities with a frequency defined by their base periodicity. AFs which meet their triggering conditions report the corresponding values and coordination will choose to which AF to pass the token.

A Generic Mechanism Based on Joint Optimization

This family of algorithms is the hardest to make it generic, and AFs can only be eligible to joint optimization at the cost of heavy design constraints. The principle is to solve a multi-objective optimization problem in a centralized way. Each AF was independently trying to optimize its own objective, whereas coordination will address a problem of optimizing N objectives which can be formulated as:

$$\min \vec{F}(\vec{x}) = \left[f_1(\vec{x}), f_2(\vec{x}), ..., f_N(\vec{x}) \right]^T$$

subject to

$$g_m\left(\vec{x}\right) \leq 0, m = 1, 2, ... M$$

where

$$\vec{x} = \left[x_1, x_2, ..., x_p \right]^T \in \Omega$$

where $\vec{F}$ represents the objective vector, g denotes the constraints and $\vec{x}$ is a P-dimensional vector representing the decision variables within a parameter space Ω. The mathematical problem can be solved by aggregating all the objectives into a single objective or optimizing one objective and treating the other as constraints. These methods produce a single solution as outcome, rather than a Pareto Optima.

During the initialization phase, coordination constructs the optimization objective and method that will be used to jointly optimize the set of AFs. Coordination also instructs AFs to disable their actuation (they'll only perform monitoring), and to report the monitored metrics when requested.

During runtime, upon request from coordination, AFs report the metrics they have monitored, then coordination proceeds to solve the multi-objective optimization problem and calculates the network parameter values that AFs will enforce on the controlled network elements. Finally, AFs enforce those values, which will remain valid until the next cycle of the centralized optimizer.

Coordination Mechanisms to Control AFs

This paragraph provides a synthetic view of the algorithms previously presented in an increasing efficiency order. The range of efficiency spans from minimizing the influence of conflicts (by avoiding concurrent actions) to jointly optimizing the utility of all AFs. Unfortunately, the increase of efficiency is gained at the cost of complexity growth both in setting parameters to the coordination algorithm and in terms of requirements on AFs API, as depicted in Table 5.

During the initialization phase, sets of AFs are assigned to instances of the coordination mechanisms. The selection and grouping of AFs under each instance depends primarily on identified conflicts, but it can additionally depend on factors such as proximity of AFs' controlled resources, policies coming from the static conflict identification. Finally, the choice of the coordination mechanism depends also on the AFs in the group, whether they are compliant with the chosen algorithm (see Table 5).

Table 5. Summary of features AFs must support to be coordinated by each of the coordination algorithms

Algorithm Name	Control the Frequency of Loop Execution	Knowledge Provided by AF to Coordination	Suspending Changes to Parameters	Forcing Values to Parameters
Random token	X			
Hierarchical coordination	X	Average convergence time		
Efficiency bids	X	Predicted utility	x	
Joint optimization	X	Utility function	x	x

MANAGEMENT FRAMEWORK HANDLING OF INFORMATION AND KNOWLEDGE

Since "a Knowledge Plane for the Internet" (Clark, Partridge, Ramming, & Wroclawski, 2003), knowledge is considered as a basis for autonomic networks, and many works on autonomic networks place knowledge at the heart of their solution (Madhyastha, Isdal, Piatek, Dixon, Anderson, Krishnamurthy, & Venkataramani, 2006), and (Mestres, Rodriguez-Natal, Carner, Barlet-Ros, Alarcón, Solé, ... & Estrada, 2017). The Management Framework presented in this section makes no exception to this trend; this section covers how knowledge and its exchange are organized in the Management Framework. All the aspects related to information and knowledge are gathered into the Knowledge block. The Knowledge block performs the duties of organizing the exchange of information (and knowledge) in the framework (and with AFs), and of building knowledge on the network behavior.

Before moving to the actual knowledge block, it is worth defining knowledge, especially because information and knowledge are sometimes confused (one is used instead of the other). The authors like considering that as long as operation performed on information consist on filtering, aggregation, correlation, these operations do not magically turn information into knowledge. Knowledge is what cannot be obtained from information solely, there is a need to understand the behavior of the system in order to build knowledge out of information

Building Knowledge Flows

The knowledge block manages information from/to the AFs and the other functions of the Management Framework and organizes communication of both information and knowledge. These organized exchanges between sources and sinks are hereafter named knowledge flows. The organization of these flows relies upon two functionalities, the first to keep track of which entity may share a given piece of information, the second to a negotiation mechanism between source and sinks. The final piece of this puzzle is the interface supporting these exchanges, the interface that is at the ends of the knowledge flows.

Information Registry

Any element in the Management Framework can act as source and/or sink of information. The elements can be either AFs or mechanisms of the Management Framework (like governance or coordination mechanisms). The sources register to the knowledge block by exposing the type of information they can share and by registering their list of "Acquired inputs", as well as their list of "Available outputs", while the sinks of information register to the knowledge block by exposing the type of information they need and by registering their list of "External inputs" (e.g., as AFs do with their Instance Manifest - see related section). The knowledge block then indexes all these 'MetricDescriptors' in a database named the information registry.

On one side, each information source should subscribe both the designation of information and their collection constraints (e.g., the maximum frequency of monitoring, or its maximum accuracy), while on the other side, each information sink should subscribe both the designation of required information and retrieval constraints with a similar process. The subscription process takes place during AF registration (or update) and is depicted in Figure 14. The information subscription handles 'MetricDescriptor' while the result of this subscription is the establishment of a knowledge flow, through which the actual metric values will be conveyed under the format of a 'KnowledgeFlowInformation' (see Appendix 2 for details on 'MetricDescriptor' and 'KnowledgeFlowInformation').

It is important to note that the workflow actors are named "knowledge sink" and "knowledge source": this underlines that these workflows are characterizing the behavior and the configuration of a Knowledge Exchange Interface, independently of the nature of the actors, which may be functions of the MF or AF.

This workflow shows the matching of constraints with requirements that takes place during a negotiation process will lead to the creation of information flow between source and sink according to the negotiated modalities.

Building and Negotiating Information Flows

Both knowledge source and sink negotiate information flow modalities which contain multiple parameters. The intermediate negotiator is the flow negotiation process held by the knowledge block. This process receives requested parameters from sink and achievable parameters form source and decides

Figure 14. Information subscription workflow

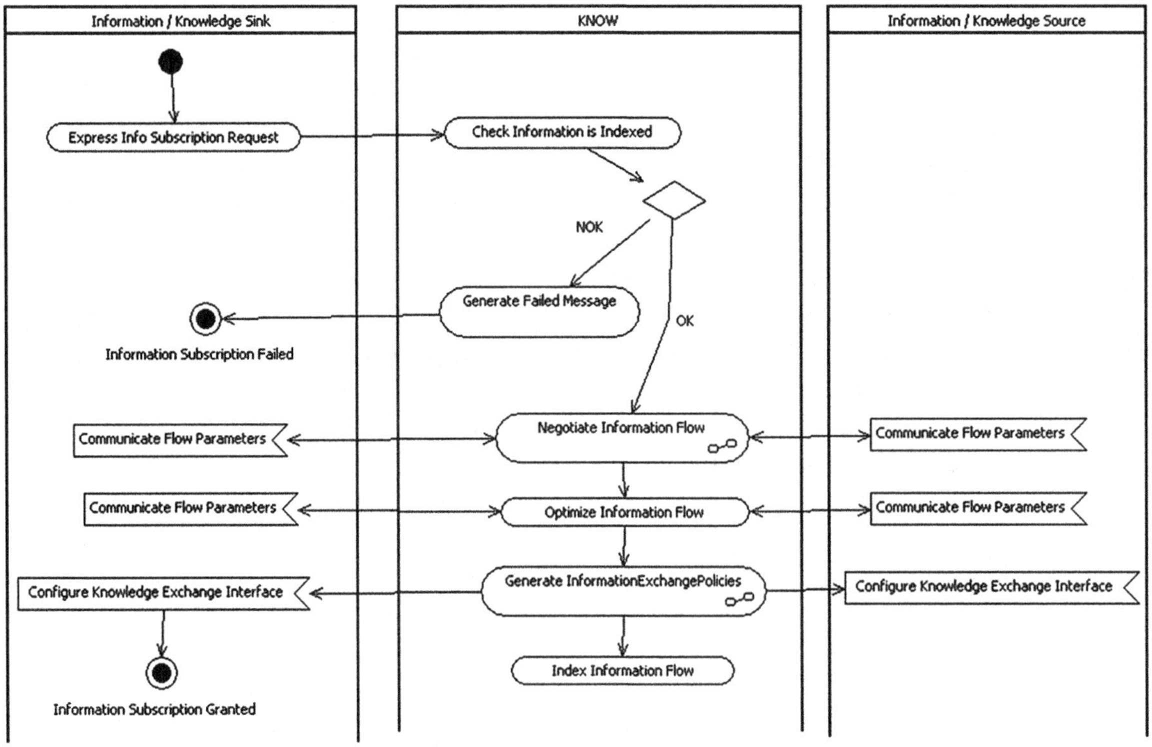

a set of negotiated values for these parameters, which will define the new flow. The flow definition is stored in a dedicated registry. After that, knowledge source can start communicating information to the knowledge sink through their Knowledge Exchange interface.

The communication of information in the flow is either based upon pull or publish-subscribe (pub-sub) methods. The choice of the method is the main parameter of the flow modalities to be negotiated. These two methods are illustrated in Figure 15, which mentions the flows with dashed lines. It shows that AF #2 pulls information from AF #1, while it is sharing information with AF #3 through pub-sub. In the pull method, both knowledge sink and knowledge source communicate directly, while in the pub-sub method an intermediate broker stays in between the sink and the source. The intermediate broker can additionally store the information for further use, which is why it is being named Intermediate Information Storage.

When many sinks are consuming the same information, the broker solution is more effective than having many independent pulls. But for local exchanges of information between neighboring entities, the pull method may be more effective.

The additional parameters of the negotiation depend on the flow method. For a pull flow, the negotiation may constrain the frequency of pulls allowed by the sink. For a pub-sub flow, the condition of update from the source may be negotiated (either by fixing a frequency of the updating rate or by determining a threshold in value change). The role of the flow builder is first to create (and later destroy) such flows between sources and sinks and then to keep track of the existence of these flows for management and optimization purposes (which is why flow definitions are being stored in the information flow registry).

Knowledge Exchange Interface

This Knowledge Exchange Interface is available at least once in each MF entity, which can then directly (or indirectly) exchange information with any other entity. This interface is only used to exchange information, while the whole registration and negotiation procedures happen through the management interface of the entity.

Figure 15. Knowledge block diagram showing established information flows

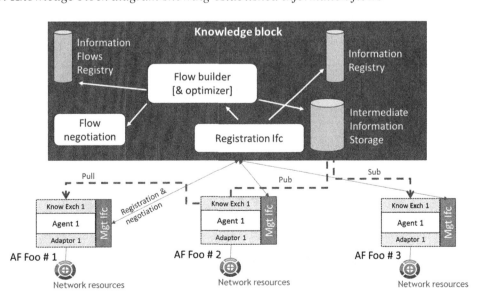

Concerning AFs, though their management interface is a single entry-point (used to manage them), this uniqueness property does not apply to knowledge exchange, as this interface may be used much more frequently than the management one. Changes in the management of an autonomic loop may happen once every few runs of its control loop, while exchange of information may happen many times even before triggering a run of the loop. It was then considered a good design choice to allow AF designers to determine the best way of implementing their autonomic function in terms of knowledge exchange. This degree of freedom is especially of interest when AF instance relies on multiple agents, as illustrated in the comparison made in Figure 16, which illustrates three different types of deployment for AFs.

AF Foo #1 relies on a single agent; hence its instance and its agent are the same thing, it is a centralized deployment. Therefore, a single knowledge exchange interface is available at this agent.

AF Foo #2 is organized out of two agents, which certainly allows proximity between the agents and the resources they handle. In the case shown, the main agent (the one containing the management interface) is also the one containing the knowledge exchange interface, but the design of the AF could have led to a different choice. In both cases, all the information exchanged with any other element of the Management Framework would happen through the agent holding the knowledge exchange interface.

Finally, the example shows the case of AF Foo #3, which is organized out of n agents, each having its own knowledge exchange interface. This deployment allows more distribution in the exchange of information as any agent can directly share and receive information on the resources handily available, without having the internal structure of the AF to carry information to/from the master agent. Under such a configuration, the negotiation phase presents an additional parameter on which it should obtain a consensus: the choice of the knowledge exchange interface.

Figure 16. Placement of Knowledge exchange interface in 3 different strategies of design of AF

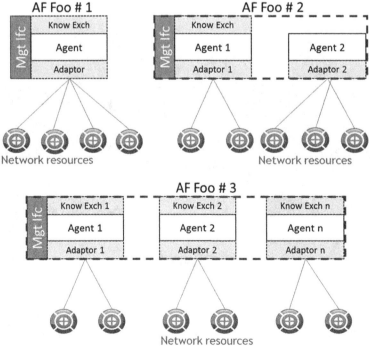

Optimization of Information Exchange

In the previous sub-section on building flows, the advantages of each information flow were discussed, showing local exchanges are often best suited with pull methods while broader exchanges that involve multiple sinks are best suited with pub-sub methods. When the flow building function is enriched with an optimization algorithm, then flows of the most appropriate type are built or updated. When additional sinks register or current sinks unregister, the type of flow may be dynamically adapted.

The role of the flow optimization algorithm is to dynamically adapt the flows and storage of information to the management network capacity and to the needs of MF entities. The criteria on which the optimization algorithm can play are:

- The choice of the information flow method;
- The choice of knowledge exchange interfaces used when AFs offer multiple interfaces;
- The actual instance of broker when having pub-sub flows (can relax the load on broker and/or reduce the flows path length by bringing broker closer), and;
- The strategies for updating values, which is a compromise between up-to-date information and management network capacity.

Building Knowledge

The second role of the knowledge block is to gather sufficient knowledge on the network to help better understand the network and the relationships between its resources. Among the applications of this "network" knowledge, the identification of conflicts before they occur (see "Identifying potential conflicts" in coordination section) is the most straightforward, but this knowledge can be of many uses in the context of autonomic networking.

Network Knowledge Map

The knowledge gathered from the network is captured in the Network Knowledge Map. Actually, the conflict map (discussed in the coordination section) is itself a subset of this network knowledge map. As previously explained in "Identifying potential conflicts", the production of the network knowledge map starts with a static map using an ontology language which details relationships between classes of network metrics and parameters. Then this static map is unfolded over the whole network by expending the edges and vertices using network topology information, which leads to the graph of the instantiated network knowledge map.

One reason for utilizing ontology languages (e.g., OWL – see (Antoniou & Van Harmelen, 2009) in producing network knowledge maps is their flexibility and their rich, yet generic enough, description/ representation (in other words "knowledge capturing") capabilities. A static network knowledge map is collected offline and it consists of some formalism, structure (in the form of graphs). and instances/ individuals reflecting the given network instantiation. Notably, the structure is designed once-and-for-all at project design-time, while the task of populating it with individuals is carried out on a per-network instance basis by the network experts in charge. This one will inject relations depending on technologies at play, network deployment specificities, etc.

The second, and probably most important, reason for choosing a Resource Description Framework (RDF) -based ontology language such as OWL is the potential it exhibits for further reasoning and integration with rules. The main idea is to capture the semantics of parameters, metrics, operators, actors (e.g., AFs), and utilities during the project design-time, so that:

- The network expert is provided with the tools to express his/her (sufficient) knowledge when instantiating a MF system.
- Reasoners (or other mechanisms) can infer additional knowledge based on those semantics, and detect additional interactions at runtime by monitoring state/configuration changes.

"Sufficient knowledge" above refers to the set of facts that will enable the reasoning mechanisms both to infer additional knowledge and to detect additional interactions. Such rules, as well as rules expressing conflicts can be formally expressed through the logical clauses of most rule- or logic programming- languages.

To elaborate a bit more, there are two concepts to be semantically enriched: namely the "influences" association between parameters and metrics, and the "coupled" association between metrics. The description of the relationships between vertices (metrics, parameters, AFs, etc.) will allow for inferring complex and potentially indirect coupling between them. Instead of using a predicate (as a verb in natural language usually dictates) to represent the relationship, in this case, a class is chosen so that it can be further linked to more properties regarding the characteristics of the relationship. That generalization class, namely "Impact", contains individuals that are used to describe the (direct or indirect) coupling of parameters. Linear dependencies can be described through a data property assignment to such individuals, namely 'hasStrength'. The value of the 'hasStrength' property in this case represents the differential of one parameter as a linear function of the other and represents the ratio of change in y over a change in x.

$$Strength = \frac{dy}{dx} = c \,,$$

where c is a constant, which can be used as a metric for the corresponding edge in the instantiated network map.

This kind of linear dependency assumption, although naive and unrealistic for the most part of the networking world, allows the reasoner to infer indirect coupling of parameters previously unknown to the system using the chain rule:

$$\text{If } \forall i \in \left\{1..k\right\} \frac{dx_i}{dx_{i+1}} = c_i \text{ then } \frac{dx_n}{dx_{m+1}} = \prod_{i=n}^{m} c_i \text{ with } 1 \leq n < m \leq k$$

The consequence of this rule can be easily inferred and calculated by a reasoner, and is what is referred to additional knowledge, since it was never manually or automatically injected into the system by the network engineer.

To complete the puzzle, the final question to address is how the ontology captures the topology relationships to use when unfolding the static knowledge map into the instantiated one. This can be achieved by completing the generic class "Impact" with properties such as 'inTheSameSubnet', 'onTheSameLink', 'onNeighbouringNodes', 'onNeighbouringLinks', 'ofTheSameLink', 'inTheSameCell', etc…. Depending on these properties, the unfolding algorithm can deduce the vertices over which impact relations are drawn, and which strength to affect to the edge.

The improvement brought by these additional properties can be illustrated with the impact of metric over the load of links. This impact would have a different strength for three different topological relations: A high strength for 'onTheSameLink', a medium strength for 'fromTheSameSourceNode', and low strength for 'inTheSameArea'.

Knowledge Building Functions

This section about knowledge could not be concluded without mentioning the knowledge building functions (KBFs). These functions are similar to AFs. However, they do not affect directly the network nor any of its resources. Their internal entities are based upon algorithms which produce additional knowledge to the one previously available in the network. To do so, KBFs can take inputs directly from resources or from any entity in the Management Framework ready to share those. Then the additional knowledge can be shared with any entity subscribing to such kind of information.

As their behavior is similar to the one of AFs, there is no need to define any dedicated specifications and the AF life cycle can be applied. For example, AF Class and Instance Manifest can be reused. The "Available Outputs" field would contain descriptors of additional knowledge proposed by the KBF, and the "Possible Actions" field would be empty. Coordination would not impose any constraints on these KBFs. Knowledge would establish flows with those as with any other entity.

These KBFs can be used to generate additional knowledge in the network knowledge map. They would monitor correlations between metrics as already depicted in the sub-section about dynamic conflict identification in Identifying potential conflicts.

These KBFs can also be used to augment the performance of existing AFs by providing those with augmented inputs, such as the following KBFs:

- IP network congestion prediction, which analyzes trends in network links load and compares it with the current network configuration to assess the risk of congestion.
- RAN traffic prediction, which tries to learn traffic patterns on RAN networks to be able to recognize those and predict traffic trends.
- Root-cause failure identification, which does Bayesian analysis of alarms to be able to identify the root cause of a failure (Bennacer, Amirat, Chibani, Mellouk, & Ciavaglia, 2015).

FUTURE RESEARCH DIRECTIONS

Over the years, an important body of knowledge has been produced in the field of autonomic networking and networks have gradually integrated more autonomic management principles and mechanisms. The current transformation sustained by software-driven and virtualization techniques enables the design and deployment of more versatile network infrastructures, requiring advanced automation and adaptation capabilities which naturally call for autonomic solutions.

However, beyond the current achievements, several areas of research and development remain to be addressed.

A first area relates quest for higher manageability and better usability of the networks. Declarative policy based management (also sometimes called intent-based networking) is a realm full of promises and challenges. Intent-driven networks configure and adapt autonomously to the user's or operator's intentions (i.e., a desired state or behavior) without the need to specify every technical detail of the process and operations to achieve it (i.e., the "machines" will figure out on their own how-to-achieve the user's goal). Designing, developing and deploying innovative technologies based on intent-driven networking has the potential to generate enormous gains in performance (doing things better and faster) and in functionality (enabling things previously impossible). To attain such a level of sophistication, numerous challenges must be addressed:

- How to represent, recognize, and interpret 'intentions' in structured and unstructured sets of data.
- How to formulate and solve the mapping of the shared goals to distributed and concurrent optimization problems, considering the contextual information and operational constraints.
- How to automatically generate and verify programs (decisions application), considering the execution constraints of/over virtual/physical infrastructures.
- How to evaluate the quality of the end-to-end process, e.g., as Quality of Intent via adequate feedback/control mechanisms, and analysis of decisions'/actions' effects.

A second area of future research direction relates to the coordination function. Achieving coordination schemes over large scale and dynamic infrastructures remains an important challenge. The coordination function not only must ensure an efficient arbitration between conflicts, but it must also cope with performance and scalability boundaries (e.g., how to coordinate the simultaneous and dynamic operation of hundreds or thousands of control loops distributed over extended networks in near real-time?), and must balance the trade-offs on criteria such as stability, robustness, security, integrity, cost/budget, etc. Those aspects raise questions on approaches for distributed and scalable clustering, avoidance of single points of failure while maintaining decision integrity and end-to-end consistency, ability to coping with uncertainties and priorities.

A third domain lies in the exploitation of the knowledge contained in an ever-increasing volume of data collected by the measurement and monitoring processes. Succeeding in generating the right insight, at the right time, with the right budget is one of key challenges for the data analytics and knowledge processing functionalities. Today, both Machine Learning algorithms and computing power are available to process large amount of data, however without proper guidance, the insights will not be useful nor actionable. It is therefore of prime importance to link the machine reasoning capabilities with the representation of the expert knowledge to maximize the results of data mining. Moreover, with proper modeling, the produced knowledge can even be used to forecast and predict future network conditions and open the floor to the vast domain of proactive and predictive care and operations.

Finally, building trust in the behavior and performance of autonomic systems is the most difficult challenge for their wide-scale adoption in the industry. Stability, robustness, and security requirements arising from future self-managing networks must be understood today to be included in their future design, standardization, and certification.

CONCLUSION

Autonomic networking aims at mastering the growing complexity of daily network operation. Important research efforts have been spent to design clean-slate and evolutionary architectures for autonomic networks, yet with limited adoption by the telecommunications industry. In order to fill the gaps between research, standards and industry, a global effort involving all stakeholders and a systematic roadmap are required. In this chapter, the authors have highlighted four essential artefacts to realize: the need for a unified management framework composed of the governance, coordination and knowledge functions in an end-to-end and multi-technology environment, and the need for standardized interfaces harmonizing the communication between autonomic functions.

The need for standards on autonomic networking is obvious: long-term solutions could only emerge from collaborative work and partnerships, and the massive adoption of autonomic networking will require interoperable systems. Therefore, the key question is what needs to be standardized. A series of recent initiatives supported and pushed by industrial players in different standard organizations or forums show an evolution of the problematic and the need to develop the standard dimension of future solutions as a key asset, which can be witnessed through ETSI Zero touch network and Service Management Industry Specification Group (ZSM ISG) (Mia, He, Pei, Martiny, Klotz, Khan, ... & Lopez, 2017), or IETF initiatives in the Network Management Research Group (Behringer, Bjarnason, Jiang, Carpenter, Pritikin, Ciavaglia, & Clemm, 2015; Jiang, Carpenter & Behringer 2015) and Autonomic Networking Integrated Model and Approach working group (Behringer, Carpenter, Eckert, Ciavaglia, & Nobre, 2018).

The ultimate goal is to have open solutions as opposed to proprietary ones, and insure interoperable functioning to broaden the market opportunities. From the vendor's point of view, the interest of standards resides in knowing that the effort invested in the design and development of a new technology will be shared, and it indicates a base agreement on how to develop interoperable implementations. On the operator's side, standardization is a key step to minimize the risk of introducing novel networking techniques and ensure that deployable solutions are available. The industry should undertake the necessary actions towards standardization organizations in order to foster the development of reference and interoperable autonomic networks implementations. Without standards, there will be no adoption of the autonomic technologies, no compatibility between systems and real progress could be hindered. It is therefore crucial to agree on a path forward with respect to standardization. An ETSI ISG has been set up to address specifically the zero-touch automation of future networks and services. The ETSI ISG ZSM has recently (2017) published its Terms of Reference and Work Plan to produce reference industry specifications for end-to-end network automation. The key items that require standard procedures are: resource models, communication interfaces, common and consistent management principles and language, context- and goal-oriented integrated systems and service management.

ACKNOWLEDGMENT

This research was supported by FP7-UniverSelf [Grant no. 257513].

REFERENCES

Antoniou, G., & Van Harmelen, F. (2009). Web ontology language: OWL. In *Handbook on ontologies* (pp. 91–110). Berlin: Springer. doi:10.1007/978-3-540-92673-3_4

Behringer, M., Bjarnason, S., Jiang, S., Carpenter, B., Pritikin, M., Ciavaglia, L., & Clemm, A. (2015). *Autonomic networking: Definitions and design goals* (RFC 7575).

Behringer, M., Carpenter, B., Eckert, T., Ciavaglia, L., & Nobre, J. (2018). *A Reference Model for Autonomic Networking*. IETF Internet draft.

Bennacer, L., Amirat, Y., Chibani, A., Mellouk, A., & Ciavaglia, L. (2015). Self-diagnosis technique for virtual private networks combining Bayesian networks and case-based reasoning. *IEEE Transactions on Automation Science and Engineering*, *12*(1), 354–366. doi:10.1109/TASE.2014.2321011

Ciavaglia, L., Ghamri-Doudane, S., Smirnov, M., Demestichas, P., Stavroulaki, V. A., Bantouna, A., & Sayrac, B. (2012). Unifying management of future networks with trust. *Bell Labs Technical Journal*, *17*(3), 193–212. doi:10.1002/bltj.21568

Clark, D. D., Partridge, C., Ramming, J. C., & Wroclawski, J. T. (2003). A knowledge plane for the internet. In *Proceedings of the 2003 conference on Applications, technologies, architectures, and protocols for computer communications* (pp. 3-10). ACM.

Combes, R., Altman, Z., & Altman, E. (2013). Coordination of autonomic functionalities in communications networks. In *Modeling & Optimization in Mobile, Ad Hoc & Wireless Networks (WiOpt), 2013 11th International Symposium on* (pp. 364-371). IEEE.

Davy, S., Jennings, B., & Strassner, J. (2007). The policy continuum–a formal model. In *Proceedings of the Second IEEE International Workshop on Modelling Autonomic Communications Environments* (pp. 65-79). IEEE.

Galani, A., Tsagkaris, K., Demestichas, P., Nguengang, G., BenYahia, I. G., Stamatelatos, M., . . . Ciavaglia, L. (2012). Core functional and network empower mechanisms of an operator-driven, framework for unifying autonomic network and service management. In *Computer Aided Modeling and Design of Communication Links and Networks (CAMAD), 2012 IEEE 17th International Workshop on* (pp. 191-195). IEEE. 10.1109/CAMAD.2012.6335330

3. GPP. (2011). Self-configuring and self-optimizing network (SON) use cases and solutions. *Third Generation Partnership Project (3GPP) specification TR36902*, V9.

Harrington, D., Presuhn, R., & Wijnen, B. (2002). *An architecture for describing simple network management protocol (snmp) management frameworks* (RFC 3411).

Iacoboaiea, O. C., Sayrac, B., Ben Jemaa, S., & Bianchi, P. (2014). SON conflict resolution using reinforcement learning with state aggregation. In *Proceedings of the 4th workshop on All things cellular: operations, applications, & challenges* (pp. 15-20). ACM. 10.1145/2627585.2627591

International Telecommunication Union (ITU-T) (2007). *Enhanced Telecom Operations Map (eTOM) – The business process framework, ITU-T Recommendation M.3050.1*.

Jiang, S., Carpenter, B., & Behringer, M. (2015). *General gap analysis for autonomic networking* (RFC 7576).

Koutsouris, N., Tsagkaris, K., Demestichas, P., Altman, Z., Combes, R., Peloso, P., . . . Galis, A. (2013). Conflict free coordination of SON functions in a unified management framework: Demonstration of a proof of concept prototyping platform. In *Integrated Network Management (IM 2013), 2013 IFIP/IEEE International Symposium on* (pp. 1092-1093). IEEE.

López, J. A. L., Muñoz, J. M. G., & Morilla, J. (2007). A Telco Approach to Autonomic Infrastructure Management. In *Advanced Autonomic Networking and Communication* (pp. 27–42). Birkhäuser Basel. doi:10.1007/978-3-7643-8569-9_2

Luo, W., Zeng, J., Su, X., Li, J., & Xiao, L. (2012). A mathematical model for joint optimization of coverage and capacity in self-organizing network in centralized manner. In *Communications and Networking in China (CHINACOM), 2012 7th International ICST Conference on* (pp. 622-626). IEEE.

Madhyastha, H. V., Isdal, T., Piatek, M., Dixon, C., Anderson, T., Krishnamurthy, A., & Venkataramani, A. (2006). iPlane: An information plane for distributed services. In *Proceedings of the 7th symposium on Operating systems design and implementation* (pp. 367-380). USENIX Association.

McKeown, N., Anderson, T., Balakrishnan, H., Parulkar, G., Peterson, L., Rexford, J., ... Turner, J. (2008). OpenFlow: Enabling innovation in campus networks. *Computer Communication Review*, *38*(2), 69–74. doi:10.1145/1355734.1355746

Mestres, A., Rodriguez-Natal, A., Carner, J., Barlet-Ros, P., Alarcón, E., Solé, M., ... Estrada, G. (2017). Knowledge-defined networking. *Computer Communication Review*, *47*(3), 2–10. doi:10.1145/3138808.3138810

Mia, J., He, G., Pei, X., Martiny, K., Klotz, M., Khan, A., ... Lopez, D. (2017). *Zero-touch Network and Service Management – Introductory White Paper*. Retrieved from https://portal.etsi.org/TBSiteMap/ ZSM/OperatorWhitePaper

Open Networking Foundation. (2016). *Intent NBI – Definition and Principles. ONF TR523*. Paolo Alto.

Stamatelatos, M., Yahia, I., Peloso, P., Fuentes, B., Tsagkaris, K., & Kaloxylos, A. (2013). Information model for managing autonomic functions in future networks. In *International Conference on Mobile Networks and Management* (pp. 259-272). Springer. 10.1007/978-3-319-04277-0_20

Telemanagement Forum – TMF. (2018). *GB922 Information Framework R17.5*. Parsippany, NJ: SID.

Tsagkaris, K., Nguengang, G., Peloso, P., Fuentes, B., Mamatas, L., Georgoulas, S., . . . Smirnov, M. (2013). *Unified Management Framework (UMF) Specifications - Release 3 – UniverSelf Deliverable D2.4*. Retrieved from http://www.univerself-project.eu/tecnical-reports

KEY TERMS AND DEFINITIONS

AF API: A software component to provide the AF developer with the MF interfaces and the skeleton for AF behavior (i.e., registration, configuration, knowledge-exchange and management) needed for interacting with the MF core and compliance with the MF specification.

AF Class: It is a piece of software that contains the logic achieving a specific autonomic function. Such class is deployed in a network running a MF system and requires being instantiated on a set of concrete network elements to effectively perform its autonomic function.

AF (Class) Instance: Allows performing a given autonomic function onto a given subset of a network. This is achieved by binding the code of an AF Class to a set of identified network resources/devices. This AF instance is identified by an instance ID and its unique interface with the MF. This AF instance at any given time handles a set of identified network resources (this set can evolve over time). Hence, there may be multiple instances of a given AF Class inside the same network e.g., one per area. An AF instance is created by the MF system it is being deployed in.

AF Instance Description: Describes a given instance of a given AF Class. This description is issued by the AF instance towards MF system, it is used for the registration of the AF and it tells which information is monitored and which actions are taken.

AF Instance Description Grammar: A subset of MF specifications describing which information must and may be provided by the AF instance when starting (and when its settings are changed) so as to register to the MF system the 1) capabilities of this AF instance regarding information/knowledge sharing, 2) requirements of this AF instance regarding knowledge inputs, and 3) conflicts of this AF instance with already running AF instances of any AF class.

AF Mandate: Is issued by the MF system to an AF instance. This AF Mandate is a set of instructions telling which devices must be handled by this AF instance and which settings this AF instance must work with.

AF Mandate Format: Is a subset of MF specifications describing which information must and may be provided by the MF system to the AF.

AF Manifest: Describes a given AF Class. This description provides guidance to the network operator in order to install and configure an instance of this AF Class – the goal of an AF manifest is similar to a datasheet. This description is issued by the AF designer towards network operators.

AF Manifest Grammar: A subset of MF specifications describing which information must and may be provided by the AF developers in order to describe their AF class.

AF Specifications: They constrain the behavior of AFs and define the generic part of their interfaces with MF elements, as the specifications of these MF elements.

Autonomic Function (AF): A functional grouping of objective(s), context and method(s) where "method" is a general procedure for solving a problem. An AF is (a priori) implemented as a piece of software that can be deployed in a network to enhance or simplify its control and management (e.g., take over some operations). An intrinsic capability of an AF is to be deployable and interoperable in a MF context (in a MF-compliant network).

Coordination Function: A core management framework (MF) component that aims to ensure the proper sequence in triggering of autonomic functions (AFs) and the conditions under which they will be invoked (i.e., produce their output), taking into account operator services and scenario requirements and at the same time the needs for conflict avoidance, stability control, and joint optimization through the corresponding functions.

Governance Function: A core MF component that aims to provide a human operator with a mechanism for controlling the network from a high-level business point of view, that is, without the need for having a deep technical knowledge of the network.

Knowledge Function: An infrastructure that uses and/or manipulates information and knowledge, including information/knowledge flow optimization within the network.

Management Framework (MF): A framework that will help produce the unification, governance, and "plug & play" of autonomic networking solutions within existing and future management ecosystems. The objective of the MF is to facilitate the seamless and trustworthy deployment of AFs.

APPENDIX 1

Detailed names of the parameters, metrics and SON functions of the conflict map of SON functions depicted in Figure 10.

Table 6. Parameters names of Figure 10

	Parameter Description
P1	Handover/(re) selection
P2	Antenna configuration (e.g., tilt, MIMO)
P3	Downlink transmit power RS+TCH
P4	Uplink transmit power
P5	Cell switch ON/OFF
P6	Scheduling (RB assignment/preferences)
P7	Inter-cell interference coordination thresholds (reporting, reference signal received power (RSRP))
P8	Parameters related to syndicated feed reception (SFR), fractional frequency reuse (FFR) schemes
P9	Random access channel (RACH) related parameters

Table 7. Metric names of Figure 10

	Metric Description (KPI)
K1	Indicators/counters composed for too late HOs, too early HOs, HOs to a wrong cell and HOs subsequent to a connection setup (HO-related)
K2	Number of HOs (incoming outgoing)
K3	Ping-pong handovers
K4	Handover success rate (HOSR)
K5	Bit error rate (BER)
K6	Block error rate (BLER)
K7	Outage
K8	Average throughput
K9	Number of calls
K10	Hours and/or data communicated
K11	Call set-up success rate (CSSR)
K12	System/cell load information
K13	Energy expenses
K14	OPEX linked to energy expenses
K15	Access delay
K16	Call setup delay
K17	Handover delay
K18	Block call rate (BCR)
K19	Drop call rate (DCR)Handover/(re) selection

Table 8. SON function (control) names of Figure 10

	SON Function Name (Control)
1	Capacity and coverage optimization (CCO)
2	Energy savings (ES)
3	Interference reduction (IR)
4	Mobility robustness optimization (MRO)
5	Mobility load balancing (MLB)
6	Random access channel (RACH)
7	Inter-cell interference coordination (ICIC)

APPENDIX 2

Recap about info model used for Metrics

- **Metric Class Descriptor:**
  - ◦ **Found in:** AF Class Manifest
  - ◦ **Example:** {class: "Load of an Ethernet link", unitClass: bit/s}
- **Metric Descriptor:**
  - ◦ **Found in:** AF Instance Manifest
  - ◦ **Exchanged:** During Information subscription flow
  - ◦ **Example:** {class: "Load of an Ethernet link", unitClass: bit/s, instantiatedOver: "UUID of between router 1.1.1.1 and router 1.1.1.2"}
- **Knowledge Flow Information:**
  - ◦ **Exchanged:** Inside Knowledge exchange flow
  - ◦ **Example:** {class: "Load of an Ethernet link", unitClass: bit/s, instantiatedOver: "UUID of between router 1.1.1.1 and router 1.1.1.2",
  - ◦ **Value:** "3600", unit: "Mbit/s"}

Chapter 4

Autonomic Networking Integrated Model and Approach (ANIMA):
Secure Autonomic Network Infrastructure

Toerless Eckert
Huawei, USA

ABSTRACT

This chapter presents the work of the Autonomic Networking Integrated Model and Approach (ANIMA) working group of the Internet Engineering Task Force (IETF). It was formed to standardize protocols and procedures for an ANIMA autonomic network (AN) and first chartered to define the ANIMA secure autonomic network infrastructure (ANI). This chapter describes the technical history and goals leading to this working group. It then describes how the ANIMA approach provides an evolutionary approach to securing and automating networks and to provide a common infrastructure to evolve into future autonomic networks. Finally, this chapter compares this approach to adjacent standards technologies and discusses interesting next steps.

INTRODUCTION

Operation, Administration and Maintenance (OAM) as well as service automation within data centers are quickly evolving and driving technology evolution and standards in Software Defined Networks (SDN) and Network Function Virtualization (NFV). Trying to apply these methods to Internet of Things (IoT), Wide Area Networks (WAN), Metro-Area Networks (MAN) or Customer Premises Networks (Enterprises, IoT and others) introduces a range of unique challenges.

OAM and service automation for the above-mentioned networks consist of a highly fragmented and complex set of technologies and practices. One important area is the remotely managed, secured, and automated initial setup of network devices, which is called Zero Touch Deployment (ZTD). Another area is the absence of a common secure and reliable infrastructure for ongoing network OAM and network

DOI: 10.4018/978-1-5225-7146-9.ch004

services control. Vendor- and device-specific solutions are common. These solutions are often complex to manage by themselves and have problems in some topologies such as a multi-layer subtended network ring structures.

The evolving architectural Internet Engineering Task Force (IETF) standards direction for autonomic networks attempts to address these challenges by enabling networks to be self-manageable and self-operational. Ultimately, any network, autonomic or not, should require only high level, so called Intent based input from the operator into the network infrastructure to instantiate its services and direct its operations.

The Network Management Research Group of the Internet Research Task Force analyzed this problem of autonomic networking and published its findings in Behringer et al. (2015) and Jiang et al. (2015). Even before finishing that work, it became clear that any autonomic network would require a common infrastructure and approach for ZTD, secure autonomic network layer communications, discovery and signaling for OAM and network services, and that these components are well enough understood to warrant standardization.

That work resulted in the formation of a working group in the IETF chartered to define and standardize an Autonomic Networking Infrastructure (ANI). This working group is called Autonomic Networking Integrated Model and Approach (ANIMA). In addition to enabling more and more distributed autonomic functions in networks, the ANI targets to support legacy centralized OAM operations as well as current and future centralized SDN methods using a common approach. This chapter presents an overview of that work.

The ANIMA ANI design is currently (2018) targeted to support the most widely deployed type of networks which are managed by professional operators and can thus support a wide range of services and large number of subscribers. These networks often need to evolve over time, adding and changing services and subscribers, and can have high degree of complexity. These networks include Service Provider Networks, Enterprise or Public Networks, but also Industrial and other OT/IoT networks (Operational Technologies, Internet of Things).

Security is a key focus of the ANI because of the recurrent experience with past protocol designs where security was often only considered as an afterthought, resulting either in the inability to deploy solutions due to missing security features and/or high degrees of complexity through later added security functionality.

The most fundamental problem for security is the management of cryptographic keying material. It is also one of the most complex problems in network management. The ANI can use a single Public Key Infrastructure (PKI) certificate on each node for all ANI functions. The Bootstrap of Remote Secure Key Infrastructures protocol (BRSKI) used by the ANI provides a zero touch solution for this problem. It also introduces a novel credential mechanism, called vouchers, to allow booting devices to authenticate the network they are connecting and therefore to mitigate remote attacks against the volatile unconfigured bootstrapping devices.

The ANI relies on a secure, zero touch built, in-band virtual management network. This so-called Autonomic Control Plane (ACP) is indestructible by operator configuration or SDN applications, including mistakes or intentional changes to connectivity/services/security. The ACP provides secure IPv6 connectivity and service discovery not only for OAM/SDN operations, but also to future intelligent distributed autonomic software, which are called Autonomic Service Agents (ASA) in the ANIMA architecture.

Finally, the ANI introduces a new signaling mechanism called Generic Autonomic Signaling Protocol (GRASP). This mechanism provides a common framework for service discovery and negotiation between autonomic or non-autonomic components, allowing to avoid the creation of specify protocols for every service or purpose.

The ANIMA ANI effort is unique in that it does not focus on the higher layers of autonomic networks, such as self-orchestration of operations and services, but instead defines and standardizes the common underlying infrastructure components necessary to enable such higher layer functions. How can a set of completely un-configured devices physically connected with each other create a secured communications network with minimal operator dependencies; and how can they autonomically provide secure IPv6 routing and forwarding as well as service discovery and negotiation functions for these higher layer functions distributed autonomic or centralized. This is what ANI does. It provides the most basic self-orchestration infrastructure for networks.

The ANI can therefore be the common basis for a wide range of current or future higher layer autonomic solution designs. ANIMA itself has laid out a high level architecture for autonomic networks (AN) as well.

This chapter describes the ANIMA AN and ANI work, starting with the historical evolution that shaped its goals, detailing core technical aspects and benefits, and finishing with a comparison of adjacent technologies and challenging options for future work. This chapter does not address or compare the ANIMA with that of other organizations such as ETSI.

BACKGROUND

This section explains the history, use-cases, and reasoning that lead to the basic architecture goals of ANIMA ANI and AN.

From Vision to ANIMA Architecture

The term "autonomic" was made popular by Kephart and Chess (2002) for the larger context of Autonomic Computing. Its main goal was that of a Self-X behavior: self-Configuring, self-Healing, self-Optimizing, and self-Provisioning (Self-CHOP). Other X used include managing, healing, and protection. Since then, network device vendors have attempted to develop Self-X solutions for various X. Especially the automated bootstrap of devices has a wide variety of vendor-specific solutions – all different from each other.

Self-X in networks is not a new idea of the 21st century. The origins of the Internet date back to the Advanced Research Projects Agency of the United States Department of Defense that funded research in the 1960th for self-healing networks where end-to-end connectivity is maintained and restored autonomously in the face of physical attacks that cause failure of components – especially of central components. Distributed routing algorithms and protocols are the result of that early work. They still are the foundation of all IP networks today and the reference for distributed autonomic behavior in networks.

In the past decades, IP networks have evolved in often non-autonomic ways. The following sections review core problems that led to the ANIMA architecture for AN and ANI.

Evolution of Network Management Network Infrastructure

In the 1980th and 1990th, non-IP networks had a physically separate management infrastructure from the actual network infrastructure itself (or "data-plane"). Originally, this management plane consisted of Telephone/Modem, ATM, Frame-Relay or X.25 networks to connect serial management ports of network devices with the NOC to allow remote management of the network devices.

Towards the end of the 1990th, operators of these non-IP networks recognized that IP networks could well serve as a management network. Therefore, the International Telecommunication Union defined the so called "Architecture and Specification of Data Communication Network" (2001) (DCN): An IP network connecting network devices via serial or Ethernet ports to the NOC. While these DCNs introduced a variety of management services, initial device bring-up and provisioning continued to be mostly a manual task, now performed across the DCN.

In IP networks, a separate DCN management network infrastructure is not necessary. Only large service providers maintain a physically separate DCN to operate at least some aspects of their IP networks. Almost all IP networks are managed by simply using the IP network itself to manage it. This is called in-band management and it causes many issues.

In-Band Management Complexity

The fundamental issue with in-band IP management is how to ensure reachability of networking devices from the NOC. A set of Ethernet switches plugged together does autonomously form a single switched Ethernet providing autonomic connectivity between all devices as well as to all Ethernet switches. There is no equivalent for IP networks except in specific IoT networks or to some extent introduced in an architecture defined by the IETF Homenet working group; see the section about adjacent technologies at the bottom of this chapter.

IP networks in general cannot create end-to-end and global connectivity autonomously for several reasons: (public) IP addresses are not assigned by manufacturers as they are in Ethernet, so some IP address prefix needs to be assigned to a network. Subdividing such a network prefix autonomously across all the network segments is difficult, especially in IPv4 because of the limited available address space. Other IP networks do not even have a common, default enabled signaling infrastructure to allow running such a distributed prefix assignment mechanism.

There is a variety of IP routing protocols, and unless a specific one is mandated for all equipment of a particular type of network, there is no mechanism for a network to agree on a single routing protocol autonomously. Common enterprise routing protocols would also be very hard to scale to large networks autonomously because they require additional administrative structuring to scale. Last but not least, operators often need to deal with complex IP address assignment policies, e.g., different prefixes for internal vs. external network segments, specific prefixes for specific type of devices, geographic regions, speed of network links, company departments, and so on. The reasons for such complex policies is that IP addresses often are the only available information in the network traffic to which policies can be tied. Further, even if all these problems were solved, network operators typically would not want to have the insecure creation of a network across arbitrary devices as it is possible with Ethernet switches.

Even if all the above problems were solved, this would still leave autonomously created connectivity brittle to configuration mistakes. As long as all the components used to provide the connectivity are subject to operator misconfiguration, mistakes can cause loss of connectivity. In today's IP networks with in-band management, the list of explicitly configured services in the network required to provide the connectivity is often several hundreds of configuration entries long and a single line misconfiguration can cause the device to be unreachable from the NOC. Various policies (e.g., addressing, routing, tunnels, QoS, security) need to be configured adequately; otherwise a misconfiguration will break connectivity to the NOC.

Another problem with in-band management is how to protect it from users attacking the management plane. Traditional, management plane protocols had almost no security and even today (2018) they only partially evolved to support end-to-end security. In most cases, that security was added as an afterthought and is difficult and error-prone to configure. Even with most common end-to-end encryption, management of keying material is often complex.

In reaction to all the in-band management problems, operators have come up with a large variety of non-standardized solutions. Primarily they attempted to isolate the data plane from the management plane to prohibit traffic between them. Virtual Local Area Networks (VLANs), Virtual Private Networks (VPNs), or Virtual Routing and Forwarding Functions (VRF) are tweaked to further isolate the management plane from the data plane.

The Autonomic Control Plane (ACP) is the component in the ANIMA architecture that provides an autonomic secure, in-band management plane that as far as possible behaves like a physically out-of-band management network.

Self-Organizing and Secure Network Services

When more and more services were added to IP networks over the last three decades, almost none of them were defined to provide autonomous self-organization or even simple network-wide policy options. Instead, it became necessary to configure more and more parameters across network devices with often-complex consistency requirements.

Security for network services is a special case of this problem. Indeed, in most network services and as mentioned earlier, security was added after the original design and many services re-invented their own security method (e.g., security in routing protocols, IP multicast security, authentication protocols management protocols and so on). Often, the security model of these services is also limited. This has led overall to a high degree of provisioning complexity for secure network services. Today, every service also employs its own keying material and most often has no way to automatically manage it.

The resulting lack of security in networks is becoming more and more a problem, because the exploitation of security breaches is highly automated today. Every "Script Kiddie" (2018) can easily buy automated attack software yet there is no automated secure management infrastructure solution for network operators. Until the ANI.

The ANIs domain certificates are intended to be re-useable keying material to solve the keying material problem. BRSKI is the solution to manage this keying material. The ACP is intended to be the common secure communications fabric to eliminate the need for each network service to design its own communications security. The Autonomic Service Agents (ASAs) are the intended software components to easily build autonomous network services.

Device Bootstrap and Zero Touch Deployment

Large-scale deployment of remote devices has led to various "zero touch" deployment technologies by vendors. These are often insecure and are primarily targeted for devices attached to the edge of fully provisioned network infrastructure which has also been provisioned to provide Dynamic Host Configuration Protocol (DHCP) and Domain Name System (DNS) information to the bootstrapping device: DHCP to provide an address, DHCP/DNS to find bootstrap and other servers.

Using these technologies to deploy actual network infrastructures such as broadband aggregation rings leads to various problems because transit links in networks to which network devices would attach are usually managed completely differently than links to attach end user devices. For example, DHCP is not typically used to assign addresses to transit network devices, and trying to support it only for the bootstrap can be a big operational issue.

When rolling out complete network infrastructures such as access network aggregation rings, the inability of today's IP networks to autonomously establish connectivity end-to-end leads to highly interlocked workflows where each device needs to be provisioned with configuration so that it can provide transit before the next device can even be reached from the NOC to be bootstrapped. The initial configuration to provide this connectivity is often fragile and highly dependent on specific hardware configuration and software versions, and licenses as well as interface types or even location in the network topology. Any mistake in these initial configuration files downloaded from the NOC can make the device itself become unreachable from the NOC or its ability to provide transit for further devices.

Many networks overcome these issues with locally installed bootstrap or "jumpstart" servers to avoid having to depend on this fragile network connectivity for often complex bootstrap and installation procedures of network devices.

BRSKI and ACP are the components to solve these issues in ANIMA. BRSKI for the fully automated secure bootstrap and ACP to provide the secure and resilient zero touch connectivity to the NOC.

The Impact of SDN

With SDN, the problem of non-automatic in-band network connectivity increases because any service automation needs to understand which configuration elements are exactly required to maintain connectivity between the NOC and the transitive set of devices being managed. An incorrect change in an Access Control List (ACL) configuration on one device might impact the NOCs connectivity to another device, for example. This ACL might not even impact the actual provisioning traffic, but just the traffic of the authentication protocol for the provisioning connection. Or the routing protocol. Or protocols to assign addresses and names to the device. Or a security protocol for the device to gain access to the network. Any of these could disconnect the device effectively from the NOC. Modelling all these dependencies into any SDN controller software is a major obstacle for reliable remote SDN manageability. Especially when more and more parties are contributing to the SDN software in a modular fashion for different parts of the device modelling and configuration (e.g., vendor, customer developers, independent third-parties) (Eckert. & Behringer, 2018).

ANIMA AUTONOMIC NETWORKING ARCHITECTURE

This section outlines the overall architecture of autonomic networks as envisioned by ANIMA. It includes both the ANI as well as a high level abstraction of the higher layers of an autonomic network.

According to (Behringer, Carpenter, Eckert, Ciavaglia, & Nobre, 2018), the reference model of an autonomic network has four layers:

1. Network Intent and Reporting;
2. ASA/Autonomic Functions;
3. ANI/ACP, and;
4. The Network OS of the device

Only the ANI layer is currently specified and standardized. The other layers are architecturally outlined.

COMPONENTS OF AN ANIMA AUTONOMIC NETWORK (ANIMA AN)

Network Intent and Reporting

In the ANIMA architecture, Intent and Reporting are the northbound API of autonomic networks to the NOC/OAM functions. Intent is a network-wide description of services and policy originating from operators or backend systems that describes the desired behavior of the autonomic network. Intent is meant to

Figure 1. Autonomic Networking Architecture with NOC and benefits

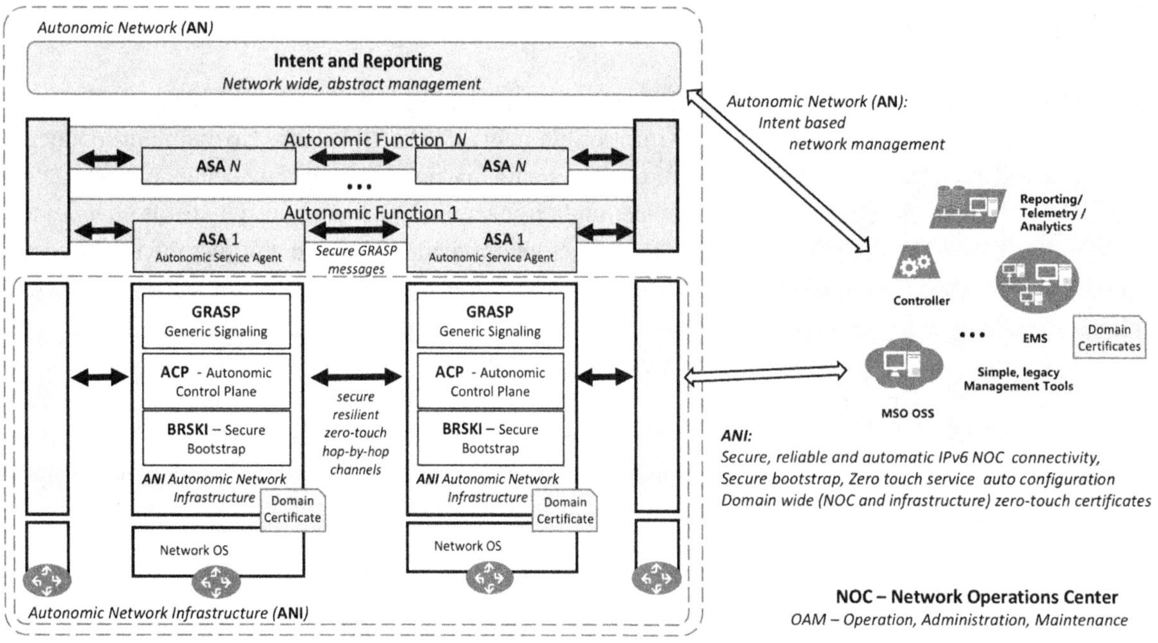

© 2018, Huawei. Used with permission

replace per-network-device configuration. As of today, there is no defined model for Intent in ANIMA. One likely future direction is for Intent to be a set of YANG modules describing network-wide service instances, operations policies and other aspects of the network behavior. Some YANG data models to define network-wide services already exist such as (Wu, Litkowski, Tomotaki, & Ogaki 2018) which defines instances of Layer 3 VPNs.

Intent is not meant to be a definition depending on an explicitly known topology and a set of resources (devices, links) in the network. Instead, it needs to be so abstract that it applies to all possible changes to the network infrastructure – extensions, capacity/equipment changes, or failures. The network operator should also only need to express Intent that he/she is interested in: If the network operator has a reason to decide via Intent, which routing protocol should be used in the network, for example IS-IS or OSPF, then Intent should allow to specify this. By default, network operators should rather not have to worry about details that an autonomic network could decide itself. Network Intent should also be survivable inside the autonomic network so that it continues to be the source of self-configuration of the network even if the NOC is disconnected from the network.

Where Intent is in the direction from the network operator to the autonomic network, reporting information is autonomously collected, potentially aggregated by the autonomic network, and provided to the OAM backend systems. It can include performance and failure telemetry, network topology and service/maintenance status, or any other information required by network operations. Like Intent, the goal is to reduce communications to the network operator to only those aspects that are required or beneficial for OAM procedures. The NOC should not need to be involved in any control loop that can safely be resolved autonomously inside the network (but reporting of diagnostics is fine if so desired).

Autonomic Functions and Service Agents (ASA)

Autonomic Functions are distributed services in the network relying on (most often) distributed algorithms to coordinate instances of the autonomic function across devices and to coordinate between autonomic functions. Routing protocols in the network are the classic example of Autonomic Functions. In the ANIMA architecture, instances of Autonomic Functions on devices are represented via software components that are called ASAs. Instances of routing protocols qualify as ASAs if they are self-configuring.

ASAs communicate via Intent/Reporting on their northbound side to the OAM components in the NOC. They use the GRASP protocol (explained further below) to communicate amongst themselves in the east/westbound direction, both within a device and between devices. Both the northbound and east/westbound communication happen via IPv6 in the Autonomic Control Plane which provides the autonomic, secure and reliable communications fabric. Finally, the ASAs need to be able to communicate with the non-autonomic network OS in network devices on their southbound side to query their status and configure them.

In a simple incremental AN implementation, ASAs could be lightweight script agents (for example, written in python) that are running on every network device, layered on top of existing non-autonomic service functions. The autonomic routing function, for example, could have a simple set of Intent parameters, such as the choice of routing protocol. This intent is distributed via GRASP from the NOC to the ASAs forming the autonomic routing function and running on every network device. These ASAs then configure on their respective device the existing routing protocol of the devices network software.

Many network services will have a range of parameters that need to be selected consistently across the devices, but that do not need to be explicitly selected by the NOC. For example, routing protocols should have security enabled, which requires mutual agreement between neighboring networking devices about the keying material. These mutual agreements are negotiated using GRASP between those neighboring ASAs and the selected keys would dynamically be configured into the networking devices routing protocols by the ASAs.

In newly developed autonomic devices where the whole network devices software is written with autonomic operations in mind, an ASA would not need to be layered on top of existing non-autonomic software but could be an integral part of a network service.

Autonomic Network Infrastructure (ANI) Only Devices

In the current thinking of many advanced, but non-autonomic network automation approaches, control loops for automation of network services are built via centralized SDN methods in which telemetry is collected by automation software running in the NOC – as part of OAM logic. This automation software is then making the automated decisions for how to provision network services and policies and how to react to incidents in the networks (maintenance, failure, etc.).

In these environments, devices would not be fully autonomic because they would not need to have ASA implementing autonomic functions nor Intent/Reporting via those ASA. These devices would still use the Autonomic Network Infrastructure (ANI) as the communications fabric between the OAM functions and the network services software in the network devices. These devices are called ANI devices to distinguish them from (fully) autonomic devices that also implement ASAs, Intent, and Reporting.

Autonomic Network Infrastructure

The ANI is the communications infrastructure of autonomic networks, their autonomic devices and the OAM communications infrastructure of non-autonomic, ANI devices. Whenever in the following discussion the behavior of autonomic devices and ANI devices is the same, this text will only refer to ANI devices.

At the core of the ANI is the ANI domain certificate that allows for an ANI device to securely identify itself to other ANI devices in the same ANI domain. These certificates are securely and zero touch bootstrapped via ANIs BRSKI protocol. These ANI domain certificates can then be used to secure any communications of the ANI devices to the OAM backend. For example, the domain certificates can be credentials for SSH or TLS authentication of NETCONF or RESTCONF connections. The certificates can equally be used for authentication between ASAs or between non-autonomic network services that support authentication via certificates.

In the current ANIMA defined ANI, this secure zero touch connectivity relies on a separate virtual in-band VPN, called the Autonomic Control Plane (ACP). It is autonomously and securely built. The ACP should be non-configurable/changeable by operator/backend, so that it is indestructible by OAM actions. The ACP uses hop-by-hop encryption to protect the networks and NOC infrastructure from injected traffic attacks and to secure any legacy, non end-to-end encrypted protocols used in the network. In contrast to the ACP, all other connectivity between devices is called the data plane. This also includes signaling between control plane services that is not carried across the ACP such as (current) routing protocol signaling packets. These packets may still be secured by the ANI domain certificate though.

In summary, the ANI consists of BRSKI, ACP, and GRASP. It provides complete lifecycle security and connectivity between ANI devices and between ANI devices and the OAM backend/NOC.

Greenfield, Brownfield and ACP Devices

"Greenfield" devices are those that have never been touched by provisioning mechanisms in before but are in so-called "mint" factory condition. BRSKI does support zero touch, secure enrolment of those devices with the ANI domain certificate followed by secure zero touch building of the ACP. ANI provides full lifecycle secure zero touch operations for greenfield devices.

"Brownfield" devices are those that have previously been configured, for example they may be part of an already operating network without ANI. To enable ANI on brownfield devices it is only necessary to enable ANI (binary configuration option) and the rest is equally zero touch as in greenfield devices. Brownfield devices therefore require only "one-touch" (enable ANI).

Enabling and operating ANI, whether in greenfield or in brownfield devices, should have no impact on the remaining operations of the devices. Instead it just provides additional connectivity between these devices and to the NOC. This connectivity can only be used by the OAM functions and ASA in autonomic devices, but it is not available to any user traffic.

When devices implement only ACP, but not BRSKI, they are called ACP only devices, but not ANI devices. In this case, some pre-existing mechanism is required to enroll them with a domain certificate. Because of the absence of BRSKI, ACP only devices cannot provide secure, zero touch "day 0" operations of greenfield devices, or secure one-touch "day 1" operations for brownfield devices, but they can still provide the secure zero touch "day-N" connectivity that the ACP provides.

ANIMA AUTONOMIC NETWORK INFRASTRUCTURE

This section describes in details the components of the ANI, how they work, and interoperate.

Figure 2 serves as a reference for the components and signaling of the ANI as explained in this chapter.

An ANI network needs one, or for redundancy, multiple Registrar devices that act as the seed devices of ANI networks. They are the central point in the BRKI enrolment process for other ANI devices and they are the best ANI devices to provide connections to the NOC. Registrars are the only ANI devices that require configuration other than the aforementioned "ANI enable" on brownfield devices. This configuration consists of defining the ANI domains name and a URL to the domains CA (Certificate Authority). The Registrar requires connectivity – typically across the Internet – to so-called "Manufacturer Authorized Signing Authorities" (MASA) used by BRSKI. The Registrar is typically a device in the NOC locally connecting to other NOC/OAM equipment.

ANI: BRSKI

Enrolment Over Secure Transport (EST)

BRSKI is a bootstrap mechanism that is based on and expanding the Enrollment over Secure Transport (EST) protocol of Pritikin, Yee, and Harkins (2013). EST is the IETF standard protocol to enroll a Pledge with a certificate in a Public Key Infrastructure (PKI).

In the PKI component model as used by EST and expanded by BRSKI, a Certificate Authority (CA) is signing a certificate for a Pledge with the private key of the CAs certificate which is called the Trust Anchor (TA). A Registration Authority (RA), also called Registrar, acts as an intermediary between CA

Figure 2. Autonomic Networking Infrastructure with NOC and signaling

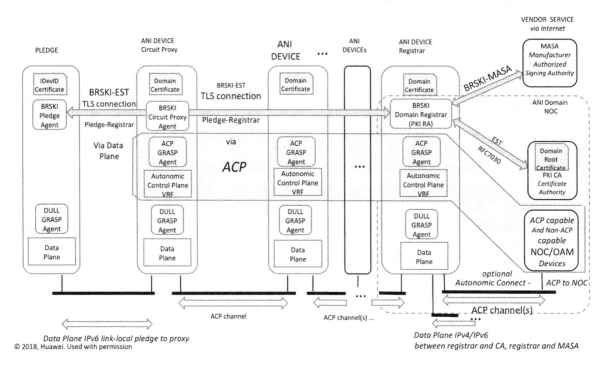

and Pledge. It is trusted by the CA and is responsible to ensure that the certificate information provided by the Pledge is correct and that the Pledge is authorized to have its certificate signed by the CA.

Using Figures 2 and 3, this section describes the BRSKI protocol as specified in Pritikin, Richardson, Behringer, Bjarnason, and Watsen (2018). It focusses on the features BRSKI introduces over EST and the problems for the ANI and autonomic networks that these extensions solve. On top of the EST components Pledge, Registrar, and CA, BRSKI adds the BRSKI proxy and the MASA. The ACP (as explained further below) provides autonomic connectivity between the BRSKI proxy and a Registrar.

Autonomic Connectivity for Bootstrap

The first problem in standard EST bootstrap is that the Pledge and the network between the Pledge and the PKI Registrar need to be configured so that the Pledge can discover the PKI Registrar address and build a secure connection to it. This involves configuring all intermediate devices to provide routing as well as the Pledge itself. There is no standard mechanism defined in EST for how to discover a Registrar.

In practice, the most common uses of EST so far are those where the network between Pledge and Registrar is non-autonomic, Pledges receive an IP address via DHCP and use manufacturer or deployment specific automation scripting to find and connect to the Registrar. There are thus a lot of possible pitfalls and manual steps involved. Specifically, for network devices, assignment of an IP address via DHCP is typically a problem, because the Pledge itself may be network device in the middle of the network and would for normal operation only use addresses provisioned by the NOC, and the neighboring routers would not be set up to allow DHCP address assignment on interfaces other than those intended to connect to user equipment.

Figure 3. BRSKI signaling sequence

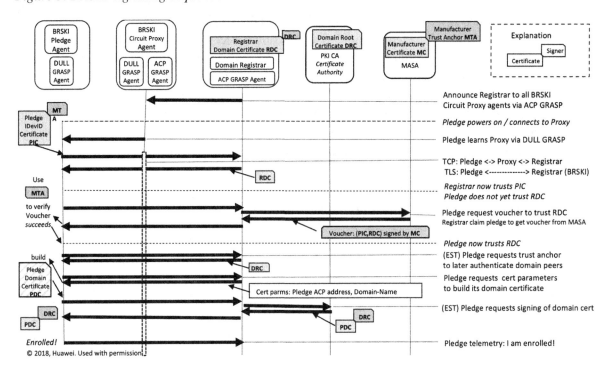

© 2018, Huawei. Used with permission.

This first problem is solved in BRSKI by using the ACP to provide zero touch enabled connectivity between the Registrar and the ANI device neighboring the Pledge. Every ANI device runs a BRSKI proxy agent used to help bootstrapping Pledges. This proxy utilizes the GRASP instance running inside the ACP (shown as "ACP Grasp agent" in Figure 2) to discover a Registrar. The proxy announces itself via a simple instance of the GRASP protocol on every interface in the data plane. These instances of GRASP are called Discovery Unsolicited Link-Local (DULL) GRASP. In result, the Pledge which is also running DULL GRASP simply needs an IPv6 link-local address on its interface to start the BRSKI bootstrap process. It discovers the proxy and then establishes a TCP connection to that proxy's IPv6 link local address. The proxy acts as a simple TCP circuit proxy, connecting the Pledge to a Registrar and then passing on any TCP message between Proxy and Registrar. This TCP connection carries a BRSKI extended EST/TLS connection, but the proxy is not aware or part of TLS; the TLS authentication is purely between the Pledge and the Registrar.

Making Pledges Trust the Network

The second important aspect of BRSKI is the authentication used by the Pledge towards the Registrar to identify itself. EST permits a range of options. BRSKI mandates that the Pledge uses the so-called Initial Device Identifier (IDevID), a certificate installed by the manufacturer. The IDevID contains an information element called the serial number that includes information such as the product type and an actual serial identifier. The Registrar, or a backend device interacting with the Registrar for enrollments can therefore securely identify the Pledge and verify that it should receive a domain certificate.

The third and most novel aspect of BRSKI is how the Pledge can trust the Registrar and the domain it is representing so that the Pledge will want to enroll through this Registrar to receive domain certificate and associated trust anchors. If a Pledge would simply permit to receive a certificate from any Registrar that it discovers, then not only could Pledges easily be stolen and abused, but even when connecting to the correct network of the organization owning the Pledge, men-in-the-middle attackers with access to the LAN to which the Pledge connects can easily fake a Registrar and take over the Pledge. In the absence of malicious parties, it is still a big problem to let the Pledge not authenticate the Registrar, especially in environments where multiple domains may exist, and a simple wrong wiring or connection of a Pledge could lead to the Pledge being enrolled into the wrong domain. Examples are office parks, data centers or other multi-party installation sites.

In EST deployments, the Pledge typically trusts the Registrar because a manual process is used to configure the URL or the IP address of the Registrar on the proxy, and this ensures that both the physical attachment and IP address of the registrar will lead to the desired enrollment of the Pledge. If this part is automated without further considerations, then errors above mentioned errors can occur.

In BRSKI, the logic by which the Pledge trusts the Registrar is by leveraging a service that is provided or authorized by the vendor of the Pledge: the MASA. During manufacturing, IDevID and respective trust-anchors (manufacturer root certificates) are installed into the Pledge. This allows the Pledge to authenticate and trust information signed by those manufacturer certificates. Therefore, the only way to indicate to the Pledge in a trusted way who its intended domain and owner are, is to leverage these manufacturer-installed trust-anchors in the Pledge.

Vouchers and MASA

The way BRSKI therefore solves this issue is via a novel digital artifact called a voucher as defined in Watsen, Richardson, Pritikin, and Eckert (2018). At its core, a voucher contains the serial number of a Pledge and the certificate of a Registrar. It is then signed with a manufacturer certificate (Watsen, Richardson, Pritikin, & Eckert, 2018).

When a Pledge connects to the Registrar, it initially simply accepts the Registrar's certificate presented in the TLS authentication exchange but cannot authenticate it. The Registrar then connects to the MASA responsible for the Pledge and requests a voucher for this Pledge (after deciding to accept the Pledge into the domain). The MASA returns this voucher, the Registrar passes it on to the Pledge and finally the Pledge verifies it: Is the signature on the voucher from its manufacturer? Is the serial-number in the voucher its own serial number? Is the certificate of the registrar in the voucher the certificate used by the Registrar on this TLS connection? If all these checks pass, the Pledge has authenticated the Registrar and continues with EST enrolment to receive a domain certificate and corresponding trust anchors of the domain.

Two key aspects of the Registrar-MASA interaction are considered:

1. The Registrar can automatically find and connect to the MASA for a Pledge by looking up the new BRSKI defined MASA information field in the IDevID of the Pledge. This IDevID was presented by the Pledge to the MASA during TLS connection setup. For vendors whose Pledges use legacy IDevIDs without a MASA field, the Registrar will need to be configured for the URL of the MASA for this vendor.

2.   The MASA can use different methods to verify whether the Registrar should receive a voucher for the Pledge. In one instance, the MASA simply hands out a voucher to the Registrar without any checks, but it creates an audit log-entry on the MASA. In this method, the Registrar would retrieve the log from the Registrar together with a voucher and decide whether to trust that the Pledge is untampered with based on the logging entries. If there are no prior log entries, the Registrar can be certain. If prior log entries show vouchers handed out to any (other) Registrar in this domain, the Registrar will likely also want to trust that the pledge is untampered with. Otherwise it might refuse to enroll the Pledge – based on policies set by the domain operations.

A MASA can be simple and lightweight, because it requires no so-called "sales-integration", whereby the vendor tracks who has actually bought an individual pledge. Instead, it may only force the creation of audit-log records, revealing that somebody else did try to enroll the Pledge. This is in most cases a sufficient indication that the device is not in virgin state from the manufacturer. The Registrar can also determine from the audit-log if the prior attempt to enroll the Pledge was from another trusted entity, such as another Registrar of the same organization. This provides a good initial security protection against attacks.

To add the ability to track devices easier, the MASA could accept voucher requests only from organizations or individuals registered with the MASA service. The audit-log entries would then allow to identify the requesters of vouchers and therefore reduce the risk of theft of Pledges. The MASA can furthermore provide sales-integration: The MASA then only provides vouchers to that organization or individual that owns the Pledge according to the sales integration information. This can be a highly complex operation process for vendors, especially those with complex reseller structures, therefore it is only an option. It can also be a unique selling point especially for vendors that are positioning themselves as trusted/secure vendors.

Further Features

If Internet connectivity to Pledges is an issue, vouchers can be made to have long lifetimes and be provisioned into the Pledge through different means than an on-demand connection to the MASA when the Pledge connects. If vouchers are transferred from MASA to the Registrar via an offline method such as a USB stick, the whole domain including Pledges and the Registrar would need no Internet connectivity at all.

Various extensions to BRSKI are possible. For example, a final reseller of Pledges could install a voucher on behalf of the customer into the Pledge so that the Pledge and the Registrar need no further Internet/MASA connection when the Plege is shipped to the customer. BRSKI could also be extended to support Pledges behaving as "ducklings" – insecurely accepting any Registrar they connect to without requesting a voucher. In this case, no MASA would ever be needed for those type of devices, but they would be subject to all the initially described security issues in zero touch deployment scenarios.

The vouchers method has further optional features in BRSKI. For example, if so desired, the MASA could verify that the Registrar has an active connection to the Pledge and is not just a remote attacker that knows the serial-number of a Pledge, trying to retrieve a voucher and create a bogus audit log entry.

The third improvement in BRSKI over EST is for Pledges to provide telemetry. With the whole BRSKI operation fully automated, it is crucial to also automatically discover any errors. Therefore, the Pledge provides status telemetry of operations up to and terminating with a success status for having received a domain certificate and the associated domain trust anchors and stored them locally on the Pledge. This ultimately finishes the BRSKI enrolment process and allows the domain operator to know that this device is now ready for further deployment operations (such as building the ACP).

ANI: Domain Certificates

BRSKI enrolls devices with ANI domain certificates. If BRSKI is not used, but only ACP, these are called ACP domain certificates. In either case, the domain certificate and associated domain root certificate of the PKI CA as the trust anchor are meant to allow any software on the devices to mutually authenticate with other domain member devices. In the ANI, this is used by the ACP.

Simple PKI authentication of a peer certificate only verifies whether the peers certificate is signed by the expected trust anchor. If the PKI CA for an organization supports multiple domains, this is not sufficient. Therefore, ANI/ACP domain certificates include the ACP/ANI domain name. When authenticating a peer to be part of the same domain, their domains need to match. This domain name would typically be a DNS domain name. The use of a DNS domain name is a simple way to create a globally unique name that can also easily be identified for diagnostics. When, for example, in a multi-tenant building a networking device is incorrectly cabled into a different domain, the exchange of certificates during ACP authentication would not only fail because domain names or PKI CA do not match, but the domain names in the certificate also provide diagnostic about the peer device. A domain cannot be attacked by faking the domain name because the authentication always also checks the peers trust anchor.

BRSKI can work with any pre-existing PKI CA unaware of BRSKI features. All the domain information extensions are handled between Registrar and Pledge. The PKI CA just needs to trust the Registrars to only permit the correct domain information to be included into certificates. If Registrars of a domain cannot be trusted by the PKI CA, a separate PKI CA for such a domain needs to be used.

The domain information field also encodes the intended IPv6 address of the Pledge in the ACP. This is a specific IPv6 address, called Unique Local Address (ULA), whose prefix can be automatically derived from the domain name. It is made unique for each Pledge with a serial number assigned by the Registrar. Tying the ACP address to the domain certificate of a device makes it a unique identifier for the device that will not change even if the device moves in the network. It also allows devices to cryptographically prove ownership of their ACP address with their certificate.

ANI: Autonomic Control Plane

Once a device has an ANI/ACP domain certificate, (and associated trust anchors), it is no longer a Pledge and will start to build the ACP. The ACP is specified in Eckert, Behringer, and Bjarnason (2018). It is a Virtual Routing and Forwarding (VRF) instance in the device. The ACP is supporting only IPv6 and requires only one routable IPv6 address, the aforementioned ACP address. It is assigned to an internal interface in the ACP VRF, the ACP loopback interface. It can also be a prefix, so that an ACP device could have multiple virtual contexts, each with a different address and therefore easily managed separately.

The ACPs connections between devices are called secure ACP channels: Secure tunnels to neighboring ACP devices that are auto-discovered, auto-built, authenticated, and encrypted.

To discover candidate ACP neighbors on its interfaces, each ACP device runs DULL GRASP (see below). This is a simple discovery mechanism using only IPv6 link-local addresses. It is the same mechanism as used by a BRSKI Pledge to discover a connected ANI device running the BRSKI proxy. The ACP needs to discover that the neighbor also supports the ACP.

Every ACP device announces via DULL GRASP that it is capable of running the ACP and which protocols for the secure ACP channel protocols it supports. This enables flexibility for security. The current mandatory mechanism is IPsec. Once a candidate ACP neighbor is discovered, the ACP domain certificate is used to mutually authenticate and establish the secure channel connection. Finally, the secure channel is linked into the ACP VRF as a virtual ACP interface. No routable IPv6 addresses are wasted on these virtual interfaces.

IPv6 routing across the ACP uses the IPv6 Routing Protocol for Low-Power and Lossy Networks (RPL) routing protocol defined in RFC6550. RPL was designed for IoT networks and low end devices. It scales very well to large networks (20,000 nodes or more) with minimum memory and CPU footprint. In the recommended profile for the ACP, it will build a spanning-tree like topology rooted in the NOC. Every ACP device injects its ACP address as one prefix into the RPL routing table. If it is a single address, it is a /128 prefix, but as mentioned above, the Registrar may assign a prefix to a device, in which case that prefix is announced.

RPL automatically deals very efficiently with large routing tables. It automatically creates a "default" route toward the root (NOC) and does only populate routes that do not go to the same link as the default route. Therefore, the closer a device is to the edge, the smaller its routing table. This matches well the typical network design whereby devices further toward the edge may be smaller and less powerful than those in the core.

RPL is used in the ACP because it is deemed to be important to have a simple, secure and stable addressing scheme in which ACP device addresses are identifiers and are therefore not depend on where devices are in the network topology. There are also no simple and proven algorithms to dynamically and autonomously self-organize an address space in a distributed fashion otherwise. Inventing such a mechanism for the ACP would certainly be feasible, but it would be very risky to build a reliable management infrastructure on that premise. Using RPL in the way the ACP does leverage deployment experience from many large scale IoT networks and simply applies it to the ACP use case. Last but not least: the routing table of the ACP has in the core (towards the root) as many entries as devices, something which could be a problem for other more heavy-weight routing protocols in larger ACP networks.

ANI: ACP Security

The choice of hop-by-hop encryption and decryption of ACP traffic is a rather challenging requirement against many current networking devices. When a device can only support encryption in software, it can reduce the forwarding performance in the ACP compared to forwarding not via the ACP. When encryption is supported in hardware, the number of cryptographic associations supported may be limited and the need to have another cryptographic association per neighbor may be a challenge. Nevertheless, without hop-by-hop encryption, it is not possible to fully protect the infrastructure, and in face of the following considerations, the ACP chooses to require hop-by-hop encryption:

Attackers with physical access to links of the infrastructure can easily inject spoofed packets and attack both the bandwidth of the infrastructure as well as the software stacks on all the reachable devices. Theoretically the software stacks of network devices could all be self-protecting, but in practice this is very difficult to achieve and even more difficult to prove. With the wide variety of infrastructure devices and software stacks and the high possible gains of attacking them, finding the weakest element is also a lot easier for attackers than trying to ubiquitously raise the lowest common security denominator across the infrastructure. Therefore, the ANI did strive to define a very well defined minimum attack-surface – it solely consists of DULL GRASP and the secure channel signaling protocol for IPsec (IKEv2). In addition, hop-by-hop encryption also protects all those management plane software stacks that are insecure or have limited degrees of security or complex to maintain security.

The more the management plane software stacks can evolve into a single end-to-end security protocol and stack used across all protocols in a device, such as a single TLS/DTLS stack on each network device, the more easier it will become to create comparably easy to verify security of the full management software stack, and in that case more lightweight, non-hop-by-hop encrypted options for an ACP variation would become feasible and less taxing to the infrastructure. Nevertheless, the problem of prohibiting the injection of attack traffic and to isolate the sources of such attacks will still exist in those solutions and that needs to be solved better than through todays standard design of "clamshell-security": Expect attacks only from the outside, protect only the edge but have little security against attacks from the inside. That model will not survive the ongoing evolution of current trends in infrastructure creation where more and more locations cannot be made physically secure because they are in shared colocation spaces and links cannot be considered to be physically protected anymore just because they use fiber.

In conclusion, the desirable evolution of the ANI security concept is to use the currently defined ACP security model with extensible hop-by-hop security as the start, but promote the abovementioned evolution of software stacks to similar light attack surface by using common end-to-end encryption (the ANI certificates) and promote the ubiquitous support of fully hardware supported, non-performance impacting hop-by-hop encryption options such as MACSec/802.1AE.

ANI: GRASP

ANI and Autonomic Networks use a common signaling protocol called GRASP specified in Bormann, Carpenter, and Liu (2017). This section describes the purpose of GRASP, the problem it addresses, and the solutions it provides.

GRASP is meant to be used in various places in an Autonomic Network and is already used in the ANI itself in two types of instances: the DULL GRASP and the ACP GRASP instances. These instances of GRASP are also sufficient for full Autonomic Networks to support communications between ASAs across the ACP, and for communications between ASAs and the OAM services in the NOC across the ACP.

The more interesting use of GRASP is to enable self-coordination of the ASAs in an easily developed and consistently signaled fashion. An example of such a function and its proposed use of GRASP is the Autonomic IPv6 Edge Prefix Management in Large-scale Networks described in Jiang, Du, Carpenter, and Sun (2018).

Today, many network protocols, especially those standardized by the IETF are based on unique binary TLV (Type, Length Value) encoded protocol messages specified through ASCII pictures of message elements in 32 bit units. These specifications cannot be formally verified, and the uniqueness of TLV encoding is labor intensive in development, standardization, implementations, and operations. Development of software to support these protocols cannot rely on common encoding/parsing libraries.

GRASP addresses these issues. GRASP messages are CBOR data-structures (Concise Binary Object Representation, RFC7049). CBOR provides similar encoding efficiencies to handcrafted TLV data structures. Creation and parsing of CBOR has also been shown to be feasible in very limited code-space using readily available CBOR libraries. CBOR data structures can be defined via CDDL (Concise Data Definition Language) and therefore also formally be checked.

CBOR is a binary encoding variation of JSON which is the way how the JavaScript language expresses data structures. JavaScript is the most common programming language for web development. This can help to make ASA development easier for developers with backgrounds in web development and therefore more "mainstream" than today's network services development is.

GRASP consists of a small set of message types. The payload of messages is defined by the autonomic function/ASA, the message type and headers support different exchange patterns.

The simplest GRASP communication pattern is that of a point-to-point negotiation and exchange of information between two GRASP peers where at least one is able to know the other and can therefore establish a unicast GRASP connection to it.

The more interesting GRASP communication patterns are those where information needs to be learned without knowing a peer. One solution is DULL GRASP in which only link-local multicast GRASP messages are used to announce or request information. BRSKI proxies and ACP use this to announce themselves. This is similar to, but more lightweight and flexible, than mDNS and it can also be used to announce and discover DNS servers.

The most advanced communication pattern in GRASP is that of network wide announcements and discovery. It relies on hop-by-hop, network-wide flooding of unsolicited information or of information requests followed by unicast responses. Looping of flooded messages is prevented by recognizing already received messages via network wide unique message identifiers. Flooding of information requests can also stop by message diameter and/or at nodes that do have the requested information – to make it more efficient and constrained in scope. The ACP instance of GRASP uses this communications pattern to announce Registrars to BRSKI proxies. GRASP TLS connections ensure reliability and security of these announcements.

Reliable automatic service announcement and discovery has long since been a major problem for networks and GRASP can help to solve this. The lack of easily deployed, reliably and easily operated and scaling solutions has hampered incremental automation of network-services self-orchestration severely. The use of unicast DNS servers for dynamic service information between network equipment has not succeeded to see significant adoption. mDNS is limited to single-hop, and is not transported reliably, even in extensions trying to support it across multiple hops. Most solutions that attempted to provide network wide service discovery tried to use IP multicast as the underlying transport, which immediately rendered these approaches little successful because of the operational and deployment complexity of IP multicast – and the unreliability of its datagram-only replication mechanism.

ANI: NOC/OAM Connectivity and Integration

In a non-AN ANI network, the NOC simply needs to be set up to have IPv6 connectivity into the ANI via some ANI router that exposes the ACP VPN unencrypted to NOC tools/systems. For example, such an ANI router in a NOC would be the registrar as shown in Figure 2. The Registrar could be a router running as software in a VM or container, co-located with other NOC tools that today also are typically running in a such a context. Operationalizing the ANI in this fashion could allow to automatically start and configure the Registrar-VM/container from another NOC-tool such as the network orchestrator/controller and automatically setting up the virtual network connections inside the NOC between the Registrar and the NOC VM/containers that need access to the ACP.

To support complete device zero touch provisioning workflows via BRSKI, the Registrar should be able to indicate to NOC back-ends when there is a new Pledge to be enrolled, allowing such NOC tools to exercise policy whether or not to accept the pledge into the domain. From the Perspective of an SDN centric NOC design, the Registrar can be seen as a VM/NFV based SDK to integrate with CA and MASA services, operate the BRSKI protocol and provide a secure, zero touch and reliable/indestructible VPN-style access to the network via the ACP.

Beside traditional NETCONF configuration of devices across the ACP, a more easily scalable and probably more reliable way to configure the network to use core services of the NOC reliably across the ACP is to use GRASP for service announcements: Servers in the NOC, having access to the ACP, would simply use GRASP to announce their services and network devices would auto-configure themselves for the services they need. This approach would simply use GRASP across the ACP as a reliable network-wide mechanism to distribute DNS-SD service announcements from these servers: Radius/Diameter, NTP, syslog/SNMP-notifications DHCP, DNS, firmware-upgrade-server, flow-collectors (IPFIX, sflow or others), and so on.

In a cloud-native approach of developing a NOC, services would not have to be single instances or operate on a VM with fixed address, instead multiple instances may exist and will be restarted upon failure on other nodes in the NOC with different addresses and potentially different parameters to provide an ongoing level of redundancy and load distribution. Having those services VM announce themselves and network devices track these services via GRASP is a more distributed, self-orchestrating and arguably more resilient approach than having a single controller try to track all active service instances in the NOC and update all network devices for all known active instances of all such services any time a VM is started in the NOC on a new address.

IMPLEMENTATIONS

Software components required for the ANI exist as open source packages, ranging from demo prototypes to production quality. For example, "LIBEST" (2018), which provides EST and BRSKI extensions, "GRASPY" (2018), which provides GRASP code and "SNBI" (2018), which provides an experimental and unfinished design for an ANI solution centered on exploring how it could be integrated with the Open Daylight management and orchestration SDN framework.

A pre-ANIMA-standard, commercial implementation of an ANI is available in products using IOS (Internetwork Operating System), the network software from Cisco Systems Inc. It is documented in "Autonomic Networking Configuration and Deployment Guide, Cisco IOS XE Everest 16.6" (2017). This solution was important input to ANIMA work. Its primary differences from the mechanisms described here is that it does not use the GRASP protocol but a variation of mDNS (Multicast DNS) and a vendor-specific protocol and the older SCEP (Simple Certificate Enrollment Process) protocol instead of BRSKI/EST. The components of MASA and use of secure enrolment via IDevID where gaps in this implementation that lead to the definition of BRSKI.

ADJACENT IETF TECHNOLOGIES

ANIMA's Autonomic Networking and ANI are adjacent to a range of other IETF technologies. This section provides a comparison, current as of May 2018.

Homenet, like ANIMA, is an IETF working group targeting to design an IPv6 and routing-centric next generation, fully autonomic home networking architecture without the need for any operator. ANIMA does not target home networks but instead well-managed networks such as Enterprise, service provider and IoT where an operator interacts with the network via Intent and Reporting. In Homenet, there is no concept of a separation between management plane and data plane. The only functions in the data plane are those that Homenet defines and they are all meant to be fully autonomic. One could think of a Homenet as a very simple version of a fully autonomic network while the ANIMA model is one that starts with the ANI as an autonomic management plane supporting non-autonomic existing network services in the devices first. It can then evolve easily into an autonomic network by incrementally introducing ASAs. Last but not least, ANIMA has a stronger security focus with certificates as a basis for zero touch enrollment and hop-by-hop secure channels.

IoT networks such as those seen as use cases in a variety of IETF working groups share a couple of technologies with ANIMA. RPL was built for IoT networks and IoT networks often also use a variety of automatic IPv6 addressing of network devices similar to the one used by the ACP. CBOR was developed also with IoT networks in mind. Likewise, CoAP instead of TLS/HTTPs signaling is also a target option for ANIMA bootstrapping to better fit IoT networks. Like any other existing type of networks, IoT networks so far do not have the notion of an in-band autonomic management plane (ANI) separate from a configured data plane. This is novel with ANIMA. and one could think of simplified ANIMA IoT versions, where these is no such separation to make the ANI design fit better lightweight IoT networks. Finally, one main difference between many IoT solutions and ANIMA is the use of strong cryptographic security. This will evolve also into IoT networks when more and more IoT equipment will become performant enough to support this type of security.

The netmod working group in the IETF is defining a solution for secure zero touch device bootstrap via its call-home functionality (Watsen, Abrahamsson, & Farrer, 2018). This work is aligned with ANIMA bootstrap architecture relying on the common concept of vouchers to assign devices to operators. NETCONF does protect with the secure bootstrap method the download of arbitrary configuration, while ANIMA mandates the enrolment with a certificate as the first step. NETCONF relies on its own protocols for communicating with the enrolling device, while ANIMA relies on BRSKI.

FUTURE DIRECTIONS

There are important missing components for full ANIMA autonomic networks including the aforementioned Intent/Reporting aspects and standardized network service definitions with automated self-configuration and self-maintenance as ASA with GRASP signaling. A potentially more short-term question is how to architect the ANI in the software infrastructure of network devices.

Experience gained with pre-standard implementations of ANI functionality has shown that the logical desirable behavior of the ANI as a VRF inside a network device is the right abstraction from the perspective of specifying the external behavior in standards. It is not an ideal approach to actually implement the ANI inside the existing devices network OS software though. It leads to an entanglement between that network OS software and the ANI and makes it extremely difficult to build an ANI that is indestructible by any misbehavior of that network OS software or inhibit that any possible configuration of this software cannot break the ACP.

A more appropriate network device software architecture would be to consider a design with a (micro) kernel that supports the ANI and can also act as a hypervisor for the actual network OS software. This not only provides full isolation between ANI and the network OS software, it also allows network OS software to be managed and operated as easily on any network device in any location as it is today only possible for NFV style software in a data center.

While this type of network device software architecture sounds easy from this level of abstraction, it can be actually quite challenging in the face of the wide range of hardware typically on network devices such as forwarding ASIC, NPU or intelligent NICs, that would have to be managed across between the NFV network OS device software and the hypervisor/ANI.

CONCLUSION

The ANIMA framework for autonomic networks and its currently evolving standards for the autonomic networking infrastructure is a significant proposal to evolve the management infrastructure of networks in the short term, and the development of network software longer term. ANI can support and help build better SDN-enabled networks and simplify the evolution of network management ultimately enabling to architect and design fully autonomic networks.

ANI is modular in design and each of its three components, BRSKI, ACP, and GRASP not only constitute a significant evolution for how to build network solutions, but they can also each be used and adopted individually or in combination. ANIMA/ANI is therefore not just a frozen solution, but rather a solution framework.

ACKNOWLEDGMENT

The work for ANIMA ANI was possible through the contributions of many individual, including, but not limited to the following: Alexander Clemm, Amit Dutta, Bing Liu, Brian Carpenter, Balaji BL, Benoit Claise, Bruno Klauser, Carsten Bormann, Frank Brockners, Ignas Bagdonas, Kent Watsen, Laurent Ciavaglia, Max Pritikin, Michael Behringer, Michael Richardson, Parag Bhide, Pascal Thubert, Ravi Kumar Vadapalli, Richard Li, Sebastian Meissner, Sheng Jiang, Steinthor Bjarnason, Terry Manderson, Vijay Anand R, William Atwood, Yash Pahuja, and Yves Hertoghs.

REFERENCES

Architecture and specification of data communication network. (2001). ITU-T Recommendation G.7712/Y.1703, International Telecommunication Union.

Autonomic Networking Configuration and Deployment Guide. (2017). Cisco IOS XE Everest 16.6. Retrieved from https://www.cisco.com/c/en/us/td/docs/ios-xml/ios/auto_net/configuration/xe-16-6/an-auto-cfg-deploy-16-6.html

Behringer, M., Carpenter, B., Eckert, T., Ciavaglia, L., & Nobre, J. (2018). *A Reference Model for Autonomic Networking*. Retrieved from https://tools.ietf.org/html/draft-ietf-anima-reference-model-06

Behringer, M., Pritikin, M., Bjarnason, S., Clemm, A., Carpenter, B., Jian, S., & Ciavaglia, L. (2015). *Autonomic Networking: Definitions and Design Goals. RFC7575*. Internet Research Task Force. doi:10.17487/RFC7575

Bormann, C., Carpenter, B., & Liu, B. (Eds.). (2017). *A Generic Autonomic Signaling Protocol (GRASP)*. Retrieved from https://tools.ietf.org/html/draft-ietf-anima-grasp-15

Eckert, T., & Behringer, M. (2018). *Using Autonomic Control Plane for Stable Connectivity of Network OAM. RFC8368*. Internet Engineering Task Force.

Eckert, T., Behringer, M., & Bjarnason, S. (2018). *An Autonomic Control Plane (ACP)*. Retrieved from https://tools.ietf.org/html/draft-ietf-anima-autonomic-control-plane-13

GRASPY. (2018). Retrieved from https://github.com/becarpenter/graspy

Jiang, S., Carpenter, B., & Behringer, M. (2015). *General Gap Analysis for Autonomic Networking. (2015). RFC7576*. Internet Research Task Force. doi:10.17487/RFC7576

Jiang, S., Du, Z., Carpenter, B., & Sun, Q. (2018). *Autonomic IPv6 Edge Prefix Management in Large-scale Networks*. Retrieved from https://www.ietf.org/id/draft-ietf-anima-prefix-management-07.txt

Kephart, J., & Chess, D. (2003). The Vision of Autonomic Computing. *IEEE Computer*, *36*(1), 41–50. doi:10.1109/MC.2003.1160055

LIBEST. (2018). Retrieved from https://github.com/cisco/libest

Pritikin, M., Richardson, M., Behringer, M., Bjarnason, S., & Watsen, K. (2018). *Bootstrapping Remote Secure Key Infrastructures (BRSKI)*. Retrieved from https://tools.ietf.org/html/draft-ietf-anima-bootstrapping-keyinfra-13

Pritikin, M., Yee, P., & Harkins, D. (2013). *Enrollment over Secure Transport. RFC7030*. Internet Engineering Task Force.

Script Kiddie. (2018). Retrieved from https://en.wikipedia.org/wiki/Script_kiddie

SNBI. (2018). Retrieved from https://wiki.opendaylight.org/view/SNBI_Architecture_and_Design

Watsen, K., Abrahamsson, M., & Farrer, I. (2018). *Zero Touch Provisioning for Networking Devices*. Retrieved from https://tools.ietf.org/html/draft-ietf-netconf-zerotouch-21

Watsen, K., Richardson, M., Pritikin, M., & Eckert, T. (2018). *Voucher for Bootstrapping Protocols. RFC8366*. Internet Engineering Task Force. doi:10.17487/RFC8366

Wu, Q., Litkowski, S., Tomotaki, S., & Ogaki, K. (2018). *YANG Data Model for L3VPN Service Delivery. RFC8299*. Internet Engineering Task Force. doi:10.17487/RFC8299

KEY TERMS AND DEFINITIONS

Autonomic Control Plane (ACP): An autonomic created and maintained secure virtual management network to support autonomic and traditional, distributed or centralized management functions of the network on which it runs. ACP uses only IPv6. ACP nodes authenticate with each other via cryptographic certificates. These certificates can be installed (enrolled) via BRSKI.

Autonomic Network Infrastructure (ANI): The ANI is an infrastructure to enable autonomic networks and to support a secure, automatic and reliable management infrastructure for current non-autonomic networks using SDN based management. The ANI consists of ACP, BRSKI, and GRASP.

Autonomic Networking Integrated Model and Approach (ANIMA): ACP, BRSKI, and GRASP are products of the IETF ANIMA working group.

Bootstrapping Remote Secure Key Infrastructures (BRSKI): A protocol extending EST to enable secure zero-touch bootstrap of nodes called Pledges in conjunction with ACP. The most important extension over EST is a mechanism through which the Pledge can trust the network in which it gets enrolled (Voucher/MASA).

Enrollment Over Secure Transport (EST): IETF standard protocol for enrollment of a node, called Pledge with a certificate. BRSKI is based on EST.

Generic Autonomic Signaling Protocol (GRASP): An extensible signaling protocol designed to simplify future signaling between instances of distributed network protocols. In this function, GRASP is used by BRSKI and ACP. In the ANI, GRASP provides also network wide service and other instance discovery for future autonomic network protocols and services.

Manufacturer Authorized Signing Authority (MASA): A service run by a manufacturer or contractor of the manufacturer. The MASA is responsible for the creation and logging of vouchers.

Voucher: A signed digital object similar to a public key certificate that declares on behalf of the manufacturer of a network device who owns or claims to own a particular device from this manufacturer. Vouchers are signaled in BRSKI to the device in question (called pledge) so that it will trust the network it connects to.

Chapter 5
Automating Network Management With Artificial Intelligence:
In Software Networks and Beyond

Imen Grida Ben Yahia
Orange Labs, France

Jaafar Bendriss
Orange Labs, France

Teodora Sandra Buda
IBM, Ireland

Haytham Assem
IBM, Ireland

ABSTRACT

Artificial intelligence (AI) and in particular machine learning are seen as cornerstones to automate and rethink network management operations in the context of network softwarization (i.e., SDN, NFV, and Cloud). In this regard, operators and service providers target the creation of service offerings, the customization of network solutions, and the fast adaptation to rapidly changing market demands. This translates into requirements for increased flexibility, modularity, and scalability in network management operations. This chapter presents a detailed specification of a cognitive (AI-based) network management framework applicable for existing and future (software-defined) networks. The framework is built upon the combined state-of-the-art on autonomic, policy-based management and big data. It is exemplified with two detailed use cases: the urban mobility awareness for today's mobile networks and SLA (service level agreement) enforcement in the context of NFV and cloud.

DOI: 10.4018/978-1-5225-7146-9.ch005

INTRODUCTION

Mobile communications are one of the areas that has grown tremendously in the Information and Communication Technologies (ICT) market. It is expected that trillions of various devices, such as smartphones and tablets, medical devices, traffic and security cameras, etc., will connect to cellular networks by 2020. As a result, future mobile networks need to support the huge amount of resources that will be consumed, which will lead to a dramatic increase of network traffic (Cisco, 2016). Meanwhile, the emergence of new types of devices enables various new applications that affect different spheres of human life. Likewise, the ongoing deployment of the Internet of Things will foster the development of machine-to-machine communications, which complement the dominating human-centric communications of today (2018).

This would subsequently lead to a diversity of communication characteristics. Both trends will raise new requirements on network scalability, data rates, latency and reliability. The forecasted huge increase in demand for network capacity, and strict and diverse requirements raised from new communication patterns may not be adequately addressed along with the evolution of existing technologies. Therefore, research on new technologies is necessary in order to complement current ones. Additionally, techniques for the virtualization of network functions are becoming more and more mature. Such techniques will undoubtedly play an important role in the new generation of networks: for example, 5G promoters are investigating how virtualization and orchestration capabilities can be used to dynamically accommodate ever-changing resource demands.

5G networks will also rely upon other technologies, such as network densification and infrastructure sharing, to address the challenges and requirements faced by today's wireless networks (including cellular networks). It is not hard to foretell that the complexity of network management will become one of the biggest challenges to be addressed by 5G infrastructures, because of the conglomeration of technologies. To cope with similar challenges in 3G and 4G networks, self-administering and self-managing networks have been extensively researched, as presented later in the chapter. The fundamental work in the area of automation or advanced and smart automation is known as autonomic computing and autonomic networking where self-x (e.g., self-configuring, self-healing) functions were defined to ease, simplify and automate network operations since 2001 by IBM Manifesto (Kephart, 2003).

Both the come-back of Artificial Intelligence (AI), in particular Machine Learning (ML) and deep learning owing to the increasing computation power and the transformation of networks towards more softwarization, attracted much academic and industrial attention to cognitive management of networks.

This chapter primarily discusses the effort conducted by the European collaborative project CogNet (CogNitive Networks): Towards automation with Artificial Intelligence, a cognitive management framework and its inner modules are presented. The project aims at making a major contribution towards the automation of network and infrastructures management by investigating existing and devising novel ML algorithms tuned for available network data in order to yield insights, detect meaningful events and conditions, and respond correctly to them.

The chapter is structured as follows. The background section presents the autonomic and cognitive management, policy-based management, the concept of big data as well as an overview of current projects related to automated network management. Then, the authors present a cognitive management framework aiming to realize an automated control loop for the management operations with Artificial Intelligence. To exemplify this framework two use cases namely, Urban Mobility Awareness in 3G/4G networks and SLA Enforcement in an NFV (Network Function Virtualization) context are detailed. For both use cases, the workflows are presented to show how the framework building blocks interact together. In addition, a focus on the data and algorithms shows how to automate network management with machine learning and deep learning techniques.

BACKGROUND

Autonomic and Cognitive Management

"Autonomic" is the adjective derived from autonomy, which means self-governing or independent. "Autonomics" therefore denotes the science of autonomic systems.

Autonomics is intended to extend the concept of Self-Organizing Networks (SON) that is used in cellular networks to any kind of network segment, including core and MEC (Mobile Edge Computing) networks. As a reminder, IBM was the pioneer with the foundation of Autonomic Computing in 2001. Autonomic Computing is mainly IT-oriented (both software and hardware) (Kephart, 2003).

Soon after, the same principles were adopted for various network control and management operations and the concept of Autonomic Communication/Networking was thus introduced.

The IBM scale extended to networks is presented in Figure 1. It illustrates the different levels of automation up to the autonomic level.

An autonomic system includes an autonomic manager (engine) and a managed element. It implements the MAPE control loop. MAPE stands for Monitoring, Analysis, Planning and Execute. A managed element could be a business process, a network function (virtual or physical), a web application, a database, a server, etc.

The autonomic engine controls and manages one or more managed elements (Figure 2). Autonomic managers receive inputs from "sensors" (e.g., inputs from end-users, network data, log files) to monitor the managed elements and use effectors to execute actions on such a managed element (Salehie, 2009).

On the other hand, autonomic systems must enable self-* (also called self-star, self-x, or auto-*) properties to fulfill requirements at runtime, in response to exogenous and endogenous changes in the operating environment.

An autonomic system has self-* properties. The most well-known properties are:

Figure 1. IBM scale extended to networks and services

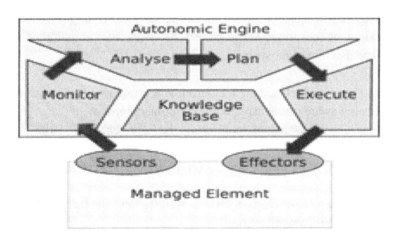

Figure 2. Autonomic System

	Basic level	Managed level	Predictive level	Adaptive level	Autonomic level
Characteristics	Multiple data/info from network elements and service platforms	Consolidation of data/info and operations and through management tools	Management tools monitor, correlate and recommend operations	Management tools monitor, correlate and execute operations	Integrated management tools dynamically managed by business rules/policies
Skills	Requires extensive, highly skilled staff	Staff analyzes and takes action	Staff approves and initiates actions	Staff manages performances against SLAs	Staff focuses on enabling business needs
Benefits		•Greater network awareness •Improved productivity	•Reduced dependency on deep skills •Faster/better •Decision making	•Balanced human/System interaction •Agility and resiliency	•Business policy drives management •Business agility and resiliency

Autonomic

- **Self-Configuration:** The ability to autonomously and dynamically reconfigure components.
- **Self-Healing:** The capability of self-discovering, self-diagnosing and self-repairing (i.e., reacting) to disruptions.
- **Self-Optimization (Also Known as Self-Tuning):** The capability of managing performance and resource allocation to satisfy the requirements (e.g., end-to-end response time, throughput, resource utilization and workload) of different users.
- **Self-Protection:** The capability of detecting security breaches and recovering from their effects by providing the means to defend the system against attacks and anticipating problems by taking proactive actions to either avoid such problems or mitigate/soften their effects.

Some properties at this level might depend on others, e.g., self-healing might either use self-configuring to repair a detected failure or self-protecting to protect resources from a malicious attacker.

Other properties are also important such as:

- Self-context (also known as self-situated, environment-awareness, and context-awareness), which is the ability of being aware of the exogenous operating environment.
- Self-monitoring which is related to monitoring the endogenous and the exogenous operating environment.
- Self-adjustment consists of executing actions on the endogenous environment using effectors.

Chapter "*A Unifying Framework Design for the Management of Autonomic Network Functions*" provides sample examples of these capabilities.

Policy Based Management

Policy Based Management (PBM) (Moore, Ellesson, Strassner, & Westerinen, 2001) was usually combined with autonomic-based management in the context of network, service, and system management. In PBM, this is usually the role of network operational teams to define the events, conditions, and actions while taking into account several dimensions such as the constraints, the nature of the managed elements, and the type of events. With the definition of those rules and the conditions to trigger them, it helps to determine the behaviours of networks and services. In addition, PBM intends to abstract the low level configurations by ensuring a mapping between high level objectives (e.g., reduce power consumption) and low level actuations (e.g., scale in/out). In this context, both the Internet Engineering Task Force (IETF) and the Distributed Management Task force (DMTF) defined the PCIM (Policy Core Information Model) model (IETF, 2002).

PCIM defines three key concepts of PR (Policy Repository), PDP (Policy Decision Point), and PEP (Policy Enforcement Point). Policies can be grouped in two categories: imperative and declarative policies. The imperative policies are usually low-level action policies depending on the domain, device and system. The policy languages allow expressing the Event-Condition-Action (ECA) or Condition-Action (CA) (Nicklish, 1999) (Kephart & Walsh, 2004). Actions determine two policy categories: Authorization Policies (define what a manager is permitted or not permitted to do) and Obligation Policies (define what a manager must or must not do). The declarative policies include the overall goal and utility function policies (e.g., Business constraints).

Most relevant policy languages for network management use the PCIM model to represent (network) device configuration. The following are the most representatives:

- PFDL (Policy Framework Definition Language) (Strassner & Schleimer, 1998) defines a hierarchy of rule classes.
- PDL (Policy Description Language) by (Lobo, Bhatia, & Naqvi, 1999) is a declarative language, domain-independent and formulated with ECA rules.
- Ponder (Damianou, Dulay, Lupu, & Sloman) is declarative, object-oriented and uses Role-Based Access Control (RBAC) to group policies into roles and meta-policies to prevent conflicting actions.
- CIM-SPL (Simplified Policy Language for CIM) is a general purpose policy language published as a standard by DMTF that complements and renders the policy model included in CIM (Common Information Model), and its rules are CA-based. It has an external event model and a RBAC extension.
- XACML (OASIS, 2005) is a declarative XML-based policy language for access control management in distributed systems.
- Congress is an open-source framework for governance and regulatory compliance across cloud environments used by Openstack. The policy language for Congress is Datalog, a declarative language that is SQL-based whose syntax is close to traditional programming languages.
- In 2016, the Simplified Use of Policy Abstractions (SUPA) IETF working group (now disbanded) published a draft that describes a YANG module for defining ECA policies that are independent of the level of abstraction of the content and meaning of a policy.

Policy conflict is a general issue that is present in all policy languages. The implementers of policy systems must provide conflict detection and avoidance capabilities, or resolution mechanisms to prevent such situations. Intra-policy conflicts appear when the conditions of two policies to be applied in the same domain are satisfied but their respective actions contradict each other (i.e., a PEP cannot enforce them simultaneously). Inter-policy conflicts occur when conflicts appear among policies that pertain to different domains. Conflicts can be resolved statically beforehand or dynamically when a PDP detects at run time that multiple actions generate a conflict.

Lambda Architecture

The lambda architecture (Bijnens & Hausenblas, 2017) is depicted in Figure 3. It represents a framework for designing big data applications, and which serves a variety of use cases with different latency requirements.

The architecture leverages for each query a combination of answers retrieved from two layers:

- A Batch Layer which maintains views of historical data, and
- A Speed Layer which maintains views of freshly-added data.

Thus, the architecture ensures low latency through the computation of the response to a query by combining the answers retrieved from both layers to get a holistic answer.

The lambda architecture consists of three layers:

- **Batch Layer:** It manages the master dataset, which is an immutable, append-only set of raw data, and also offers pre-computing batch views on the dataset.
- **Serving Layer:** It indexes the batch views so that these views can be queried in an ad-hoc way with low latency.
- **Speed Layer:** It accommodates all requests that are subject to low latency requirements. This layer compensates for the high latency of updates to the Serving Layer and it only processes recent data.

Figure 3. Lambda Architecture

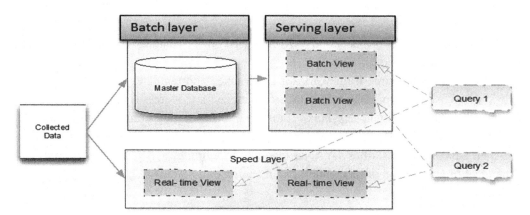

Cognition for Software-Based Networks

Before presenting the framework elaborated by the CogNet project, this section introduces other initiatives that are also related to cognitive software networks.

There is a vast amount of efforts that have been conducted on network management by research. NetOS (López et al., 2014) has presented an experiment in this area showing a vision based on software, where any virtual function can be managed, updated, and moved efficiently. Moreover, (Soares, Dias, Carapinha, Parreira, & Sargento, 2014) and (Soares et al., 2015) present end-to-end platforms for NFV to facilitate the creation, modification, and withdrawal of network functions. (Szabo, Kind, Westphal, Woesner, Jocha, & Csaszar, 2015) and (Csoma et al., 2014) present a framework named UNIFY, which integrates NFV with SDN, to enable the direct control of elastic resources for the network functions. Instead of providing a complete management solution for the whole NFV architecture, (Yoshida, Shen, Kawabata, Minato, & Imajuku, 2014) present a plug-in on the NFV Infrastructure (NFVI) to deal with resource requirements and stakeholder policies. This plug-in uses a multiple object generic solution to provide optimal solutions based on possibly conflicting objectives, which potentially enhances the NFV management. (Chen, Qin, Lambe, & Chu, 2015) posed a Virtual Network Function Manager (VNFM) Integration API based on the European Telecommunications Standards Institute (ETSI) NFV MANO architecture at the VNFM southbound interface to integrate external systems to facilitate the lifecycle management of VNFs. Additionally, other works related to NFV MANO have been presented in (Shen, Yoshida, Minato, & Imajuku, 2015) (Donadio, Fioccola, Canonico, & Ventre, 2014) (Bolla, Lombardo, Bruschi, & Mangialardi, 2014) (Giotis, Kryftis, & Maglaris, 2015).

Figure 4 summarizes the related existing 5G Infrastructure Public Private Partnership (5G PPP) projects and relevant Open source and industrial solutions.

The 5G PPP is a joint initiative between the European Commission and the European ICT industry. In its phase 1, 19 projects have been funded. Collaboration across all projects, including CogNet, resulted in relevant white papers for the 5G architecture, such as View on 5G Architecture (Architecture, 2016) and Cognitive network management for 5G (5GPPP Network Management & Quality of Service Working Group, 2017).

Figure 4. 5G PPP Projects

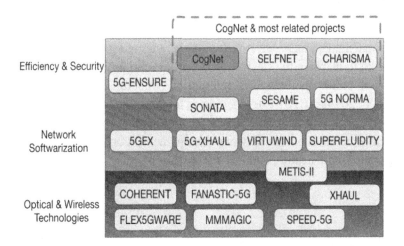

Figure 4 shows how the CogNet project relates to other research European projects in the area of cognitive network management. Projects related to CogNet are reviewed hereafter.

CHARISMA (CHARISMA, 2016) is an EU H2020 5GPP project that investigates an architecture solution offering end-to-end security across all layers of the converged and virtualized network with low latency (<1ms). CHARISMA tries to provide a cloud infrastructure platform with increased spectral and energy efficiency and greatly enhanced performance compared with existing telecom networks. Similar to the CogNet solution, the CHARISMA architecture solution complements the MANO stack with additional functionality on data collection and analysis. Their processing power stays close to data that facilitates real-time operations. However, this solution may be limited by the available computational power available and cannot therefore support heavyweight data analysis.

The SELFNET reference architecture (Neves et al., 2016) addresses self-organized network management on Software-Defined Networks (SDN) and Virtualized Network Functions (VNFs). It integrates technologies that enable 5G networks, such as Self-Organizing Network, Cloud Computing and machine learning to implement an automatic network management system to address challenges for management tasks. The Monitoring and Analyzer Sublayer of the architecture collects network state information, aggregates it, and generates knowledge from collected records. The output of the analysis is consumed by the Autonomic Management Sublayer to select and enforce management policies on the network infrastructure. Compared to the CogNet architecture, the SELFNET architecture puts the analysis power not close to functional components, which raises strict requirements on the processing time of the analysis and policy enforcement when dealing with real-time management.

The SESAME project (Giannoulakis et al., 2016) provides a platform to enable network slicing based on the deployment of Cloud-Enabled Small Cells (CESCs), which are formed by small cell devices with virtualized functions and which are connected to micro-servers. The management system of SESAME is designed to handle both 4G and 5G network infrastructures, but also CESCs and CESC clusters. It is built on top of VIM that integrates NFVO with SLA and cluster management, and it embeds a component named Element Management System covering fault, configuration, accounting, performance and security to facilitate network management.

The 5G NORMA (NORMA, 2015) presents a mobile network architecture that provides the necessary adaptability on resource management. It is designed to handle fluctuations in traffic demands resulting from heterogeneous and dynamically charging service portfolios. This architecture tries to achieve its goals by means of orchestration and slicing based upon network softwarization. The NORMA project aims to complement MANO mainly through service and slice orchestration.

The SONATA project (SONATA, 2016) tries to fill the gap between business requirements of telecom networks and operational management systems. It provides an orchestration framework associated with a service development kit to increase the flexibility and programmability of 5G networks. The SONATA orchestration framework builds upon the ETSI reference architecture for NFV management and orchestration within the (ETSI, 2014a) (ETSI, 2014b), aims to leverage the NFVO and VNFM and additionally offers the management functionalities requested by the architecture. Although the SONATA design can potentially enable real-time autonomous network management, it does not offer analytic capabilities to support self-configuration, self-healing and self-optimization.

Cognitive Management Framework and Modules

This section presents the Cognitive Management framework and its main modules, namely, the Analysis Module and the Data Collection and Pre-processing module. It also introduces the policy engine.

The section also describes the managed environment that relies upon SDN and NFV techniques, since they are the basic constituents of 5G infrastructures (CogNet, 2017).

Managed Environment

NFV is a technique that virtualizes network functions, which are currently supported by proprietary and often dedicated hardware. NFV's foreseen/claimed benefits include cost savings on both CAPEX and OPEX and optimized network configuration in near real-time (ETSI, 2014). The main concept of NFV is the decoupling of functionality from capacity (the physical infrastructure on which they run) (ETSI-NFV, 2016). The shift that is envisaged to generate savings is moving from proprietary hardware towards commodity hardware, as depicted in Figure 5. However, the deployment of NFV is likely to dramatically distort how the network is designed, deployed, and operated, and therefore challenges the network management system to adapt to claimed NFV's flexibility and dynamics.

There has been considerable effort made by standardization bodies and researchers on NFV management and orchestration (NFV MANO). The ETSI, as one of the major standardization bodies in the area, has worked on the NFV standard since 2012. ETSI-NFV is the ETSI Industry Specification Group (ISG) devoted to the standardization of the virtualization of Networks Functions. It intends to define the complete architecture required to accommodate the challenges of the new virtualization approach. Its architecture covers runtime and management aspects, capable of managing the entire lifecycle of a VNF. Furthermore, it also comprises the management of network services, which are built by chaining multiple VNFs, according to a Forwarding Graph in some cases, by using a catalogue-driven approach. The ETSI NFV architectural framework that is most commonly used is presented in (ETSI, 2014).

The ETSI NFV MANO framework (ETSI, 2014) defines three functional blocks that belong to NFV Management and Orchestration, how other functional blocks interact with NFV MANO, and reference points that enable communication among different functional blocks. These three functional blocks are:

- The Virtualized Infrastructure Manager(s) (VIM) manages all physical and virtual hardware resources in a given domain. An NFV architecture may contain one or multiple VIMs, each managing resources for an infrastructure provider.
- The VNF Manager (VNFM) manages the lifecycles of individual VNF instances. VNFM operations include instantiation, scaling, updating and/or upgrading VNFs, and termination of VNFs.
- The NFV Orchestrator (NFVO) is responsible for managing the lifecycles of network services and for controlling NFVI resources. The NFV coordinates service orchestration with resource orchestration. It has the ability to coordinate, authorize, release, and engage NFVI resources independently of any specific VIM. In addition, The NFV orchestrator creates end-to-end services by composing different VNFs.

The ETSI framework also identifies the external functional blocks that share reference points with NFV MANO. This includes Operations Support System (OSS), Business Support System (BSS), and Element Management (EM).

The NFV MANO architecture framework is intended to help vendors integrate their various solutions into one ecosystem. However, it is argued by (Szabo, 2015) that the framework does not take into account any infrastructure abstraction enabling automated resource orchestration and self-management.

To fill this gap, there are active research projects referenced above as 5G phase 1 projects within the context of EC's Horizon 2020 program.

ITU-T Recommendation Y.3300 (ITU-T, 2014) defines SDN as "a set of techniques that enable to directly program, orchestrate, control and manage network resources, which facilitate the design, delivery and operation of network services in a dynamic and scalable manner".

The SDN specification effort has been contributed by Open Network Foundation (ONF) (OpenFlow, 2017) to enable the separation of the data plane from the control plane. Most SDN-labelled solutions assume a logically centralized control plane, which is represented by a so-called SDN controller. SDN architectures reflect the 3-layer reference model shown in Figure 6.

SDN separates the data plane from the control plane, the latter being logically centralized. The user-data plane is responsible for forwarding traffic. The control plane is responsible for programming the network by means of dynamic resource allocation and policy enforcement techniques. SDN is therefore often seen as a set of (automation) techniques that facilitate the overall service delivery and operational procedures. Within the NFV architectural framework introduced by ETSI, SDN solutions might be used in the infrastructure domain, in the tenant domain or both, as follows: (1) in the infrastructure domain, where the SDN controller acts as the controlling element of the network infrastructure, which is responsible for providing the programmable network interfaces that enable the establishment of connectivity within the domain; (2) in the tenant domain, which is responsible for handling the network services provided at the service tenant layer.

COGNITIVE MANAGEMENT FRAMEWORK: GLOBAL VIEW

The cognitive 5G framework (Xu, 2016), namely CogNet (Cognitive Networks), is built upon the previously presented state-of-the-art that brings together Autonomics, Big data, and Policy-Based Management. Furthermore, in this framework, ML is used to reach advanced levels of automation.

The Cognitive framework consists of the following main building blocks (Figure 5):

- **Data Collection and Pre-Processing:** The Data Collector ensures the data extraction and gathering from different network probes, monitoring agents, etc. The data pre-processing will ensure that data is filtered, normalized, e.g., ranging all the data values between 0 and 1, etc., depending on the analysis required.
- **Analysis:** The collected information is forwarded for analysis to the CogNet Smart Engine (CSE) which is composed of agents that perceive the network state and its external environment. The CSE is responsible for receiving the state and resource consumption records, pre-processing the records, selecting suitable algorithms, and then applying selected models to further process the received data. The CSE is enhanced by a Batch Engine that processes data in batches, and by a

(Near) Real-time Engine (NRE) that processes data in a lower latency manner. The CSE supports various machine learning modules that in turn help deliver different CogNet services. These include data gathering services, forecasting and prediction services, anomalies and fault recognition services, and action recommendation services for the policy engine.

- ○ **Light CSE (LCSE):** It is a processing component that offers similar functionalities as the CSE, but is only equipped with the (Near) Real-time Processing Engine. Such a component is designed to be embedded into the MANO that is located as close to data collectors as possible so that the data can remain local. Thus, access and processing latency can be minimized.

- ○ **Proxy:** It forwards the concrete actions from the Policy Engine to related components constituting the MANO stack, but also converts the actions into a format that can be consumed by these components directly. The components connected to the Proxy, including NFVO, VNFM and VIM, are equipped with built-in policy enforcement mechanisms, which can adjust or re-configure the network elements managed by them.

- **Policy Engine:** The output of the analysis is sent to the Policy Engine, which fulfils the role of the planning part in the MAPE control loop. In this regards, it recommends network policies to enact a desired alternation in the network infrastructure. The policy engine is mainly responsible for mapping insights from the LCSE/CSE into appropriate policy actions that can be directly understood by related components in the managed environment.

- **Managed Environment:** Consequently, these actions are sent to the managed environment here exemplified as NFV- and SDN-based networks. The CogNet architecture leverages ETSI's NFV architecture. One key architectural innovation of CogNet is the adoption of network intelligence by NFV MANO. Specifically, the MANO stack is enhanced by the LCSE, as a processing component that offers similar functionality as the CSE, but is only equipped with NRE. Such a component is designed to be embedded into MANO, located close to data collectors as possible to reduce access and processing times. The smart engines analyze gathered data for various purposes, such as dynamic resource allocation, security threats and performance degradation detection, and then adjust resource usage and VNF behavior accordingly.

The output of the LCSE/CSE consists in some key values that will be applied by the Policy Engine for policy recommendation purposes. The Policy Engine not only maps values from the LCSE/CSE into policies, but also recommends actions to be taken by the MANO stack. The components of the CogNet architecture are specified in more detail in the following sub-sections.

Analysis Module

The Analysis module is composed of two main components: the Cognitive Smart Engine and the Automated Model Selection.

The CSE depicted in Figure 6, is responsible for receiving the state and resource consumption records, pre-processing the records, selecting suitable algorithms, and then applying selected models to further process the received data. The objective of the CSE is to support the various Machine Learning modules that in turn contribute to the delivery of various services of the CogNet solution. These services in turn have associated policies that are instantiated in the Policy Repository of the Policy Engine.

Figure 5. CogNet architecture overview with main modules: Data Collection and Pre-processing, Cognitive Elements, Policy Engine Elements.

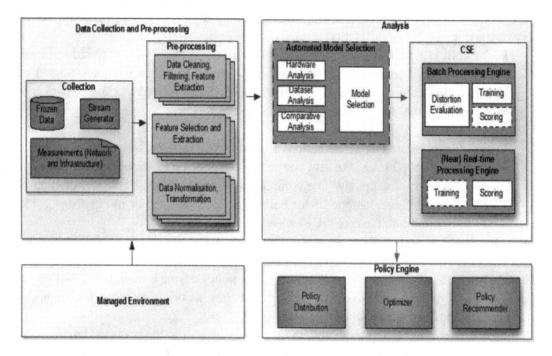

The input of the CSE is a data stream on the relevant events that flows from both the resource provider's side and the consumer's side, whilst the CSE output will be scored on the states of given components in the architecture. This is intended to increase the openness and transparency of services delivered by 5G networks. Moreover, the outputs of the CSE are prediction scores, which can be divided into:

- Thresholds for specific policies, such as the maximum CPU usage before degrading service performance, or
- Metric data at timestamp t, such as predicting the: %CPU (numerical), or presence of an anomaly or fault (categorical).

Algorithm Selection

Similar to the Data Pre-processing, this component can identify the model(s) that will be deployed on the CSE processing engines automatically or based on customer's requirements. In the automatic mode, it will take into account the features of given datasets, the performance of candidate algorithms, and the available resources of the processing engine to ensure the learning phase. Particularly, the Automated Model Selection component checks the availability of processing engines' hardware resources, and then evaluates the performance of machine learning models based on the configuration for a specific task (e.g., classification, association, regression anomaly detection, etc.) requested by a user. Instead of comparing all available models recursively, the work can be processed based on certain selection criteria. The model that offers the desired performance will be deployed on selected processing engine(s).

Batch Processing Engine

It retrieves consumption and state data from the Data Storage, and applies these data to train a model or generate scores. In the former case, the Batch Processing Engine will evaluate the distortion of the current model. If the model has become stale or no model is available, it will generate a new model from scratch to facilitate the work of the NRE. In the latter case, this engine works independently to analyze collected records in a more accurate but higher latency manner. Note that the scoring in both the Batch Processing Engine and (Near) Real-time Processing Engine is not to simply apply one machine learning model but may rather involve a sequence of models associated with post-processing. For example, to detect network anomalies, one may need to score a number of records and then draw a conclusion based on a linear combination of generated scores.

Distributed File System

It stores models generated by the Batch Processing Engine that will be deployed on the (Near) Real-time Processing Engine. Note that this component is optional since the Batch Process Engine may forward generated models directly, e.g., through message queues/RESTful Web Services or the two processing engines may not share data with each other without writing it to an external storage system if they are implemented and deployed in some cluster computing systems, such as Apache Spark.

(Near) Real-Time Processing Engine

It consumes the data from the sources directly, and scores the received data within a short period of time. This can be achieved by applying the model generated by the Batch Processing Engine, or lightweight online learning approaches directly, such as some online clustering algorithms.

This component can generate scores either in real-time if it is implemented and deployed in a distributed real-time computation system, such as Apache Storm, or near real-time if it is powered by a mini-batch system, such as Spark Streaming.

As depicted in Figure 7(c), if LCSE is assigned as the processing component in a given task, which is only equipped with a (Near) Real-time Processing Engine, then it collects monitoring information directly from a data collector component hosted in the MANO stack since the MANO has the knowledge on all components constituting the NFV architecture. This forms the basis for low latency analysis. The output of the LCSE will be consumed by the Policy Engine.

If the CSE is assigned the processing task, both the Batch and (Near) Real-time Engine may be requested to cooperate with each other or work individually. Figures 7(a)(b)(d) depict how these engines work in different modes. In the case Figures 7(a), where only the (Near) Real-time Processing Engine is activated, data are pre-processed and models are selected and deployed on this engine. The (Near) Real-time Processing Engine then operates based on its configuration, and its analysis results are forwarded to the Policy Engine. In the Figures 7(b), the Batch Processing Engine works independently; it consumes models from Automated Model Selection and data from Data Storage instead of the Data collector directly. Its outputs will also support the operation of Policy Engine. In Figures 7(c), where both engines are selected, the Batch Processing Engine trains selected models and then forwards these models directly or indirectly to the (Near) Real-time Processing Engine. The models will be applied to generate analysis results by the (Near) Real-time Processing Engine.

Figure 6. CogNet Analysis Module

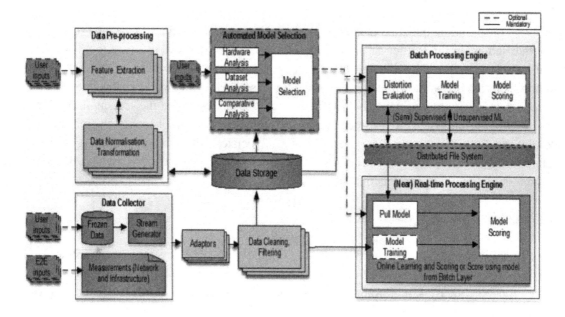

In practice, historical data may contain sufficient knowledge for network management to work properly. However, the amount of these data, in the order of petabytes, can prohibit the learning of predictive models in a timely manner. The hybrid mode unifies both batch and real-time processing. It enables the framework to process massive amounts of data in order to build predictive models based on previous network behavior. It also brings the ability to process fresh network data for predicting customer or network behaviors based on the historical models within a short period of time.

Data Collection and Pre-Processing Module

Data Collection & Adaptors: it collects data from multiple resources, and maps collected data into those that can be processed directly by the following components:

- **Data Cleaning & Filtering:** It cleans and refines received data, and then stores it into the Data Storage or forwards it to the (Near) Real-time Processing Engine.
- **Data Storage:** It stores historical data, and makes them available for multiple components of the CSE.
- **Data Pre-processing:** It can work in either automatic or manual modes to pre-process collected data stored in the Data Storage and make them ready for the Batch Processing Engine. Feature extraction can be achieved by Deep Neural Networks, which can generate highly informative features automatically. Such functionality is essential to support the overall flexibility of the architecture and to keep it adjustable to constantly changing environments. It controls the noise and reduces the processing time of analytic works in the big data context.

Figure 7. Processing Engines

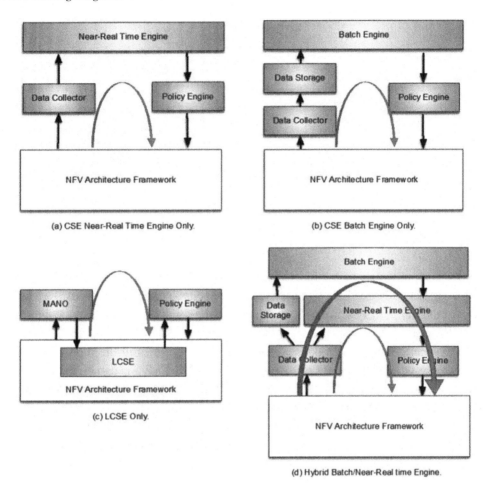

The Data Pre-processing flow is illustrated in Figure 8. Initially, collected records are cleaned by some lightweight approaches that aim to reduce the size of data for storage. The feature extraction may also be performed on the cleaned records based on the request from the Data Pre-processing if the records are forwarded to the (Near) Real-time Processing Engine. Afterwards, processed records are stored in the Data storage or consumed directly by the (Near) Real-time Processing Engine.

The Data Pre-processing will further process the stored data by normalization and extraction. The former operation consists in adjusting values measured on different scales to a theoretically common scale, which is essential for certain machine learning algorithms, such as classifiers that calculate the distance between two points by the Euclidean, and can potentially facilitate the convergence of some machine learning approaches, such as gradient descent. The latter one covers methods that transform raw data into informative features for machine learning algorithms.

Data extraction is intended to increase the accuracy of machine learning models by extracting salient features from the raw input data but also potentially remove noise and redundancy from monitoring records. It also simplifies and facilitates model selections since if relevant features can be extracted, even a simple model can offer remarkable results. Additional goals include lowering the dimension of data to facilitate training speed and visualization.

Figure 8. Data Pre-processing

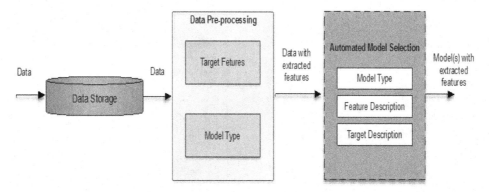

Policy Engine Module

This component is mainly responsible for mapping the output from the LCSE/CSE into the policy actions that can be directly understood by the related components in the MANO stack, Tenant Controller and OSS (Operation Support System)/BSS. It consists of the following sub-components:

The Policy Recommender matches events that represent system state of interests in the context of business objectives and their operational realization with the policies in the repository, to determine which policy is relevant. The events are received from the LCSE/CSE and can be in the form of (i) predictions such as resource utilization (e.g., expected CPU/RAM consumption) or anomalies detected (e.g., network intruder alert, or performance degradation detection), or (ii) thresholds optimized for specific monitoring values, such as: considering the dynamic environment a CPU consumption exceeding 80% might cause degradations at a point in time t, however with the changes in the dynamic environment this amount might vary at t+1. The Policy Recommender is a decision point that takes into account the state of individual network elements, but also helps to achieve business objectives by suggesting how to manage the overall resources required for network services. By integrating the predicted results from LCSE/CSE, the Policy Recommender can make policy decisions dynamically to respond to a situational context, as well as changes to the network environment due to ongoing operations. In addition, the recommender can optionally feed the repository with adapted/new policies. The Recommender can be extended to adapt/ recommend new policies based on the experience gathered from applying previously existing policies. Hence, it will be analyzing historical data of the effect of existing policies, by looking at performance indicators, such as delay, throughput, degradations caused, resource consumption patterns, etc.

The Policy Repository stores policies related to all network components. These policies are bindings of policy events with policy actions. They contain parameters and data structures that the Policy Recommender needs to evaluate for policy recommendations.

The Optimizer consumes what is in the repository, and is responsible for dealing with the fine tuning of the parameters/conditions. The Policy Optimizer receives policy decisions from the Policy Recommender, and then transforms the abstract actions specified in selected policies into concrete ones based on the state and configuration information from the MANO stack. This information can be static, such as source or destination addresses, or dynamic such as currently available network resources.

The Policy Distribution invokes APIs offered by the components that are hosted in the MANO stack, Tenant Controller and OSS/BSS based on specified actions. It recommends actions according to the decisions made by the Policy Recommender and current network conditions.

The CSE or LCSE sends its outputs, which can be predicted values on specific events, such as the CPU usage of a given server, to the Policy Engine. As illustrated in Figure 9, upon receipt of these inputs, the Policy Recommender evaluates conditions of all policies stored in the Policy Repository and then identifies the policies that will be triggered. Afterwards, the selected policies are sent to the Optimizer that maps the high-level action specifications of policies into concrete ones based on the state information from the NFV architecture. The concrete actions will be forwarded to the Policy Distribution and then the Proxy provides recommendations to the MANO/SDN controller about how to adjust resource provisioning in order to avoid the violation of network management rules.

Cognitive Policy Engine

The traditional policy engine illustrated in Figure 10 receives events generated by either the monitoring system (usually in the form of alarms) or from the CSE as input data. The policy engine includes the engine itself, which selects from the policy repository the most appropriate set of actions as a function of the nature of the event and on the system conditions. Additionally, the policy engine can distribute actions to the different components. The policy engine may be extended to take other responsibilities (conflict resolution, withdrawal of policies, optimization of policy parameters, etc.); however, these responsibilities (including policy generation/adaption) are out of the scope of the project (and also this chapter).

Figure 9. Policy Engine

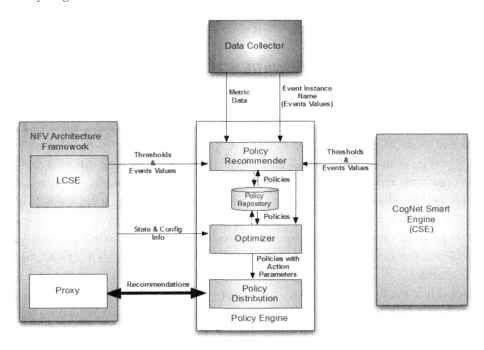

Figure 10. Policy-Based Management based on Cognitive generated events

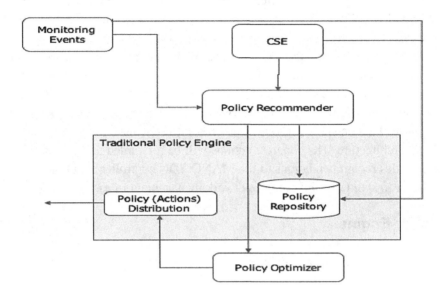

The policy engine includes a policy repository where the policies are stored. The policy engine uses the stored policies to determine the appropriate actions. The policy recommender has currently the role of retrieving the violated policies and will aim to adapt the existing policies in the policy repository with new ones that are customized for the specific deployment. This could be the addition of new policies or the adaptation of the parameters in the policies (e.g., threshold levels). The policy recommendation could be based on the direct monitoring of the events, on the history/status of the system and especially on the machine learning insight (which provides dynamic statistic results on specific events). The cognitive processing flow includes monitoring, CSE, policy engine, distribution of actions.

USE CASE 1: URBAN MOBILITY AWARENESS

Use Case Description

Urbanization and modern civilization lead to different functional regions of the city, e.g., residential areas, shopping areas, business districts and educational areas, which all have different needs and serve as a valuable organizing input for framing detailed knowledge of a certain metropolitan area. Such regions are either designed by urban planners or naturally formed according to the people's lifestyle, and would change functions and territories with the development of a city. Among different scenarios that can be considered in the future for cities, the focus was made on the particular case where discovering regions of different functionalities can enable a variety of valuable insights for better managing the network infrastructure.

It is expected that the load on the network will vary from one region to another according to its "functionality". In the business district of the city, the service demand and the load on the network is expected to be less than shopping districts since probably the users at the shopping districts might rely on the augmented reality applications that can aid them for shopping and which will increase the load and may lead to congestion. In a real situation, when users move across different areas of the cities, the network is expected to automatically allocate resources according to the mobility patterns of these users according to their predicted network consumption based on the used applications which is expected to vary from one area to another, according to the region's functionality. Hence, in this scenario the target is to perform the clustering of cities into regions based on their functionalities and for each region, classifying the network traffic. Based on traffic classification, recommendations can be made for migrating some network resources or dynamically configuring the network topology.

The Urban Mobility Awareness (UMA) scenario focuses on predicting the network demand according to the spatial/temporal variation of the different regions of the city, and according to the crowd mobility patterns as well. The ability of understanding patterns across cities and their impact on network demand can obviously create new and valuable insights into the dynamicity of customers' patterns and hence, smart placement and migration strategies of network resources accordingly.

Data

The data utilized by this scenario is the historical network demand in a region over time, along with social network data that can be used to capture the flows of users in a region as discussed by (Assem, Buda, & O'Sullivan, 2017) and the "functionality" of that region described here (Assem, Buda, & O'Sullivan 2016), which can also be captured from other data such as Points of Interest (PoI). The Points of interest data can be obtained from open street maps' points of interest data for Manhattan, which is publicly available[1]. The functional regions of Manhattan over 24h periods are depicted in Figure 11, which shows the corresponding visualization for the functional regions illustrating how some regions can change over time.

Moreover, the raw network data contained the network demand in the Manhattan region for a period of 6 months (July-December 2016). The dataset used for the case study was obtained from Truconnect Technologies Inc. The dataset contains more than 2*1012 anonymized geotagged mobile network sessions in Manhattan with some key performance indicators. Figure 12, shows a strong weekly periodicity of the data.

Figure 11. Temporal functional regions visualization based on hierarchical clustering

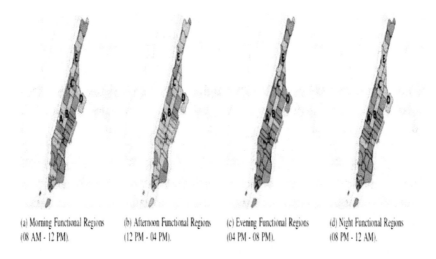

(a) Morning Functional Regions (08 AM - 12 PM).   (b) Afternoon Functional Regions (12 PM - 04 PM).   (c) Evening Functional Regions (04 PM - 08 PM).   (d) Night Functional Regions (08 PM - 12 AM).

Figure 12. Hourly maximum demand for the weeks plotted on top of each other to show the strong weekly periodicity in the data

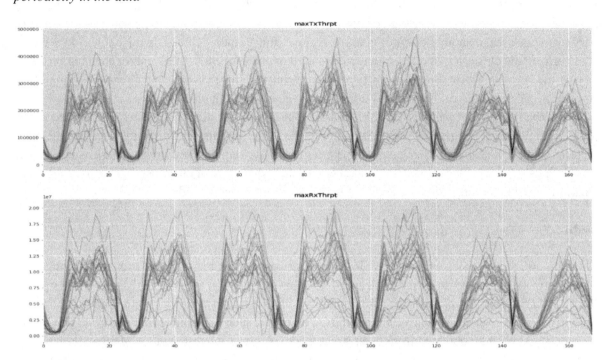

Given real-time data, the trained models can predict the network demand one step ahead in order to allow for the detection of regions with unexpected levels of network demand. The step ahead in the experiments data was hourly (i.e., the model predicted the network demand in the next hour). Depending on the availability of the data during real-time this can be adjusted to other step values.

Workflow, Algorithms, and Results

The UMA scenario's sequence diagram is depicted in Figure 13 which shows the CSE employing recurrent crowd urban patterns and sector detection based upon the social network data forwarded by the Data Collector. The CSE will then map the network demand data received from the data collector in order to detect the network demand for a particular region/crowd. Furthermore, the events detected are transmitted to the Policy Engine, which in turn sends the actions to the NFVO which performs the runtime adaptations.

Data are received and processed by the CSE through clustering for detecting functional regions and prior trained models on historical network demand data to predict the network demand. This is further sent to the Policy Engine which will react based on the events with recommended actions to the Orchestrator.

In the CSE phase, the clustering techniques are applied to group regions with similar functionality in the Manhattan region. To achieve this from PoI data, the Manhattan region is decomposed into a 32x32 grids, and the points of interest are counted for each grid cell to create a PoI count vector with a size equal to the functionalities for each portion of the grid and normalized it for the clustering algorithm. Afterwards, the grid is clustered into functional regions.

Figure 13. Workflow involving the cognitive management modules for Urban Mobility Awareness

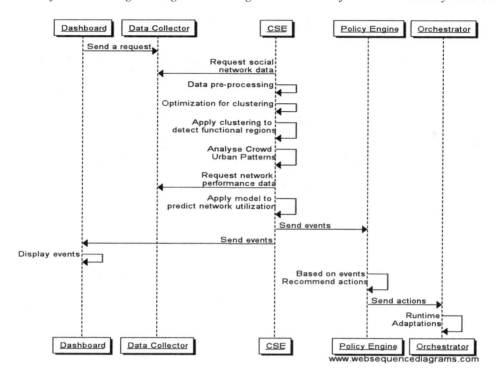

In this use case, the CSE encompasses hierarchical, spectral and k-means clustering. They were evaluated on a silhouette score, which reflects the quality of the clusters. It is observed that the highest silhouette score is obtained with hierarchical clustering.

Moreover, various time window splits are explored in order to determine the optimal split for the quality of the clusters and in addition various k values (i.e., number of clusters) for obtaining optimal results in terms of silhouette score and thus in terms of region functionality.

Figure 14 shows results from exploring the optimum number of clusters k for the 4 hours interval resulting in 6 time slots. As it can be observed, the optimum number of clusters for hierarchical clustering for the 4 Hours interval are k=13, represented by a dashed vertical line (Assem, Buda, & O'Sullivan, 2017).

As a learning algorithm, a Long Short Term Memory (LSTM) neural network is used to predict the expected demand for each region with a different functionality. LSTM networks are special types of recurrent neural networks that remember information passed to them for a time window and are well-suited for various time series forecast scenarios The LSTM architecture comprises of one input layer representing the past network demand, one hidden layer of 16 neurons and an output layer representing the one step ahead network demand.

The network demand in the Manhattan region is processed for a period of 6 months (July-December 2016) to evaluate the UMA framework for the prediction of network demand. In the generic model, the prediction of the network demand is made for the whole region. In a functional region based model, the prediction of the network demand is made for each functional region. In this use case, the mean absolute scaled error (MASE) is used as the primary performance measure. After training the model for the first three months (July-September), authors tested the model output for the next three months (October-December). The model performance is depicted in Figure 15.

Figure 14. Clustering results with varied number of clusters when applying hierarchical clustering

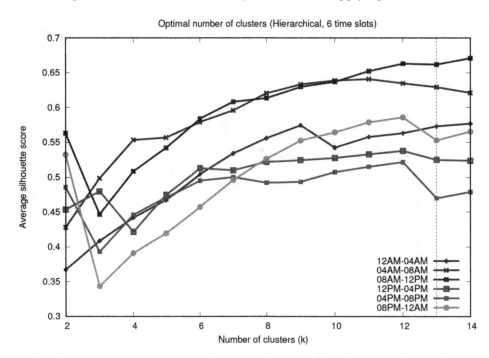

Figure 15. Network Demand Prediction Performance on Test Dataset

```
Model=lstm_full RMSE=663766.2201 MAPE=17.4071 MASE=0.9761 R^2=0.3164
----5Factors
Model=lstm-1/5- RMSE=1450887.0065 MAPE=18.9535 MASE=0.7821 R^2=0.3131
Model=lstm-2/5- RMSE=2014798.5348 MAPE=68.6180 MASE=0.7283 R^2=0.1009
Model=lstm-3/5- RMSE=1087525.8595 MAPE=19.9857 MASE=0.9281 R^2=0.2694
Model=lstm-4/5- RMSE=3183796.3181 MAPE=129.5212 MASE=0.7645 R^2=0.0470
Model=lstm-5/5- RMSE=1620350.9928 MAPE=28.8126 MASE=0.7632 R^2=0.2275
```

For each region, MASE was better than the generic model which is denoted by "lstm_full".

In the policy engine phase, an operator might have portable base stations that provide mobile data coverage for an area of a specific size. The location of these portable base stations can be optimized based on the predicted network demand from the CSE. For instance, given a detected crowd movement to a specific area perhaps due to an event in the region, the placement of the portable base stations can be adjusted to account for this event.

The UMA framework allows predicting the network demand in a dense urban area for a flexible time unit. Forecasting the network demand aids a network operator in planning for the changes in user demand. In addition, it helps service providers in identifying potential bottlenecks in their service ahead of time to achieve higher operational performance. Through UMA, an increased accuracy is observed for predicting network demand based on certain external features, such as the functional regions.

USE CASE 2: SLA ENFORCEMENT

Use Case Description

SLA agreement generally comprises parameters describing the service functional behavior and non-functional properties such as the minimum acceptable QoS values (referred to as SLOs- Service Level Objectives). As an example, SLOs for a VoIP (Voice over IP) service could be the following:

SLO_1: Service Availability ratio;
SLO_2: Response time ratio;
SLO_3: Capacity, downlink throughput ratio, etc.

The "SLA enforcement" use case shows how ML technology can help anticipating and thus preventing SLO violation from occurring; avoiding any potential penalties and extra costs as well as maintaining nominal behavior for the service and networks. This helps operators to ensure service resiliency and availability. More details about SLA violations are discussed in Chapter "*A Perspective on the Standardization of Autonomic Detection of Service Level Agreements Violations*".

The use case is exemplified in the context of VNF, where a network service relies upon a set of chained VNFs. VNFs could be atomic or composite. Composite VNFs are deployed as a set of one or multiple VNF Component (VNFC). Clearwater, a composite and open source VNF, is selected. Clearwater delivers a Multimedia connection, including VoIP service, using IMS (IP Multimedia Subsystem). The VNF is composite and relies upon five VNFCs namely, Bono, Sprout, Homer, Homestead, and Ralf as represented in Figure 16:

- Ellis is a provisioning portal providing sign-up, password management, and SIP (Session Initiation Protocol) identity management.
- The IMS I-CSCF (Interrogating-Call Session Control Function) and S-CSCF (Serving-Call Session Control Function) components are implemented in Sprout.
- Bono is the Clearwater edge proxy, it uses Sprout (SIP Router). It implements the P-CSCF (Proxy-Call/Session Control Functions) component. It is the entry point of SIP clients, which in turn forwards SIP requests to Sprout.
- Homer is a XDMS, a standard XML Document Management Server, it stores multimedia telephony service (MMTel). It runs a Cassandra database.
- Homestead (HSS Mirror) relies upon HTTP RESTful interfaces and Cassandra as the data store. It is used by Sprout to retrieve authentication credentials and user profile. It also delivers some I-CSCF and S-CSCF features.
- Ralf (CTF) is responsible for charging and billing.

Clearwater has different properties that are useful for the use case like the scale-out capability of all the VNFCs and its build-in stress generator namely SIPp, (Opensource tool, n.d.) which the authors used to emulate SLO violations. 30,000 different SIP profiles were created and stored using Homestead in the local Cassandra database. These profiles are used to generate traffic and anomalies when they are launched simultaneously. The monitoring tool used by the framework is Monasca (Hewlett-Packard

Figure 16. Description of the Testbed. Clearwater virtual IMS functional architecture in the box lower right. Upper left the Cognitive Smart Engine (CSE). The experimental process is: (1) Stress testing for SLA violation generation. (2) System-level supervision. (3) Reporting SLO violations. (4) Data labeling, merging observations on the SLO state and the system-level metrics

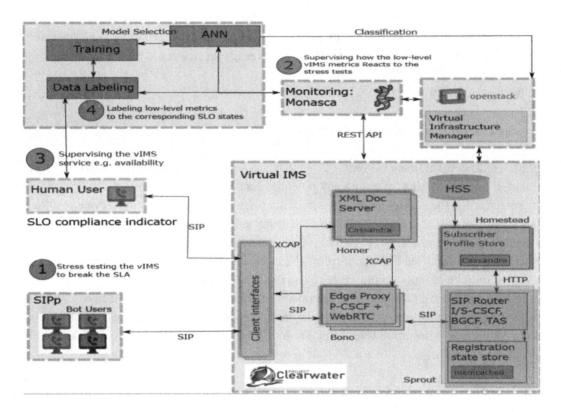

Enterprise, 2015). Monasca is a MaaS, Monitoring-as-a-Service solution from HP, built as a highly scalable Openstack service.

Data

Table 1 shows a subset of the collected metrics. Monasca collects mainly low-level system metrics. 30,000 bot SIP users were generated to simulate service degradation and violate the SLA. Monasca by default collects 30 metrics per VM (Virtual Machine), four of which are of no use in this use case (e.g., idle values or Null values). Only 26 metrics per VM are considered, which correspond to 156 metrics with all the 6 VMs (Bono, Ralf, Sprout, Homer, Homestead, Ellis). The window of observation was set to 2 months, with a sampling rate of 15 seconds (i.e., collecting data each 15 seconds). The preprocessing phase in this use case consists mainly in removing corrupted lines, empty cells, and redundant lines.

Figure 17 shows twelve whisker plots representing different low-level metrics of the core IMS nodes. It displays some difference in the distribution of the same metric in different VNFCs (for example "ralf-cpu" and "homer-cpu"). This means that the stress test impacts different VNFCs with different degrees.

Table 1. List of collected raw data

Metric Name	Semantics
cpu.idle_perc	Percentage of time the CPU is idle when no I/O requests are in progress
cpu.wait_perc	Percentage of time the CPU is idle AND there is at least one I/O request in progress
cpu.stolen_perc	Percentage of stolen CPU time, i.e. the time spent in other OS contexts when running in a virtualized environment
disk.total_space_mb	The total amount of disk space aggregated across all the disks on a particular node.
io.read_kbytes_sec	Kbytes/sec read by an io device
net.in_bytes_sec	Number of network bytes received per second
io.read_req_sec	Number of read requests/sec to an io device
load.avg_1_min	The average system load over a 1-minute period
mem.swap_free_perc	Percentage of free swap memory that is free
net.out_packets_sec	Number of network packets sent per second
net.in_errors_sec	Number of network errors on incoming network traffic per second

Figure 17. A subset of the data set distribution

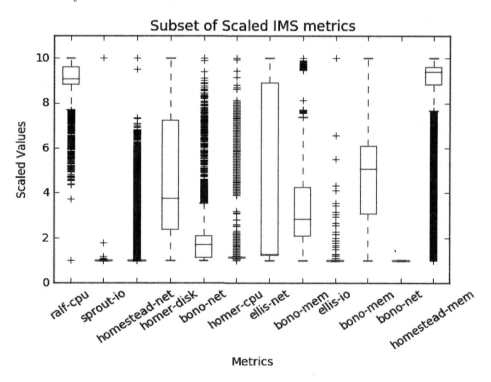

The dataset describes both normal SLA state and the violation state. The scale of the time series varies widely from one metric to another. Therefore, the normalization stage is performed to rescale the metrics to the [0-1] range. The classifier considers all the metrics with no scale bias.

Workflow, Algorithms, and Results

This section describes how the framework building blocks are considered in this use case. The sequence diagram is presented hereafter: firstly, the monitoring phase takes place where the Data Collector retrieves metrics from the NFV components of the architecture (MANO, NFVI, etc.). The CSE queries the metrics data from the Data Collector and further processes the received data. The CSE applies forecasting techniques in order to detect potential SLO violations on the forecasted values. If a violation is detected, the CSE SLA enforcer is notified and it will compute proactive management actions in order to avoid the SLO breach.

In this regard, the CSE reports an event to the Policy Engine which checks the rules and actions associated with the SLA enforcement use case. In order to apply the actions, the Policy Engine requests the topology from the NFVO and it forwards the request of allocating/withdrawing resources to/from the VIM and to setup the NFV Infrastructure topology to the NFVO and the SDN controller. The latter further initiates the setup of the NFV. Next, the dashboard receives the performance report (Figure 18).

In this use case to generate the violation, the number of SIP connections is linearly and abruptly incremented to simulate the performance degradation until the service fails. This procedure is repeated multiple times as depicted in Figure 18 with label '1'.

The labeling of input features is made thanks to the observations from the SLO compliancy indicator (see Figure 18 label 3). The SLO compliancy indicator watches the behavior of the testbed and determines the system state with respect to three SLOs (represented in the equation of Figure 19). Next to that, the monitoring data and the labels are merged based on the timestamps of the observations (see Figure 19). This merge allows labeling the inputs into the three SLO categories.

In the equation shown in Figure 19, the values of the Ys are either 'True' or 'False', for SLA Violation and Non-Violation respectively.

The data is split into three parts, the training set at 70%, the test set at 20% and the validation set at 10%. It is labeled based on the experiments made beforehand and while taking into account the three SLO definitions.

The 3 SLOs targets, respectively, the response time of the service, the availability of the proxy and the database transaction. In this use case, two types of Artificial Neural Networks (ANN) are used.

The role of the ANN is to identify from the observations the relevant metrics to watch for each SLO and to identify effectively when an SLO breach is occurring. The three considered SLOs are the following:

- **SLO1 Response Time:** This service objective targets the response time of the SIP proxy VNFC (i.e., Bono). The overload tests generate a large amount of connections forcing the proxy to drop multiple connection requests. This in turn, reduces the mean time necessary to answer a connection request.
- **SLO2 Database Transaction:** This SLO targets mainly Ralf and Homestead nodes. The SLO in this context is defined as the Cassandra database performance.

Figure 18. Workflow involving the cognitive management modules for SLA enforcement use case

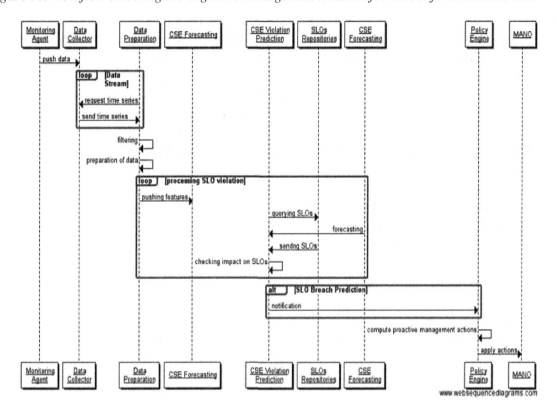

Figure 19. Annotation process

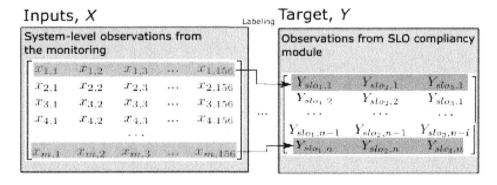

- **SLO3 Service Availability:** This SLO monitors the behavior of the service as a whole. When the communication service is down, a label is assigned to the corresponding dummy variable with 1, 0 otherwise.

The learning algorithms in this use case are generated randomly. 200 different LSTMs and FFNN (Feed Forward Neural Network) were generated and tested. For all the neural networks, an implementation of an early stopping based on the loss is made. The training stops when the loss stabilized to optimize the training time. Each experiment consists of 20 trials over the same hypothesis.

The ANN successfully managed to learn the underlying complex patterns of the dynamic environment expected in future networks. Figure 20.A shows the distribution of the training time of all the ANNs with respect to the sample size. Figure 20.B shows that those overall, training epochs have a strong influence on the model accuracy.

The more time necessary for the training the lower the global score. It is noticed that the high LSTM accuracy averages out with its long training time giving a similar global score of FFNN and LSTM, although training on a GPU configuration benefits more to the FFNN than to the LSTM.

The results of this use case are described in more details in (Bendriss & Grida, 2017a) (Bendriss & Grida, 2017b). With respect to the machine learning, an empirical approach to machine learning was investigated. It consists of generating multiple random ANNs with different factors of variation for the SLA use case within the context of NFV.

The CogNet framework was followed to automate network management with ML. A real test case, using a virtual IMS to instantiate the NFV framework is used to assess the challenges of managing VNFs. The results could be summed up as follows:

Figure 20. C compares between FFNN and LSTM architecture over two metrics, the validation score and the global score. The validation score is the score obtained after training the model on the training set and testing it on the test set. The global score is a customized metric that takes into account the log of the training time and the accuracy of the model.

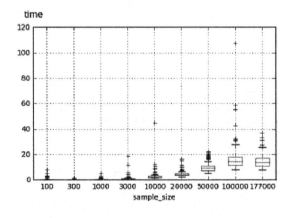

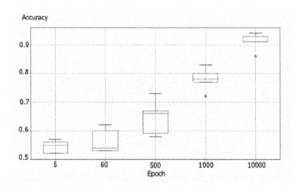

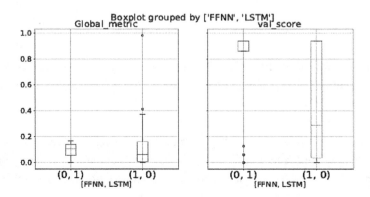

- FFNN and LSTM, if properly configured, can yield high accuracy (up to 94%).
- Overall, LSTM is more performant than FFNN but is more prone to overfitting when incrementing the number of epochs.
- The framework building blocks, namely data collector, data pre-processing, model selection were developed in this use case to correspond to the problem solved and to the collected dataset.

CONCLUSION

In this chapter, the background and the pillars for cognitive management with Artificial Intelligence to automate network management operation were presented: Autonomics, Policy-Based Management, Lambda architecture, and a state-of-the-art of ongoing initiatives in the context of the 5G program, phase 1.

Based on this background, a cognitive management framework was detailed with its modules and their interactions as the output of the CogNet project. Mainly three modules were presented: the Data Collector and Pre-processing, the Analysis module, and the Policy Engine.

The aim is to facilitate the management of current networks, software-defined networks, and beyond, but also to embed the intelligence to cope with the massive connectivity and heterogeneity challenges and activate automation techniques that rely upon machine learning to ensure pro-active modes.

Two use cases of relevance to the diversity and expected resiliency and availability in current and future networks were selected and presented in this chapter. Urban Mobility Awareness aims to enable an adaptive network management based on predicted network demands, considering various features such as functional regions and crowd mobility. In addition, the SLA enforcement use case was presented to anticipate SLO violations through machine learning. The goal was to show that the framework is applicable to current mobile networks and also to software-defined networks.

Particularly, intelligence will help to scale up and down and to proactively detect any network events, leading to a significant reduction of CAPEX and OPEX budgets, let alone service deployment times.

The cognitive management framework is agnostic and is being expanded to cover the slice concept within the 5G SliceNet project (SliceNet, 2018).

ACKNOWLEDGMENT

This work was supported by the EU project CogNet, 671625 (H2020-ICT-2014-2, Research and Innovation action).

REFERENCES

Architecture, 5GPPP. (2016). *View on 5G Architecture.* Retrieved from https://5g-ppp.eu/wp-content/uploads/2014/02/5G-PPP-5G-Architecture-WP-July-2016.pdf

Assem, H., Buda, T., & O'Sullivan, D. (2016). *Spatio-Temporal Clustering Approach for Detecting Functional Regions in Cities.* EEE ICTAI. doi:10.1109/ICTAI.2016.0063

Assem, H., Buda, T., & O'Sullivan, D. (2017). *RCMC: Recognizing Crowd Mobility Patterns in Cities based on Location Based Social Networks Data. ACM Transactions on Intelligent Systems and Technology.*

Assem, H., & O'Sullivan, D. (2015). Towards Bridging the Gap between Machine Learning Researchers and Practitioners. *IEEE International Conference on Smart City/SocialCom/SustainCom (SmartCity).* 10.1109/SmartCity.2015.151

Bendriss, J., & Grida, I. (2017). Forecasting and anticipating SLO breaches in programmable networks. *20th Conference on Innovations in Clouds, Internet and Networks (ICIN)*, 127-134. 10.1109/ICIN.2017.7899402

Bendriss, J., & Grida, I. (2017). AI for SLA Management in Programmable Networks. *DRCN 2017-Design of Reliable Communication Networks; 13th International Conference; Proceedings of*, 1-8.

Bijnens, N., & Hausenblas, M. (2017). *Lamnda Architecture.* Retrieved from http://lambda-architecture.net/

Bolla, R., Lombardo, C., Bruschi, R., & Mangialardi, S. (2014). *DROPv2: energy efficiency through network function virtualization.* IEEE Network.

CHARISMA. (2016). *CHARISMA Project.* Retrieved from http://www.charisma5g.eu/index.php/overview/

Chen, Y., Qin, Y., Lambe, M., & Chu, W. (2015). Realizing network function virtualization management and orchestration with model based open architecture. *11th International Conference on Network and Service Management (CNSM).* 10.1109/CNSM.2015.7367393

Cisco. (2016). *The zettabyte era - trends and analysis.* Retrieved from http://www.cisco.com/c/en/us/solutions/collateral/service-provider/visual-networking-index-vni/VNI_Hyperconnectivity_WP.htm

CogNet. (2017). *CogNet final requirements, scenarios and architecture.* Author.

Csoma, A., Sonkoly, B., Csikor, L., Németh, F., Gulyás, A., Jocha, D., ... Sahhaf, S. (2014). Multi-layered Service Orchestration in a Multi-domain Network Environment. *Third European Workshop on Software Defined Networks.* 10.1109/EWSDN.2014.32

Damianou, N., Dulay, N., Lupu, E., & Sloman, M. (2001). *The ponder policy specification language.* In *Policies for Distributed Systems and Networks.* Springer Berlin Heidelberg.

Donadio, P., Fioccola, G. B., Canonico, R., & Ventre, G. (2014). A PCE-based architecture for the management of virtualized infrastructures. *IEEE 3rd International Conference on Cloud Networking (CloudNet).*

ETSI. (2014). *Network Functions Virtualisation (NFV); Management and Orchestration v1.1.1.* Retrieved from http://www.etsi.org/deliver/etsi_gs/NFV-MAN/001_099/001/01.01.01_60/gs_nfv-man001v010101p.pdf

ETSI GS NFV 002 V1.2.1. (2014). *Network Functions Virtualisation (NFV); Architectural Framework.* Retrieved from http://www.etsi.org/deliver/etsi_gs/NFV/001_099/002/01.02.01_60/gs_NFV002v010201p.pdf

ETSI-NFV. (2016). Retrieved from http://www.etsi.org/technologies-clusters/technologies/nfv

Giannoulakis, I., Xylouris, G., Kafetzakis, E., Kourtis, A., Fajardo, J. O., Khodashenas, P. S., & Vassilakis, V. (2016). *System architecture and deployment scenarios for SESAME: Small cEllS coodinAtion for Multi-tenancy and Edge services. In IEEE NetSoft Conference and Workshops.* NetSoft.

Giotis, K., Kryftis, Y., & Maglaris, V. (2015). Policy-based orchestration of NFV services in Software-Defined Networks. *1st IEEE Conference on Network Softwarization (NetSoft).* 10.1109/NETSOFT.2015.7116145

5. GPPP Network Management & Quality of Service Working Group. (2017). *Cognitive Network Management for 5G.* Retrieved from https://5g-ppp.eu/wp-content/uploads/2017/03/NetworkManagement_WhitePaper_1.pdf

Hewlett-Packard Enterprise. (2015). *Monasca, Monitoring tool.* Retrieved from http://monasca.io/

IETF. (2002). *Policy Framework (policy).* Retrieved from http://www.ietf.org/html.charters/policy-charter.html

IETF. (2016). *The Open vSwitch Database Management Protocol.* Retrieved from https://tools.ietf.org/html/rfc7047

Intanagonwiwat, C., Govindan, R., & Estrin, D. (2000). *Directed Diffusion: A scalable and robust communication paradigm for sensor networks.* ACM MOBICOM. doi:10.1145/345910.345920

ITU-T. (2014). *Framework of software-defined networking. 5G connectivity to meet demanding services: examples of connected cars and mobile health.* Retrieved from https://ec.europa.eu/digital-agenda/events/cf/ict2015/item-display.cfm?id=15141

Kephart, J. (2003). *The vision of autonomic computing.* Academic Press.

Kephart, J., & Walsh, W. (2004). An artificial intelligence perspective on autonomic computing policies. *Proceedings 5th IEEE Workshop on Policies for Distributed Systems and Networks (Policy 2004)*, 3–12. 10.1109/POLICY.2004.1309145

Lobo, J., Bhathia, R., & Naqvi, S. (1999). A policy description language. *Proceedings 16th National Conference on Artificial Intelligence (AAAI-99)*, 291-298.

López, V., Dios, O. G., Fuentes, B., Yannuzzi, M., Fernández-Palacios, J. P., & López, D. (2014). *Towards a network operating system. Optical Fiber Communications Conference and Exhibition.* OFC.

Moore, B., Ellesson, E., Strassner, J., & Westerinen, A. (2001). *Policy core information model – version 1 specification.*

Neves, P., Cale, R., Costa, M. R., Parada, C., Parreira, B., Calero, J. M., & Barros, M. J. (2016). *The SELFNET Approach for Autonomic Management in an NFV/SDN Networking Paradigm.* IJDSN.

Nicklish, J. (1999). *A rule language for network policies.* Policy.

NORMA. (2015). *5G NORMA Deliverable D3.1 Functional Network Architecture and Security Requirements.* Retrieved from https://5gnorma.5g-ppp.eu/wp-content/uploads/2016/01/5G_NORMA_D3.1.pdf

OASIS. (2005). *Extensible access control markup language (xacml) version 2.0. 2011-09-24.* Retrieved from http://docs oasisopen org/xacml/2.0/access_control-xacml-2.0-core-spec-os. pdf

OpenFlow. (2017). *OpenFlow Home Page.* Retrieved from https://www.opennetworking.org/sdn-resources/openflow

Opensource tool. (n.d.). *SIPp, test tool / traffic generator for Session Initiation Protocol.* Retrieved from http://sipp-wip.readthedocs.io/en/latest/

Salehie, M. a. (2009). Self-adaptive Software: Landscape and Research Challenges. *ACM Trans. Auton. Adapt. Syst., 4*(2), 14:1–14:42.

Shen, W., Yoshida, M., Minato, K., & Imajuku, W. (2015). vConductor: An enabler for achieving virtual network integration as a service. *IEEE Communications Magazine, 53*(2), 116–124. doi:10.1109/MCOM.2015.7045399

SliceNet. (2018). *SliceNet Project.* Récupéré sur SliceNet Project: https://slicenet.eu/

Soares, J., Dias, M., Carapinha, J., Parreira, B., & Sargento, S. (2014). Cloud4NFV: A platform for Virtual Network Functions. *IEEE 3rd International Conference on Cloud Networking (CloudNet).* 10.1109/CloudNet.2014.6969010

Soares, J., Gonçalves, C., Parreira, B., Tavares, P., Carapinha, J., Barraca, J. P., ... Sargento, S. (2015). Toward a telco cloud environment for service functions. *IEEE Communications Magazine, 53*(2), 98–106. doi:10.1109/MCOM.2015.7045397

SONATA. (2016). *SONATA project.* Retrieved from https://sonata-project.org/

Strassner, J., & Schleimer, S. (1998). Policy framework definition language. Internet Engineering Task Force, Internet Draft draft-ietf-policy-framework-pfdl-OO. txt, vol 17.

Szabo, R., Kind, M., Westphal, F. J., Woesner, H., Jocha, D., & Csaszar, A. (2015). Elastic network functions: Opportunities and challenges. *IEEE Network, 29*(3), 15–21. doi:10.1109/MNET.2015.7113220

Xu, L. (2016). CogNet: Network Management Architecture Featuring Cognitive Capabilities. *European Conference on Networks and Communications (EUCNC 2016).* 10.1109/EuCNC.2016.7561056

Yoshida, M., Shen, W., Kawabata, T., Minato, K., & Imajuku, W. (2014). MORSA: A multi-objective resource scheduling algorithm for NFV infrastructure. *16th Asia-Pacific Network Operations and Management Symposium (APNOMS).* 10.1109/APNOMS.2014.6996545

KEY TERMS AND DEFINITIONS

Cognitive Management: Management of networks is said cognitive when it embeds or uses artificial intelligence (and in particular machine learning) techniques to ensure faster deployment, proactive detection of fault, and performance degradation.

Machine Learning: An application of the field of artificial intelligence that relies on statistical, mathematical, and computer-based techniques to learn from a given data without being specifically programmed.

Network Function Virtualization: Is a network-based architecture that leverages IT and virtualization techniques to virtualize network functions.

SLA Enforcement: Is a concept to ensure SLA (service level agreement) compliancy with the use of advanced machine learning algorithms.

Software-Defined Networking: Is an approach to ensure network programmability through well-defined APIs and open networking protocols to control network elements.

Software Network: Denotes a network that relies massively upon Cloud, SDN, and NFV techniques.

Urban Mobility Awareness: Focuses on predicting the network demand according to the spatial/temporal variation of the different regions of a city, and according to the crowd mobility patterns as well.

ENDNOTE

[1]   http://wiki.openstreetmap.org/wiki/Map_Features

Section 2
Advanced Techniques for the Future Internet

Chapter 6
Slicing Challenges for Operators

Luis Contreras
Telefonica, Spain

ABSTRACT

The advent of 5G introduces the concept of network slicing which is meant to permit network service providers to overcome the great challenge of forthcoming 5G services: how to support and operate different kinds of services with very distinct needs onto the same infrastructure. Deploying altogether on the same network makes it quite difficult to define a common architecture capable of keeping the diverse requirements of all of them. The network slicing concept foresees a number of logically independent slices, each comprising different network nodes and service functions, which are interconnected and are involved in the delivery and the operation of a specific service. By instantiating network slices, the network will be able to provide completely different services in a dynamic way over the same infrastructure. This chapter overviews the challenges raised by the implementation of the network slicing concept and which will be faced by the network operators.

INTRODUCTION

An initial idea of network slices in standardization[1] was introduced in 2011 by the ITU-T (ITU-T, 2011) in the form of logically isolated network partitions (LINP), with a slice being considered as a unit of programmable resources such as network, computation and storage. Later, in 2016, the concept of network slicing has been formulated by the NGMN in (NGMN, 2015) as an enabler for (hopefully) achieving an efficient logical division of network resources (either physical or virtual) and service functions for different services on the same network infrastructure. The concrete settings of resources and service functions are selected and combined together with the aim of supporting a specific application or type of service.

The different types of services are in principle the ones under consideration for 5G services, as introduced in (ITU-R, 2015). These are the enhanced Mobile Broadband (eMBB), massive Machine-Type Communications (mMTC) and ultra-Reliable and Low Latency Communications (uRLLC). The eMBB service type encompasses the challenge of providing an extremely high volume of delivered data, due to e.g., (ultra) high-definition video sharing. The mMTC kind of service focuses on applications where

DOI: 10.4018/978-1-5225-7146-9.ch006

Figure 1. Characteristics of different kinds of 5G services

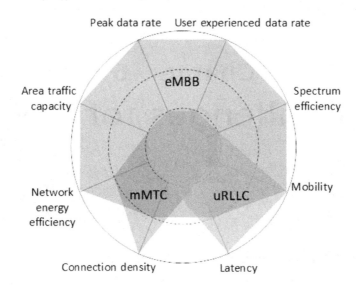

a large number of connected IoT devices, such as sensors, representing a large number of sessions collectively create a significant amount of data passing through the network. Moreover, these data are often associated with requirements like privacy, data ownership, etc. Finally, the uRLLC type refers to services that require extremely low end-to-end latency, like Tactile Internet, Interactive Gaming, Automotive, or Industrial Automation. Figure 1 summarizes some characteristics of each type of service.

Combining services like eMBB, uRLLC, and mMTC on the same network, makes it quite difficult to define a common engineering pattern capable of supporting simultaneously all the requirements of each of them. An approach to manage such deployment needs is to segregate those services into specialized network partitions or slices, designed, and optimized for each of the types of services to be provided.

Each slice is then tailored to such specific purpose, thereby avoiding unnecessary capabilities (for example, an instance of a mMTC slice may not require a TCP optimizer function, whereas an instance of an eMBB slice may need to invoke this capability). This form of flexible network resource consumption opens possibilities of new business models for network operators. However, the associated challenges are not minor, as described along this chapter.

Figure 2 provides a high-level overview of the slicing concept. Through the instantiation of distinct network slices, the operator will be able to provide completely different services in a dynamic and isolated manner despite that all of them actually run over the same physical infrastructure. Thus, the operators can initiate a transition from the existing design choices that rely upon multi-service networks deployed over one architecture conceived to fit all kinds of services (Doverspike, Ramakrishnan, & Chase, 2010), towards the approach of getting logical networks defined per service.

Network slices are intended to behave like entirely independent networks. This implies that there should be mechanisms for properly isolating the slices (if required by the slice definition), thereby avoiding interference between one slice and the others. Furthermore, in some cases, there will be situations that will require that some of the slices to be interconnected to compose a service, raising the need for interworking (stitching) such independent logical constructs.

Figure 2. Network slicing concept

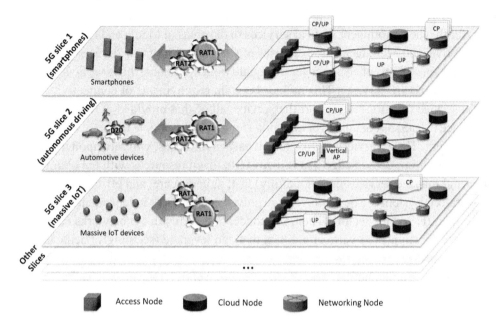

In order to be able of managing such complexity induced by the logical slice partitioning, the operator shall have technical means to take into account the specific requirements of each slice (for instance in terms of throughput, delay, and jitter), as well as suitable inter-slice information exchange mechanisms to avoid congestion issues and arbitrate resource needs, permanent or occasional.

It is clearly anticipated that the mechanisms for creating and operating the network slices will be supported by the softwarization trend enabled by the programmability of the network resources and the virtualization of the network functions, that is, leveraging Software Defined Networking (SDN) and Network Functions Virtualization (NFV) techniques. Apart from the elasticity provided by the virtualization of network functions when dynamically deploying network functions, flexible steering mechanisms (a.k.a., Service Function Chaining) are needed to shepherd the traffic flows according to the expected service behavior. In order to address these requirements, network programmability and its integration with the function virtualization described above, are considered as the baseline pieces to approach network slicing (Odini, 2017) playing an instrumental role in the control, management, and operation of future networks. Both SDN and NFV raise a number of challenges by themselves (Contreras, Doolan, Lønsethagen, & López, 2015). The author focuses here on the additional degree of complexity brought by the concept of network slicing that accompanies this technical transition initiated by the network operators.

VALUE PROVIDED BY NETWORK SLICING

Future adaptation demands of 5G networks, mainly in terms of performance and resources, cannot be achieved in a sustainable manner with existing static and inflexible approaches that are mostly based on manual interventions. The convergence of the telecom and IT industries will provide a common and very high capacity 5G infrastructure, complemented with dynamic service invocation capabilities.

5G is expected to enrich by design the customer-facing services (the so-called "vertical industries" or simply "verticals") with new capabilities and quality features. Automation will revolutionize service provisioning, for the most prominent vertical services in the areas of Media and Entertainment, eHealth, Energy, Automotive, and Manufacturing-Factories of the future (5G-PPP, 2015).

To satisfy the expectations of end-user service quality of experience, those verticals need also to rely on wholesale infrastructure services. This includes certain requirements of connectivity and the chaining of specific service functions to support the service, all of that provided in the overarching form of Slice-as-a-Service (SlaaS) as containers of network, storage, and compute resources deployed in a multi-tenancy environment. These services, unlike recent past experiences, will rely upon a fully softwarized network architecture from core to edge that utilizes virtualized resources with the claim to orchestrate, trade, deploy, and manage services in a (hopefully) fast, agile, secure, and efficient way.

The 5G overall ecosystem can be perceived as a universe of multiple independent vertical ecosystems, each targeting specific service sectors. Then, the concept of slicing in 5G networks contains a business purpose, which is the support of vertical markets that can leverage (seemingly) dedicated networks to improve their production cycles (5G-PPP, 2016).

Network slicing, as a combination of network, computing and storage resource allocation, is intended to enable value creation for vertical segments that lack physical network infrastructures, or which can complement their own resources with the ones offered by the operators. The business objective is to improve and evolve the production capabilities of those industries. Network slicing can thus be seen as the evolution of current wholesale services, by improving the way network resources are allocated and consumed in an agile and ultimately efficient manner.

At the time of characterizing the relationship with the vertical customer, the GSMA has described (GSMA, 2017) a potential value chain for the support of network slicing by network providers, as shown in Figure 3.

Three different kinds of value-added services are identified as a source of incremental value:

- **Capability Exposure:** Through this utilization model, the providers can offer Application Programming Interfaces (APIs) to the vertical business customers for granting the capability of managing their own slices. Such management actions can include e.g., dimensioning, configuration, etc.
- **Integration at Customer Premises:** Complementary network segments, in some cases pertaining to the vertical business customer, become an integral part of the solution, requiring a truly

Figure 3. Network slicing value chain
(GSMA, 2017)

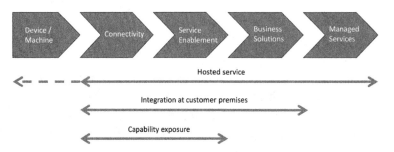

convergent network including the integration in existing business processes as defined by the vertical customer.

- **Hosting Applications:** The provider offers the capability of hosting virtualized network functions or applications, including the activation of the necessary monitoring information for those functions.

In addition to the value provided to external customers, the network slicing does also provide value to the operator for the implementation of its own or internal services and for allowing federating services on demand with other operators. For example, it seems feasible to dynamically create dedicated environments adapted to the characteristics of services that today have to co-exist. The referred services are those like content distribution (e.g., TV, VoD), communication services (e.g., VPNs with distinct purposes such as backhauling, site interconnection, or database transactions), cloud-like services (e.g., for processing capabilities), etc. All these internal services today require in most cases re-architecting the network for accommodating them, including the steering of the traffic among service nodes and the reconfiguration of the forwarding paths supported onto the transport nodes. The expectation with network slicing is to accommodate some specific services on dedicated slices, going in the direction of network adaptation instead of re-architecting it.

Environments Facilitating Network Slicing

Network providers are nowadays deploying cloud facilities, termed NFV infrastructures (NFVI) that will serve to host virtualized network functions (VNFs). An NFVI allows for deploying VNFs in a dynamic way that can be adapted to the specific needs of each requested service. In the case of Telefónica, those capabilities are based on UNICA (Analysys Mason, 2017), the NFVI architecture being globally deployed for all of its operations. The overarching architecture of UNICA is based on cloud concepts to allow large-scale deployment across multiple sites, but also covers provider' needs such as carrier grade performance, scalability, and operational capabilities.

In a generic manner, the NFVI infrastructure will be required to define several types of sites or points of presence along the operator's network to create the topology needed to satisfy the requirements of the services according to their needs in terms of latency, processing capacity, bandwidth, etc. The aim is to distribute workloads efficiently across the network.

New Business Proposition

Taking into account the similarities with the definition of wholesale service offerings today (2018), different situations can be considered when looking at SlaaS, leading to slices with different capabilities, specifically in terms of their management and control capabilities, and how much of them the network service provider hands over to the slice customer or tenant:

- Internal slices, understood as the partitions used for internal services of the provider, who remains in complete control of the corresponding slices and resources allocated to them.
- External slices, being those partitions hosting customer services, appearing to the customer as dedicated networks. In this case, a subsequent distinction applies:

○ Provider-managed slices, meaning that the provider keeps the full control and management of the slice. In other words, the customer can merely use the network resources of the provided slice, without any further capability of managing or controlling them.

○ Tenant[2]-managed slices, implying that the customer has full control of the resources and functions allocated. The tenant has access to a (limited) set of operations and/or configuration actions, and the provider just segregates the infrastructure necessary for that purpose. It is worth noting that the term "infrastructure" is used in the broadest sense that is, including all network functions that the customer can deploy and use on the slice.

It is clear that Tenant-managed slices have to be allocated one per customer, since the customer directly controls it. On the other hand, Provider-managed slices could accommodate different customers sharing the same kind of service in terms of service requirements (bandwidth, latency, number of handled sessions, etc.). Figure 4 presents these different options, illustrating that while the orchestration capability always resides in the provider side, the control of the slice or the service on top of such slice could reside in the provider and/or in the tenant sides depending on the kind of slice.

Requirements for Accomplishing Business Objectives

A number of key requirements can be deemed critical for accomplishing the business objectives as previously described. This sub-section covers some of them.

Figure 4. Types of considered slices and control responsibilities
(Contreras, & López, 2018)

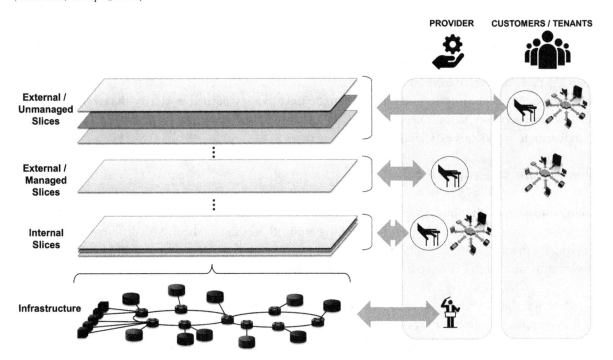

SLA (Service Level Agreement) Management

The assurance of SLAs will become a key aspect of the provisioning of services on top of 5G networks. Acknowledging the relevance of this observation for operator's internal services, this is even more evident when considering vertical customers, who will base their production totally or partially on the negotiated network slice.

Any distortion of the negotiated SLA associated to the network slice can impact not only the technical behavior of the service offered to the end-user of the vertical but also its reputation or business leadership. Even more importantly, such distortion may have legal consequences of any kind due to the incapacity of honoring the contracted service expectations (e.g., in terms of latency, bandwidth, or availability) through the network slice based on the nature of the service. A concrete case could be the result of injured people in a factory or in an assisted driving service because of the misbehavior of the network slice supporting the corresponding service. SLAs then have consequences beyond what sales agreements with strict associated penalties imply.

The negotiated terms of an SLA define a number of service indicators to be satisfied. These service indicators will be translated into network indicators (to be understood in a broad sense, that is, including computing, networking and storage resources) that will be used as inputs for the configuration and the orchestration of resources to form the slice. The deployment of a vertical service will observe interdependencies in the different classes of resources to be provisioned and configured, their location, and their forecasted availability. Furthermore, depending on the class of slice provided (e.g., provider- or tenant-managed), the vertical customer could have direct control of those resources, introducing uncertainty with regards to the future behavior of the assets provided, which may raise some inconsistency issues.

Mechanisms for a timely analysis of the real network situation (including each particular slice) and quick reaction to fulfil an SLA are then required.

High Customization of the Slice

The vertical industries are different in nature, as described before. This implies that operators should deal with a large variety of needs and requirements to accommodate the vertical services, introducing an inevitable high customization at the time of provisioning network slices, tailored to each of the requested services.

The variety of services can be categorized according to different dimensions:

- **Major Type of Requested Service:** The author has already discussed the major types of services to be supported by 5G networks, such as eMBB, uRLLC, and mMTC. Furthermore, some additional types could be considered, such as pure connectivity services (as an evolution of existing corporate communication services, for example), or even NFVI-as-a-Service services (as an evolution of the IaaS kind of services currently available in cloud environments). Finally, the same vertical customer can subscribe to services pertaining to more than one of these major types, and then require some interconnect of the provisioned slices to offer a smooth service experience for the vertical customer.
- **Particular Type of Requested Service:** The major type of services described above can be seen as some kind of macroscopic description of the main characteristics of the service. Beyond such description, particular services will require specific conditions that eventually motivate a distinc-

tion at the time of provisioning the required slice. For instance, latency requirements of uRLLC services can differ allowing for more relaxed conditions in some cases (Cominardi, Contreras, Bernardos, & Berberana, 2018).

- **Vertical Customer Differentiation:** Obviously, a competitive industrial market will look for differentiation as a form of a competitive advantage compared to similar vertical competitors. Then, specific requirements coming from different customers pertaining to the same industrial sector at the time of requesting a network slice can also be expected.
- **Location:** It is also clear that different vertical customers will also have distinct geographical footprints, hence the need for extending the network slice coverage in a different and customer-specific way.
- **Vertical Service Evolution:** Finally, the business of each vertical customer can evolve at a different pace, requiring upgrading and scaling resources at different speeds and with distinct constraints, including the need for invoking various kinds of slice instances over time.

As a consequence, the operator must endow itself with automation mechanisms as a means to simplify and foster the provisioning of the slices. These mechanisms will reside in the orchestration and management artifacts used to handle the resources (either physical or virtual) constituent of the slices. Programmability and virtualization (of functions and infrastructure) will be essential to reduce time to market, which essentially is the same as reducing the time to revenue. They will be essential to guarantee chances of capturing the market of 5G vertical services too, since conventional forms of service provision will not sufficiently scale to support this high customization (in terms of flexibility, speed, granularity, etc.).

Service Segregation

The critical importance of ensuring isolation among the slices provided and supported on top of the same infrastructure has been already mentioned.

The need for service segregation has been satisfied in the past by different means. A very basic option consisted in physically separating network infrastructures, each one being dedicated to enterprise, fixed residential, and mobile services, respectively. This design is clearly neither cost-efficient nor sustainable anymore.

Alternatively, logical separation has been also performed by means of the deployment of overlay solutions, e.g., in the form of VPNs. However, traditional tools and mechanisms for VPN provisioning are neither flexible nor agile, as previously pointed out in the high customization discussion.

Once again, it is required to evolve towards scenarios where dedicated resources (including network functions) can be automatically allocated according to the needs of the service, ensuring isolation, on top of the same infrastructure.

SURVEY ON SLICING INITIATIVES IN STANDARDIZATION

An important number of Standards Development Organizations (SDOs) and some other industrial associations are looking at the network slice concept from different angles and perspectives. From an operator's point of view, there is a risk of fragmenting the conceptual approach to network slices, since small differences can provoke incompatibilities among the different approaches. It is therefore necessary to reach consensus on common terms, definitions, rationale, ideas, and goals in order to properly normalize the network slice concept.

The NGMN Alliance provided a primary description of the network slice concept as mentioned in the introductory section. The NGMN view is that of a 5G slice as a composition of a collection of 5G network functions and specific Radio Access Technology (RAT) settings that are combined for the specific use case or business model while leveraging NFV and SDN concepts. The network slice concept is organized in a layered manner (NGMN, 2016), differentiating the service instance layer, comprising the end-user of business services; the network slice instance (NSI) layer, as a set of functions forming a complete instantiated logical network; and the Resource layer, consisting of both physical and logical resources. In this layered view, the NSIs can be potentially shared among multiple service instances.

The 3GPP differentiates (3GPP TS 23.501, 2017) among network slices and network slice instances. On one hand, a network slice represents a logical network providing specific network capabilities and network characteristics. On the other hand, a network slice instance is defined as a deployed network slice, that is, a specific set of network function instances and associated resources.

ETSI NFV maps some of the ideas of 3GPP onto its own architectural framework (ETSI GR NFV-EVE 012, 2017) concretely the network slice management artifacts defined as Communication Service Management Function (CSMF), which is responsible for translating communication service requirements into network slice requirements and the Network Slice Management Function (NSMF), which is responsible for the management (including lifecycle) of NSIs. These management functions are considered to be part of the OSS/BSS segment in ETSI NFV framework.

The BBF is also approaching network slicing (BBF, 2018) by augmenting the previous management functions by defining new and complementary ones, like Access Network Slice Management (ANSM), Core Network Slice Management (CNSM), and Transport Network Slice Management (TNSM). Each of them is intended to take care of the slice lifecycle management of each particular network slice sub-instance (i.e., access, core, or transport).

Also, ITU-T has defined (ITU-T, 2011) the concept of LINP composed of multiple virtual resources (i.e., abstraction of physical or logical resources), which is actually a realization of a network slice. The LINPs are isolated from other LINPs, having their own programmable control plane and data plane.

Last, the IETF is approaching the ideas of network slicing exploring management frameworks and architectural models (Geng, Qiang, Ordonez, Adamuz-Hinojosa, Ameigeiras, Lopez, & Contreras, 2018).

CHALLENGES FOR NETWORK OPERATORS

The fundamental aspect of network slicing is that each slice will behave as if it were an independent network. Taking this into account, this section describes a list of key challenges from a provider's perspective.

Scalability

Scalability in the context of network slicing exhibits two dimensions: the scalability of the slice itself, and the overall scalability, as a function of the total number of slices.

The first dimension is related to resource allocation and accounting (including resources necessary for satisfying protection and availability), directly related with the kind of service requested and negotiated with the customers. Furthermore, the deployed slices can scale up or down over time, depending on several factors that include commercial success and optimization, e.g., following seasonal demand.

This scalability dimension requires orchestration mechanisms that dynamically add or remove assets to the slice in a consistent manner, based upon either computing or networking capabilities (or a combination thereof). Additionally, on the customer's side, these new resources have to be accounted as part of the provided solution. If the customer is responsible for the control and the management of the provided resources, then those that have been introduced (to scale up) or removed (to scale down) have to be added or removed according to the decisions applied by the control and management functions of the customer. Charging should also be adapted dynamically according to the consumed capabilities at any given time.

The second scalability dimension refers to the global scalability that the operator can support in terms of quantity and types of slices to be orchestrated and managed. A too much fine-grained offering of slices can provoke an unmanageable number of artifacts to be orchestrated by the provider, making them unpractical. Some kind of aggregation or grouping will be needed for achieving tractability. Scalability can be much impacted by the number of external tenant-managed slices offered.

In order to partition network resources in a scalable manner, it is required to clearly define to what extent slice customers can be served or not by an existing slice. A proper application of different SLAs with the translation of service parameters into network ones (including compute needs) will be essential to understand to what extent a new demand can be accommodated with existing slices, from the service point of view. In addition, if the customer requires the responsibility of control and management capabilities, then the customer-specific "individualization" of the slice is a must.

Arbitration

In order to resolve conflicts and to ensure negotiated service levels, the provider needs to incorporate some arbitration mechanisms to allow an efficient usage of resources (including functions), preventing on the one hand resource over-dimensioning, and on the other hand service degradation or disruption. These mechanisms have to be in place not only among the different slices that are being deployed over the same infrastructure, but also within the individual slices themselves (like the three main classes described in the above categorization, as shown in Figure 4), since the relationship between a customer and a slice is not necessarily 1:1 (unlike the external, provider-managed slice case).

Arbitration will have to be applied not only to slice creation or customer activation, but also (and more importantly) when scaling and/or failure events happen, so resources are properly (re-)assigned according to the applicable SLAs. Such inter-slice arbitration may negatively influence the performance of other slices that share the same infrastructure, hence the critical importance of adequate arbitration solutions. Note that SLAs should enclose technical clauses which govern slice availability and the expected maximum duration before getting the slice running as expected. Such clauses need also to be taken into account.

The role of arbitration is to some extent equivalent to the role that existing QoS mechanisms play on current networks. QoS is primarily effective in situations of network congestion, when the availability of resources becomes compromised and their scarcity has to be managed to minimize any kind of impact on the service delivery. Similarly, arbitration needs to be in place when events in the network limit the availability of the resources that compose the different slices supported by the network, or their internal components.

This arbitration capability can collide with the requirement of slice isolation. That is, the arbitration of resources should maintain the principle of isolation among slices, to avoid any kind of degradation or interference from one slice to another, especially when such isolation is imposed by the associated SLA.

The arbitration is foreseen as an internal capability of the operator, transparent to the customer that can influence the decisions and arbitration criteria only through the negotiated SLAs.

Finally, it can be expected that some prioritization could happen in the event of massive failure or outage. The criteria for establishing priorities could be diverse, ranging from the type of service to be ensured, the customers to be protected, the percentage of slice affected, the critical SLAs to be guaranteed, the associated penalties, etc. Commercial, regulation and security aspects could motivate distinct options to be taken into consideration by each operator.

Slice Planning and Dimensioning

Over-dimensioning has often been the default design principle to deploy and operate networks for avoiding any kind of congestion. Through slicing, the location of the traffic sources and destinations becomes much less predictable, if predictable at all. This is especially relevant for the case of external tenant-managed slices, where the final decision of where to deploy traffic sources and destinations (as well as some intermediate service functions that could alter or modify the traffic profile) lies in the hands of the customer.

Two different time scales can be distinguished during these processes: microscopic and macroscopic planning and dimensioning. Microscopic planning and dimensioning refers to the process applied to each individual slice. On the contrary, macroscopic planning refers to the global process applied to the overall infrastructure, including resources and functions.

In the microscopic case, a primary source of information for the dimensioning process will be the SLA agreed with the customer, which specifies the expectations for the service to be provided. A number of network and compute KPIs will be derived from the service parameters expressed in the SLA. These will serve as inputs for determining and tweaking the required resources for honoring the requested service (as well as for identifying engineering parameters of the slice, like redundancy, etc.). This for sure is needed for data plane related resources, but also for control plane resources, including associated licenses or processing needs (e.g., for database dimensioning purposes). A certain level of over-allocation/overbooking can be expected in order to mitigate issues related to unexpected demands, failures, etc. Additionally, some excess could be derived from the resource quantization process (e.g., bandwidth granularity allocated in Gbps units, or licenses allocated in blocks of thousands of users).

The planning in the microscopic case will require some (traffic) forecast inputs from the slice tenant, either internal or external. The formalization of those inputs could vary, from being part of the negotiated SLA (renewed periodically) up to a different/specific administrative process. Adherence to the planned resources derives from a commercial obligation for the operator towards the customer. Then, an assessment of the allocated capabilities should be performed as well. The concept of in-operation network planning (Velasco, Castro, King, Gerstel, Casellas, & López, 2014) can be also assumed as valid for the network slicing case as a means to adjust any kind of resources to the observed demand evolution.

At a macroscopic level, the dimensioning process will take into consideration all the slice demands, the ones already in place plus the slices that are being instantiated. A punctual need coming from an aggregated demand could require borrowing resources from other slices (e.g., capabilities allocated for resource protection purposes) in order to satisfy the overall demand while the operator builds the necessary infrastructure for all the demands. Furthermore, overbooking is certainly an option when the probability of congestion is actually low or the scarcity of resources does not allow for an immediate upgrade of the slice in terms of resources.

The planning procedures will also take into consideration the forecasted evolution of the existing slices plus the evolution of the (marketing and business) plans provided by the commercial and service units. The multi-tenancy approach facilitated by the slicing concept is fundamental to define rational investments for serving the expected demands, but also the programmability and virtualization techniques will be solicited to make a better use of the available resources by reconfiguring services in a flexible manner.

Proper planning, dimensioning, and enforcement are needed to make the transition towards this new form of service sustainable, starting with an appropriate data collection on resource usage, especially the virtual ones which need abstract models for usage reporting.

Multi-Domain

Multi-domain can be interpreted in different ways, since the notion of "domain" can reflect different concepts. For slice provisioning, two meanings are considered: technological domain, taking into account the applicability of slicing to different technologies, and administrative domain, where more than one provider is involved in the provisioning of network slice(s) to a customer.

Slice-based services will necessarily require the integration of different technology domains. The complete end-to-end nature of slices involves distinct computing environments and transport technologies (data switching, optical, etc.), and linking them will require a consistent orchestration approach. For those services making use of radio access technologies, the slice concept has also to be extended to the Radio Access Network (RAN) and the Core Network (CN), with their own slicing specificities (Kaloxylos, Mannweiler, Zimmermann, Di Girolamo, Marsch, Belschner, ... Nikaein, 2018).

The deployment of slices in the networking technological domains will be necessarily different since the forms of traffic segregation are specific to each of the technologies. Furthermore, a combination of logical (e.g., VLAN tag-based in Ethernet systems, label-based in MPLS, etc.) and physical (e.g., lambda-based in optical, slot-based in Flexible Ethernet, etc.) separation methods can be expected. Complementary computing capabilities have to be added with their own form of separation (e.g., hypervisor-based or container-based). The form of combining and integrating them for a single slice will require the combined action of multiple controllers, including an overarching system that maintains a global, systemic view of all the resources, including those that are available.

The interaction with different technologies is clearly fundamental for slice provisioning. Notwithstanding, vertical customers could require no restriction for the slice requested in terms of coverage, service capability, resource constraints, geographical footprint, etc., avoiding any potential limitation of the network provider with whom they have a commercial relationship as their privileged provider. This leads to the necessity of enabling multi-domain slicing, which implies functional and commercial interfaces to be normalized for the sake of massive adoption.

Both business and technical implications can be deemed necessary for such multi-operator slice provisioning context. From the business side, the following implications can be listed:

- **Coordination Models:** There is a need for business coordination to define how multiple stakeholders interact for the provisioning of a multi-domain slice in order to trade low-level resources and elementary services combined and orchestrated to deploy slices end-to-end.

- **Inter-Provider SLAs:** Each provider in each administrative domain should have its own SLA assessment capabilities internally, including interfaces with SLA aggregation components that automate the multi-domain aggregation process.
- **Pricing Schemes:** Bilateral negotiation can be expected as a regular mechanism to establish pricing agreements. Even for simple pricing formulas, the values of the parameters under consideration should be dynamically adapted, e.g., according to demand or resource/service availability.
- **Service Specification and Customer Facing Advertisement:** Each provider may consider not only its own capabilities in its domain but also slice offerings and capabilities available in neighboring domains. Therefore, catalogue synchronization is required to be performed across domains.

From a technical standpoint, implications include:

- **Multi-Domain Orchestrator:** From the provider-to-provider's viewpoint, only certain entities within each domain should interact with each other for handling the inter-domain activities in order to keep the slice provisioning consistent end-to-end. Those entities can be identified as multi-domain orchestrators. This kind of orchestrator will be in charge of abstracting the underlying infrastructure in its domain before it announces (to neighboring providers) what capabilities and functions the operator can provide.
- **Slice Decomposition:** The vertical customer will request a slice to a provider, the latter becoming the origin provider for that customer. The origin provider should then incorporate sufficient logic for decomposing the slices across the different domains.
- **Discovery of Domains:** Although manual configuration can be used, automatic procedures are desirable for speeding up service provisioning in the network softwarized era.
- **Common Abstraction Models:** A common understanding of the description of the resources (i.e., network, compute and storage) and the capabilities per domain is needed.
- **Standard Interfaces, Protocols, and APIs:** These will be required for remote control and management of functions and slices in other domains.

Orchestration and Control of the Slices

The request for network slices that is sent by customers will require the orchestration of resources in order to address the said request. SDN and NFV techniques can be used by an operator to orchestrate slices (Ordonez-Lucena, Ameigeiras, López, Ramos-Munoz, Lorca, & Folgueira, 2017). Such orchestration needs to have full control and visibility of the nodes, topology, functions, and capabilities (such as bandwidth or compute power) to make decisions. Example situations can be found in (Bryskin, Liu, Guichard, Lee, Contreras, Ceccarelli, & Tantsura, 2018).

End-to-end slices are a service management issue. The enablers of management and orchestration are the usage of open and standard interfaces for interacting with the nodes and systems, as well as the definition of normalized models for service and devices. An overview of network management and orchestration can be found in (Contreras, López, Vilalta, Casellas, Muñoz, Jiang, ... Toka, 2018).

The result of the orchestration process is the allocation of the resources, as well as the management of their lifecycle, including service assurance and fulfillment. Then, the constituent blocks of the slice are controlled by the operator.

Different customers can require distinct levels of control for the resources they have requested to the provider. Extreme cases can be customers that do not require any capability of control and management of the allocated assets (just pure communication service), and on the other end, customers requiring full control of their assets. A gradual level of control can be found in between.

Then, the operator should provide configuration and administration capabilities to the customers according to the levels of control that they request. These capabilities could come by simply exposing some interfaces for that required control actions (e.g., APIs), up to granting direct access to the resources (e.g., IP address to access the element console). The more abstracted way, the less invasive for the operator.

3GPP (3GPP TR 28.801, 2017) defines a number of management functions needed to manage network slices to support communication services. These functions are:

- **Communication Service Management Function (CSMF):** Which is responsible for translating the communication service-related requirements into network slice-related requirements.
- **Network Slice Management Function (NSMF):** Which is responsible for the management and the orchestration of an instance of a network slice.
- **Network Slice Subnet Management Function (NSSMF):** Which performs the same task as the NSMF, but at a sub-instance level.

Both NSMF and NSSMF can be considered as functionally similar. ETSI NFV (ETSI GR NFV-EVE 012, 2017) has mapped these management functions with ETSI's NFV orchestration framework. The resulting mapping locates this functionality as part of the broader OSS/BSS components.

Regarding the programmable control of the slices, two levels of SDN control can be considered for a given slice. On one hand, there is the tenant's controller that permits to configure the involved functions. On the other hand, there is the infrastructure controller that is used to program the underlying infrastructure resources to provide end-to-end connectivity. These two levels of control facilitate interplay of actions at both service function and connectivity infrastructure levels, enabling flexibility on the slice instantiation and provisioning, assuming cross-layer coordination.

Figure 5. Service and connectivity control

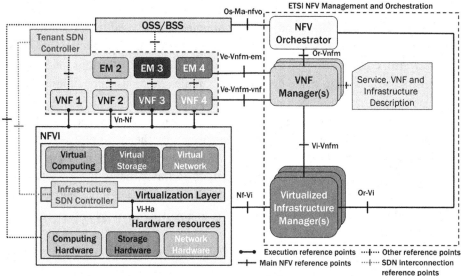

In the NFV framework, such a double control level is proposed in (ETSI GS NFV-EVE 005, 2015) that describes the usage of SDN in NFV environments. Figure 5 shows this approach. The infrastructure controller relates to the Transport SDN controller, while the tenant controller is equivalent to the service controller, as proposed in (Contreras, Bernardos, López, Boucadair, & Iovanna, 2015).

Slice Operation

The operation of slices, once instantiated, share many aspects with conventional networks. However, some new mechanisms and artifacts will be needed. This section considers monitoring and maintenance as relevant aspects of the operation of a network, identifying how the application of maintenance and operational procedures related to a slice can raise new requirements.

Monitoring and performance information is essential for a healthy operation of a network. Monitoring data are usually associated to specific resources, either network ones (e.g., packet errors) or compute ones (e.g., CPU load). This can be complemented with indicators of the service functions that compose the service (e.g., number of active users of the service). Some mechanisms have to be defined in order to properly display and abstract the information for each slice tenant (or user). To this respect, external slices have a higher degree of complexity since the information to be exposed, and the constraints to access it, have to be defined or even better, agreed between the provider and the customers.

At the time of creating a slice, a number of resources are allocated to a given customer. As a consequence, the monitoring information associated to the allocated resources has to be extracted in order to ensure proper operation of the slice. All or some of them will be presented to the customer in order to provide the necessary information. It is important to preserve privacy as the information related to other slices must not be leaked into other slices. The monitoring and performance-related information would also serve as a reference for assessing the compliance of what has been delivered with what has been agreed in the SLA.

Then, the monitoring information has to be properly processed to be provided to the customer (possibly according to a specific format and semantic). Only the information strictly associated to the customer's resources has to be exposed, which implies some filtering on the global indicators. Furthermore, slices can be supported on top of virtual resources. This means that the physical resources can change over time while the virtual ones allocated for the slice will appear as unchanged, even though they may have been, for example, migrated from one virtual machine to another. This implies that the monitoring information could be originated from different sources, thereby requiring dynamic aggregation and association during the slice lifetime.

All the received information has to be processed and correlated in the same manner as in today's legacy networks. This implies the replication of operational procedures per slice, hence raising a scalability issue. Two approaches could be followed: (1) initial processing of all the indicators and further personalization per slice, or; (2) initial separation per slice of the corresponding indicators for further individual processing and correlation. The first approach seems to be more scalable and practical, but requires more coordination and integration from the OSS/BSS point of view.

Slice Marketplace

The interaction with the vertical customers is a critical feature for understanding the needs of the service to be provided. From that interaction, the provider will obtain the necessary information for creating (or reusing) a slice and mapping the customer service to the allocated resources.

The level of detail in the request sent by the customer will impact the functionality required on the provider's side to address such request. The customer requests could be expressed in terms of service or resources. The former will imply that the request identifies the characteristics of the service to be delivered, without any further details about what is needed in terms of resources to be allocated (also known as intent-based requests). In contrast, the latter will imply that the request details the resources identified as needed by the customer. Clearly, the provider should be able to translate the service semantics into resource semantics for the actual allocation of the slice resources, based upon a computation logic that can take into account the outcomes of the possible negotiation between the customer and the provider as input data, but also the network planning policies, the status of the network, its resources, the location of the end-user, whether the end-user is in motion or not, etc.

Different kinds of customers can have different levels of know-how and skills, thereby determining what approach to follow. From the provider's perspective, service semantic requests can allow to reach a broader market, the one formed by vertical customers neither specialized nor skilled in the knowledge of what communication services are needed for their specific business. Considering the type of slices shown in Figure 4, most probably the external, customer-managed slices will be requested through the resource semantics approach, while the external, provider-managed slices will be requested through service semantics. The support of the different slice classes will require a consistent set of abstractions either at service or resource levels to allow the aforementioned semantics to be expressed consistently. As a consequence, proper abstractions and templates have to be defined to ensure the provisioning of a service portfolio providing a consistent view of the network and its resources, as well as their integration with the internal network management and orchestration systems.

Security

In any shared infrastructure, security is a key element to guarantee proper operation to each user. Slice customers must be appropriately authenticated, their rights enforced by authorization mechanisms, and the operations they perform accounted for, so that further auditing can be applied in case of any problem. This becomes crucial when considering the external, customer-managed slices, since the possibility of altering the behavior or status of the allocated functions and resources increases.

Each vertical customer will offer services to his/her end-users thanks to the slices that have been deployed (similar to the current MVNO service offerings). This means that the vertical customer has also the responsibility of enforcing security measures in order to protect the service (and the end-users, indirectly), which affects the security exposure of the allocated resources. The security measures of every vertical customer will be multiple and diverse, thereby requiring the provider to harden the allocated resources in order to prevent whatever issue (e.g., attacks generated from within a slice managed by a tenant). Even if the provider can influence the security implemented by the vertical customer, the control will not be total. Generic guidelines and best (current) practices should be defined and updated according to new threats and security problems as they are met.

Another key issue is the privacy of customer data, as well as the privacy of the end-users' data making use of the service offered by the vertical customer. All this information has to be properly stored and encrypted (whenever applicable) in order to prevent any exposure of such data to the provider in general, or to other customers who use the provider's infrastructure. This is essential when some of the functions and resources can be shared between different customers in the same slice or across slices.

Beyond this, measures have to be in place to proactively detect and mitigate active security attacks, thereby avoiding that a security breach that affects one slice does not propagate into the infrastructure and other slices.

Slice Aging

The same dynamicity for the allocation of slices to tenants, leveraging SDN and NFV techniques, applies as well to the slices' lifecycle. One of the promises of automation is the possibility of invoking and deploying services faster than today, thereby overcoming the currently weak service agility. This facility in the creation of services opens new business opportunities since targeted services, scoping events and situations of short duration, can be made available easily. The duration of the existence of a slice can be certainly variable, so differentiating between short versus long is relative: long slices are those created as a semi-permanent service. Hourly, daily, or even seasonal slices can be considered as short-aged ones.

Furthermore, the frequency at which a given slice is requested can be another timing parameter to be taken into consideration. Depending on the frequency of slice requests, some resources can be freed or should be kept as booked until a new forthcoming service request shows up (that is, the resources may remain unavailable for any other slice request, except for temporary needs, for example).

This dynamic situation (motivated by allocating and freeing resources), implies that whatever the decision or the action made by the operator with respect to using some resources, the operator should consider not only the resource view and status at the time of the specific request but also over a broader timeline, since any decision at the moment of the request can negatively influence future decisions.

Slices based on calendaring considerations (e.g., day/night operation) will need some guarantees, thus motivating a certain level of resource booking. The matching of the resource availability with the time duration request will introduce more constraints as far as resource allocation for slices is concerned.

Whatever the duration of a slice, the creation and operation of a slice will require a non-negligible number of administrative and technical registers. Administrative notifications, data and billing records, systems configurations, etc., are proportional to the number of slices.

A mix of long- and short-lived slices co-existing on top of the same infrastructure should be expected. This will impact providers in several manners, from resource planning (slice demand forecast including traffic and resources to be consumed) to security (data preservation per tenant).

Slice Isolation

This main requirement for isolation constitutes the essential feature any network service provider has to support in order to deliver slices to its customers. The degree of isolation achieved will be critical in determining the ability of a certain provider to address the different classes of slices discussed above, and how they can be requested and used by its customers.

The isolation has to be applied at different levels, such as control plane and data plane isolation, as well as resource and function isolation. Even the sharing of constituent elements within each of these planes can be allowed, the allocated capabilities have to be segregated in order to avoid any kind of misbehavior induced by any other customer in the system.

Data plane isolation can be achieved by several means, and with different degrees. The encapsulation of data in different tunnels, one per vertical customer, can be a primary measure for achieving such isolation in a shared environment. More extreme situations, like strict allocation of assets (as enabled e.g., by the concept of calendar slots in Flexible Ethernet (OIF, 2017)) will allow the exclusive allocation of a specific amount of resources to slices. It will also be possible to find several options with a higher or lower level of isolation.

For the control plane, the separation can be achieved even by supporting such separation in the actual control plane capabilities or alternatively by replicating control plane capabilities dedicated to specific customers per slice. The first approach requires the control plane element to implement such isolation mechanisms, e.g., via the creation of different virtual spaces per customer. The second approach naturally grants isolation since the different replicas act as independent control elements.

A pairing among the form of managing the data plane and the control plane has to be defined. For instance, sharing the data plane capabilities while dedicating control plane ones can be problematic. Multiple replicas of control elements (i.e., hard isolation at the control plane level) acting on the same data plane elements that isolate traffic by means of encapsulation in an overlay model context (i.e., soft isolation at the data plane level) can lead to inconsistencies, hence jeopardizing the isolation.

As for resource isolation, the implications reside in the level of partitioning that the provider is willing to or can implement. Resource isolation can apply to compute nodes, ranging from the dedication of specific compute resources like the bare-metal approach versus the sharing of computing capabilities by means of hypervisors. It can also apply to transport resources, like the allocation of specific lambdas in optical nodes to specific slices versus the accommodation of traffic of different customers carried by the same lambda.

Function isolation will basically consist in the instantiation of separated service function instances per vertical customer versus the sharing of a given service function instance to be used by multiple verticals. An intuitive example could be a firewall. Implications like the number of compute capabilities associated to each option, the connectivity with the rest of the service functions per each customer, the number of licenses to be consumed, etc., have to be taken into consideration.

PROSPECTIVE APPROACHES

This section presents some prospective approaches covering some of the aforementioned aspects.

Slicing Across Multiple Administrative Domains: The 5G-Exchange Project

Even in the existing networks, the majority of the services involve more than one administrative domain, from basic Internet access to services provided by Over-The-Top players, up to inter-domain VPN services deployed for multinational companies. This multi-administrative interaction requires increasing computing capabilities that providers start to offer for internal and external services, and needs solutions for interworking between partners in a standard manner, e.g., for trading and operational procedures as well as resource allocation among providers.

The 5G-Exchange (5GEx) project[3] has developed an architectural framework for multi-domain orchestration among providers that enables the overarching service category of SlaaS. The framework is an extension of the ETSI NFV model for orchestration purposes across multiple administrative domains. Initial steps towards the specification of this model have been reported in (ETSI GR NFV-IFA 028, 2018).

Three are the services that can be provided by 5GEx under the umbrella of SlaaS: (1) the NFVI-as-a-Service (NFVIaaS), where one provider makes a specific amount of infrastructure resources available to another provider; (2) the VNF-as-a-Service (VNFaaS), where one provider makes a number of VNFs available to another provider, and; (3) the enriched connectivity service, where assured quality forwarding paths for medium-to-large traffic aggregates and value-added forwarding paths at the flow level are provided. In all these cases, providers also offer the necessary capabilities for the configuration and the administration of the services provided in the remote domain as part of the service.

The starting point for 5GEx has been the idea of enabling a logical exchange (as an analogy with the physical exchange environments that exist nowadays e.g., for peering purposes) for a global and automated orchestration of multi-domain 5G services. The objective is to enable mechanisms for trading resources (including service functions) together with the necessary orchestration, management, and control capabilities between partnering providers, and which are not necessarily directly and physically interconnected.

Figure 6 shows the high-level architecture of 5GEx. The providers that are involved in the delivery of a service each operate a different administrative domain. The interaction among providers is done through multi-domain orchestrators (MdOs). The MdO is a functional extension of the MANO NFVO used for the orchestration of services across multiple administrative domains.

Each MdO enables the offering of resources of its own domain, and at the same time coordinates the resource and service orchestration in other domains, via the interaction with other MdOs.

Figure 6. 5GEx reference architectural framework

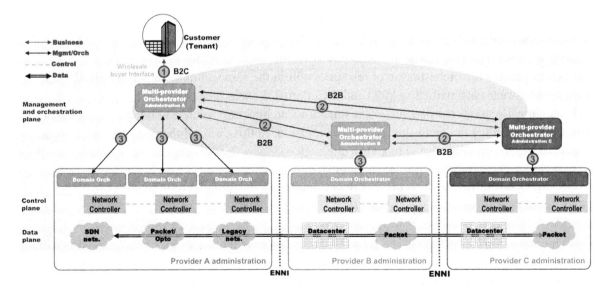

Figure 7. Functional architecture of 5GEx

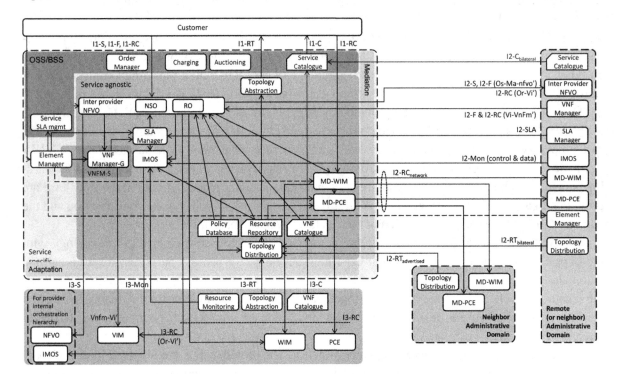

The domain orchestrators in each of the administrative domains are responsible for performing virtualization, service orchestration, and/or resource orchestration within their domain, and the corresponding tasks are coordinated by the MdO. These domain orchestrators use the abstractions exposed by the underlying resource domains according to a variety of technologies, both for network and compute resources.

There are three main interworking interfaces identified in the 5GEx architecture framework. The interface I1, which is focused on Customer-to-Business (C2B) interactions, exposes service specification APIs allowing business customers to specify their requirements for a service to the MdO. The interface I2, which is scoped for Business-to-Business (B2B) relationships, allows the interactions among MdOs of distinct providers to request and orchestrate resources across administrative domains. Lastly, the interface I3 permits the orchestration of resources within the same administrative domain through the interaction between each particular MdO and the internal domain orchestrators.

ThisFigure 7 presents the detailed 5GEx functional architecture where a number of components are identified for enabling the multi-domain SlaaS provision. In this case, all the providers are assumed to support the same components and modules, although in Figure 7, the complete view is only shown for the provider on the left for the sake of simplicity.

Hereafter are briefly described some of the most relevant components of Figure 7. A full description can be found in (5GEx, 2016) (5GEx, 2017).

- The *Inter-Provider NFVO* is the NFVO that implements multi-provider service decomposition, and is responsible for performing the end-to-end network service orchestration. The Network Service Orchestrator (NSO) and Resource Orchestrator (RO) capabilities are contained here.

- The *Topology Distribution* module exchanges topology information with its peer MdOs.
- The *Resource Repository* keeps an abstracted view of the resources at the disposal of each domain reachable by the MdO.
- The *Topology Abstraction* module performs topology abstraction by elaborating the information stored in the Resource Repository and Topology Distribution modules.
- The *SLA Manager* is responsible for reporting the performance of its own partial service graph (that is, its piece of the multi-domain service).
- The *Policy Database* that contains policy information (for instance, topology information to be advertised to other providers).
- The *Resource Monitoring* module dynamically instantiates monitoring probes on the resources of each domain involved in the implementation of a given service.
- The *Service Catalogue* is in charge of exposing the available services to customers and to other MdOs operated by other providers.
- The *MD-PCE* (Multi-Domain Path Computation Element) is devoted to compute traffic-engineered paths and to set up the connections between domains.

From an interface perspective, the functional split is related to service management (-S functionality), VNF lifecycle management (-F), catalogues (-C), resource topology (-RT), resource control (-RC), and monitoring (-Mon). Candidate solutions have been proposed for the implementation of these interfaces in (5GEx, 2016) (5GEx, 2017).

The left MdO is the entry point for a service request coming from the customer, through the I1 interface. Using I1-C, I1-S and I1-F, the vertical customer will be able to request VNF instantiation and configuration, apart from expressing how these VNFs should be chained by means of a service forwarding graph.

The MdO will decompose the service by the NFVO of provider A. The NFVO will make use of resources offered by other providers if provider A cannot satisfy the service needs itself. The availability of resources from other parties is collected via I2-RT, and the availability of services offered by such parties is obtained through I2-C.

The MdO from provider A will make use of I2-S and I2-RC for requesting and controlling the necessary resources and services. This MdO will also make use of I3 interface for governing its own resources accordingly, in a similar manner.

In order to accomplish the negotiated SLA between the parties (both the customer and the entry provider, and the providers participating to the delivery of the end-to-end service), monitoring capabilities are deployed and monitoring information is collected, using I1-Mon, I2-Mon, and I3-Mon for the respective capabilities.

As a reference of the different roles in the exchange, note that provider B (the one in the middle) participates to the delivery of the end-to-end service only by providing data plane connectivity between providers A and C.

Preparing the Network to be Consumed in the Form of Slices: The 5G-TRANSFORMER Project

The delivery of services to vertical customers should be facilitated, so that they do not have to worry about the actual (technological) implementation of a service. The 5G-TRANSFORMER project[4] explores how to progress the current state-of-the- art developing solid and efficient solutions for orchestration and management of the vertical services.

The architectural proposition of the 5G-TRANSFORMER is built upon three major components: (1) Vertical Slicer (VS); (2) Service Orchestrator (SO), and; (3) Mobile Transport and computing Platform (MTP), as represented in Figure 8. These three modules aim to allow any vertical industry to obtain an end-to-end slice tailored to its needs.

The vertical slicer is the common entry point for all the vertical customers into the system. Services for vertical customers are offered through a high-level interface that is designed to allow the verticals to focus on the service logic and requirements, without the need to worry about how they are eventually deployed at the resource level that is, providing service semantics for the service request. The VS offers a catalogue of vertical service blueprints, based on which the service requests are invoked by the vertical customer. After the appropriate translation of service requirements into slice-related requirements, a decision is made at the vertical slicer level on whether the service is included in an already existing slice or if a new one needs to be created. The network slice manager is the core component of the VS, and it is in charge of the lifecycle management of network slice instances.

The vertical slicer is the component of the system that is aware of the business needs of the vertical, its SLA requirements, and how they are satisfied by mapping them with existing slices. In case that one customer is served with more than one slice, a prioritization policy may be enforced between slices delivered to such customer, based upon considerations about the agreed SLA.

The VS sends request towards the SO to create or update the NFV-based network services (NFV-NS) that implement the slices. In turn, such NFV-NS will be created or updated through a Network Service Descriptor (NSD), which is a service forwarding graph composed of a set of service functions (e.g., in the form of VNFs) chained with each other, and the corresponding fine-grained instantiation parameters (e.g., deployment flavor) that are sent to the SO.

Figure 8. 5G-TRANSFORMER system architecture

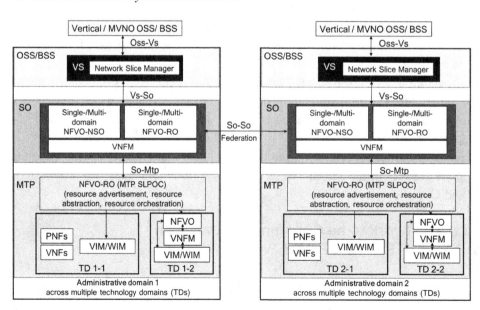

The SO is responsible for providing the end-to-end orchestration of the NFV-NS across multiple administrative domains by interacting with the SOs of other administrative domains, besides interacting with the local MTPs. The SO interacts with SOs of other federated administrative domains in a peer-to-peer fashion to make decisions about the end-to-end (de)composition of virtual services.

Even if a service is deployed across several administrative domains, a vertical customer still uses a single VS to access the system, the one of the primary provider. The federation is opaque to the vertical customer, which has no notion of the multi-domain provisioning resources, since the SO hides this information.

The SO embeds the network service orchestrator (NFV-NSO) and the resource orchestrator (NFVO-RO) with functionalities equivalent to those of a regular NFV orchestrator. Since the slices handled at the VS will in general serve complex end-to-end services, the corresponding network service will be generally a composition of nested NFV-NSs. The lifecycle management of this complex NFV-NS is the role of the NFV-NSO.

Eventually, a resource-related request is generated towards the underlying NFVO-RO to assign virtual resources towards the deployment of the (constituent) NFV-NS. The NFVO-RO functionality of the SO handles resources coming from the local MTP (physical or virtual) and from the SOs of other administrative domains (in an abstracted manner).

The MTP is responsible for the orchestration of resources and the instantiation of VNFs over the infrastructure under its control, as well as for the management of the underlying physical transport network, and computing and storage infrastructures. In general, there will be multiple network/resource segments inside an MTP (e.g., data centers, mobile network, or wide area network).

Regarding the way the customer requests services, the vertical slicer offers Vertical Service Blueprints (VSB) and Descriptors (VSD), enabling the modeling of vertical services by using parameters adapted to the information and capabilities of the vertical (i.e., model services without detailing the infrastructure resources required to support such service). 5G-TRANSFORMER uses an extended version of ETSI NSDs (ETSI GS NFV-IFA-014, 2018) as a notation for network slice templates.

To instantiate a vertical service, a vertical first selects a blueprint, complements the blueprint with the missing information to prepare a VSD. The vertical slicer maps this with an NSD, which describes the network slice for this vertical service. The VSBs are then parameterized versions of VSDs. Details on VSBs, VSDs, and gaps compared to ETSI NSDs can be found in (5G-TRANSFORMER, 2018).

Lightweight Slicing Methods for Limited Environments: The NECOS Project

The multiplicity of services with a variety of properties and characteristics will imply the need for deploying functions and using resources spread across the network. These environments can present episodes of resource scarcity either temporary (e.g., for unexpected events) or almost permanently (e.g., because of limitations on space and energy towards the very edge of the network). Developing forms of creating and operating slices in a lightweight mode is essential to make the infrastructure compatible with these operational situations.

The NECOS project[5] aims to realize an integrated platform encompassing cloud and network management, service orchestration, and distributed resource monitoring to support slicing across cloud capabilities. The target is to propose a lightweight approach for automating the process of optimal cloud slicing configuration, identified as Lightweight Slice Defined Cloud (LSDC). The purpose of LSDC is to automate the process of cloud configuration by creating cloud-based slices across all the available resources in a set of federated data centers. The objective is also to provide a uniform management of the currently separated computing, connectivity and storage resources. The main characteristics of LSDC are:

- Slice-as-a-Service as a service model to be offered to customers. A slice as a grouping of physical or virtual (network, compute, storage) resources can act as a sub-cloud, sub-network and can accommodate service components, seemingly independent of other slices. The management software can dynamically map service components on top of the already available cloud platform features and functions, creating slices on-demand, and (re)configuring them as appropriate to provide the end-to-end service. The slice management takes over the control of all the service components, virtualized network functions and system programmability functions assigned to the slice.

- Configuration of slices across physical resources spanning multiple cloud infrastructures (from large centralized data centers to the computing capabilities located at the edge), in order to better accommodate the various service demands. Adaptation and reconfiguration are done at the slice level, rather than the whole cloud. This configuration is achieved by using specially-designed software that can describe and manage the various aspects of slices within the cloud environment. The actions performed in each aspect that comprises the cloud environment – from the networking between virtual machines, to the SLAs of the hosted applications – are to be managed via software. This reduces the complexity related to configuring and operating the infrastructure, which in turn eases the management of the cloud infrastructure. Such infrastructure tends to expand at large scales, and is commonly composed of thousands of servers and network elements, which support tens of thousands of virtual machines, virtual networks, and applications.

- Lightweight and uniform management and virtualization systems as the target design, with small footprint components, and which can be deployed over a large number of small servers and cloud systems both at the core and the edges of the network. These lightweight elements enable the integration of core data centers and mobile edge into cloud networks.

As service providers offer more applications on the cloud and as consumers' demand increases at an exponential rate, eventually even the largest cloud infrastructure will run out of computing, networking, and storage resources. While cloud infrastructures can be over-provisioned to handle spikes on demand, this is hugely expensive and not scalable.

Figure 9 depicts the platform design that represents the LSCD concept and which exposes interfaces for resource allocation and service deployment purposes. It includes as components the Cloud Manager, the Network Manager, and the Control Element for VMs, and the Service Orchestration.

This view is complemented by Figure 10 which depicts the NECOS native integration of cloud computing and advanced networking enabling cloud networking slicing capabilities in multi-domain scenarios.

CONCLUSION AND FUTURE DIRECTIONS

Network slicing is a promising approach for the provisioning of network services, and it aims to deal with the diversified demand of 5G services with very stringent requirements, and which ambitions to support new wholesale offerings. While leveraging recent but well-established technology substrates such as NFV and SDN seems a straightforward path to achieve network slicing, there are still several

Figure 9. NECOS platform

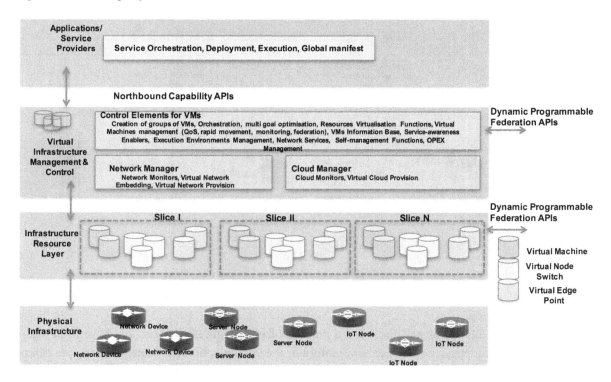

Figure 10. NECOS high-level architecture

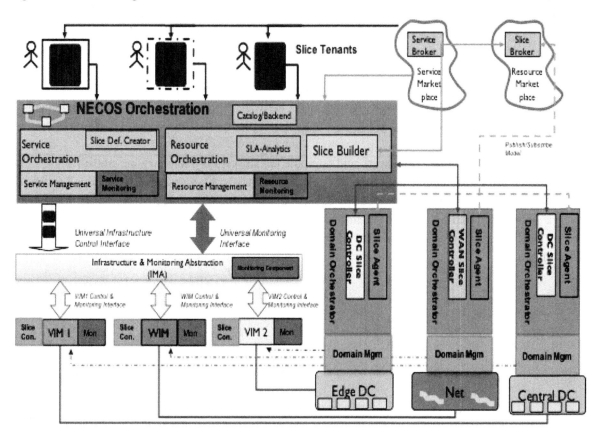

Figure 11. End-to-end slicing of the operator's infrastructure

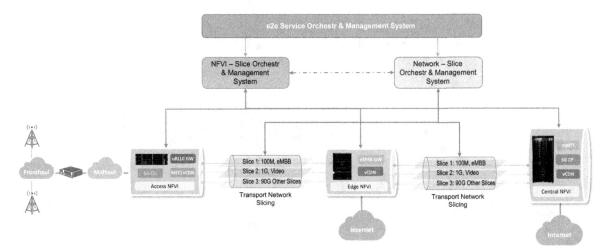

important challenges that have to be addressed to make the concept operationally feasible, viable and deployable for providers.

In this chapter, the author has discussed a number of issues and challenges that have to be taken into consideration for ensuring practical operability of the slicing solutions. Some other points can be equally important, but have not been addressed for the sake of conciseness. These are aspects like the interface between the customer and the provider, details on the interfaces for federating infrastructures, regulation, roaming, charging and billing, etc.

Network slicing is currently more an objective than a reality since the implications of creating a network (the slice) within a network (either physical or virtual) affects all the dimensions of current service delivery procedures. Control, management, and data planes are affected by these changes, thereby making their evolution intricate and inter-related.

The final target can be similar to what is depicted in Figure 11: an infrastructure operated as a network that can host some other networks within, these networks being run and operated independently, with the necessary isolation, and probably in conjunction with other resources and functions offered by alternative providers.

Coordinated orchestration of network and compute capabilities is necessary but not sufficient. The exposure of control and management capabilities to the vertical customers through standard interfaces will be the next step in order to cover the business expectations generated by the broad concept of network slicing. Supporting dynamic means to capture slice requirements will accelerate and ease the slice provision (including foster recursive slice instantiation when multiple domains and providers are to be solicited).

ACKNOWLEDGMENT

This work has been partly funded by the European Commission through the H2020 projects 5GEx (Grant Agreement no. 671636) and 5G-TRANSFORMER (Grant Agreement no. 761536), and EUB project NECOS (Grant Agreement no. 777067). This information reflects the consortia views, but neither the consortia nor the European Commission are liable for any use that may be done of the information contained therein.

REFERENCES

Analysys Manson. (2017). *Telefónica's UNICA architecture strategy for network virtualization*. Retrieved from http://www.analysysmason.com/telefonica-UNICA-architecture-strategy-for-network-virtualisation-report

BBF. (2018). *End-to-End Network Slicing*. SD-406 (work in progress).

Boucadair, M., Lévis, P., Griffin, D., Wang, N., Howarth, M., Pavlou, G., ... García-Osma, M. L. (2007). A Framework for End-to-End Service Differentiation: Network Planes and Parallel Internets. *IEEE Communications Magazine*, *45*(9), 134–143. doi:10.1109/MCOM.2007.4342868

Bryskin, I., Liu, X., Guichard, J., Lee, Y., Contreras, L.M., Ceccarelli, D., & Tantsura, J. (2018). *Use Cases for SF Aware Topology Models*, draft-bryskin-teas-use-cases-sf-aware-topo-model-03 (work in progress).

Cominardi, L., Contreras, L. M., Bernardos, C. J., & Berberana, I. (2018). Understanding QoS applicability in 5G transport networks. *Proc. of the 13th IEEE International Symposium on Broadband Multimedia Systems and Broadcasting*.

Contreras, L.M., Bernardos, C.J., López, D.R., Boucadair, M., & Iovanna, P. (2015). *Cooperating Layered Architecture for SDN*, draft-contreras-sdnrg-layered-sdn-04.

Contreras, L. M., Doolan, P., Lønsethagen, H., & López, D. R. (2015). Operation, organization and business challenges for network providers in the context of SDN and NFV. *Elsevier Computer Networks*, *92*, 211–217. doi:10.1016/j.comnet.2015.07.016

Contreras, L. M., & López, D. R. (2018). *A Network Service Provider Perspective on Network Slicing*. Retrieved from https://sdn.ieee.org/newsletter/january-2018/a-network-service-provider-perspective-on-network-slicing

Contreras, L. M., López, V., Vilalta, R., Casellas, R., Muñoz, R., Jiang, W., ... Toka, L. (2018). Network management and orchestration. In P. Marsch, Ö. Bulakci, O. Queseth, & M. Boldi (Eds.), 5G System Design: Architectural and Functional Considerations and Long Term Research. John Wiley & Sons. doi:10.1002/9781119425144.ch10

Doverspike, R. D., Ramakrishnan, K. K., & Chase, C. (2010). Structural Overview of ISP Networks. In C. R. Kalmanek, S. Misra, & Y. R. Yang (Eds.), *Guide to Reliable Internet Services and Applications*. *Springer-Verlag*. doi:10.1007/978-1-84882-828-5_2

ETSI GR NFV-EVE 012. (2017). *Report on Network Slicing Support with ETSI NFV Architecture Framework*. V3.1.1.

ETSI GR NFV-IFA 028. (2018). *Report on architecture options to support multiple administrative domains*. V3.1.1.

ETSI GS NFV-EVE 005. (2015). *Report on SDN Usage in NFV Architectural Framework*. V1.1.1.

ETSI GS NFV-IFA-014. (2018). *Management and Orchestration; Network Service Templates Specification*. V2.4.1.

Galis, A., Abramowicz, H., Brunner, M., Raz, D., Chemouil, P., & Pras, A. (2009). Management and Service-aware Networking Architectures (MANA) for Future Internet - Position Paper: System Functions, Capabilities and Requirements. *IEEE 2009 Fourth International Conference on Communications and Networking in China –ChinaCom.*

Galis, A., Denazis, S., Brou, C., & Klein, C. (Eds.). (2004). *Programmable Networks for IP Service Deployment*. Artech House.

Geng, L., Qiang, L., Ordonez, J., Adamuz-Hinojosa, O., Ameigeiras, P., Lopez, D., Contreras, L.M. (2018). *COMS architecture*, draft-geng-coms-architecture-02 (work in progress).

5.   GEx. (2016). *5GEx Initial System Requirements and Architecture*. Deliverable 2.1.

5.   GEx. (2017). *5GEx Final System Requirements and Architecture*. Deliverable 2.2.

3.   GPP TR 28.801. (2017). *Study on management and orchestration of network slicing for next generation network* (Release 15).

3.   GPP TS 23.501. (2017). *System Architecture for the 5G System.*

GSMA. (2017). *An introduction to network slicing*. Retrieved from https://www.gsma.com/futurenetworks/wp-content/uploads/2017/11/GSMA-An-Introduction-to-Network-Slicing.pdf

ITU-R. (2015). *IMT Vision – Framework and overall objectives of the future development of IMT for 2020 and beyond*. Recommendation M.2083-0. Retrieved from https://www.itu.int/dms_pubrec/itu-r/rec/m/R-REC-M.2083-0-201509-I!!PDF-E.pdf

ITU-T. (2011). *Framework of network virtualization for future networks*. Recommendation Y.3011.

ITU-T. (2012). *Framework of Network Virtualization for Future Networks, Next Generation Network –future Networks*. Recommendation Y.3011.

Kaloxylos, A., Mannweiler, C., Zimmermann, G., Di Girolamo, M., Marsch, P., Belschner, J., . . . Nikaein, N. (2018). Network Slicing. In P. Marsch, Ö. Bulakci, O. Queseth, & M. Boldi (Eds.), 5G System Design: Architectural and Functional Considerations and Long Term Research. John Wiley & Sons. doi:10.1002/9781119425144.ch8

NGMN. (2015). *5G White Paper*. Retrieved from https://www.ngmn.org/uploads/media/NGMN_5G_White_Paper_V1_0.pdf

NGMN (2016). *Description of Network Slicing Concept*. NGMN.

Odini, M.-P. (2017). *SDN and NFV Evolution Towards 5G*. IEEE Softwarization. Retrieved from https://sdn.ieee.org/newsletter/september-2017/sdn-and-nfv-evolution-towards-5g

OIF (2017). *Flexible Ethernet Implementation agreement*. OIF-FLEXE-01.1.

Ordonez-Lucena, J., Ameigeiras, P., López, D., Ramos-Munoz, J. J., Lorca, J., & Folgueira, J. (2017). Network slicing for 5G with SDN/NFV: Concepts, architectures, and challenges. *IEEE Communications Magazine*, *55*(5), 80–87. doi:10.1109/MCOM.2017.1600935

5G. PPP. (2015). *White papers on vertical industries*. Retrieved from https://5g-ppp.eu/white-papers/

5G. PPP. (2016). *5G empowering verticals*. Retrieved from https://5g-ppp.eu/wp-content/uploads/2016/02/BROCHURE_5PPP_BAT2_PL.pdf

5G. TRANSFORMER. (2018). *Definition of vertical service descriptors and SO NBI*. Deliverable 3.1.

Velasco, L., Castro, A., King, D., Gerstel, O., Casellas, R., & López, V. (2014). In-Operation Network Planning. *IEEE Communications Magazine*, *52*(1), 52–60. doi:10.1109/MCOM.2014.6710064

KEY TERMS AND DEFINITIONS

5G: Fifth generation of mobile systems conceived to support the needs of a hyper-connected society demanding very high data rate access, requiring a wider coverage, and offering an increasing number of almost permanently connected devices.

Network Functions Virtualization: Networking approach that envisages the instantiation of service functions on commodity hardware, breaking the traditional monolithic approach of functional software and hardware.

Network Functions Virtualization Infrastructure: Set of compute, storage, and networking assets hosting and connecting the virtualized service functions as enabled by the NFV architecture.

Network Slice: Logical division of network resources (either physical or virtual) and service functions for different services sharing the same network infrastructure.

Orchestration: Coordination of systems and actions that permit the instantiation of functions and/or the control and allocation of resources in order to compose a network service.

Software-Defined Networking: Networking approach that proposes the decoupling of both the control and data planes in network equipment and logically centralizing that control while leaving the network element to forward traffic, and enforcing policies according to instructions received from a controller.

X-as-a-Service: On-demand instantiation of service X by a given provider, as requested by a customer of such provider.

ENDNOTES

[1]   Some research works introduced seminal ideas on network slicing even before, like (Boucadair et al. 2007), (Galis, Denazis, Brou, & Klein, 2004), (Galis et al., 2009).

[2]   Tenant and customer are used indifferently through the chapter as the consumer of the network slice, as opposed to end-user, which is referred as the user served by the tenant.

[3]   http://www.5gex.eu/

[4]   http://5g-transformer.eu/

[5]   http://www.h2020-necos.eu/

Chapter 7
Future Networks:
Overview of Optimization Problems in Decision-Making Procedures

Nancy Perrot
Orange Labs, France

Amal Benhamiche
Orange Labs, France

Yannick Carlinet
Orange Labs, France

Eric Gourdin
Orange Labs, France

ABSTRACT

This chapter gives an insight into some challenging combinatorial optimization problems that have to be tackled to deliver efficient and appropriate decision algorithms to manage future networks. The first part of the chapter is dedicated to variants of routing optimization problems in future IP networks, and the second part is dedicated to two optimization problems related to network virtualization and 5G network slicing, the virtual network embedding problem and the service function chaining problem. Each of these optimization problems is described along with the main challenges to overcome, and a recent and extensive related state of the art is given, so as to highlight the most recent and promising approaches to solve them.

INTRODUCTION

With the emergence of the Software Defined Networking (SDN) and virtualization techniques, future networks are expected to be more flexible, dynamic, open, and service-oriented. However, this evolution brings new challenging problems to design and manage networks. The virtualization of network functions and the programmability of the control plane will lead to architectures composed of several virtual

DOI: 10.4018/978-1-5225-7146-9.ch007

network layers on top of a shared physical infrastructure, in many network segments. Although a key rule in the administration of large networks is to avoid complexity, mainly so that human administrators can stay in charge, the complexity of the tasks on the one hand, and the constantly improving efficiency and reliability of software on the other hand, will undoubtedly to rely more and more on automated processes. Thus, on the road towards automated networking, many challenging optimization problems have first to be tackled to deliver efficient and appropriate decision-making algorithms.

In this chapter, the authors present some of these optimization problems, essential to deliver and operate robust services on top of the future network architectures. Our purpose is to provide a State-of-The-Art (SoTA) of the optimization and decision-making challenges such as efficient routing and forwarding, physical and virtual resource allocation, and virtual network function placement. Along with the SoTA, an insight on the complexity of the underlying optimization problems is provided.

The chapter is divided into two main parts associated to two major optimization challenges: first, the routing policies in software-defined networks, second the optimization challenges that arise with the emergence of 5G and more generally virtualized networks: the virtual network embedding onto a physical infrastructure and the virtual network function placement and routing in the context of Service Functions Chaining.

ROUTING OPTIMIZATION IN SOFTWARE-DEFINED NETWORKS

In spite of the promises of the MPLS forwarding scheme, most IP networks still heavily rely on shortest-path rules where weights are assigned to links by network administrators and the routers are then able to compute shortest routing paths. It has been acknowledged for a long time that this indirect control (by setting administrative weights only) on the overall routing scheme makes the TE (Traffic Engineering) tasks very difficult to execute. On the contrary, MPLS-based mechanisms allow network administrators to deploy almost any possible routing pattern. However, the introduction of such a powerful tool shifts the problem from "how do I set weights so that traffic uses (more or less) the routes I want?" to a new kind of problem, namely "how do I find the best set of routes?" Indeed, if traffic between any o-d (origin-destination) pair can be forwarded along any combination of paths, deciding the routes for all o-d pairs at the same time seems an intractable problem.

Fortunately, such problems are extremely well solved using sophisticated optimization techniques and powerful algorithmic tools. The rise of SDN is a major opportunity to wisely combine all these optimization approaches in order to derive efficient routing and forwarding policies.

Some Building Blocks

Most of the problems requiring somehow the computation of optimal routes within a telecommunication network can be closely related to well-known and intensively studied problems in optimization and graph theory. The shortest-path problem is one of the most studied problems in graph theory and hundreds of extremely powerful algorithms have been designed in the past to address almost every possible variant (Schrijver, 2002). The so-called multi-commodity flow problem consists in deciding how to send flows in a graph between various pairs of end-nodes (called commodities) and without exceeding the edge capacities (Minoux, 2008). This problem is obviously particularly well-suited to model traffic demands routed within a telecommunication network.

Again, there are many variants of the multi-commodity flow problem. First, many different objective functions have been considered: many of them are concerned with a so-called routing cost, trying to capture in a single objective function the monetary impact of using edges. Another type of objective functions is focused on the edge loads: if f_e is the total flows routed over edge e (resulting from a certain choice of routing strategy) and C_e is the capacity of that edge, then the load is simply defined by $load_e = f_e/C_e$. A very popular model along this line is the Maximum Concurrent Flow (MCF) problem where the commodities have to be routed within the network in order to minimize the load over the most loaded edge. Hence, the MCF model is very well-suited for traffic engineering purposes since it will concentrate all the effort on lowering the load on heavily congested links.

The MCF problem has been extensively studied (Shahrokhi & Matula, 1987, 1990). It can be modeled as a compact LP (Linear Program), using standard arc-flow variables. However, it has been acknowledged as a problem difficult to solve in practice (Bienstock & Raskina, 2002). As a result, non-compact formulations, based on paths, trees or other aggregations of paths, had been proposed and shown to be very efficient, when used within a column generation scheme (Bauguion, Ben-Ameur, & Gourdin, 2015), (Jones, Lustig, Farvolden, & Powell, 1993). Such techniques are efficient for solving large instances of MCF in practice. In a more practical setting, focusing only on the most loaded edge might be a little restrictive. Indeed, the nature of the problem is such that the load on the most loaded edge is minimized, but possibly at the expense of increasing unnecessarily the load on other edges. A way to cope with this issue is to solve several MCF problems in sequence, to reduce as much as possible the load on the most loaded, second most loaded, third most loaded, etc., edges. Another issue to address in practical setting is the length of the routing paths. Assuming there is no congestion and only transmission delays are experienced along the edges, it is wise to check that the end-to-end delays over the paths remain reasonable, or even bounded by some value. Using column generation techniques, one has to check that the delay on the paths produced remains bounded, hence relying on a *Resource Constrained Shortest Path problem* (Beasley & Christofides, 1989; Irnich & Desaulniers, 2005; Karsten, Pisinger, Ropke, & Brouer, 2015).

There are also many variants of multi-commodity flow problems that have tried to restrict the routing possibilities for each demand. One family of such problems is the unsplittable or k-splittable flow problems in which each demand can only be routed, either on a single path, or on at most k paths (Barnhart, Hane, & Vance, 1997; Dinitz, Garg, & Goemans, 1999; Donovan, Shepherd, Vetta, & Wilfong, 2007). Going one step further, many researchers have designed models capturing more closely the engineering constraints imposed by various routing protocols. Some of these models will be detailed in the following sub-sections.

Another important field of research concerns the ability of the network, and potentially the routing strategy, to resist against failures (Grötschel, Monma, & Stoer, 1995). For instance, a significant amount of attention has been devoted to the end-to-end path protection in the literature, especially through the so-called *k-Edge (Node) Disjoint Paths problem*. This problem consists, given an initial network with weights on the edges and a set of origin-destination nodes, in designing a sub-network with k edge (respectively node) disjoint paths between every origin-destination pairs, where *k* is a positive integer, so that the total cost is minimum and survivability to k – 1 failures is consequently guaranteed. Most of the exact approaches proposed for these problems were based on polyhedral results allowing to strengthen the relaxations and leading to cutting plane algorithms (see for instance Magnanti & Raghavan, 2005; Kerivin & Mahjoub, 2005; and the references therein). More recent work focuses on the hop-constrained version of the k edge (node) disjoint problem, thus enabling that a certain level of Quality of Service (QoS), in addition to the survivability, is guaranteed (see Diarrassouba, Mahjoub, Mahjoub, & Yaman, 2018).

Traffic Engineering

One goal of Traffic Engineering is to design mechanisms for better managing network resources and as a consequence, deliver better services. Typically, a major issue in such a context is to find routing strategies such that the experienced traffic flow on links remains significantly below the capacities (maximum allowable bandwidth). There are many other criteria to assess the "quality" of a routing (path lengths, number of hops, costs associated with link usage, etc.), but the load (defined here as the ratio of flow over capacity) is often a good way to capture the quality of a routing scheme. Given a set of information related to the network's current and (forecasted) future status (topology, traffic, TE rules, etc.), a first issue is to derive an approach allowing the computation of an "optimal" routing solution. However, once a theoretical set of routing paths is designed, it still remains to check whether this solution can be realized in practice. Indeed, the way traffic is forwarded in IP networks relies on various routing protocols being more or less restrictive in the choice of allowable paths. This second issue of determining how to effectively deploy routing paths might be quite challenging. To summarize, a Traffic Engineering approach for routing can be decomposed into two steps:

1. **Compute an Optimal Feasible Routing Solution:** Optimal = according to a given set of optimization criteria, feasible = complying with a set of constraints.
2. **Setup the Routing Protocol:** So that the routing paths effectively used in the network correspond to the optimal solution provided in (1).

Note that the optimal solution computed in step (1) might not be compatible with a given routing protocol. One way to reduce this potential flaw of the approach consists in adding some of the routing protocol mechanisms of step (2) into the set of constraints of step (1).

OSPF/IS-IS Traffic Engineering

The "classical" (and still widely used) Interior Gateway Protocols (IGPs) – such as OSPF or IS-IS – allow each individual router to maintain an updated view of the whole Autonomous System (AS) topology and use shortest-paths algorithms (mainly Dijkstra) to build and update its routing table, i.e., the choice of outgoing interfaces to use to reach any destination within the AS. On a broad view, one can consider that the network computes shortest paths for sending the traffic for each origin-destination pair. However, the very concept of shortest-path is obviously related to link length or weights. Assuming a weight w_{ij} is associated to each link (i,j), the shortest path between routers o and d is the path that minimizes the sum of individual link weights:

$$W_{od}^* = \min_{p \in P(o,d)} \sum_{(i,j) \in p} w_{ij}$$

Note that w_{ij} does not necessarily represent a physical quantity. In fact, the administrative weights w_{ij} should be seen as the indirect control the administrator has over the network to implement a set of efficient routes. The control is indirect because the administrator cannot really choose any set of routes, but only routes for which there exists link weights such that each route is a shortest-path. Assuming an optimal set of routes has been computed in step (1), the problem of step (2) is known as the inverse shortest-path problem (Burton & Toint, 1992):

- **Inverse Shortest-Path Problem:** *Given a graph G=(V,E) and a set of paths P=$(p_{od})_{(o,d) \in V \times V}$ find a set of weights $(w_{ij})_{(i,j) \in E}$ such that each path in P is a (unique) shortest-path according to the weights (w_{ij}).*

Despite its apparent complexity, this problem is relatively easy to solve (Ben-Ameur & Gourdin, 2003). Note that the optional term "unique" in the above problem can make quite a difference: the problem is harder, but the solution provided is more practical because it avoids ambiguity between several shortest-paths (only one of them being required).

There have been many attempts to include IGP shortest-path routing constraints within the problem of determining an optimal set of routes (in other words, to solve simultaneously steps (1) and (2) (Bley, 2008; Bley, Fortz, Gourdin, Holmberg, Klopfenstein, Pióro Michałand Tomaszewski, & Ümit, 2010). These attempts are more or less successful, mainly because the associated decision problems are always NP-hard. Other routing extensions proposed by shortest-path routing, such as ECMP (Equal Cost Multi-Paths) that allows balancing the traffic load over several shortest-paths, have also been investigated and massively adopted in practice, but mainly to balance the load among parallel links.

It was observed in (Fortz & Thorup, 2000) that almost optimal routing performances can be achieved while using shortest-path based routing. However, many tasks, such as, avoid temporarily congested links or distribute the load among alternative paths, cannot easily be handled with these routing protocols. Hence, their general lack of flexibility caused the production of a new routing approach.

MPLS Traffic Engineering

The MPLS approach was originally introduced to avoid look-up of complete IP addresses and hence enforce a consistent forwarding policy for all packets within a same flow. The interest of the IP community then quickly shifted to another potential benefit of MPLS networks compared to standard OSPF/IS-IS networks, namely the huge flexibility offered by label switched routing, allowing to push in the network almost any possible routing scheme. However this flexibility came with a cost: the complexity of the route design problem, since everything became possible and the need to rely on some safe and secured automated rules to deploy or update routes within the network. This is the reason why many MPLS-based networks rely mostly on legacy shortest-path based routing protocols to establish their routes, called LSP (Label Switched Paths) with limited additional routes designed by the network administrators.

The flexibility of MPLS is such that solutions provided by most of the routing optimization algorithms (such as MCF, for instance) could be directly deployed as MPLS-based routing schemes. To become fully operational, the solutions provided by optimization algorithms still need to comply with two main additional requirements:

1. Remain efficient (even if somewhat sub-optimal) when the traffic demand evolves over time, and
2. Address the issue of potential network failures, with convergence times compatible with real-life telecommunication services.

Robustness Against Varying Traffic Conditions

One of the main challenges when designing an efficient routing scheme is to implicitly take into account future demand matrices while only past demand is known (or even partially known). In a typical setting, a set Δ_{past} of past traffic matrices is available. There are many ways to use this information for designing a new routing:

- Use a statistical model to derive an estimation of the future traffic matrix D_{future} and run the optimization model with this single matrix;
- Assume all past matrices are likely to appear again and hence run an optimization model taking into account all matrices $D \in \Delta_{past}$. This approach is sometimes tagged as *"conservative"* because the routing scheme is optimized for the worst past situation;
- Since linear models are often used in the optimization approach, the previous case is equivalent to consider any traffic matrix that lies within the convex hull of previous matrices:

$$D_{future} = \sum_{t \in past} \alpha_t D_t \text{ with } \sum_{t \in past} \alpha_t = 1 \text{ and } \alpha_t \geq 0$$

- More generally, the approaches where the routing scheme is optimized for the worst case traffic matrix when the matrices span a compact subset (hyper-rectangle, ellipsoid, polytope,...) can often be successfully handled by "robust optimization" techniques.

In their pioneering work, the authors of (Duffield, Goyal, Greenberg, Mishra, Ramakrishnan, & van der Merive, 1999) propose the "hose model" where upper-bounds are provided on the total traffic leaving and entering the end-nodes. This simple approach was then generalized in (Ben - Ameur & Kerivin, 2005) to take into account any possible linear constraints on the traffic matrix elements, thus leading to a polyhedral description of the uncertain traffic matric region.

The optimal routing obtained in the extreme situation where all possible traffic matrices are taken into account is known as *"oblivious routing"* (Azar, Cohen, Fiat, Kaplan, & Räcke, 2004; Räcke, 2002; Wang, Xie, Qiu, & Yang, 2006). The idea of oblivious routing is to compute a routing pattern that is the best possible for all possible traffic matrices. Consider a matrix demand D and a routing f and denote by FLOW(e,f,D) the resulting flow on edge e. Then the maximum load over the whole network is:

$$\text{MAX-LOAD}(f, D) = \max_e \frac{\text{FLOW}(e, f, D)}{\text{CAPA}(e)}$$

Recall that, given a demand D, the aim of the Maximum Concurrent Flow (MCF) problem is to find a routing f that minimizes the maximum load, and hence, to compute:

$$\text{MCF}(D) = \min_f \text{MAXLOAD}(f, D)$$

The oblivious performance ratio of a given routing f is the worst possible ratio of the maximum load over the optimal load, over all possible demand matrices:

$$\text{OBLIV-PERF}\left(f\right) = \max_{D} \frac{\text{MAX-LOAD}\left(f, D\right)}{\text{MCF}\left(D\right)}$$

Finally, an oblivious routing f_{obliv} is a routing that minimizes the oblivious performance and is therefore a solution of:

$$\text{OBLIV-OPT} = \min_{f} \text{OBLIV-PERF}\left(f\right)$$

It was shown in (Räcke, 2002) that this optimal ratio is of the order of magnitude $O\left(\log^{3} n\right)$ (where n is the number of nodes in the networks), which is rather reasonable, considering that it is the worst case over all possible traffic matrices. A polynomial time algorithm was proposed in (Azar, Cohen, Fiat, Kaplan, & Räcke, 2004) to compute such an oblivious routing. Another polynomial approach is proposed in (Applegate & Cohen, 2006) together with results of extensive numerical experiments showing that the routing solutions obtained in practice are often very efficient (near-optimal). (Applegate & Cohen, 2006) also considered interval restrictions on the demand and some experiments with link failures.

The assumption that any traffic matrix might suddenly appear is somewhat extreme and the main benefit of oblivious routing is to provide worst-case bounds and backup solutions. In practice, it has been observed that traffic matrices follow, most of the time, a very stable pattern. Some rare events might occur from time to time, causing more severe variations. This is why several papers have proposed a mixture of solutions to cope with various situations: for instance, in (Wang, Xie, Qiu, & Yang, 2006), the authors propose a robust approach where the uncertainty set is built around the convex envelope of recently observed traffic matrices. An additional parameter allows the extension of the scope beyond this convex envelope. Some papers have considered this case, especially when a decision made at one time slot has an impact on all consecutive time slots (Amiri & Pirkul, 1999; Ben-Ameur, 2002).

Note that the references cited above, although dealing with traffic uncertainty, mainly address static TE techniques. Actually, this type of approaches takes into account the traffic variations and provides a feasible routing for any possible scenario; it may nevertheless suffer from performance loss for significant deviations from the worst case scenario. Dynamic TE techniques have been proposed to overcome these limitations, and seek for a new routing solution every time a change in the traffic occurs. Examples of dynamic TE include mechanisms based on MATE algorithms (Elwalid, Jin, Low, & Widjaja, 2001) for joint congestion control and traffic engineering. In the recent work presented in (Sanvito, Filippini, Capone, Paris, & Leguay, n.d.), the authors propose an iterative algorithm called Clustered Robust Routing (CRR) which, given a set of TMs (Traffic Matrices) and routing configurations, performs a partitioning of the TMs into the possible routing configurations (clusters) so as to minimize the maximum link utilization. A robust routing is then computed over each cluster and eventually reconfigured in an online fashion if the traffic evolves. The latest work is an example of a semi-static TE approach where a limited number of reconfiguration operations is performed on the network to cope with the traffic variation.

Resilience Against Network Failures

The issue of network element failures has been considered for a long time, as soon as practical telecommunication networks had to be designed and operated. Every new technology comes with protocols or mechanisms to make the network resilient, to a certain point, to failures. The ring topology is often used in backhaul networks because the network remains connected when a node or an edge fails and the rerouting strategy is obvious. The topology information exchanges occurring in IP networks allow each router to be updated on the current network topology and to re-compute shortest-paths when necessary, thereby contributing to maintain the connectivity. However, these operations may take some time that is often incompatible with an efficient service delivery.

It is beyond the scope of this chapter to cover all topics related to network resilience issues. The first issue concerns the topology. There are some minimal connectivity requirements to satisfy during the network design phase to make resilience mechanisms possible. The design of minimal cost topologies exhibiting various connectivity requirements have inspired many research activities (as already mentioned in the building blocks section). Once the topology is defined, the dimensioning phase can take place. In this phase, capacities need to be installed on the network elements (most often, the edges) to ensure an efficient transmission of traffic data. Survivability issues should be also taken into account during this phase, so that sufficient remaining capacities are always available. During the TE phase, the network topology is given and properly dimensioned (although the dimensioning should be adapted to the chosen routing/rerouting strategy). The question then consists in defining a routing OR/AND rerouting strategy that can sustain most failures (or at least, a subset of the most probable failures). Broadly speaking, there are two main streams of approaches: (1) protection approaches, where some actions are taken before the failure occurs and; (2) restoration approaches, where actions are taken after the failure occurs.

The choice of a given strategy is driven by a tradeoff between cost and efficiency: if cost is not an issue, then extremely resilient strategies can be deployed by over-dimensioning the network and duplicating all traffic flows over disjoint paths. On the contrary, if cost matters but efficiency is less important, then standard IGP rerouting mechanisms could be used, but with very slow convergence times and the risk of losing many packets or even connections. In most real situations, both cost and efficiency matter and some wiser mechanisms need to be designed.

There has been several works in the optimization community investigating the problems arising in path protection and restoration for IP/MPLS networks. An example of studies handling local restoration can be found in (Chekuri et al., 2002) where the authors consider several problems of primary and/ or backup allocation in the case of a fixed number k of edge failures and no resource limitation in the base network. The first problem studied is the so-called *Constrained Steiner Network Problem* (CSNP) and consists, given a primary network and a single failure scenario (k=1), in finding for each edge e of this primary network a backup path P(e) with a capacity greater or equal than the capacity of e over all the edges, and such that the total cost of the backup provisioning is minimum. The results obtained for the CSNP problem are extended for k > 1 failures and then for the case of simultaneous primary and backup allocation problems. The authors further address the problem of backup allocation in the case of a primary network having a tree topology. They provide approximation algorithms with worst-case guarantees for these problems. In particular, they present an $O(1)$ approximation algorithm for the backup allocation problem and an $O(log(n))$ (with n being the number of nodes in the base network) approximation algorithm for the simultaneous primary and backup allocation problem. Finally, they show how the single-commodity backup allocation can be used to tackle the online version of the problem, with demands arriving dynamically.

One of the most efficient resilience mechanisms is MPLS Fast-Reroute (Awduche, Berger, Gan, Li, Srinivasan, & Swallow, 2001). Fast-Reroute consists in setting-up, in advance, specific backup paths for each possible failure event. For instance, to prevent the failure of an edge (a,b), a backup path is predefined between a and b. If the edge (a,b) fails, the traffic flowing on this edge is instantaneously switched on the backup path. Defining the backup paths and computing the required capacity amounts to solve another type of optimization problems (Hock, Hartmann, Menth, Pióro, Tomaszewski, & Zukowski, 2013). Another interesting question is to decide how to migrate from one MPLS routing solution to another using the so-called make-before-break paradigm (Józsa & Makai, 2003; Klopfenstein, 2008).

- **Traffic Engineering and Minimum Interference Routing:** *Consider a graph G = (V,E) modeling a network, with V being the set of nodes (routers) and E the set of edges connecting them. Every edge is associated a capacity that is the available bandwidth. Denote by P the subset of nodes possibly generating or receiving traffic requests, and assume that those requests arrive one at a time. Let (s,t) be the current demand. The Minimum Interference Routing (MIR) problem is then to find a routing for (s,t) that minimizes the decrease of the maximum flow for the remaining pairs of P\(s,t).*

The MIR problem has been shown to be NP-hard by a reduction from 3SAT (Kar, Kodialam, & Lakshman, 2000) and most of the works on this problem propose heuristic approaches to solve it. In (Kar, Kodialam, & Lakshman, 2000) and (Kodialam & Lakshman, n.d.), the authors provide an algorithm named MIRA (Minimum Interference Routing Algorithm) which consists, for each arriving demand (a,b), in computing a set of maximum flow values for all the remaining demands and derive a weight system enabling to identify "critical" links then finally use these weights to find an appropriate (shortest path) routing for (a,b). The complexity of MIRA is bounded by one of the max flow algorithms used. In (Figueiredo, da Fonseca, & Monteiro, 2004), the authors provide a heuristic approach named Light MIRA that use a modified version of the Dijkstra algorithm for critical link identification, thus avoiding max flow computation and reducing the worst case complexity.

Traffic Engineering Using Segment Routing

Recent trends in the networking community present Segment Routing (SR) as a promising solution for traffic engineering in networks (Filsfils, Nainar, Pignataro, Cardona, & Francois, 2015). The SR approach consists in splitting the routing/forwarding path between an origin and destination into a sequence of segments in order to allow a better distribution of the traffic and thus avoid congestion due to the over-utilization of some links (see example in Figure 1). In particular, this is done by inserting one or several intermediate nodes, not involved in the shortest paths, between an origin and a destination. Routing within each segment is then performed using the standard shortest path routing algorithms with IGP link weights, either single path or multiple paths routing (namely ECMP). This is referred to by *Segment Routing Domain* the set of nodes in the network having the required capabilities to perform SR. More formally, the TE using Segment Routing problem can be stated as follows:

Figure 1. Illustration of a packet forwarded using two segments s-D-B and B-E-t (green path) while the shortest path (blue) is given by s-D-E-t

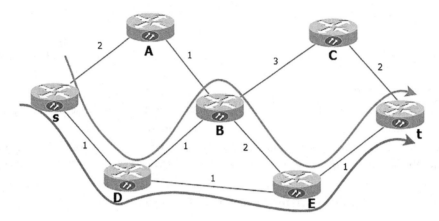

Consider a given graph $G = (V,E)$ representing an IP network, with V being the set of nodes (routers) and E the set of edges (direct links) connecting them. Every edge e is associated with a weight $w(e) \geq 0$ and a capacity $c(e) \geq 0$ being the bandwidth available over the associated link. Let K denote a set of traffic demands, where each element k is defined by an origin node o^k, a destination node d^k and a traffic amount t^k to be routed through the network. For every pair (o, d) and every node u, suppose the (fractional) value $g_{od}^u(e) \geq 0$ is given, which results from the equal cost multiple shortest path computation from o to d using node u. The values g depend only on the graph topology and weights, they do not relate to the traffic amounts. In its general setting, the Segment Routing problem consists in finding for each demand k a set of routing paths using one or several intermediate nodes so as to minimize the maximum link utilization.

As SR implementation details are still being standardized by the IETF, there is a recent interest for the optimization problems arising in SR-based traffic engineering and the associated algorithmic aspects. In (Bhatia, Hao, Kodialam, & Lakshman, 2015), authors address the problem of minimizing the maximum link utilization in a network using 2-segment routing. They study three versions of the problem and use tools from linear programming to solve them. In particular, they address the: (1) *Traffic Matrix Aware Segment Routing,* where a traffic matrix is supposed to be known and the problem consists in finding, for every traffic demand, the 2-segment routing paths using an intermediate node; (2) *Traffic Matrix Oblivious Segment Routing* where a sample of traffic matrixes is used to derive an efficient oblivious segment routing scheme and; (3) *Online Segment Routing* where traffic demands are supposed to arrive dynamically over time. An online algorithm based on a primal-dual scheme is provided for the last problem. A similar modeling and solving approach is proposed in (Bhatia, Hao, Kodialam, & Lakshman, 2015) where failure-aware segment routing is considered for one intermediate node (2-segment routing). The authors first address the case of single path routing where only one link failure can occur at a given time and propose a primal-dual FPTAS (Fully Polynomial Time Approximation Scheme) algorithm for the segment routing problem with restoration. They further show how to extend their results to the case of multiple path routing (ECMP) with Shared Risk Link Group Failures.

A more recent work (Cianfrani, Listanti, & Polverini, 2017) addresses the problem of designing a Segment Routing Domain (SRDD) where cardinality constraints are to be satisfied. This consists, given a graph, a traffic matrix and a maximum *domain* size, in identifying a subset of nodes that should be used as intermediate nodes for a segment routing solution that minimizes the maximum link utilization. In this problem, the demands are not necessarily routed using IGP weights. The identified nodes, along with the associated origin-destination pairs, are candidate to receive the required capabilities to perform their SR functions, while the remaining nodes remain classical IP nodes. The authors propose a 0-1 ILP formulation for this problem and a branch-and-bound algorithm to solve it. They assess the efficiency of their approach by analyzing several indicators including the comparison with a full SR solution (the number of intermediate nodes is not minimized).

Note that recent research provides some features of Segment Routing-based TE implementation via SDN. For instance, in (Davoli, Veltri, Ventre, Siracusano, & Salsano, 2015), the authors propose and implement a network architecture embedding TE and SR modules within a logically centralized SDN controller. Further implementation details for SR are described in (Sgambelluri, Paolucci, Giorgetti, Cugini, & Castoldi, 2015) for networks using SDN techniques (e.g., with nodes being OpenFlow-enabled switches) and within a Path Computation Element (PCE) framework (with nodes being IP/MPLS routers). Both works show through their experiments that Segment Routing based TE is quite suitable for the forthcoming network architectures. Additional analysis on the impact of SDN on routing protocols design can be found in (Gopi, Cheng, & Huck, 2017; Feamster, Rexford, & Zegura, 2014; Kreutz, Ramos, Veríssimo, Rothenberg, Azodolmolky, & Uhlig).

Traffic Engineering in Future Networks

Numerous mathematical models and optimization algorithms are readily available to efficiently handle various situations where the forwarding paths in a given network should be updated in order to better use the available network resources. Instead of running these algorithms in an offline fashion and then push the routing solutions within the network, one could imagine that these algorithms are embedded in a path control element (for instance, an SDN controller or the so-called PCE) that is able to automatically update some routing and forwarding parameters (such as, IGP weights, MPLS LSPs, segments, …) to switch from a current routing pattern to an updated one, better suited to significantly modify network or traffic conditions. Of course, a special care should be paid to maintain as much as possible the stability of the network (which is crucial to provide regular traffic conditions to the end-users), but there is no reason why such a requirement could not be included within the optimization algorithms (for instance, minimizing the number of path modifications, or restricting this number, can be part of the model). On the other hand, if such automated approaches become more and more customary in the management of Wide Area Networks (WANs), then network administrators might become more and more confident to trust them also on a more dynamical setting, similarly to the SON (Self-organizing Networks) mechanisms that are now deployed in the radio access networks.

OPTIMIZATION CHALLENGES IN VIRTUALIZED AND 5G NETWORKS

One of the main objectives of the future 5G networks is to integrate several different services in a common shared physical network in such a way that each service has its own logical network, isolated from the other logical networks. Network slicing allows logically-isolated network partitions, each slice being defined as a unit made of programmable resources such as network, computation, and storage. Thus, network slicing is considered as the key technology to meet the different service requirements on a shared infrastructure composed of heterogeneous equipment. The recent advances in network slicing open a number of algorithmic challenges to operate the future networks: how to deploy and optimize a slice to guarantee the quality of service required by the corresponding services and tenants? How to allocate and share the physical resources to the different slices taking into account the isolation properties? How to design the orchestration policies within each network slice? Once the slices are designed, there are also operational challenges to tackle: how to compose the Virtual Network Functions for each service, how to place them, and how to route the flows so that the service is correctly delivered. These challenges, even considered independently, correspond to complex combinatorial optimization problems.

Forthcoming Mobile Networks and Emerging Services

The next generation of mobile networks promises increasingly intelligent, flexible, and cost-effective solutions to address the massive growth and wide range of traffic demand. They have the ambition to respond to emerging new service types such as enhanced Mobile BroadBand (eMBB), Ultra-Reliable and Low Latency Communications (URLLC), and massive Machine Type Communications (mMTC), along with the related Internet of Things (IoT) services. Hence, future 5G systems have to be capable of efficiently delivering services with different and various requirements, on top of a common infrastructure (Architecture & Group, 2017). Besides, network operators will have to cope with the so-called verticals, with various technical requirements, corresponding to different business domains such as Healthcare, Smart city, Smart Factory, Automotive, or Energy. In order to tackle these challenges, the following design principles were defined for 5G networks: multi-tenancy, scalability by means of shared infrastructure, efficient orchestration of network functions and services, fragmentation of administrative domains. In this context, *Network Slicing* appears as a key concept, inseparable from the deployment of future 5G mobile networks.

Network Slicing

In 5G systems, "network slicing" implements a logically-isolated network partitioning, where a slice represents a unit of combined programmable resource composed of network, computation and storage resources ((NGMN Alliance, 2015), ("22261-g20," n.d.)). Network Slicing is thus a concept that enables the provisioning of dedicated custom virtual networks for different *verticals,* according to their specific requirements in terms of latency, security level or storage capacities for instance ("draft-geng-coms-problem-statement-01 - Problem Statement of Supervised Heterogeneous Network Slicing," 2017).

Once a slice is defined, it corresponds to a *virtual layer,* composed of a set of *virtual nodes* hosting specific network functionalities and interconnected by *virtual links.* Thanks to network slicing, several virtual layers can be instantiated simultaneously and independently from each other, hosted on a common physical network infrastructure. The provider of the physical infrastructure shares and allocates the resources needed to create each slice, determines a set of orchestration policies (e.g., for security or performance requirements) and, in some cases, guarantees the protection against possible failures (redundancy of resources) and/or security against vulnerabilities (with slice isolation). The slice provider may possibly re-configure the slices (notably through an update of its resource provisioning policy), if the technological requirements change throughout its lifecycle, however, intra-slice communications could be managed by the slice tenant.

Several resource allocation stages should be considered for network slicing, at different time scales. At a macro time scale, the physical resources have first to be shared (under fairness considerations or following a priority rule) among the slices, according to their needs and their expected requirements and usage. Actually, efficient resource allocation is a key enabler to realize slicing and covers two mutually dependent problems:

1. **Inter-Slice Resource Allocation:** It consists in finding a mapping of virtual networks onto a common physical infrastructure (see example in Figure 2). This problem is related to the so-called Virtual Network Embedding (VNE) Problem and its variants.
2. **Intra-Slice Resource Allocation:** It consists in assigning the virtual network functions, the service function chains and the request flows of the slice users to the part of the physical resources reserved for this particular slice (see Figure 3). This problem is related to the so-called Service Function Chaining (SFC) Problem.

Then, at micro time scale, dynamic or even real-time allocation strategies should be considered for both inter-slice and intra-slice resource allocation, to react to security breaches and physical failures, to reduce congestion problems and to manage potential slice conflicts/anti-affinities that may not have been previously predicted (scaling and healing).

Figure 2. Inter-slice resource allocation

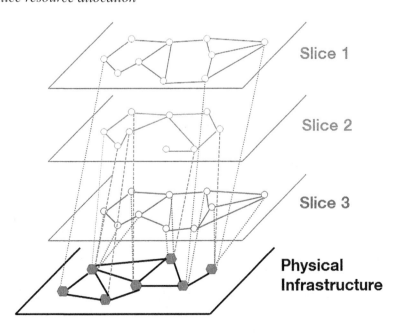

Figure 3. Intra-slice resource allocation

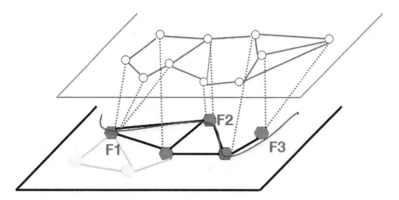

In the next section, the authors detail the Virtual Network Embedding problem and the associated challenges, and provide a review of the recent state-of-the-art for this problem and its variants.

Inter-Slice Management: Virtual Network Embedding Problem

Given a physical *substrate* network and a set of requests for virtual networks (for example, network slices), the VNE problem consists in deciding whether a virtual network request may be *accepted* or *rejected,* and in finding a feasible "mapping" of the accepted virtual networks onto the physical substrate, in such a way that a profit function, usually reflecting the substrate network operator interests, is maximized (see example in Figure 4). In this context, the mapping consists, first, in allocating enough resources within the substrate nodes so as to host the virtual nodes with respect to their technical requirements; second, in assigning every virtual link to one or several routing paths in the substrate network, depending on the strategy applied by the substrate network operator (either *unsplittable* or *splittable* routing). A virtual network request may not be accepted for several reasons, for instance if it is not possible to satisfy some technical requirements, if the resources constraints are too tight, if the different security requirements cannot be accommodated, etc. Nevertheless, this possibly occurs after the completion of a service/slice parameter negotiation cycle. A mapping is said to be feasible if the resources available on the links and nodes of the substrate network can be efficiently shared among the accepted virtual network requests. This specificity is referred to as *admission control.* In case all the virtual network requests have to be satisfied, the problem is to find a substrate resource sharing (that is mapping the virtual nodes and links with the substrate network) among the virtual networks, that maximizes a profit (or minimizes a cost) function.

The Virtual Network Embedding Problem

Given a graph $G = (V, E)$ representing the substrate network, with V being the set of nodes and E the set of edges. Every edge e in E is associated a bandwidth capacity, denoted $C_e \geq 0$ and every node v is associated a set of capacities $C_v^j \geq 0$, where $j = 1 \ldots n$ is the resource type (storage, processing, battery state, etc.). To every node v in V and edge e in E are associated nonnegative profits, denoted p_v and p_e respectively. Those profits correspond to the net revenue received by the substrate network operator from allocating one unit of node or link resource. Now let $G_i = (V_i, E_i)$ be the graph corresponding to the virtual network request i, $i = 1 \ldots m$. To every node v in V_i and link e in E_i is associated a certain

Figure 4. An example of two virtual networks Virtual Network 1 and Virtual Network 2, embedded onto the Substrate Network

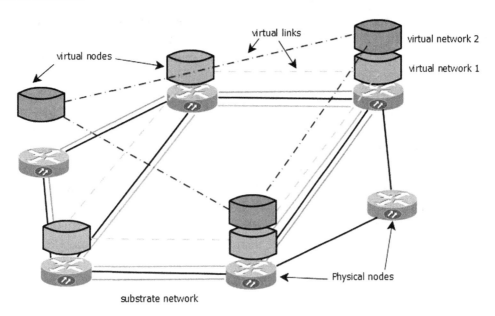

demand denoted d_v and d_e, respectively, in terms of computing resource or bandwidth. In addition, a virtual network can also be associated with a set A_i of *affinity rules,* corresponding to conflict constraints or preferences that possibly forbid packing the virtual nodes of G_i with other virtual nodes.

The VNE problem consists then in finding: 1) an assignment of the virtual network nodes of {G_1 to G_m} into the nodes of G, and; 2) a path in G for every link of {G_1 to G_m}, between the physical assigned nodes of G, such that all the capacity constraints are satisfied and the profit of the mapping is maximized.

Note that this section focuses on the *offline* version of the problem, where all the virtual network requests are assumed to be known in advance, or arrive by batches, and the resources could be reserved in advance.

The offline VNE problem and its multiple versions have received a fair amount of attention in both the network virtualization and Operations Research (OR) communities. This problem is proven weakly NP-hard by a reduction to the 0-1 *knapsack problem* (Coniglio, Koster & Tieves, 2016) while its strong NP-hardness is shown by means of a reduction from the *Maximum Stable Set problem* (Amaldi, Coniglio, Koster, & Tieves, 2016) and is still NP-hard even if a node mapping is given. The latter result follows from a reduction from the *unsplittable network flow problem.* A more recent work extends the state-of-the-art results on NP-completeness for VNE variants including specific node placement, routing or latency restrictions (see (Rost & Schmid, 2018)). Consequently, a large part of the literature addressing this problem develops heuristic algorithms for solving it. In particular, a common approach is to decompose the VNE problem into two blocks, namely *node mapping* and *link mapping*, that are solved independently, as in (Zhu & Ammar, 2006; Mosharaf, Chowdhury, Rahman, & Boutaba, 2009). In (Mosharaf, Chowdhury, Rahman, & Boutaba, 2009), both blocks are solved using deterministic and randomized rounding procedures over the solution of the linear relaxation. A MILP (Mixed Integer Linear

Programming) formulation using path variables and including both node and link mapping constraints is given in (Mijumbi, Serrat, Gorricho, & Boutaba, 2015), and solved heuristically using a column generation algorithm. Further heuristic approaches are presented in (Fischer, Felipe Botero, Till Beck, de Meer, & Hesselbach, n.d.). In (Yu, Yi, Rexford, & Chiang, 2008), the authors adopted an alternative approach; they redesigned the substrate network so as to allow simpler embedding algorithms, while keeping the problem space unrestricted. The approach consists in firstly splitting some virtual links over multiple substrate paths, and secondly in using path migration in order to re-optimize periodically the substrate network when new requests arrive.

Although a significant amount of attention has been dedicated to the VNE problem and its multiple variants, only few papers in the literature propose exact approaches for the problem. Even though exact approaches are often time consuming even on small instances, these are necessary to assess the quality of the solutions provided by heuristic algorithms. Furthermore, exact solving methods often allow deriving near optimal heuristic algorithms. Among the earliest references, the authors can cite the work of (Houidi, Louati, Ben Ameur, & Zeghlache, 2011) that provides a MILP formulation for a VNE problem with multiple substrate networks while minimizing the embedding costs. This formulation is used within an embedding algorithm that handles VN requests arriving dynamically (online VNE). In (Inführ & Raidl, n.d.), the authors propose a multi-commodity flow-based ILP formulation for the VNE problem considering the delay, among other resource constraints, for the forwarding of virtual requests. More recent work in (Coniglio, S., Koster, A., & Tieves Coniglio et al., 2016) addresses the case of uncertainty in Virtual Network requests and proposes a robust optimization approach through an exact Γ-robust MILP formulation that is further used to devise heuristics for larger instances.

- **Energy-Aware Virtual Network Embedding:** Energy-efficiency is one of the many challenges that 5G tackles. Virtualization can benefit energy-efficiency by sharing hardware resources, as opposed to dedicate hardware to each instance. As a consequence, energy can be saved by mapping virtual network resources onto hardware, in a way that allows putting into sleep mode unused hardware. Energy consumption is used in (Botero, Hesselbach, Duelli, Schlosser, Fischer, & De Meer, 2012) and (Fischer, Beck, & De Meer, 2013) as an optimization criterion to be minimized. In particular, authors in (Botero, Hesselbach, Duelli, Schlosser, Fischer, & De Meer, 2012) provide a MILP formulation that minimizes the energy consumption by switching off as many nodes and links as possible. The authors of (Marotta, Kassler, & Zola, n.d.) investigated whether Γ-robustness yields solutions that minimize the total power consumption of the network (through activated nodes and links), when facing demand uncertainties.

- **Considering Failures:** Further studies encompass resiliency or survivability aspects in the requirements for the VNE problem. Among the available references, the authors cite the work presented in (Houidi, Louati, & Zeghlache, 2015) that addresses a version of the VNE problem where three optimization criteria are considered, namely the embedding costs, the power consumption of both the substrate nodes and links, and the load balancing among the hosting substrate nodes. An exact VNE algorithm is provided and used to derive an adaptive algorithm for energy-aware and fault-tolerant cases. In (Zhang, Phillips, & Chen, 2011), the authors provide an exact algorithm for the VNE problem that guarantees enhanced QoS and resilience in the solutions. They propose a MILP formulation including delay constraints and routing constraints that ensure a working and a backup path for every virtual link request in the substrate network.

Interested readers are invited to check the surveys in (Fischer, Felipe Botero, Till Beck, de Meer, & Hesselbach, n.d.) and (Mosharaf, Chowdhury, Boutaba, & Cheriton, 2008), and the references therein, for a comprehensive review of the technical features inducing further versions of the VNE problem.

Once the slices are mapped onto the physical infrastructure, each one must be managed in order to provide the desired services. This intra-slice management includes the precise definition of the services, and the placement of the atomic parts of the services. Then, flows must be routed within this slice. This step is detailed is the next section.

Intra-Slice Management- Service Function Chaining Problem

Intra-slice resource allocation problem consists in finding the optimal placement of VNFs onto the physical resource nodes, and the request routing paths under link and node capacity constraints, so that the overall resource utilization cost is minimized. This optimization problem is related to the Service Function Chaining Problem.

Service Function Chain

Current network services deployed by operators are often composed of several Service Functions (SFs). For instance a VPN (Virtual Private Network) service could be composed of the following SFs: authentication, admission control, firewall, encryption, and traffic shaping, not necessarily in a strict order but some functions are better applied (or must be applied) before others (see Figure 5). For instance, it is better to execute the authentication function first, in order not to overload the other functions if the user fails to authenticate. For a given service, its composition and the order of invoking the atomic SFs that compose this service is called a Service Function Chain (SFC).

SFs being now virtualized, they could be executed in virtual machines deployed in any commodity off-the-shelves servers. Thus, a "softwarized" network architecture, coupled with virtualization, will allow in a near future to manage traffic flows within the network, while deploying the "on-demand" SFs only along the traffic paths when required. The high flexibility arising from these technologies leads to a huge number of possibilities for deploying the network services. A key challenge for operators and service providers is to build the service function chains in an efficient manner, by rationalizing the network, computing, and storage resources.

Figure 5. VPN Service example

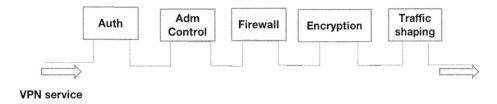

VPN service

The Service Function Chaining Problem

Consider a given graph $G = (V, E)$ representing the network, where V is the set of nodes and E is the set of edges; and traffic matrices that have to be routed on G so as to satisfy requests for a set of given services. Traffic flows pertain to a service, and as such, have requirements for the chain of VNFs that the flows must process. Services may require that the service function chains have strictly ordered VNFs, partially ordered VNFs, or may not require any specific order, and in that case, service function chaining brings little benefit. The nodes in V have both the capability to forward traffic flows, and to host and execute the VNFs. The network nodes have limited capacities in terms of memory, CPU, storage and throughput resources, while VNFs have requirements for the same set of resources. The links have a limited bandwidth capacity. A SFC may also specify anti-affinity rules for some of its VNFs, in order to improve the reliability of the service.

The Service Function Chaining Problem in a pure virtualized network context consists in determining 1) how to place the VNFs of each service onto the network nodes and 2) how to route all the traffic flows of each service through its VNFs, while taking into account the network capacity constraints and the requirements of the service function chains. The objective of the problem is usually a function of the network costs (both installation costs and/or routing costs) to minimize or a function of the routed flows to maximize.

Challenges

The SFC problem could be seen as a variant of the VNE problem, where the service function chains are modeled as point-to-point virtual network requests. However, the SFC problem is quite different from the VNE problem as it should allow mutualizing virtual network functions between several service chains to reduce deployment cost; and it allows considering partially ordered set of functions.

In order to tackle the SFC problem, there are actually three different optimization problems to solve: the service composition, the VNF placement, and the service flow routing problems.

There are usually solved sequentially: first the services are composed, then the associated VNFs are placed onto the physical nodes and finally the flows are routed according to the chain requirements and to the VNFs already deployed in the network. However, the problems are linked to each other as solutions of any of these problems have an impact on the solutions of the others (and could deteriorate the solution cost - as illustrated in Figures 6 a-c), and eventually could lead to unfeasibility of the global problem. Furthermore, each of these problems, even considered separately, represents challenging combinatorial optimization problems.

The challenges that arise for the composition of SFCs are numerous. Indeed, the order of the VNFs must take into account inter-dependencies that can be mandatory in some cases, and recommended in some other cases. Service composition should improve load balancing and QoS indicators, such as one-way packet delay.

Besides service composition, the problem of VNF placement similarly raises a lot of challenging questions. In its simplest form it is related to the well-known Facility Location Problem (FLP). Given a set of facility sites (network nodes) that can be open and a set of demand points to serve from the facilities, the FLP consists in determining the subset of facilities to open, so as to minimize the sum of distances from each demand point to its nearest facility, plus the sum of opening costs of the facilities. The basic FLP is NP-Hard (Krarup & Pruzan, 1983), and its extension to the VNF placement could be hard to solve in practice in large network topologies where there exists a combinatorial number of feasible solutions. In addition, VNF placement should improve reliability of the service. This is done, for instance, with redundancy or anti-affinity rules, so that two critical VNFs are not on a same physical infrastructure, which can be subject to failure. It should also take into account energy consumption, privacy, and performance. Security issues should also be taken into account, leading then to a challenging optimization problem.

Then, once the service is composed and the service VNFs are placed onto the network nodes, the flow routing has to be determined. It is then related to a classical Network Design Problem (NDP) or to a Multi-Commodity Flow Routing Problem (see Traffic Engineering Section). In the NDP, given a weighted graph, the goal is to find a subgraph that connects all original vertices and minimizes the sum of the routing costs between all vertex pairs, subject to a budget constraint on the sum of its edge weights. These problems are NP-complete problems (see Johnson, Lenstra, & Kan, 1978 for NDP). For the routing in the context of a service function chain, these problems have to be extended to take into account the service specificities: the routes should traverse all the VNFs that compose the corresponding service, in the right processing order, and while respecting the technical and topological constraints. In addition, to address service requirements such as low latency, it could be necessary to impose a maximal delay on the end-to-end path or on segment path between two successive functions.

Considering these three decision-making problems embedded in a single joint problem to answer the global SFC Problem is a real challenge: to find a good mathematical formulation that could make sure that a wide range of constraints can be accommodated, and then to propose efficient procedures to solve it in a reasonable timeframe. As a consequence, it is often necessary to rely on heuristics for solving (meaning, finding good solutions) real-life applications.

Example

Figures 6-a, 6-b, and 6-c depict a small network topology composed of 7 nodes, and two requests F_1 and F_2 for two different services: F1 has its origin in node S1 and should be delivered to destination node D1 while processing a Firewall, a Proxy and a DPI SFs; and F2 should be delivered from S2 to D2 while processing a DPI and a Proxy.

Considering that the VNFs are already placed in the network (as the result of a VNF placement algorithm for instance) (see Figure 6-a), the problem reduces to solve a capacitated routing problem with ordered imposed nodes in the path. A solution of this problem is illustrated in Figure 6-b. However, lower cost solutions could be obtained by placing the virtualized network functions only where needed along the flows. Figure 6-c is an illustration of a solution in which both flows and functions are shared so as to minimize both the routing cost and the function deployment cost as a single objective.

Three kinds of approaches, relying on a problem decomposition, are developed in the state-of-the-art: 1) the partial problem studies that consist in treating separately at least one of the three aforementioned problems; 2) the joint VNF placement and routing problem, and finally; 3) the global service function chaining problem, denoted as global SFC optimization.

Figure 6. a) A small network instance with some VNFs already deployed in some networks nodes; b) A routing solution for two SFCs; c) Optimized solution where flows and VNFs are aggregated to minimize the routing and deployment costs

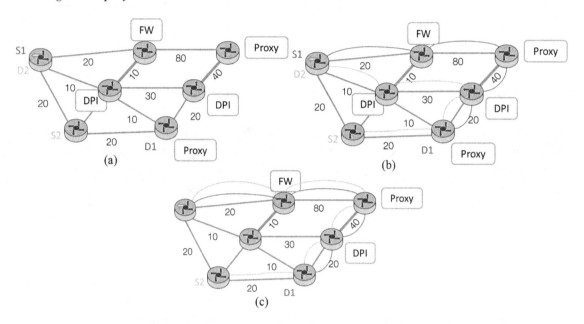

Partial Problem Studies

In the service composition problem, demands from users for particular network services are considered. These network services (i.e., the resulting services of instantiating Service Function Chains) are composed of VNFs. The order of the VNFs in a service function chain can be changed to some extent, and each VNF can have dependencies on other VNFs. Consequently, several different chains can provide the same service. Given the specifications of the network services, and a set of resource constraints, the service composition problem consists in finding the best VNF chain for each user demand. A formulation for this problem as an Integer Linear Programming (ILP) has been given in (Gil-herrera, Isolani, Neves, Zambenedetti, Botero, Barcellos, & Gaspary, 2017). The considered objective function is to minimize the number of VNF instances in the resulting SFC. Scalability issues were not evaluated.

The problem of VM placement in a network of Data Centers is very similar to the VNF placement, except that there is no consideration of Service Chain. In this problem, the aim is to place a set of VMs in a set of Data Centers so as to minimize the communication costs in between the VMs. This problem defines capacities for the DCs (in terms of number of VMs) and for the links between DCs, latencies and costs to transfer data between DCs. Each pair of VMs has a demand in terms of bandwidth and maximum latency. A study of this problem can be found in (Stefanello, Buriol, Aggarwal, & Resende, n.d.), in which the authors extend a formulation of the Generalized Quadratic Assignment Problem (GQAP) with a set of cuts to decrease the solving time.

To solve both the VNF placement and routing problems, several works in the literature relies on a sequential solving approach. First the VNF placement problem is solved and then the request scheduling problem, with additional constraints to force the request flows to go through the previously placed

VNFs. This approach is developed in (Zhang, Xiao, Liu, Lui, Guo, & Wang, 2017), where the objectives are first to minimize the number of computing nodes in service, and second to minimize the average response latency for each service. The authors propose a priority-driven algorithm for VNF placement (inspired by the bin-packing problem), and a heuristic for request scheduling. They evaluate the proposed heuristics with a 50-node graph, 1000 requests and one 6-VNF SFC.

Another sequential approach consists in solving the VNF placement once the flow routing paths are fixed. In (Sang, Ji, Gupta, Du, & Ye, 2017), the authors study the problem of VNF placement, considering fixed service function chains and fixed flow routing. This is a joint problem of placement and allocation, since a decision about where to locate the VNFs is to be made, and also about how to allocate the computing resource to the different VNF instances, in order to process the flows going through the nodes. The authors designed a greedy heuristic for this problem that is asymptotically optimal, when the number of flows is large. They also propose a greedy heuristics for the particular case where the graph is a tree. The authors show that it is optimal. However the scalability of the approach remains to be demonstrated, as only one VNF type was considered, in a 40-node graph and up 400 flows.

Joint VNF Placement and Routing

The studies mentioned in this subsection all tackle the joint problems of VNF placement and routing, but do not consider the issue of service composition. Given a graph, and a set of demands characterized by a source/destination pair with associated required network service, bandwidth and maximum latency, the problem consists in finding the optimal placement of VNFs and routing of demand flows in the graph, so that the VNFs crossed fulfill the required service function chain.

Several objective functions could be considered. In the classical variants it consists generally of the minimization of the VNFs deployment and/or routing costs (as a budget or as an energy consumption function). Two different objective functions are considered in (Addis, Belabed, Bouet, & Secci, 2015): the minimization of the maximum link utilization, in order to prevent risks of bottlenecks due to traffic variations, and the minimization of the number of core CPUs used by the VNF, because it is the main source of energy consumption. The model does not take into account any order of VNF for the demands. (Hmaity, Savi, Musumeci, Tornatore, & Pattavina, 2016) study the joint problems of VNF placement, routing, with resiliency guarantees against node and link failures. The objective function is to minimize the number of VNF nodes. They solve the problem to optimality with an instance with a 14-node graph, 2 service function chains and 2 traffic flows.

In (Huin, Jaumard, & Giroire, 2017), the authors aim at minimizing the bandwidth provisioned for the (fixed) SFC. They model the problem with an ILP and also a decomposition model based on column generation. They solve the problem to optimality for rather large instances (50-node graph, 4 service function chains, 10 000 traffic flows). In (Gupta, Jaumard, Tornatore, & Mukherjee, 2016), the authors also use a decomposition model to solve the problem to optimality in a 14-node graph, with 13 service function chains and 20 traffic flows.

Again, because of the scalability issue, it seems necessary to design heuristic approaches. In (Luizelli, Bays, Buriol, Barcellos, & Gaspary, 2015), the authors formulate an ILP model of the problem. They propose a heuristics based on binary search in order to find the lowest possible number of NFV instances. An efficient heuristic method is proposed in (Mechtri, Ghribi, & Zeghlache, 2016) is based on Eigen decomposition of adjacency matrices. The advantage of this approach is its scalability: it can find a solution for a graph of thousands of nodes, with any number of service function chains. The authors in (Mohammadkhan et al., 2015) present an ILP (Integer Linear Programming) with the following objective function: minimize the bandwidth and CPU core used. They propose heuristics to solve the problem for larger instances. They propose a multi-step greedy algorithm, and solve the ILP iteratively for groups of flows. They claim they can support up to 9000 flows. The authors in (Tastevin, Obadia, & Bouet, 2017) also give an ILP formulation for the problem. The objective function is cost-driven, in which the costs of VNF deployment and operation, and the costs of each hop for the traffic flows, are taken into account. They solve the ILP and they also propose a heuristic based on the graph properties. The authors estimate that their heuristic is 1000 times faster than the ILP and very close to the optimal, on small instances.

Global SFC Optimization

The most general problem of joint service composition, VFN placement and routing is considered in (Allybokus, Perrot, Leguay, Maggi, & Gourdin, 2018). The authors consider that the VNF in a service function chain have a partial order, because some VNFs may depend on others but not necessarily all others. They also introduce anti-affinity rules, so that the chain is more robust in the case of a node failure. The objective is to minimize the operational costs. The authors proposed a greedy algorithm that processes nodes one by one. They also propose a heuristic algorithm based on the linear relaxation of the ILP.

CONCLUSION

The SFC problem is NP-hard, so it does not scale well with the number of flows, the number of different types of VNFs nor with the number of nodes in the network. However, in order to apply the results of research studies on real-life instances, the proposed solutions have to tackle these scalability issues. Indeed, a typical SFC such as for a VPN service for instance, can use more than 10 types of VNFs. A typical network can be composed of several thousands of nodes and the number of simultaneous flows is in the order of tens of thousands for each service. So far, no work has really overcome these issues.

Besides, the objectives of this problem can have a lot of different forms. Some authors consider only the bandwidth provisioned for the service function chains (in average or at the peak), some others consider the number of VNF instances, or the number of CPU cores. They are all valid and useful approaches, however, the most general approach is to attribute a cost for each resource consumed and then minimize the cost globally.

Network Slicing From a Business Perspective

In order to achieve the full technological promise of 5G mobile networks and to offer the expected bandwidth and very constrained QoS requirements while keeping the prices affordable for end-users, 5G operators will have to rely on cost-efficient solutions such as infrastructure sharing with other actors. Indeed, specific partnerships will be established between mobile operators and other mobile operators (MNOs), mobile virtual network operators (MVNOs) leasing capacities from another MNO, over-the-top (OTT) service providers or vertical industries actors (Samdanis, Costa-perez, & Sciancalepore, 2016).

As a consequence, mobile operators have to rethink their strategies and business models in light of these technological advances, so as to sustain competitiveness and profitability.

This question, although very timely, has begun to attract some interest, mainly in the networking community within a network economics framework, including cooperative game theoretical approaches and auction-based models. In (Guo, Liu, Lui, & Jin, 2016), the authors address the problem of bandwidth allocation for Infrastructure-as-a-Service (IaaS) datacenters under fairness considerations. This problem consists, given a set of "tenants" with specific bandwidth requirements that seek to access shared (and limited) resources in datacenter networks, in finding an allocation of the bandwidth to the Virtual Machines (VMs) that satisfies the requirements of each tenant while guaranteeing fairness among the VMs. The authors provide a Nash bargaining game model for the problem and develop two optimization algorithms to solve its offline and online versions, respectively. This work, although focusing on IaaS, gives a methodological framework that may apply to the case of bandwidth allocation for multiple slice requests, provided that the additional constraints like QoS or security requirements are embedded in the model. More recently, the work in (Vincenzi, Antonopoulos, Kartsakli, Vardakas, Alonso, & Verikoukis, n.d.) has considered the strategic aspects behind resource sharing for multi-tenant slicing. In particular, the authors investigate the problem of determining whether it is most profitable for MNOs to deploy their 5G networks independently, or to create a coalition by pooling their resources, using tools from coalitional game theory (a tutorial on coalitional game for communication network could be found in (Saad & Han, n.d.).

In (Samdanis, Costa-perez, & Sciancalepore, 2016) and (Vincenzi, Antonopoulos, Kartsakli, Vardakas, Alonso, & Verikoukis, n.d.), a focus is made on the slicing orchestrator, which is a logically centralized entity (for instance, an SDN controller), and provides the third party (slice tenant) with the management capabilities according to the policy rules defined by the infrastructure owner (e.g., MNOs). This entity is supposed to stand between the infrastructure provider and the slice tenants and can also, define the bandwidth allocation strategy to some extent. In (Vincenzi, Antonopoulos, Kartsakli, Vardakas, Alonso, & Verikoukis, n.d.), this entity is referred to as slice auctioneer and is assumed to manage and allocate bandwidth to the slice requests, while also implementing a billing mechanism (for resource renting purposes). A coalitional game theory model is used to analyze the impact of the slice auctioneer (and resource sharing) on the performance within a slice and the MNOs profit.

Finally, (Yang, Liu, Chou, & Cuthbert, 2017) and (D'oro, Galluccio, Mertikopoulos, Morabito, & Palazzo, n.d.) propose auction-based models for resource allocation management in 5G networks with multiple slice tenants. In particular, authors in (Yang, Liu, Chou, & Cuthbert, 2017) propose an auction mechanism that performs resource allocation while maximizing the network revenue.

CONCLUSION

The arising of SDN and virtualization techniques provides a valuable opportunity to rethink how networks are designed and operated. This chapter illustrates sample key issues for future networks design via a broad range of optimization problems that are challenging from an algorithmic point of view.

Traffic Engineering, although widely studied, still raises numerous questions when considered in the context of future IP networks. Indeed, the rise of SDN offers the possibility to make an efficient use of optimization approaches in order to derive efficient routing and forwarding policies. Several potential challenges can be foreseen to support the evolution of routing mechanisms such as the design of efficient TE algorithms, embedding Segment Routing capabilities. Besides, the future TE mechanisms will have to cope with uncertain traffic demands and handle possible failures. These requirements are quite often associated to NP-hard problems, for which it is still possible to improve the existing optimization approaches.

Network slicing is the key for enabling 5G networks to fulfill its design principles, namely multi-tenancy, scalability by means of shared infrastructure, efficient orchestration of network functions and services, fragmentation of administrative domains. The challenges associated with network slicing can be divided into two components: inter-slice management (which is described as a VNE problem) and intra-slice management (which is described as an SFC problem).

In spite of the growing recent literature on virtual networks embedding and on service function chaining problems, there are still important optimization challenges to cope with before being able to efficiently manage future virtualized and 5G networks. One of the main challenges concerns the scalability of the optimization techniques to deal with dense network topologies (for instance in the context of IoT use cases), and with multiple slice types with various requirements. Some of these requirements, like the isolation property, should still be formalized to be taken into account in the optimization models. Another challenging area will be to adapt the optimization models adequately.

REFERENCES

22261. g20. (n.d.).

Addis, B., Belabed, D., Bouet, M., & Secci, S. (2015). Virtual network functions placement and routing optimization. *2015 IEEE 4th International Conference on Cloud Networking (CloudNet)*, 171–177. 10.1109/CloudNet.2015.7335301

Allybokus, Z., Perrot, N., Leguay, J., Maggi, L., & Gourdin, E. (2018). Virtual function placement for service chaining with partial orders and anti-affinity rules. *Networks*, *71*(2), 97–106. doi:10.1002/net.21768

Amaldi, E., Coniglio, S., Koster, A., & Tieves, M. (2016). On the computational complexity of the virtual network embedding problem. *Electronic Notes in Discrete Mathematics*, *52*, 213–220. doi:10.1016/j.endm.2016.03.028

Amiri, A., & Pirkul, H. (1999). Routing and capacity assignment in backbone communication networks under time varying traffic conditions. *European Journal of Operational Research*, *117*(1), 15–29. doi:10.1016/S0377-2217(98)00162-3

Applegate, D., & Cohen, E. (2006). Making routing robust to changing traffic demands: Algorithms and evaluation. *IEEE/ACM Transactions on Networking*, *14*(6), 1193–1206. doi:10.1109/TNET.2006.886296

Architecture, P. P. P., & Group, W. (2017). View on 5G Architecture (Version 2.0).

Awduche, D., Berger, L., Gan, D., Li, T., Srinivasan, V., & Swallow, G. (2001). *RSVP-TE: Extensions to RSVP for LSP Tunnels*. RFC Editor.

Azar, Y., Cohen, E., Fiat, A., Kaplan, H., & Räcke, H. (2004). Optimal oblivious routing in polynomial time. *Journal of Computer and System Sciences, 69*(3), 383–394. doi:10.1016/j.jcss.2004.04.010

Barnhart, C., Hane, C. A., & Vance, P. H. (1997). Integer Multicommodity Flow Problems. *Network Optimization*, 17–31. doi:10.1007/978-3-642-59179-2_2

Bauguion, P.-O., Ben-Ameur, W., & Gourdin, E. (2015). Efficient algorithms for the maximum concurrent flow problem. *Networks*, *65*(1), 56–67. doi:10.1002/net.21572

Beasley, J. E., & Christofides, N. (1989). An algorithm for the resource constrained shortest path problem. *Networks*, *19*(4), 379–394. doi:10.1002/net.3230190402

Ben-Ameur, W. (2002). Multi-hour design of survivable classical IP networks. *International Journal of Communication Systems*, *15*(6), 553–572. doi:10.1002/dac.551

Ben-Ameur, W., & Gourdin, E. (2003). Internet routing and related topology issues. *SIAM Journal on Discrete Mathematics*, *17*(1), 18–49. doi:10.1137/S0895480100377428

Ben-Ameur, W., & Kerivin, H. (2005). Routing of Uncertain Traffic Demands. *Optimization and Engineering*, *6*(3), 283–313. doi:10.100711081-005-1741-7

Bhatia, R., Hao, F., Kodialam, M., & Lakshman, T. V. (2015). Optimized network traffic engineering using segment routing. *Proceedings - IEEE INFOCOM*, *26*, 657–665. doi:10.1109/INFOCOM.2015.7218434

Bienstock, D., & Raskina, O. (2002). Asymptotic analysis of the flow deviation method for the maximum concurrent flow problem. *Ser. B*, *91*, 479–492. doi:10.1007101070100254

Bley, A. (2008). Routing and capacity optimization for IP networks. *Operations Research Proceedings*, *2007*, 9–16. doi:10.1007/978-3-540-77903-2_2

Bley, A., Fortz, B., Gourdin, E., Holmberg, K., Klopfenstein, O., Pióro Michałand Tomaszewski, A., & Ümit, H. (2010). Optimization of OSPF Routing in IP Networks. In A. Koster & X. Muñoz (Eds.), *Graphs and Algorithms in Communication Networks: Studies in Broadband, Optical, Wireless and Ad Hoc Networks* (pp. 199–240). Berlin: Springer Berlin Heidelberg; doi:10.1007/978-3-642-02250-0_8

Botero, J. F., Hesselbach, X., Duelli, M., Schlosser, D., Fischer, A., & De Meer, H. (2012). Energy Efficient Virtual Network Embedding. *IEEE Communications Letters*, *16*(5), 756–759. doi:10.1109/LCOMM.2012.030912.120082

Burton, D., & Toint, P. L. (1992). On an instance of the inverse shortest paths problem. *Mathematical Programming*, *53*(1–3), 45–61. doi:10.1007/BF01585693

Chekuri, C., Gupta, A., Kumar, A., Naor, J., Raz, D., & Kleinberg, J. (2002). *Building Edge-Failure Resilient Networks*. Academic Press.

Cianfrani, A., Listanti, M., & Polverini, M. (2017). Incremental Deployment of Segment Routing into an ISP Network: A Traffic Engineering Perspective. *IEEE/ACM Transactions on Networking*, *25*(5), 3146–3160. doi:10.1109/TNET.2017.2731419

Coniglio, S., Koster, A., & Tieves, M. (2016). Data Uncertainty in Virtual Network Embedding: Robust Optimization and Protection Levels. *Journal of Network and Systems Management*, *24*(3), 681–710. doi:10.100710922-016-9376-x

D'oro, S., Galluccio, L., Mertikopoulos, P., Morabito, G., & Palazzo, S. (n.d.). *Auction-based Resource Allocation in OpenFlow Multi-Tenant Networks.* Retrieved from http://mescal.imag.fr/membres/panayotis.mertikopoulos/files/OpenFlowAuction.pdf

Davoli, L., Veltri, L., Ventre, P.L., Siracusano, G., & Salsano, S. (2015). Traffic engineering with segment routing: SDN-based architectural design and open source implementation. *Ieeexplore.ieee.org, 2015*(1).

Diarrassouba, I., Mahjoub, M., Mahjoub, A., & Yaman, H. (2018). *k-node-disjoint hop-constrained survivable networks: Polyhedral analysis and branch and cut.* Academic Press. doi:10.100712243-017-0622-3

Dinitz, Y., Garg, N., & Goemans, M. X. (1999). On the single-source unsplittable flow problem. *Combinatorica, 19*(1), 17–41. doi:10.1007004930050043

Donovan, P., Shepherd, F. B., Vetta, A., & Wilfong, G. (2007). *Degree-constrained network flows.* Academic Press.

draft-geng-coms-problem-statement-01 - Problem Statement of Supervised Heterogeneous Network Slicing. (2017). Retrieved from https://tools.ietf.org/pdf/draft-geng-coms-problem-statement-01.pdf

Duffield, N. G., Goyal, P., Greenberg, A., Mishra, P., Ramakrishnan, K. K., & van der Merive, J. E. (1999). A flexible model for resource management in virtual private networks. *Computer Communication Review, 29*(4), 95–108. doi:10.1145/316194.316209

Elwalid, A., Jin, C., Low, S., & Widjaja, I. (2001). MATE: MPLS adaptive traffic engineering. *Proceedings IEEE INFOCOM 2001. Conference on Computer Communications. Twentieth Annual Joint Conference of the IEEE Computer and Communications Society (Cat. No.01CH37213), 3*, 1300–1309. 10.1109/INFCOM.2001.916625

Feamster, N., Rexford, J., & Zegura, E. (2014). The Road to SDN: An Intellectual History of Programmable Networks. *ACM Sigcomm Computer Communication, 44*(2), 87–98. doi:10.1145/2602204.2602219

Figueiredo, G. B., da Fonseca, N. L. S., & Monteiro, J. A. S. (2004). A Minimum Interference Routing Algorithm. *IEEE International Conference on Communications, 4*(c), 1942–1947. 10.1109/ICC.2004.1312859

Filsfils, C., Nainar, N. K., Pignataro, C., Cardona, J. C., & Francois, P. (2015). The segment routing architecture. *2015 IEEE Global Communications Conference, GLOBECOM 2015.* 10.1109/GLOCOM.2015.7417124

Fischer, A., Beck, M. T., & De Meer, H. (2013). An Approach to Energy-efficient Virtual Network Embeddings. *Integrated Network Management (IM 2013), 2013 IFIP/IEEE International Symposium on*, 1142–1147.

Fischer, A., Felipe Botero, J., Till Beck, M., de Meer, H., & Hesselbach, X. (n.d.). *Virtual Network Embedding: A Survey.* Retrieved from http://www.fim.uni-passau.de/fileadmin/files/lehrstuhl/meer/publications/pdf/Fischer2013a.pdf

Fortz, B., & Thorup, M. (2000). Internet traffic engineering by optimizing OSPF weights. *Proceedings IEEE INFOCOM 2000. Conference on Computer Communications. Nineteenth Annual Joint Conference of the IEEE Computer and Communications Societies (Cat. No.00CH37064), 2*, 519–528. 10.1109/INFCOM.2000.832225

Gil-herrera, J., Isolani, P. H., Neves, M. C., Zambenedetti, L., Botero, J. F., Barcellos, M. P., & Gaspary, L. P. (2017).. . *Security of Networks and Services in an All-Connected World, 10356*, 62–76. doi:10.1007/978-3-319-60774-0_5

Gopi, D., Cheng, S., & Huck, R. (2017). Comparative analysis of SDN and conventional networks using routing protocols. *IEEE CITS 2017 - 2017 International Conference on Computer, Information and Telecommunication Systems*, 108–112. 10.1109/CITS.2017.8035305

Grötschel, M., Monma, C. L., & Stoer, M. (1995). Design of Survivable Networks. *Handbooks in Operations Research and Management Science, 7*, 617–672. doi:10.1016/S0927-0507(05)80127-6

Guo, J., Liu, F., Lui, J. C. S., & Jin, H. (2016). Fair Network Bandwidth Allocation in IaaS Datacenters via a Cooperative Game Approach. *IEEE/ACM Transactions on Networking, 24*(2), 873–886. doi:10.1109/TNET.2015.2389270

Gupta, A., Jaumard, B., Tornatore, M., & Mukherjee, B. (2016). *Multiple Service Chain Placement and Routing in a Network-enabled Cloud*. Retrieved from http://arxiv.org/abs/1611.03197

Hmaity, A., Savi, M., Musumeci, F., Tornatore, M., & Pattavina, A. (2016). Virtual Network Function placement for resilient Service Chain provisioning. *Proceedings of 2016 8th International Workshop on Resilient Networks Design and Modeling, RNDM 2016*, 245–252. 10.1109/RNDM.2016.7608294

Hock, D., Hartmann, M., Menth, M., Pióro, M., Tomaszewski, A., & Zukowski, C. (2013). Comparison of IP-based and explicit paths for one-to-one fast reroute in MPLS networks. *Telecommunication Systems, 52*(2), 947–958. doi:10.100711235-011-9603-4

Houidi, I., Louati, W., Ben Ameur, W., & Zeghlache, D. (2011). Virtual network provisioning across multiple substrate networks. *Computer Networks, 55*(4), 1011–1023. doi:10.1016/j.comnet.2010.12.011

Houidi, I., Louati, W., & Zeghlache, D. (2015). Exact multi-objective virtual network embedding in cloud environments. *The Computer Journal, 58*(3), 403–415. doi:10.1093/comjnl/bxu154

Huin, N., Jaumard, B., & Giroire, F. (2017). Optimization of network service chain provisioning. *IEEE International Conference on Communications*. 10.1109/ICC.2017.7997198

Kreutz, D., Ramos, F., Veríssimo, P.E., Rothenberg, C. E., Azodolmolky, S., & Uhlig, S. (2015). *Software-Defined Networking: A Comprehensive Survey*. Academic Press. doi:10.1109/JPROC.2014.2371999

Inführ, J., & Raidl, G. R. (n.d.). *Introducing the Virtual Network Mapping Problem with Delay, Routing and Location Constraints*. Retrieved from https://rd.springer.com/content/pdf/10.1007%2F978-3-642-21527-8_14.pdf

Irnich, S., & Desaulniers, G. (2005). Shortest Path Problems with Resource Constraints. In *Column Generation* (pp. 33–65). New York: Springer-Verlag; doi:10.1007/0-387-25486-2_2

Johnson, D. S., Lenstra, J. K., & Kan, A. H. G. R. (1978). The complexity of the network design problem. *Networks*, *8*(4), 279–285. doi:10.1002/net.3230080402

Jones, K. L., Lustig, I. J., Farvolden, J. M., & Powell, W. B. (1993). Multicommodity network flows: The impact of formulation on decomposition. *Mathematical Programming*, *62*(1–3), 95–117. doi:10.1007/BF01585162

Józsa, B. G., & Makai, M. (2003). On the solution of reroute sequence planning problem in MPLS networks. *Computer Networks*, *42*(2), 199–210. doi:10.1016/S1389-1286(03)00189-0

Kar, K., Kodialam, M., & Lakshman, T. V. (2000). Minimum interference routing of bandwidth guaranteed tunnels with MPLS traffic engineering applications. *IEEE Journal on Selected Areas in Communications*, *18*(12), 2566–2579. doi:10.1109/49.898737

Karsten, C. V., Pisinger, D., Ropke, S., & Brouer, B. D. (2015). The time constrained multi-commodity network flow problem and its application to liner shipping network design. *Transportation Research Part E, Logistics and Transportation Review*, *76*, 122–138. doi:10.1016/j.tre.2015.01.005

Kerivin, H., & Mahjoub, A. R. (2005). Design of Survivable Networks: A survey. *Networks*, *46*(1), 1–21. doi:10.1002/net.20072

Klopfenstein, O. (2008). Rerouting tunnels for MPLS network resource optimization. *European Journal of Operational Research*, *188*(1), 293–312. doi:10.1016/j.ejor.2007.04.016

Kodialam, M., & Lakshman, T. V. (n.d.). Minimum Interference Routing with Applications to MPLS. *Traffic Engineering*.

Krarup, J., & Pruzan, P. M. (1983). The simple plant location problem: Survey and synthesis. *European Journal of Operational Research*, *12*(1), 36–81. doi:10.1016/0377-2217(83)90181-9

Luizelli, M. C., Bays, L. R., Buriol, L. S., Barcellos, M. P., & Gaspary, L. P. (2015). Piecing together the NFV provisioning puzzle: Efficient placement and chaining of virtual network functions. *Proceedings of the 2015 IFIP/IEEE International Symposium on Integrated Network Management, IM 2015*, 98–106. 10.1109/INM.2015.7140281

Magnanti, T. L., & Raghavan, S. (2005). Strong formulations for network design problems with connectivity requirements. *Networks*, *45*(2), 61–79. doi:10.1002/net.20046

Marotta, A., Kassler, A., & Zola, E. (n.d.). On the energy cost of robustness for green virtual network function placement in 5G virtualized On the Energy Cost of Robustness for Green Virtual Network Function Placement in 5G Virtualized Infrastructures. *Computer Networks, 125*, 64–75. doi:10.1016/j.comnet.2017.04.045

Mechtri, M., Ghribi, C., & Zeghlache, D. (2016). A scalable algorithm for the placement of service function chains Djamal Zeghlache. A scalable algorithm for the placement of service function chains. *IEEE eTransactions on Network and Service Management*, *13*(3), 1–14. doi:10.1109/TNSM.2016.2598068

Mijumbi, R., Serrat, J., Gorricho, J.-L., & Boutaba, R. (2015). A Path Generation Approach to Embedding of Virtual Networks. *IEEE eTransactions on Network and Service Management*, *12*(3), 334–348. doi:10.1109/TNSM.2015.2459073

Minoux, M. (2008). *Programmation Mathématique. Théorie et Algorithmes*. Lavoisier.

Mohammadkhan, A., Ghapani, S., Liu, G., Zhang, W., Ramakrishnan, K. K., & Wood, T. (2015). Virtual function placement and traffic steering in flexible and dynamic software defined networks. *IEEE Workshop on Local and Metropolitan Area Networks*. 10.1109/LANMAN.2015.7114738

Mosharaf, N. M., Chowdhury, K., Boutaba, R., & Cheriton, D. R. (2008). *A Survey of Network Virtualization*. Retrieved from https://cs.uwaterloo.ca/research/tr/2008/CS-2008-25.pdf

Mosharaf, N. M., Chowdhury, K., Rahman, M. R., & Boutaba, R. (2009). Virtual network embedding with coordinated node and link mapping. *Proceedings - IEEE INFOCOM*, 783–791. doi:10.1109/IN-FCOM.2009.5061987

NGMN Alliance. (2015). *NGMN 5G White Paper*. Retrieved from https://www.ngmn.org/uploads/media/NGMN_5G_White_Paper_V1_0_01.pdf

Räcke, H. (2002). Minimizing Congestion in General Networks. *Proceedings of the 43rd IEEE Symposium on Foundations of Computer Science*, 43–52.

Rost, M., & Schmid, S. (2018). *NP-Completeness and Inapproximability of the Virtual Network Embedding Problem and Its Variants*. Retrieved from http://arxiv.org/abs/1801.03162

Saad, W., & Han, Z. (n.d.). *Coalitional Game Theory for Communication Networks : A Tutorial*. Academic Press.

Samdanis, K., Costa-perez, X., & Sciancalepore, V. (2016). *From Network Sharing to Multi-Tenancy: The 5G Network Slice Broker*. Academic Press.

Sang, Y., Ji, B., Gupta, G. R., Du, X., & Ye, L. (2017). Provably efficient algorithms for joint placement and allocation of virtual network functions. *Proceedings - IEEE INFOCOM*. doi:10.1109/INFO-COM.2017.8057036

Sanvito, D., Filippini, I., Capone, A., Paris, S., & Leguay, J. (n.d.). *Adaptive Robust Traffic Engineering in Software Defined Networks*. *Academic Press*.

Schrijver, A. (2002). *Combinatorial Optimization: Polyhedra and Efficiency*. Springer Berlin Heidelberg.

Sgambelluri, A., Paolucci, F., Giorgetti, A., Cugini, F., & Castoldi, P. (2015). SDN and PCE implementations for segment routing. *2015 20th European Conference on Networks and Optical Communications, NOC 2015*, 1–4. 10.1109/NOC.2015.7238607

Shahrokhi, F., & Matula, D. W. (1987). On solving large maximum concurrent flow problems. In *Proceedings of the 15th Annual Conference on Computer Science, St. Louis, Missouri, USA, February 16-19, 1987* (pp. 205–209). ACM. 10.1145/322917.322949

Shahrokhi, F., & Matula, D. W. (1990). The Maximum Concurrent Flow Problem. *Journal of the Association for Computing Machinery*, *37*(2), 318–334. doi:10.1145/77600.77620

Stefanello, F., Buriol, L. S., Aggarwal, V., & Resende, M. G. C. (n.d.). *A New Linear Model for Placement of Virtual Machines across Geo-Separated Data Centers*. Academic Press.

Tastevin, N., Obadia, M., & Bouet, M. (2017). A graph approach to placement of Service Functions Chains. *Proceedings of the IM 2017 - 2017 IFIP/IEEE International Symposium on Integrated Network and Service Management*, 134–141. 10.23919/INM.2017.7987273

Vincenzi, M., Antonopoulos, A., Kartsakli, E., Vardakas, J., Alonso, L., & Verikoukis, C. (n.d.). *Multi-tenant slicing for spectrum management on the road to 5G*. Retrieved from https://upcommons.upc.edu/bitstream/handle/2117/111753/IEEE WCM Slicing 5G 2017.pdf

Wang, H., Xie, H., Qiu, L., & Yang, Y. (2006). COPE: Traffic engineering in dynamic networks. *ACM Sigcomm*, 99–110. doi:10.1145/1151659.1159926

Yu, M., Yi, Y., Rexford, J., & Chiang, M. (2008). Rethinking virtual network embedding: Substrate support for path splitting and migration. *Computer Communication Review*, *38*(2), 19–29. doi:10.1145/1355734.1355737

Zhang, Q., Xiao, Y., Liu, F., Lui, J. C. S., Guo, J., & Wang, T. (2017). Joint Optimization of Chain Placement and Request Scheduling for Network Function Virtualization. *Proceedings - International Conference on Distributed Computing Systems*, 731–741. 10.1109/ICDCS.2017.232

Zhang, X., Phillips, C., & Chen, X. (2011). An overlay mapping model for achieving enhanced QoS and resilience performance. *2011 3rd International Congress on Ultra Modern Telecommunications and Control Systems and Workshops (ICUMT)*, 1–7.

Zhu, Y., & Ammar, M. (2006). Algorithms for Assigning Substrate Network Resources to Virtual Network Components BT. *Infocom IEEE International Conference on Computer Communications*.

KEY TERMS AND DEFINITIONS

5G Standardization: The fifth generation of mobile network is currently (2018) in the process of being standardized by 3GPP (3rd generation partnership project). The IETF (internet engineering task force) is also working on a lot of topics closely related to 5G networks, namely overlay networks, traffic engineering, service function chaining, etc.

ILP Formulation: An integer linear programming (ILP) formulation is the mathematical formulation of an optimization problem in which variables are restricted to integer values and the constraints and objective function are linear. Mixed integer linear programming (MILP) refers to optimization problems in which some of the variables are continuous.

Optimization Problem: A problem that is described by: a set of parameters (inputs of the problem), a set of continuous or discrete decision variables, a set of constraints (in the form of equalities or inequalities over the parameters and variables), and an optimization criterion that is expressed as an objective function to be optimized. The goal is to find the best solution of the problem, that is the values of the variables that optimize (i.e., minimize or maximize, depending on the problem) the objective function, among all the feasible solutions (the solutions that fulfill the set of constraints).

Optimized Routing: A routing pattern in an IP network that optimizes a given criterion (end-to-end one-way delay, network load, cost, etc.) while complying with a set of constraints.

Shortest Path: A path in the network between an origin node and a destination node that minimizes the sum of the weights of its composing edges.

Survivable and Robust Networks: A network is said to be survivable if it implements one or several protection mechanisms allowing for resilience against link or node failures. The notion of robustness can be used for fault-tolerance but refers more often to the ability to effectively cope with uncertainties about traffic (or other input data).

Traffic Engineering: A set of mechanisms for better managing network resources and performance in order to deliver better services.

Chapter 8
Dynamic and Scalable Control as a Foundation for Future Networks

Zoran Despotovic
Huawei, Germany

Xun Xiao
Huawei, Germany

Ramin Khalili
Huawei, Germany

Maja Curic
Huawei, Germany

Artur Hecker
Huawei, Germany

ABSTRACT

The authors see problems with current network control models. Their control networks (i.e., control channels, necessary for control operation) are not thought of as part of the control model itself. Current network control is not transactional. Network updates are neither atomic nor isolated, and the application is not aware of the details of an update outcome. This chapter presents an alternative design in which the control channel is an integral part of the network control model. Its key part is a robust, in-band resource connectivity layer that interconnects all available network elements, including the controller(s). The control is also transactional. Applications can safely assume that their updates will not clash in the network, as well as that they will always affect the right, intended fraction of the network. Building on these two postulates, the authors see service scheduling as its third essential part of network control. The scheduling takes service requirements into account and assigns the services network resources that will meet their requirements.

DOI: 10.4018/978-1-5225-7146-9.ch008

INTRODUCTION

Network systems are becoming more and more customizable and programmable. This change has been exemplified through the development and the adoption of the three key technologies: Software-Defined Networking (SDN), Network Function Virtualization (NFV) and Service Function Chaining (SFC). NFV leverages virtualization technologies to implement Network Functions (NFs) on general purpose hardware platforms, in order to enable rapid creation, removal, or migration of NFs. SFC enables operation of composite services by steering traffic through an ordered set of network functions, thus providing network operators with the ability to more easily introduce new services and dynamically customize/change their runtime operation, e.g., to enforce various traffic forwarding policies for the sake of optimization. In that context, SDN emerges as an important automation and dynamicity enabler. As a technology that promotes programmability of transport network devices, it provides support for the said automation in the lower layers of the protocol stack.

Even though the three technologies exhibit important differences, often seeing the network from different angles (e.g., either merely using the network as is or rather interfering with the basic network primitives), the acquired levels of flexibility and efficiency, built on these three pillars, would represent a significant departure from the conventional networks, which are typically built upon closed hardware silos interconnected through overlays laid upon static, manually configured transport networks.

The authors believe that, taken together, SDN/NFV/SFC depict contours of the next network transformation: in this view, network becomes an execution environment (runtime) for requests of various kinds and requirements. In this chapter, the authors broadly refer to such requests as "jobs". Such jobs could be, classically, to transport bits from point A to point B, possibly with transformations of the bits on the fly (e.g., header and address changes, filtering, compression), and, more generally, it could involve in-network processing of all bits and generation of replies. SFC, through both standardization efforts within the IETF (notably in the IETF SFC WG) and the ongoing academic research, sets up a model for what such jobs can be, and shows how the job execution progress is encoded and communicated in a chain of nodes that collaboratively execute it. In this light, SDN and NFV present the underlying network as a pool of resources that are to be instructed to execute individual parts of the entire job.

The upcoming 5G presents a perfect deployment environment for the just outlined vision. The three technologies, SDN/NFV/SFC, are current hot candidates for the realization of network slicing (An, et al., 2016), recently standardized by the 3GPP in their initial 5G-relevant Release 15 (TS23.501, 2017). Indeed, instead of simply defining a new particular system architecture, 5G bets on system flexibility. Release 15 supports finer-grained modularization, allows different flavors of standard-equivalent modules and opens up mobile systems of the future for the possibility to dynamically scale-in and scale out modules in operation. In particular, a network slice is a public land mobile network (PLMN) service, however composed not of standard physical entities, but instead of network functions that could be of different flavors and different realizations. In this way, the very same 5G infrastructure could be shared by several seemingly independent PLMNs corresponding to different business requirements. The proposed finer-grained modularization, the existence of the different flavors of network functions and their instantiation in different numbers of instances (scale-in and -out) ultimately all lead to an explosion of number of overall active modules in the system and the paths between them, every single one of which could play a critical role in the particular service provisioning.

In a simple view, NFV platforms could create, deploy and start/stop all the necessary 5G modules as virtual network functions (VNF), while specially crafted SDN control applications on an SDN controller could be used to route flows between those VNF instances. Note however that both the interactions between such individual VNFs and the performance of each VNF instance in the 5G scope should be better than best effort. Problem is that both recent NFV and SDN specifications and the popular NFV and SDN implementations do not directly support guarantees; in particular, they do not so far have any assurance mechanisms in their own realizations, raising doubts with respect to their suitability for 5G realizations, especially at the projected typical 5G scales.

From a resource-specific angle, the question of effective network slicing solutions comes up (Sciancalepore, Samdanis, Costa-Perez, Bega, Gramaglia, & Banchs, 2017). While SDN, NFV and SFC provide frameworks for handling VNFs, paths, etc. in a particular service-specific ordering, the attribution of resources to a request is an orthogonal question. Highly related to the question of assignment of requests to running flow paths and instances, this question has become the main focus in the cloud operating systems of major cloud providers (Boutin, Ekanayake, Lin, Shi, Zhou, Qian,. . . Zhou, 2014; Verma, Pedrosa, Korupolu, Oppenheimer, Tune, & Wilkes, 2015), because it has a potential for huge cost savings and quality of experience improvement.

Trying to answer both questions above, contrary to the state of the art, in the authors' view, a network slice in operation is nothing else than a set of service function chains with particular extra-functional end-to-end requirements, deployed and (re-)dimensioned by a non-real time, relatively slow network management loop, with a runtime scheduling process trying to satisfy all particular requirements of the incoming jobs by: a) making sure that the walkthrough of individual functional blocks fulfills the job functional requirements and; b) assigning them to appropriate active service functions on selected resources making sure that the end-to-end extra-functional requirements are respected. Hence, the so-called service scheduling, i.e., scheduling of networked jobs on the available network resources, emerges as a first critical issue. It should be noted that service scheduling is different from the virtual network embedding (VNE) (Guerzoni, Trivisonno, Vaishnavi, Despotovic, Hecker, Beker, & Soldani, 2014; Fischer, Botero, Beck, de Meer, & Hesselbach, 2013), a relatively well-addressed topic in the literature the goal of which it is to decide, which virtual resource (e.g., a virtual machine or a path between nodes) should be assigned to which physical resource(s) (a number of servers or physical links) in the deployment phase. In other words, VNE solves the problem of an initial deployment of network function instances and paths between them on a set of interconnected network resources. Note that VNE could in principle deploy hundreds of equivalent NF instances, just as well as it could deploy virtual networks with path redundancy. In contrast, the task of service scheduling, as introduced here, is the runtime assignment of jobs (i.e., flows with specific processing requests) to already deployed, active service functions, i.e., to usable paths and running NF instances, as derived from a job classification (e.g., per policy at the ingress node). In other words, while VNE might consider, which virtual machines should be deployed on which physical compute nodes according to some initial service understanding and planning, the service scheduling will have to choose an appropriate running virtual machine instance (among potentially many equivalent ones) to serve an actual incoming request.

The second critical issue is that such scheduling has to be network-suitable, i.e., in particular scalable and highly distributable in the implementation. The background of this is that networks, due to their geographic reach and span, are typically built from many relatively simple entities spread over a large area; hence they do not integrate well with over-centralization paradigms, requiring a unique view, centrally available and fresh state information, and the like. To this end, multiple scheduler instances should be supported in the network, e.g., collocated with the packet classifiers, access nodes or some other suitable network resources, "close" to the incoming service requests. All such scheduler instances should (loosely) cooperate to provide the expected result with the necessary scalability. Indeed, synchronization of such multiple schedulers is critical both to acquire a correct decision base and to eliminate typical distributed system artefacts due to incomplete or concurrent execution. The accent here lies on the loose synchronization; such synchronization cannot be too tight, as it would challenge scalability. A loose state synchronization can be implemented by a common yet distributed data layer (as provided by e.g. scalable databases and key value stores like NoSQL, Cassandra, DHT technologies), specifically designed for large networks with possible huge geographical footprints. Such technologies are already used in this scope, notably to enable the so-called eventual consistency of the distributed SDN control planes (e.g., ONOS uses Cassandra to eventually synchronize the states of the individual FloodLight SDN controllers it is using). In turn, the support for reliable, possibly concurrent, operations of schedulers on the same pool of entities distributed over a large area might require some form of conflict avoidance, conflict resolution and conflict recovery mechanisms, currently lacking in the merging SDN and NFV implementations. The support for such may be realized through appropriate, tunable adoptions of atomicity, consistency, isolation and durability mechanisms (ACID principles), well-known from database management systems (Gray & Reuter, 1992), and the adaptation of their implementation to the particular environment of programmable networks.

Last but not least, to be able to make and enforce scheduling decisions, it is necessary to interconnect the resources and schedulers. Depending on the scheduling mechanisms in place, the schedulers (or, seen from another angle, runtime resource controllers) therefore require a reliable, fault-tolerant and low latency communication service to communicate with any concerned network entity, the underlying resource and, if required, with one another. To increase the efficiency of scheduling, fixed assignments of resources to schedulers might turn out to be limiting; indeed, due to the dynamic nature of SFC provisioning and statistical job arrivals, it is hard to reasonably and precisely predict, how resources will be involved in the jobs, and how they should be clustered to which schedulers. In particular, the authors believe that making a separate, out-of-band network for only that purpose (as tacitly assumed in most current SDN and NFV implementations) would be prohibitively expensive and would contradict the central point of virtualization, which postulates that required resource should scale with the actual service load and not with the number of deployed services. Thus, a highly adaptive, scalable and tolerant in-band control solution that operates as a logically isolated networked system from the same resource pool, in the common infrastructure, yet providing the desired level of quality of control, is needed. To distinguish the service-specific control from the more general, resource related tasks of the latter control solution. This control solution is called a controllability layer. This distinction is novel yet handy in software networks, characterized through their acquired capability of supporting several behaviors on a common resource pool, undefined at the moment of the infrastructure deployment: while in legacy networks, the composition of different network entities yielded a particular network service (e.g., mobile networks as compositions of MME, HSS, SGW/PGW, and PCRF boxes to fixed enterprise networks as compositions of hubs, switches and routers), therefore mixing resource and service specific control, in any software network, the very same infrastructure can be used for radically different network services.

This chapter presents the above vision in more details. Note that it reflects work in progress; the authors do not claim to already have all the answers; instead, depending on the respective work progress, the authors either provide solutions and proofs, limit to arguments and justifications, or, at the very least, corroborate intuition for how this vision could and should be realized. Together, the presented ideas sketch the future software networks technologies: embracing the full network virtualization (as opposed to the host virtualization employed so far) enabled through ubiquitous resource control, these should support a seamless and autonomous resource integration and cut off, a rapid service deployment, up- and downscaling and a dynamic and efficient sharing of a dynamically composed, yet common-purpose infrastructure resource pool between radically different network services, tenants and the like. The autonomous integration and adaptation of both the resource pool and of the service implementations on top of the latter must make sure to not increase the operational expenses; the dynamic service provisioning will provide the market agility, so often sought after by the infrastructure operators; finally, the efficient, integrated and automatic scheduling together with network-wide request-to-resource multiplexing should reduce the overall overprovisioning in the infrastructure, i.e., in fine, both the capital and the operational expenses related to the required resources.

The authors start with details of how to interconnect resources and create the controllability layer integrating a common, shared data layer. Then, the authors delve into the conflict avoidance aspects and introduce transactional network control. Finally, the authors provide theoretical motivation for why runtime service scheduling could be a game changer on the way towards elastic and highly customizable networks of the future.

CONTROLLABILITY LAYER

The foundation, on which the entire architecture is built, is a resource interconnection layer. In principle, there are many existing algorithms and protocols that could be suitable for the purpose of such a resource interconnection, routing and messaging between the nodes. In order to provide a shared data layer, additional data sharing organization protocols could be integrated on top. Moreover, to limit the overall configuration effort, the related work in e.g. peer to peer systems and auto-stabilization bears a plethora of approaches for node discovery and scalable autonomic operations. However, straightforward integrations of complex systems do not always yield an optimal result and sometimes fail to achieve a goal, as was shown in the areas of peer to peer protocols in mobile ad hoc networks (MANETs), TCP over wireless, etc. For this reason, trying to prepare the ground for other suitable solutions, a list of requirements for this controllability layer is presented. Then a protocol crafted to fulfill major requirements is introduced. Yet again, other solutions remain possible, and the main point here is not to advocate for any specific solution, but: (a) to motivate the need for such a controllability layer and; (b) to show that such a controllability layer is indeed feasible at large scales.

Requirements

Primarily, the intended controllability layer must provide highly resilient and low latency communication paths between the concerned nodes in the network, while at the same time remaining relatively simple in order not to steal valuable compute and storage resources from the resource nodes. To establish communication paths between nodes on bigger scales, routing and message forwarding provisioning are needed. Given that an in-band deployment of the resource interconnect layer is targeted, i.e., its provisioning through the very same infrastructure, its consumption of the network bandwidth and of local compute resources should be modest. The resilience of the interconnection here refers to both security and reliability of the established communications. Notably, the reliability refers to the resistance to or recovery from such events as failing or non-responding nodes, ports or network interfaces, failing or overloaded paths and links, etc. The security aspect refers to the authentication of endpoints as belonging to the same network control realm, to their authorization for the intended actions and the protection of integrity and confidentiality of the included messages. These requirements are not particularly new. Similar requirements have driven the research on secure routing, MANET routing, etc.

An interesting new requirement is related to the support of radically different network densities. Routing protocols usually exhibit a specific structure of the resource interconnection, dictated by, in the simplest case, the topology of the physical network, but also by its scale, span and, in more complex use cases, the intended goal. For instance, RSTP (Rapid Spanning Tree Protocol) logically cuts some of the existing communication paths and always constructs a tree (Wojdak, 2003), while OSPF (Open Shortest Path First) constructs a hierarchy of trees (Moy, 1998). Other protocols use rings, small world graphs and tori as base. In the area of the future networks, where the authors expect virtual and physical entities to build together a common infrastructure, this raises up interesting issues: while virtual machines (VMs) could sit in big quantities in a close proximity (tens of thousands of VMs could be initiated within a data center), typical physical network node degree is much smaller (e.g., a router might have 10-20 physical neighbors, a core network router much less than this). When such entities form a network together, it is not anymore possible to directly follow the topology of the physical network, as routing, discovery and communication messages would either involve too many nodes, or the resulting structure could become too vulnerable to occasional failures or targeted attacks. Given those considerations, the authors would like the present solution, i.e., the protocol at the base of the controllability layer, to work in both dense and sparse networks, of stable and unstable topologies, with or without churn, with virtual or physical resources of yet unknown purpose (programmable network), and networks exhibiting different densities in different regions. This is called structural adaptivity.

The initial bootstrapping, the integration and cut-off of resources (i.e., the maintenance of the controllability layer), and the recovery from errors should be fully autonomous (i.e., they should not require human or central entity intervention). This requirement is crucial to limit the configuration and management efforts from the owner and to increase the overall resilience of the solution. However, more importantly, this requirement is vital to support network virtualization on all layers and from all tenants. Indeed, if the infrastructure layer itself is partly built up from virtual entities, then their lifetime and presence cannot be anymore considered eternal. Just in opposite, seeking for agility, the provider might actually migrate entities to different resources, change their realization, location, etc., which may or may not work without visible service interruptions depending on the scenario. A controllability layer conceived as an autonomous entity would transparently take care of such situations, therefore accepting and promoting the existence of similar network operation principles from any provider and consumer.

Finally, the proposed solution should directly support information-centric networking where either stable names or name resolution mechanisms are provided to map data to nodes.

Table 1 summarizes the above discussion.

Main Idea

There are different potential solutions, how to fulfill the requirements in Table 1. In the following, an integrated solution to this problem is presented.

Our resource interconnectivity layer operates on the principles of ID-based structured routing, which provides a good trade-off between resiliency and latency. The resources have identifiers from a total order set and run a self-stabilizing protocol inspired by a linearization algorithm (Onus, Richa, & Scheideler, 2007) that creates a routing overlay, in which every node maintains connections toward its

Table 1. Requirements of the controllability layer

	Requirement	Description
1	Routing	Path finding mechanisms should work on large scales and limit network state.
2	Message forwarding	Messages should be reliably transported between any two entities. Connected or datagram modes can be considered, according to the nature of the communications.
3	Security	Entity authentication, authorization, data integrity and protection.
4	Reliability	Handling of node and link churn.
5	Structural adaptivity	The structure, on which routing will look for suitable paths, should be dynamically constrained to scale well, but should provide enough degrees of freedom to survive failures and attacks, depending on the node position, situation and requirements.
6	Autonomy	Bootstrapping and continuous structure maintenance should not involve humans or be done in a centralized management way.
7	Shared data layer support	An efficient means to map data to nodes.
8	Scalability	Performance and system efficiency will not be deteriorated if the network size increases.

Figure 1. A ring-based overlay topology

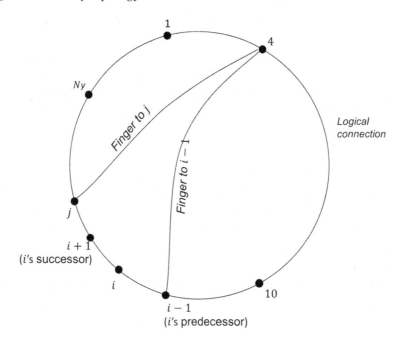

direct neighbor in the ID space where the connections to direct neighbors of all nodes together form a logical ring core structure (e.g., the connection between Node 1 and Node 4 in Figure 1), and a selected small number of other nodes in the network as shortcuts, so called fingers (e.g., the connection between Node 4 and Node j in Figure 1). This is different from structured peer-to-peer protocols like Chord (Stoica, Morris, Karger, Kaashoek, & Balakrishnan, 2001) and Kademlia (Maymounkov & Mazieres, 2002), which build a logical structure on top of underlying routing protocols. A pioneer work, Virtual Ring Routing (VRR) (Caesar, Castro, Nightingale, O'Shea, & Rowstron, 2006), tries to build a logical ring routing structure directly without relying on an existing routing protocol. However, it runs into a multiple ring separation problem, where a final broadcast step is required in order to merge multiple rings as a global one. Instead, the proposed protocol is self-stabilizing and broadcast free. For packet forwarding, similar to most structured routing protocols, the involved nodes follow a policy of greedily reducing the distance toward the destination in the ID space. The proposed protocol is called resource-to-resource (R2R) protocol in the following discussion.

The R2R protocol builds on a long line of research on routing in mobile ad-hoc, sensor networks and Distributed Hash Tables (DHTs). It is essentially a selection of good features found there, adapted to the specifics of the used environment and tuned to address the said requirements. First of all, for handling network dynamics (e.g., link failures resulting in broken paths), the affected node usually can locally route around failed paths without requiring them to be repaired because there are usually many routes between each pair of nodes. For example, consider that a node with ID *5* has connections to three peers whose IDs are 4, 6 and 8, respectively. For a packet sent to Node 9, the interface to Node 8, who is the closest to Node 9, is chosen. If Node 8 now is not available due to whatever reasons, the interface to Node 6 will be immediately selected to continue the forwarding because now Node 6 becomes the best candidate, currently the closest node to the destination Node 9.

Another interesting novel problem in this space is related to the question of structure of node interconnection. The R2R protocol features a topologically adaptive node interconnection. While every node running the R2R protocol maintains connections to its predecessor and successor whose ID values are adjacent in the logical ID space, in contrast to the prior art, the authors designed a programmable finger selection algorithm, where finger node connections (e.g., the link between Node 4 and Node j in Figure 1) are optional but provide shortcuts when forwarding, and contribute to the topological features of the constructed routing overlay. It is therefore possible to both instruct nodes administratively to change the structure of the routing overlay (i.e., a ring-based overlay structure built by the proposed R2R protocol), and to let them locally optimize the finger selection according to different locally observed metrics, like churn, connectivity, load, even energy consumptions in sensor networks etc., whatever best suits the specifics of the node.

Basic Operations of R2R Protocol

Interactions of R2R protocol uses are defined by four main protocol messages:

1. **Hello:** A node periodically broadcasts its own ID to its directly connected neighbors as a keep-alive heartbeat.
2. **NotifyNb:** A message notifying a node with information of a possible candidate of its logical neighbor.
3. **PathEst:** A node deploys a path between two nodes through hop by hop configuring forwarding rule along the path.
4. **PathTearDown:** A path is removed between two nodes.

In the following discussions, node s_i is referred to as the ID value of the *i*-th node for simplicity. Node s_i periodically sends Hello messages at the link layer to show its appearance on every local interface. In addition, Node s_i will also receive Hello messages on its local interfaces, from which it discovers physical neighbors. In this process, a node can authenticate a peer before accepting it as a physical neighbor (e.g., using public/private keys, which would be the only, and minimal, required pre-configuration). This fulfills the security requirement on entity verification. Communication security (integrity and confidentiality protection) can be derived from the initial authentication by usual cryptographic network protocols, e.g., EAP mechanisms together with IKEv2 or a VPN protocol like L2TP between the nodes.

Virtual neighbor discovery and path establishment to them are done by repeatedly executing the linearization operation. It is assumed that Node s_i knows some other nodes (initially, all the nodes are physical neighbors discovered from received Hello messages), called neighbor set N^i. Node s_i sorts its neighbor set N^i according to the ID values of its neighbors and splits it into two subsets: a left-peer set N^i_{left} where all nodes have ID values less than s_i and a right-peer set N^i_{right} where all nodes have ID values greater than s_i. For two consecutive endpoints in each peer set, node s_i sends a NotifyNb message to each endpoint of the two notifying the endpoint the information of possible logical neighbors (i.e., the other endpoint notified meanwhile). Node s_i will repeat the whole procedure above if new nodes are added to its neighbor set N^i. As an illustrating example shown in Figure 2, in Node 9's right-peer neighbor set N^9_{right}. Node 15 and Node 17 are found as two consecutive endpoints. Note that Node 11 and Node 20 will not be identified as neighbors because in the neighbor set of Node 9, Node 11 and Node 20 are not adjacent (according to their ID values). If they are not even adjacent in the local neighbor set, they are certainly not adjacent in the global ID space. Therefore, trying to notify Node 11 and Node 20 will not complete the ordered ring overlay, but builds a finger connection, which is optional. Notification messages will be sent from Node 9 to each of them (as indicated by the two arrows in Figure 2) so that the two endpoints will discover each other who might be their direct neighbor in the ID space.

The main philosophy behind the algorithm is that a node locally helps other nodes to identify their logical neighbors. Though the logical neighbor information initially might not be globally correct initially, this will be corrected progressively when more node IDs are learned so that the knowledge about the network is also growing accordingly. Recall that such a linearization operation does not require any broadcast message as in VRR. It has been proven that such an iterative process is self-stabilizing, meaning that in finite steps it will converge and every node eventually connects to its global logical neighbors (Onus, Richa, & Scheideler, 2007).

Figure 2. Neighbor set sorting and endpoint notification

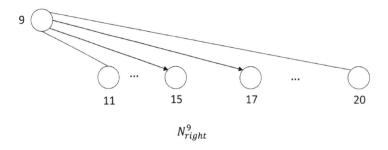

Enhanced R2R Protocol

The basic operations introduced above cannot be readily used as a distributed protocol due to some critical limitations. When linearizing two nodes (i.e., sending notification and establishing a connection) as above, from the algorithmic perspective, a new link is directly added between the two nodes and any link is directly removable. It, however, ignores path establishment/termination between the two endpoints in multi-hop distances, which cannot be simplified as adding/removing a direct link.

Another key limitation is that the algorithm assumes a centralized daemon to schedule the linearization process where at each time slot, there is only one node activated to do linearization in the network. In a fully distributed system, however, such centralized scheduling is difficult. This will cause linearization conflicts where multiple nodes linearize the same pair of nodes, which could arrive at different times over different paths. Even worse, two endpoints may asynchronously receive the notification messages from different nodes, resulting in two endpoints accepting different notifications that eventually end up with a broken path. An example is shown Figure 3, where both Node 9 and Node 20 have the same pair of neighbors in their neighbor sets, respectively, due to the lack of a central daemon to coordinate the linearization. Node 15 and Node 17 accept the notifications from different nodes (i.e., Node 15 accepts Node 9 while Node 17 accepts Node 20). In this case, neither Node 9 nor Node 20 can continue to establish the path between Node 15 and Node 17, which results in a broken path between two peers.

For the first limitation of path establishment, a PathEst message is added. This message is forwarded hop by hop. Note that when relaying the message, authentication and verification between the two consecutive nodes along the path can be done in order to prevent malicious or compromised nodes. Every intermediate node receives and processes this message, and establishes routing information for the requested path. Here, an example is provided in Figure 4 to show how it works. It is assumeed that there are two neighbors (Node 15 and Node 17. that are two hops away from Node 9 (a routing path is already established from Node 9 to each of the two). Node 9 now tries to establish a path between two nodes (i.e., Node 15 and Node 17), thereby two PathEst messages are sent from Node 9 towards each endpoint. When an intermediate node (e.g., Node s_m receives the message, it reads the destination (i.e., to Node 15), since it knows how to reach the destination thanks to the established path between Node 9 and Node 15, new routing information for Node 15 and Node 17 will be added (marked with asterisk in Figure 4). After that, the message is further forwarded to the next hop and similar actions will be taken, until the message reaches the destination. Once the two PathEst messages reach both endpoints, a path between Node 15 and Node 17 is established. Note that, removing a path follows the same way but a reverse procedure where a PathTearDown message is received and indicated routing information will be removed from. This resolves the path establishment/termination limitation.

Figure 3. Failed linearization without a central scheduling daemon

Figure 4. Hop-by-hop path establishment operation

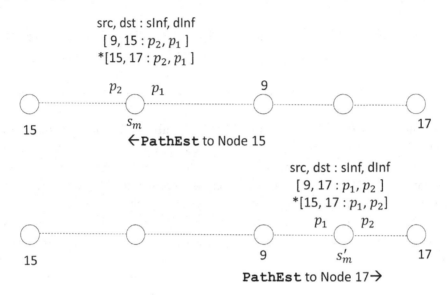

For the second limitation, the R2R protocol applies a sequential notification modification where instead of sending notifications to both endpoints at the same time, only one notification is sent to the endpoint whose ID values are the smaller ones. Still considering the failed case without a central daemon, instead of sending notification messages to both Node 15 and Node 17 at the same time, as shown in Figure 5, both Node 9 and Node 20 now send one notification message to Node 15 first. This guarantees that the smaller ID node (i.e., Node 15 here) will receive all notifications (if any) and can decide which one should be accepted. A first-come-first-serve policy is applied; where the notification that first arrives at the endpoint will be accepted and later coming notifications will be simply rejected. To accept a notification, the smaller ID node with the smallest ID sends an acknowledgement back to the notifying node. Once the notifying node (e.g., Node 9 in the example) receives the acknowledgement, it then sends the second notification to the larger ID endpoint with the greatest ID (i.e., Node 17 in this example). This guarantees that there will be always only one winner that can send the second notification, which eventually eliminates the linearization conflict.

Discussion

One advantage of the linearization process is that a node will learn some finger nodes automatically when constantly receiving NotifyNb messages from other nodes. Though this information is temporarily incorrect due to the local view of ID values of all nodes, it will lead to a connection between two nodes which may become fingers of each other. Moreover, it helps to enlarge the neighbor set of a node, which in turn facilitates the node to identify globally correct logical neighbors for other nodes. This flexibility offers an opportunity to make the built logical structure adaptive (i.e., to meet the structural adaptation requirement), because adding or removing a particular number of finger paths can generally change the node degree distributions.

Figure 5. An ordered notification eliminating linearization conflict

Another advantage is that network dynamics is automatically handled by the linearization process as the neighbor set changes (either growing or shrinking) without any special treatment. Once the underlying network infrastructure changes (e.g., due to link broken and/or interface down), nodes that are directly affected will detect connection lost to some other nodes, which eventually results in the change of the neighbor set of the node. Therefore, it instantly triggers the linearization process according to the new neighbor sets, which ultimately correct the globally order of the structured overlay. Meanwhile, the second best ID node will be chosen, if there is any in order to maintain the ongoing communication. Note that network dynamics only cause local reactions with the proposed protocol because only those nodes observe their neighbor set changes will respond with new linearization actions, while for the rest nodes that are not affected thus not observing any neighbor set changes, no action is needed.

CONFLICT AVOIDANCE

While SDN paves the way to programmatic, event-based network updates, these are not very useful to developers in the current form. Indeed, in the current SDN, there is no guarantee that the network state is not altered, while a control application tries to apply some changes. Flow events arrive at the controller in an uncoordinated fashion, and, dispatched to control applications, could result in mutually conflicting or contradictory statements. This can have a nefast overall effect, resulting in partial, conflicting, or simply incorrect cumulative policies activated in the switches. The conflict avoidance rectifies this. The authors give network updates transactional semantics and create a transactional SDN architecture, the key elements of which are: a transaction manager, a module in the controller, and a resource manager, the proposed extension in the switch. In the current design, the transaction manager coordinates network updates with help of resource managers that use the strong two-phase lock (SS2PL) scheduler. Other options such as commitment ordering (CO) are as well possible and will be investigated in the future.

Main Idea

Our standpoint is that the network control framework of the future should be transactional. To see this, let us consider an example network from Figure 6. It has eight switches (SW 1 to SW 8) and four user nodes (User 1 to User 4). It is controlled by a controller with two SDN applications, App A and App B, which compete for a given resource. Such a resource can be the bandwidth of a link or even a flow table of a switch. Let us assume the former, just to make the exposition to follow concrete. Note as well that in the latter case, the two apps can be literally any applications. So let the bandwidth budget of all links in the network be 1.5 Mbps, while the applications are about to reserve 1 Mbps paths each. If the reservations are concurrent, the following outcome can happen: one application has reserved the link SW 2 - SW 5, while the other one holds the link SW 5 - SW 7. So none of them can proceed, both will have to give up their reservations.

This issue is an artifact of concurrency, which is inherent to any SDN deployment, centralized or distributed, with one or multiple controllers. So, even though Figure 6 shows a single controller deployment, the problem remains in a multi-controller deployment as well, probably in an even more pronounced form. (Refer to Schiff, Schmid, & Kuznetsov, 2016; Jin, Liu, Gandhi, Kandula, Mahajan, Zhang, . . . Wattenhofer, 2014 for more examples.)

Requirements

Drawing a parallel to the well-known ACID properties of database transactions, (Curic, Carle, Despotovic, Khalili, & Hecker, 2017) use this example to show that network control would profit from network updates that are:

- Atomic, meaning that the network-wide updates, going beyond one single switch, either succeed completely or not at all.
- Consistent, meaning that no individual update should violate constraints that are supposed to hold in the network. Thus semantics of individual updates matters.
- Isolated, meaning that two overlapping operations, occurring at the same time and targeting the same switches, cannot result in unexpected effects. Isolation thus eliminates inconsistencies that result from the concurrency as such and not from the semantics of individual operations.

Figure 6. Example network to illustrate non-atomic and uncoordinated updates

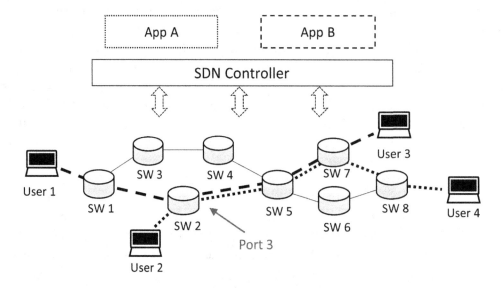

- Durable, meaning that the effect of a transaction survives indefinitely, unless it is changed by another transaction.
- Network control should thus institutionalize support for these services instead of transferring the burden to the developer, or simply neglect them, as it is the case now. Besides, that support should perform well in all relevant deployments. Table 2 summarizes all this.

Proposal

Figure 7 shows the high level architecture proposed by (Curic, Carle, Despotovic, Khalili, & Hecker, 2017) that provides this support. The additions to the standard network control models (e.g., that of Open Networking Foundation, ONF) are depicted with dotted lines. These include the transaction manager (TM) that runs in the network controller, the resource manager (RM) running in the switch and the transactional SBI (TSBI Transactional South-Bound Interface), an extension of the southbound interface for the TM-RM communications. The TM gets update requests from control applications and communicates with the required RMs on behalf of them, i.e., it handles the transactions. The RM essentially transforms the network element (switch) into a transaction-aware medium with well-defined states that can be accessed and changed only according to transactional semantics (e.g., failed transactions can be undone).

Note that the architecture incorporates the RM in the switch even though other choices, e.g., placing it in the controller, are possible. With the latter, the RMs act as images of the switches and are free to implement any concurrency control, optimistic or pessimistic, possible of different complexity (see below). However, a problem is encountered when multiple controllers are deployed: it is hard to maintain switch images in several controllers that simultaneously update the network. Thus the authors' decision to place the RMs in a switch is a deliberate choice, as it is the least constraining solution regarding the target deployment and in line with the established postulate that the control should be distributed (or, at least, distributable). A potential downside is that the switch needs to be extended, which might not be

Table 2. Requirements of the conflict avoidance

	Requirement	Description
1	Atomicity	Network-wide updates either succeed completely or not at all.
2	Consistency	Individual updates should not violate constraints that are supposed to hold in the network, i.e., maintain network wide invariants.
3	Isolation	Overlapping operations, targeting the same switches, should not result in unexpected effects.
4	Durability	Effects of transactions survive indefinitely, unless changed by other transactions.
5	Performance	High success rate of network updates and small delay of each individual update.

Figure 7. Transactional SDN architecture

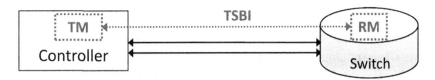

trivial. The key questions are thus what algorithms run in the TM and the RM, i.e., what the interface between them looks like, and what the performances of the resulting system are. These questions are discussed next.

Let us investigate the problem from the above example in greater detail. In concrete terms, consider an instance of the so-called "inconsistent read" (Weikum & Vossen, 2001). Let a and b denote the available bandwidth of the links SW 2 - SW 5 and SW 5 - SW 7, respectively. Then the description above is equivalent to the following pattern of interleaved read (r) and write (w) operations:

$$r_1(a)r_2(b)r_2(a)w_1(a)r_1(b)w_2(b)w_1(b)w_2(a),$$

where the subscripts denote the two apps. The authors argue that this schedule is not conflict-serializable (Weikum & Vossen, 2001; Garcia-Molina, Ullman, & Widom, 2008), i.e., it cannot be equivalent to any serial schedule. Thus, it must be eliminated by appropriate concurrency control mechanisms. In database parlance, update schedules from the equivalence class of conflict-serializable (CSR) histories are enforced.

Concurrency control can be pessimistic or optimistic (Raz, 1992). The former rules out conflicts, while the latter accepts them and reacts, if they happen. Two-phase locking (2PL) is a pessimistic mechanism. An RM uses 2PL to grant locks over data (or, resources in this case) to a single transaction, forcing the others to wait. In its basic form, 2PL guarantees serializability. Two additional variants, S2PL (strict 2PL) and SS2PL (strong 2PL), provide recoverability and cascadelessness, respectively. Commitment ordering (CO) schedulers are optimistic. They serialize the execution by building and analyzing a transaction precedence graph. This generally gives better performance than the pessimistic schedulers, but comes at an additional cost of complexity of algorithms that the RM has to run. It is necessary to provide global serializability, when transactions span multiple RMs. If all RMs are synchronized and share common info, e.g., timestamps, this can be done with a timestamp-ordering protocol. Alternatively, a TM that uses an atomic commit protocol (ACP), such as 2PC, and coordinates RMs equipped with SS2PL, will just do (Raz, 1992).

Among possible algorithms (schedulers) that provide CSR histories, the authors consider the strong two-phase locking (SS2PL) (Weikum & Vossen, 2001) as the right choice. SS2PL is easy to implement in an SDN switch, as the proof-of-concept implementation indeed shows.

Our TM also coordinates the RMs via an Atomic Commit (AC) protocol (e.g., two-phase commit, 2PC), to achieve global atomicity. Thus, the TM and the RMs achieve global serializability as well (Raz, 1992).

Results and Discussion

(Curic, Carle, Despotovic, Khalili, & Hecker, 2017) presents a proof-of-concept implementation of the proposed architecture that shows that the architecture is not only feasible but also easy to implement. The main remaining question is then: how does the solution perform? Do the switch reservations introduce an unacceptable delay for the control applications? Does their related overhead drive the system's throughput below acceptable limits? The answers are shown in Figure 8, which presents the results of the evaluations. Series of network updates are generated at a rate as high as 1000 updates/s and measure, how many of them get successfully installed. This is done on an example topology that is hierarchical and gives us the possibility to tune the path diversity by adjusting the number of links between the core and aggregation clusters. In an attempt to install a network update, a control application may find one or more switches reserved by other applications. When that happens, an attempt is either declared unsuccessful or re-tried again after a random small time. The latter is referred to in Figure 8 as "with backoff", the former "without backoff". The results show that with back-offs and in presence of small path diversity, the overall throughput, the ratio of successfully performed network updates, remains almost unaffected.

SERVICE SCHEDULING

The main functionality of service scheduling is to schedule a job request (e.g., an incoming network flow) on available resources. In contrast to the VNE, the goal here is not to decide which NF should be assigned to which physical resource, but rather to assign a job request to a running NF instance. Regardless of VNE (which is related to planning and longer-term activities), given the typical bursti-ness of the incoming requests, the resource utilization in the network can be further improved by using runtime scheduling. Here, runtime scheduling for mixed network/compute environments is introduced. Its potential gains are illustrated through suitable examples and simulations.

Requirements

In a distributed mixed compute/networking environment, the integrated scheduling has to be distributable so as to scale to larger settings. The proposed architecture therefore must support scheduler placement on every node in the network and, in principle, any scheduler organization, ranging from fully distributed

Figure 8. Network update success rate for different values of the core-aggregation connectivity in a hierarchical example network

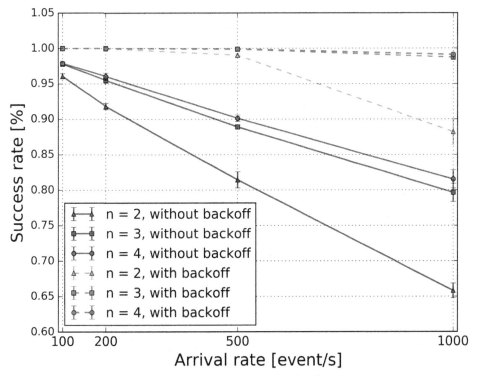

For a more accurate representation see the electronic version.

schedulers (every capable node runs a local scheduler) to hierarchical approaches (global schedulers delegate rules to local modules, which blindly apply them). A controllability layer and conflict avoidance mechanisms, as discussed in previous sections, are necessary components to provide such flexibility and to support concurrent operations of scheduler instances on the same set of resources.

To schedule a job, which will in a general case require some packet (header and, eventually, payload) processing, a scheduler instance needs to know the job classification and the state of the resources in the network. The job classification is determined by a classifier, which is assumed to be either collocated with the scheduler (a reasonable assumption, given that schedulers can be placed almost everywhere) or expressed by a relatively simple tag attached to the flow. It specifies the service function chain of the job: an ordered set of service functions that should be invoked by the job and the set of QoS requirements of the job, including latency, compute, and storage QoS expectations (Halpern & Pignataro, 2015).

The resource state contains information about the set of NF instances running in the network, the average service rate of each of these NF instances (in packets per second), the usage of each resource (e.g., CPU and RAM usage), and the latency of communication paths connecting these resources. The scheduler instances can obtain this information by directly querying the resources (see the following subsection for an example of such). In a large network, a shared data layer may however be preferred; this shared data layer stores and provides this information to the scheduler instances. Such a shared data layer can be built on top of the controllability layer discussed before. Note that this information is not required to be complete or up-to-date, as the design targets the distribution of tasks under the constraints but not an ideal distribution of tasks.

Main Idea

When a new job request arrives at a scheduler instance, it enquires the classification of the job and the resource state in the network and makes a runtime decision to assign the job to a sequence of NF instances in the network that satisfy the set of requirements of that job. To shed more light on how the scheduling process works in practice, and to demonstrate the benefit of applying runtime scheduling in future networks, an illustrative example is provided.

Consider a network with one ingress node, one egress node, and two servers S1 and S2 as shown in Figure 9. There are two types of users attached to the ingress node, generating packets that should be served by NFs running on these servers. Flows of type1 users (referred to as type1 flows) need to be served over an instance of the SFC1 chain, which is composed of NF1 only, and flows of type2 users (referred to as type2 flows) need to be served over an instance of SFC2 chain, which is NF2-NF3. An instance of each NF is running on each server. For the sake of simplicity, in this example stateless NFs are considered. A packet of type1 flows can be therefore served by the NF1 instance running on S1 or the other instance running on S2. There are four possible chain instances for SFC2 in the network, each can be used to serve a packet of type2 flows. The decision of which of these instances to use is performed by a scheduler which is running on the ingress node.

The scheduler uses three buffers to store incoming packets that need to be scheduled: one buffer for type1 packets to be scheduled over one of the NF1 instances; one buffer for type2 packets, which need to be scheduled over one of the available NF2 instances; and one buffer for type2 packets in the middle of their service, which are already processed by one of the NF2 instances in the network and now need to be scheduled over one of the NF3 instances. The assumption here is that NF2 instances return the

Figure 9. A simple scenario with one ingress node, one egress node, and two servers hosting instances of NFs

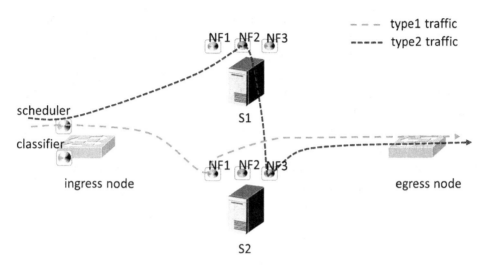

packets to the scheduler after processing. The ingress node therefore performs similarly to the Service Function Forwarder (SFF) introduced in RFC 7665 (Halpern & Pignataro, 2015).

One way to perform the scheduling is to determine fractions of resources assigned to each NF instance at each server (which is performed offline), and to perform load balancing among instances of the same NF (which is performed in runtime). The VNE solutions fall into this category. Such solutions require a priori information about the average arrival rates of flows and the average service rates of each NF instance, which might not be available in many cases. Complete re-planning is required, even if the setting is only slightly changed (for instance, due to NF migration or changes in network capacity and traffic rates). The computational complexity of such re-planning is exponential in the number of nodes (Amaldi, Coniglio, Koster, & Tieves, 2015), which is not desirable as they cannot be performed in runtime in large networks. Heuristics for VNE can perform much better in practice, yet they do not reach the optimum and still their complexity is a high order polynomial.

The authors here opt for a runtime solution, which requires an immediate decision. Therefore, the authors do not target optimality; the aim is to do better than non-runtime pre-assignment and simple runtime straightforward approaches. A typical straightforward runtime approach would be random assignment. However, it cannot maintain any guarantees for the end-to-end flow treatment. A better alternative is to apply greedy mechanisms, such as back-pressure, which the authors advocate for in this work. In particular, for illustration purposes here the authors adopt a delay-based version of the back-pressure algorithm proposed in (Dai & Lin, 2008) to perform the scheduling. It schedules packet X over server Y, if (waiting time of the job)*(the rate it would receive at Y) is the highest among all waiting packets in the buffers residing at the scheduler. The algorithm requires information about the current waiting time of packets in the queues and current service rates of NFs, which can be acquired from servers and queues in runtime, i.e., no a priori information is required. Service rate information can be collected by running an agent process on each server, which collects and reports the service rates provided by each NF instance on the server to the scheduler. The waiting time of the packets in the queues can be tracked locally by the scheduler. Moreover, it does not require any forward planning, has a computational complexity of O(1), and can dynamically adapt to the changes in the network in runtime.

Preliminary Results and Discussion

The scenario described above is assessed using a simulator and evaluate the performance of these solutions. S1 and S2 are considered as identical servers, i.e., they have similar processing capacity $C1=C2=N*C$, where C is the unit of processing capacity and N is a factor used to scale the capacity of these servers. $\mu1$, $\mu2$, and $\mu3$ denote the average service rates, in packets per second, which NF1, NF2, and NF3 instances running on S1 (or S2) can provide, if a unit of processing capacity of S1 (or S2) is assigned to them. The actual service rate of an NF is however time-varying, modelled by a two-state Markov chain (Suresh, Canini, Schmid, & Feldmann, 2015). The flow arrivals in the network are also bursty and modelled by a two-state Markov chain (Neely, 2009).

The following QoS requirements are used: the end-to-end latency, one way, seen by a packet of type1 or type2 flows should be less than D seconds. If this QoS requirement is not satisfied for a packet, it will be dropped, even if it is in the middle of its service (Kulkarni, Zhang, Hwang, Rajagopalan, Ramakrishnan, Wood, . . . Fu, 2017). The success rate is defined as the fraction of packets (of type1 or type2 flows) that are successfully processed in the network. The goal is to answer the following two questions:

Q1: Given the processing capacities of S1 and S2, what is the success rate using any of these solutions? Clearly, the higher the success rate, the better is the solution.

Q2: What is the required processing capacities at S1 and S2 to guarantee a certain success rate (e.g., 99.9%) using any of these solutions? Clearly, the lower the required capacity, the better is the solution, as it implies a lower cost.

The answers to Q1 and Q2 are provided in Figure 10 and Table 3, respectively. The results for C=1, $\mu1=0.01$ pkts/sec, $\mu2=0.02$ pkts/sec, $\mu3=0.01$ pkts/sec, D = 2 seconds, and when the average arrival rates of type1 and type2 flows to the networks are $\lambda1=\lambda2=0.15$ flows/sec are provided. For the sake of simplicity, it is also considered that each flow consists of a single packet.

Observation from the results shows that it is feasible to provide a runtime scheduling solely based on the current state information and that such mechanism significantly outperforms embedding solutions, especially when higher success rate is required (refer to the tail of the curves depicted in Figure 10). Specifically, it is observed that to guarantee 99.9% success rate, the embedding solution requires twice as much resources as the runtime scheduler (refer to Table 3). This shows the advantage of online optimization versus (offline) network planning.

A simple scenario with one ingress node and stateless NFs is considered in this example. The extension to more complex settings, with multiple ingress nodes, is possible by running the instances of the scheduler over the network in a distributed fashion. Besides, machine learning algorithms, such as Reinforcement Learning (Sutton & Barto, 1998), can be used when NFs are stateful. These are the topics of authors' future work.

CONCLUSION

Network control gives network developers right tools (e.g., programmability, APIs) to make the evolution of their networks more dynamic and essentially enable them to keep up with the technological trends. The authors, however, see problems with current control models, such as ONF. The main problems lie

Figure 10. Success rate as a function of capacity assigned to S1 and S2, using different scheduling solutions

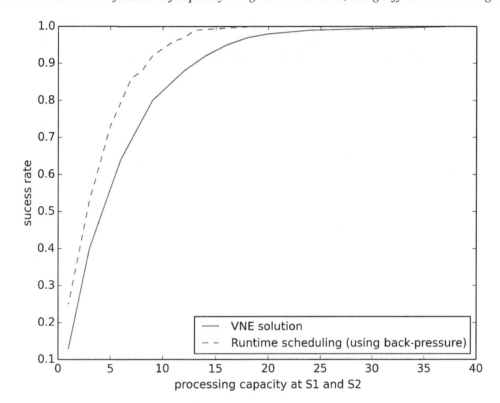

Table 3. Required processing capacities at S1 and S2 to guarantee a certain success rate

Success Rate	90%	99%	99.9%
Runtime scheduling	10C*	13C	18C
VNE solution	13C	24C	37C

in the design with too many externally made assumptions, i.e., their non-holistic approach. Current control networks, or precisely control channels and control end points, necessary for control operation, are not thought of as part of the control model itself. This defeats the original promises of control as such. Besides, current control frameworks are not transactional. Network updates are neither atomic nor isolated, the application is unaware of the details of an update outcome. That places burden and strong requirements on the network application developer, which essentially defeats the initial promise of a "trial and error" approach to developing network control applications.

The control network described here is an integral part of the control model itself. Its main part is a robust connectivity layer that autonomously, (i.e., without any external control or additional means) interconnects all available network elements, including the controller(s). It is capable of handling failures, i.e., maintaining control invariants in presence thereof. The proposed control is also transactional. Applications can safely assume that their updates will not clash in the network, as well as that they will always affect the right, intended fraction of the network.

Building on these two postulates of control, service scheduling is seen as its third essential part providing an essential value to the network owner (e.g., to the operator). The scheduling takes service requirements into account and assigns the network resources that will meet their requirements with potentially less effort, less previous knowledge and with less overprovisioning than any applicable pre-planning approach.

REFERENCES

Amaldi, E., Coniglio, S., Koster, A. M., & Tieves, M. (2015). On the computational complexity of the virtual network embedding problem. In *International Network Optimization Conference (INOC)*. Warsaw, Poland: Elsevier.

An, X., Zhou, C., Trivisonno, R., Guerzoni, R., Kaloxylos, A., Soldani, D., & Hecker, A. (2016). On end to end network slicing for 5G communication systems. *Transactions on Emerging Telecommunications Technologies*, *28*(4), e3058. doi:10.1002/ett.3058

Boutin, E., Ekanayake, J., Lin, W., Shi, B., Zhou, J., Qian, Z., . . . Zhou, L. (2014). Apollo: scalable and coordinated scheduling for cloud-scale computing. In *USENIX Symp. on Operating Systems Design and Implementation, OSDI*. USENIX.

Caesar, M., Castro, M., Nightingale, E. B., O'Shea, G., & Rowstron, A. (2006). Virtual Ring Routing: Network Routing Inspired by DHTs. In *Proceedings of the 2006 Conference on Applications, Technologies, Architectures, and Protocols for Computer Communications* (pp. 351-362). New York, NY: ACM. 10.1145/1159913.1159954

Curic, M., Carle, G., Despotovic, Z., Khalili, R., & Hecker, A. (2017). *SDN on ACIDs. In CAN '17 (CoNEXT)*. New York, NY: ACM.

Dai, J. G., & Lin, W. (2008). Asymptotic Optimality of Maximum Pressure Policies in Stochastic Processing Networks. *Annals of Applied Probability*, *18*(6), 2239–2299. doi:10.1214/08-AAP522

Fischer, A., Botero, J. F., Beck, M. T., de Meer, H., & Hesselbach, X. (2013). Virtual Network Embedding: A Survey. *IEEE Communications Surveys and Tutorials*, *15*(4), 1888–1906. doi:10.1109/SURV.2013.013013.00155

Garcia-Molina, H., Ullman, J., & Widom, J. (2008). *Database Systems: The Complete Book*. Upper Saddle River, NJ: Prentice Hall Press.

Gray, J., & Reuter, A. (1992). *Transaction Processing: Concepts and Techniques*. San Francisco, CA: Morgan Kaufmann Publishers Inc.

Guerzoni, R., Trivisonno, R., Vaishnavi, I., Despotovic, Z., Hecker, A., Beker, S., & Soldani, D. (2014). *A novel approach to virtual networks embedding for SDN management and orchestration. NOMS*. Krakow, Poland: IEEE.

Halpern, J., & Pignataro, C. (2015). *Service Function Chaining (SFC) Architecture. RFC 7665*. IETF. doi:10.17487/RFC7665

Jin, X., Liu, H., Gandhi, R., Kandula, S., Mahajan, R., Zhang, M., & Wattenhofer, R. (2014). *Dynamic Scheduling of Network Updates. In SIGCOMM'14.* New York: ACM.

Kulkarni, S. G., Zhang, W., Hwang, J., Rajagopalan, S., Ramakrishnan, K., Wood, T., & Fu, X. (2017). *NFVnice: Dynamic Backpressure and Scheduling for NFV Service Chains. Sigcomm.* Los Angeles, CA: ACM. doi:10.1145/3098822.3098828

Maymounkov, P., & Mazieres, D. (2002). Kademlia: A peer-to-peer information system based on the xor metric. *International Workshop on Peer-to-Peer Systems*, 53-65. 10.1007/3-540-45748-8_5

Moy, J. (1998). *OSPF Version 2.* IETF. Retrieved from http://www.rfc-editor.org/rfc/rfc2328.txt

Neely, M. J. (2009). Delay Analysis for Maximal Scheduling With Flow Control in Wireless Networks with Bursty Traffic. *IEEE/ACM Transactions on Networking, 17*(4), 1146-1159.

Onus, M., Richa, A. W., & Scheideler, C. (2007). Linearization: Locally Self-Stabilizing Sorting in Graphs. *ALENEX, 7*, 99–108.

Raz, Y. (1992). *The Principle of Commitment Ordering, or Guaranteeing Serializability in a Heterogeneous Environment of Multiple Autonomous Resource Mangers Using Atomic Commitment. In VLDB* (pp. 292–312). San Francisco, CA: Morgan Kaufmann Publishers.

Schiff, L., Schmid, S., & Kuznetsov, P. (2016). In-band synchronization for distributed sdn control planes. *Computer Communication Review, 46*(1), 37–43. doi:10.1145/2875951.2875957

Sciancalepore, V., Samdanis, K., Costa-Perez, X., Bega, D., Gramaglia, M., & Banchs, A. (2017). Mobile traffic forecasting for maximizing 5G network slicing resource utilization. In *IEEE INFOCOM 2017 - IEEE Conference on Computer Communications.* IEEE.

Stoica, I., Morris, R., Karger, D., Kaashoek, M. F., & Balakrishnan, H. (2001). Chord: A scalable peer-to-peer lookup service for internet applications. *Computer Communication Review, 31*(4), 149–160. doi:10.1145/964723.383071

Suresh, P. L., Canini, M., Schmid, S., & Feldmann, A. (2015). *CaC3: Cutting Tail Latency in Cloud Data Stores via Adaptive Replica Selection. In NSDI.* USENIX.

Sutton, R., & Barto, A. (1998). *Reinforcement Learning: An Introduction.* MIT Press.

TS23.501. (2017). *System Architecture for the 5G System.* 3GPP.

TS29.500. (2017). *5G System; Technical Realization of Service Based Architecture; Stage 3.* 3GPP.

Verma, A., Pedrosa, L., Korupolu, M., Oppenheimer, D., Tune, E., & Wilkes, J. (2015). Large-scale cluster management at Google with Borg. *Proc. European Conf. on Computer Systems, EuroSys.* 10.1145/2741948.2741964

Weikum, G., & Vossen, G. (2001). *Transactional Information Systems: Theory, Algorithms, and the Practice of Concurrency Control and Recovery.* San Francisco, CA: Morgan Kaufmann Publishers Inc.

Wojdak, W. (2003). *Rapid Spanning Tree Protocol: A new solution from an old technology.* Reprinted from CompactPCI Systems.

KEY TERMS AND DEFINITIONS

Controllability Layer: A set of resources interconnected and configured to enable the controller-controlee (resource) communication.

Job Classification: The service function chain of a job; an ordered set of service functions that should be invoked by the job and the set of QoS requirements of the job.

Job Request: An incoming network flow with a specific processing request.

R2R Protocol: A protocol used to create the controllability layer (i.e., autonomously establish inter-connectivity among a set of network resources).

Self-Stabilizing Control Plane: A control plane always converges from an arbitrary status to a stable correct status in finite steps.

Service Scheduling: Assignment of job requests to deployed, active network entities such that a preset goal is met.

State of Resources: Information about the set of active network entities, their service rates, and their traffic loads.

Transactional Network Updates: Network updates that execute as a whole and isolated from other updates.

Section 3
Sample Service Automation Deployments

Chapter 9
Network Security Policy Automation:
Enterprise Use Cases and Methodologies

Myo Zarny
vArmour Networks, USA

Meng Xu
vArmour Networks, USA

Yi Sun
vArmour Networks, USA

ABSTRACT

Network security policy automation enables enterprise security teams to keep pace with increasingly dynamic changes in on-premises and public/hybrid cloud environments. This chapter discusses the most common use cases for policy automation in the enterprise, and new automation methodologies to address them by taking the reader step-by-step through sample use cases. It also looks into how emerging automation solutions are using big data, artificial intelligence, and machine learning technologies to further accelerate network security policy automation and improve application and network security in the process.

BACKGROUND

Policy automation is a broad term—both policy and automation could mean many things to many people. This chapter discusses specifically about network security policy automation, looking into what network security policies mean; how they are derived and enforced in practice in larger enterprise environments; what the most common use cases driving network security policy automation are; and finally, what the emerging automation approaches are. The authors will take the reader through a few sample use cases to illustrate the most common methods.

DOI: 10.4018/978-1-5225-7146-9.ch009

The use cases are based on real-world scenarios from larger enterprises that have already begun the journey to automation. Their requirements include not only the functionality but also other key aspects such as scale, performance, resilience, and redundancy. The solutions described here should be familiar to many in the standards community, and some of them are already productized to various degrees by commercial vendors. Because many solutions and their adoption in the market are still relatively new, the goal is to give readers a better understanding of these solutions.

What Are Policies?

The term policy could have different meanings depending on the context. It could refer to broad high level Information Technology (IT) policies that support business objectives; detailed technical and procedural requirements for specific areas of IT; or anything in between. In colloquial usage, the term policy is often used interchangeably with similar terms like standards and guidelines although in more formal (academic) usage, the terms are not always interchangeable (Kim, 2016, p. 41; SANS, 2018).

The following is a simplified description of what policies could mean in different settings:

- General IT policies are a set of (codified) high level requirements, procedures and guidelines for all IT that enable the business. Such policies may cover topics like service availability, disaster recovery, business continuity planning, regulatory compliance, information security, or end-user training. Managers and senior technical architects tend to be the intended audience.
- IT security policies define what it means to be secure for IT technologies including applications, databases, systems, and networks. According to Wikipedia (Wikipedia, 2018), IT security policies codify practices that aim to prevent "unauthorized access, use, disclosure, disruption, modification, inspection, recording or destruction of information", "regardless of the form the data may take (e.g., electronic, physical)."
- IT security policies can be further broken down into sub-areas like network security, systems security, application security, legal liability, etc. Each sub-area can be divided further still—e.g., how strong the customer passwords ought to be; when and where customer data needs to be encrypted at what minimum strength; who from what networks can access to which systems in what networks and perform what functions; how frequently compliance audits ought to take place; etc. The main consumers of "low-level" policies are IT engineers, who will need to implement the policies.
- In theory, most specific policies support their higher level policies, which in turn ultimately support the business objectives.

Depending on the organization, the breadth and depth of IT policies differ greatly. Large firms, especially those that need to demonstrate regulatory compliance, typically maintain teams whose main responsibilities include developing/updating IT security policies and performing regular audit reviews. On the other hand, smaller firms may not have the technical and financial wherewithal to maintain such a staff; not all (or none) of the policies may be formally codified or documented as practices that should/ must be adhered to.

To be sure, codified authoritative policies need to exist for policies to be automated. It is a best practice to formally document all approved IT policies, and disseminate updated policies throughout the IT organization on a regular basis. In practice, however, even large organizations with dedicated Info Sec teams have trouble formally documenting their myriad IT policies, and keeping the documented ones up-to-date, let alone ensuring their proper implementation.

What Are Network Security Policies?

Network security policies are a formal set of rules, principles, procedures and guidelines to prevent unauthorized access to resources on the network (Bastien & Degu, 2003). The main areas of concern in the enterprise include access control, intrusion detection and protection, encryption, network infrastructure equipment security, and wireless security.

Here are a few sample network security policies:

- All traffic to/from external networks must traverse a perimeter "DMZ" (De-Militarized Zone) network (that typically contains, among others, layers of various security devices).
- All traffic to/from external networks must be encrypted.
- Only anti-virus-patched corporate computers can get on the corporate wireless network.
- Only authenticated and authorized users from local internal networks may access App-X.

The policies are still broad: each policy can have multiple implementations. Take the last policy. If a company has three regional internal networks, e.g., in the Americas, EMEA (Europe Middle East and Africa) and AP (Asia-Pacific), the policy could have at least three implementations.

- **In the Americas Data Centers:** Only users authenticated and authorized by Firm's AAA (Authentication, Authorization and Accounting) service, originating from local networks (10.1.1.0/24, 10.1.2.0/24 and fd99:aaaa:1234:1000::/48), may access App-X located at the virtual IP addresses (VIPs) of 172.16.1.100/32 and fd99:aaaa:bbbb:1::/128).
- **EMEA:** Only users authenticated and authorized by Firm's AAA service, originating from local networks (10.2.1.0/24,10.2.2.0/24 and fd99:aaaa:1234:2000::/48), may access App-X located at the VIPs 172.16.1.100/32 and fd99:aaaa:bbbb:1::/128).
- **AP:** Only users authenticated and authorized by Firm's AAA service, originating from local networks (10.3.1.0/24, 10.3.2.0/24 and fd99:aaaa:1234:3000::/48), may access App-X located at the VIPs 172.16.1.100/32 and fd99:aaaa:bbbb:1::/128).

The above is an example of how network security policies are *implemented* in practice. As you may have noticed, any change in the higher level policy will require implementation changes in three different regions, on multiple devices. Ensuring that the subsequent changes across regions stay consistent is a major problem. It is a major motivation for automation.

Most common network security policies by far are those controlling access to servers and applications. Access control policies are often implemented as "policy rules" on firewalls, which are systems that monitor and control incoming and outgoing network traffic. The rules tell firewalls which traffic to allow, which to block, which to redirect to another system, which to log, and so on.

So pervasive are firewalls and firewall rules that many network security engineers tend to think of firewall rules when they hear "network security policies". Technically, access control policies are not the only network security policies. Other types of network security policies—e.g., all external network traffic must be encrypted—do exist, and are in fact implemented in larger enterprises.

Why Network Security Policy Automation?

At a high level, network security policy automation means automation of implementation of codified network security policies in a dynamic manner—ideally without requiring any human intervention. Security automation could cover the entire or a portion of the security policy lifecycle—planning, review, deployment, monitoring, updates, decommissioning, etc.—across several network security enforcement points, potentially located in different geographic regions, business units, public clouds, etc.

Policy Implementation Pain Points

Implementing network security policies takes time and effort. In many enterprises, network security policy implementations are often excruciatingly time-consuming operations that involve several functional teams. An abridged firewall policy implementation process may look something like this:

- An application developer (owner) wants to deploy a new application in a data center.
- The application owner requests the network security firewall administration team to allow communications between the application instances and their counterparties.
- In larger organizations, an IT information security team may review the request.
- The firewall team reviews the request for technical feasibility, e.g., identify the firewalls where the rules need to be deployed; write the necessary rules that need to be created and/or updated; ensure that the policies are not in conflict with existing ones; and so on. Some organizations may also require a peer review of the planned configuration and the firewalls involved, and/or senior members of the team to sign off on the implementation plan.
- The firewall operations team then schedules the implementation change on all the necessary firewalls, e.g., perimeter firewalls, data center firewalls, regional firewalls, etc.—within the respective authorized maintenance windows of those firewalls.
- The firewall team then updates the rules during those maintenance windows, each of which may be a few days or weeks apart.

If you are a network security administrator, you are probably quite familiar with variations of this unwieldy and error prone process. Depending on the number of firewalls involved, all the necessary changes to provide access to the application may not be in effect for several days or weeks—*even if* everything goes according to plan. If something goes wrong—e.g., someone fat-fingered an IP address in one of the policies—the change may need to be reverted, and post mortems and root cause analyses may need to be written and reviewed before the next change can be scheduled, pushing out the application rollout by yet a few more weeks.

Why is the process so cumbersome? Larger enterprises have instituted some versions of procedural controls because they have needed to. Unvetted policies could result in service disruptions to the business, or in security loopholes that can be exploited. Increasingly, many firms have another reason: governmental, international and industry regulations. For example, the Payment Card Industry Data Security Standard (PCI-DSS) specifies a set of security standards that must be met by all firms handling credit card transactions (PCI, 2016). The European Union's General Data Protection Regulation (GDPR) data protection regime covers all firms processing data of all EU residents (EU GDPR, 2018). Firms are typically required to demonstrate compliance to the regulations through regular audits.

DevOps and Demands of Modern Data Centers

While regulatory requirements for more stringent security controls are increasing, demands to deliver services and applications faster are increasing even higher. Application developers increasingly employ DevOps (development and operations) practices, which include more automation, continuous monitoring, shorter "agile" development cycles and increased deployment frequencies (451 Research, 2010; Huttermann, 2012, pp. 7-8).

Developers increasingly demand near-instant deployment times they have become accustomed to in the public cloud in their internal environments. But many IT teams cannot deliver the kind of dynamic service of public cloud providers since they have not adopted similar automation techniques and practices.

When security cannot keep up with the increasing pace of change, the firm's overall security posture invariably deteriorates. Tired of waiting, some application owners seek ways to get around security controls. They might, for example, ask for access to a larger set of IP addresses than currently necessary so that they would not have to go through the gauntlet the next time they bring up another application instance. They might run their application inside already opened ports (e.g., SSL on TCP port number 443) on firewalls. Or worse yet, they might run their own "shadow IT" inside the public cloud, bypassing their enterprise network altogether.

Stale Security Policies

So far, the authors have discussed the difficulties of deploying new policies to accommodate new applications. But what happens when existing applications or servers are decommissioned or moved elsewhere? How do the associated access control rules also get updated or even removed?

The answer is that they do not. *Unused firewall policies rarely get removed, if ever!* In many enterprises, application, server and network security teams are usually not in sync with one another's plans. The server team might not be aware of unused older versions of applications on their servers; or application owners might not be aware that one of the servers their application is hosted on was decommissioned by the server team months ago. Even when they are aware, the server or application team might still not inform the network security team in time because the downside of mistakenly shutting down access to an application/server in production is high. The result is that network security rules are not updated in time, or in many cases, at all. This is a major issue since unused policies are in fact security loopholes waiting to be exploited.

Overview of Common Use Cases

Let us now take a look at the kinds of use cases that greatly benefit from security policy automation. The use cases are common scenarios from larger enterprises that have already begun the journey to automation. While by no means an exhaustive list, it is nonetheless a set of use cases most enterprise network security admins should be familiar with, and should give the general reader an understanding of the key drivers for security policy automation.

Use Case 1: Dynamic Deployment of Applications

This is perhaps the main driver for policy automation. Let us first go over the basics of how applications are deployed in modern enterprise data centers and in the public cloud. At a high level, applications run on operating systems (OSes) hosted on traditional servers (also called "bare-metal" or "physical" servers), or on virtual machines (VMs), which ultimately run on physical servers. Increasingly, applications—typically, smaller, modular ones, some of which are known as "microservices"—are deployed inside containers (virtualized OS partitions) on bare-metal servers or VMs. Note that not all containerized applications are microservices; applications of all sizes can be deployed as containers. Furthermore, in Kubernetes, a common open-source container orchestration and management system, containers are placed inside "pods", which are then deployed (Kubernetes, 2018). For simplicity, the term container (not pod or any other implementation-specific term) is used as the generic basic unit of deployment of containerized applications in this chapter.

Prior to the advent of VMs and containers, applications were typically deployed only on bare-metal servers. Deploying new applications often meant first deploying the required servers, which could take weeks: new servers needed to be ordered, racked-and-stacked, connected to the network, etc. The long server installation times gave the application and network security teams a few weeks to prepare the security rules for the app, get the rules reviewed and approved, and deploy them when new servers come online—in a way that was consistent with business objectives (Network Heresy, 2014). Policy automation in this stop-and-go world was arguably a nice-to-have, but not a must-have.

The advent of VMs and containers (both of which are also referred to as workloads) has changed that. Workloads hosting applications can now be deployed dynamically—within minutes for VMs and within seconds for containers. The trend has been popularized by public cloud providers like Amazon Web Services and Microsoft Azure. Cloud providers have trained users to be able to order their desired virtual compute, network, storage services in real time—*here and now, not weeks later.* Users could even order just compute functions (and not worry about the infrastructure management) through "serverless computing" or Function as a Service (FaaS) offerings.

Application owners in many enterprises increasingly demand their internal IT departments to deliver the same capabilities. Enterprise IT departments are responding with varying speeds. In larger enterprises, server virtualization is already quite common, and application owners can deploy their applications on VMs much quicker than before. The use of containers, while still relatively low, is increasing.

As a result, the bottleneck has shifted to the network security team's ability to keep up with the pace of new workloads coming on line. What happens when the network security team cannot keep pace? Bad outcomes await:

- New applications will have no network security (firewall) protection, or;
- Conversely, if the company's firewall policies are to block all unknown traffic, the new applications will not be usable until the network security team gets around to granting access to them.

In practice, the first outcome is far more probable for most firms do not have firewalls everywhere to be able to enforce policies.

The challenge for the network security team is how to dynamically apply the required security policies to applications as they are brought up.

Use Case 2: Dynamic Decommissioning of Applications

A key ability of an effective policy management system is to monitor the deployed rules, and remove unused policies. Just as an application/workload can be deployed dynamically, it can be decommissioned dynamically as well. When an application/workload is removed, the policies associated with the application/workload also need to be updated/removed.

Furthermore, it is increasingly common for workloads to come into existence only for a short duration. For example, it is now possible to dynamically add new VMs to the server pool when the utilization of the current server pool exceeds a threshold, and remove the excess VMs when the utilization goes back below the threshold. With containers, it is customary for given containers on a server to be destroyed, and rebuilt anew on a new server. Indeed, some containers may live only for *a few seconds* before they get removed!

The challenge for the network security team is to update the security policies as dynamically as applications and workloads are brought down.

Use Case 3: Dynamic Migration of Applications

A common use case in modern data centers and in public clouds is the dynamic migration of applications from one server to another. The more common reasons are:

- Routine maintenance of the underlying server. Workloads (and their applications) on the to-be-serviced server are moved off to another server so that applications on the workloads can continue operating. When the maintenance is over, the migrated applications may or may not be migrated back to the original server.
- Failure of the underlying server. Workloads (and their applications) on the failed server, if configured to do so, will be automatically migrated to another server. When the failed server recovers, the migrated workloads may or may not be migrated back to the original server.
- Permanent migration from one server to another – for whatever business or technical reason. For example, a containerized application is moved from the development network to the production network; an application and its VM are moved to another server with more memory and CPU; etc.

Typically, workload migrations take place within the same data center or within the same public cloud network. It is certainly possible for workloads to be migrated between the on-premises data center and the public cloud. Note that migration of workloads between two public cloud providers is possible but requires more sophisticated orchestration capabilities. It is not yet a common use case.

The task for the network security team is to ensure that the existing security policies dynamically follow the application to its new location, whether in the data center or in the public cloud.

Use Case 4: Dynamic Changes in Application Ownership

Let us now move on to more complex use cases. The need to dynamically apply policies extends to user identity as well. That is, the security policy for a given application may change depending on who is using the application.

A common use case is with the virtual desktop infrastructure (VDI) infrastructure. For example: users from their home computers remotely log into their company's VDI servers. Once authenticated, each user is assigned his/her own VDI server, which is permitted to access certain assets on the network. Depending on policy, users may use the VDI server only for a set period of time, e.g., until they log off. After a given user has logged off, the VDI server is now available to serve the next user. The next user of the VDI workload might not have the same rights as the previous one. For example, the first user of the VDI server belongs to the database team, and is authorized to access IT database servers while the new user is from Accounting, and is not authorized to access any IT assets.

The task for the network security team is to dynamically apply policies on the same set of applications based on the identities of users and their privileges.

Use Case 5: Dynamic Context-Aware User Identification

Just as the same application running on the same workload can be applied with different security policies based on who is using it, the same user can be subject to different security policies based on the surrounding contexts.

The contexts vary from firm to firm. For example:

- A firm's IT security policy may state that only authenticated users from the Finance Department using devices located in the internal network may access the department's databases. Finance department users cannot access the databases from home, or from anywhere else outside of the "internal network". Here, the policy is both user identity- and network-aware.

- Another policy may state that authenticated Finance Department users armed with the company-issue laptops may access the internal network. Therefore, a Finance Department user using his/her own laptop must not be allowed to access the internal network. The policy is both user identity- and device-aware.

These are not esoteric policies that only exist in the large enterprise world. Many readers most certainly have already encountered context-aware security policies in their daily life. Many e-commerce sites already enforce multi-factor authentication: e.g., even after you have correctly entered your username and password, if the site does not recognize the device you are using, or if it sees that you are accessing from a location deemed suspicious, it will challenge you to further identify yourself via email or mobile phone on record.

The task for the network security team is to dynamically apply appropriate policies using multiple contexts. It means the security policy system working together with multi-factor authentication systems.

Summary of Common Use Cases

The above five use cases are by no means exhaustive. But they are some of the most common scenarios in the enterprise that can greatly benefit from policy automation. Table 1 is a summary of the use cases.

Table 1. Summary of common use cases

Use Case	Description	Security Requirements
Policy for dynamically deployed applications	Applications can be instantiated dynamically in the data center and in the public cloud	Dynamically apply network security policies as applications are brought up
Policy for dynamically decommissioned applications	Applications can be decommissioned dynamically in the data center and in the public cloud	Dynamically update network security policies as applications are brought down
Policy for dynamically migrated applications	Applications can be migrated to another hypervisor/host	Ensure that the policies for the applications follow to the new host/hypervisor
Policy for dynamic changes in application ownership	Security policy for certain applications depends on the identity of the user. E.g., some VDI servers serve their users for a set duration. The next user may not have the same rights as the previous one.	Apply policies based on the user identity, not just on the app's network location
Context-aware policy	Users are authenticated and assigned entitlements based on several factors. Users may be assigned different rights depending on where they are logged on, the type of device they are using, etc.	Apply policies in accordance with the currently assessed entitlement rights, which can be held on an AAA system, an identity and access management (IAM) system, etc.

POLICY AUTOMATION SOLUTIONS

Group-Based Policy Overview

The most common network policy automation solutions today are based on the Group-Based Policy (GBP) framework (pioneered by various open source organizations, including OpenStack and OpenDayLight.)

Though several commercial solutions have extended/modified the GBP approach, at a high level, the solutions perform the following functions:

- Using the metadata associated with a given application/workload to determine the group or groups the application/workload belongs to;
- Placing the application/workload in the appropriate group (or groups);
- Assigning a common policy ruleset to each group, and;
- Deploying group-based policy rulesets on policy enforcers.

But why is this seemingly mundane process considered an automation solution? The answer is that by monitoring the changes with metadata of the applications/workloads, and adjusting the membership of policy groups, the solutions enable network security teams to deploy/update policies in the same speed as application and server teams can make changes to the metadata of their applications and workloads.

All of this will become clearer when going through a few sample workflows later. First, let us take a look at the basics of GBP. Figure 1 illustrates is a simplified view of the GBP architecture (based on OpenStack's Group-Based Policy Model in its whitepaper on the topic (OpenStack 2018)).

The key components are:

- Groups whose members are treated with the same policy;
- Sources of metadata of applications/workloads that determine the applications/workloads' group membership;

Figure 1. A simplified view of the GBP architecture

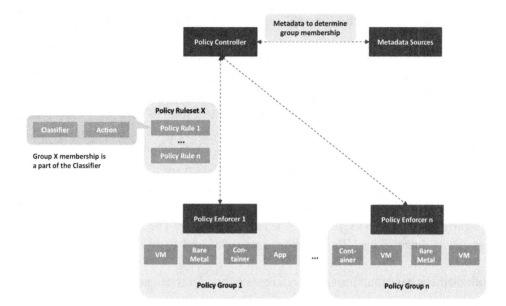

- A Policy Controller that determines policy rulesets, and monitors deployed rulesets;
- Policy enforcers that enforce the rules.

Groups

The first fundamental concept of GBP is the group. A group is simply a collection of applications or workloads (or any kind of network endpoint). Group membership requirements are fairly loose. Member applications or workloads of a group can be hosted on a mix of platforms (bare-metal servers, VMs, containers/pods, etc.), and can be in different locations or networks. The only requirement of the group construct is that all members be treated with the same set of policies.

Moreover, group membership is not restrictive. An application or workload may belong to more than one group. For instance, a VM hosting an application used by the Finance Department in Data Center 1 (DC1) can be a member of a group called Finance-Servers as well as a member of a group called DC1-Servers. The implication here is that the VM can be subject to two sets of policies—for Finance-Servers and DC1-Servers.

In general, an application or workload can be subject to as many policy rulesets as the number of groups to which it belongs. You may ask which ruleset will take precedence when an application/workload belongs to more than one group? It is an *extremely important* question. Policy prioritization is discussed in a later section.

Policy Metadata

The metadata is the lynchpin that enables network security policy automation. The idea is to use the metadata (attributes) associated with applications/workloads to determine the policy group of the applications/workloads.

Methods of Retrieval

There are two main methods of getting an application's or workload's metadata.

- The first is to find it in the data packets. The metadata in the packets can be values of common header fields (e.g., web cookie), proprietary header fields (e.g., Cisco Security Group Tags), or in the payload, e.g., signatures (byte sequences).
- The second method is to retrieve from external metadata sources such as workload management systems; identity and access management (IAM) systems; authentication, authorization and Accounting (AAA) systems; etc. The metadata here are different from those found in the packets, and vary widely depending on the source. The metadata from workload managers will typically be "labels" or "tags" associated with the workloads; and/or IPs and FQDNs (fully qualified domain names) of the workloads. Meanwhile, the metadata retrieved from AAA and IAM systems will typically be related to usernames, roles and privileges. The metadata from threat analytics services can be threat scores, IP reputation scores, etc. And so on.

While both methods have their uses, the preferred method for most automation solutions is to get the metadata from their authoritative metadata sources. There are a couple of key reasons for it:

- First, identifying the desired metadata from the packets is computationally intensive as it requires deeper, more thorough inspection of packets. Identifying content such as malware signatures (byte sequences that indicate the presence of malicious code) is even more resource intensive. And firms may not possess a sufficient number of (or any) devices capable of performing deeper packet- and session-level inspections. (Indeed, many operators still run their firewalls to inspect only up to the network-transport layers even when their firewalls are capable of inspecting up to the application layer because of the impact of deeper inspection on the performance of their firewalls.)
- Secondly, the use of external metadata is far more flexible. In theory, there are no limits to the kinds of metadata that can be used to select types of policy groups.

This is not to say that packet level inspections have no place. Far from it. It is in fact quite desirable to update the metadata sources with what is actually happening on the ground. For example, a configuration management database (CMDB) may think that Server-A is running only App-1. But if it is observed that Server-A is also running App-2, an alert can be raised for examination by admins. If it is decided that App-2 should be running on Server-A, then the CMDB can be updated to reflect the actual facts on the ground. This is discussed a bit more in detail in the Infrastructure Feedback section.

Common External Metadata Sources and Types

Table 2 lists a few of the external metadata sources in use in enterprises today (2018).

Some of the metadata are directly related to technical attributes like the IP and FQDN of the workload, or the identifier of the user. But other attributes are simply labels/tags that can describe anything. For example, a "DC-1" tag can be used to identify workloads that are located in Data Center 1 while a "Finance" label may signal workloads that are owned by the Finance Department. Similarly, a reputation score of an external IP can be used to sort IPs into different groups that can be applied with different policies.

Table 2. Sample external metadata sources

Source	Sample Commercial Sources	Sample Metadata
VM management systems	VMware vSphere vCenter Microsoft SCVMM Amazon Web Services Microsoft Azure Google Cloud Platform	VM tags, VM FQDN, VM IP, etc.
Container management systems	Kubernetes Docker Swarm Amazon Web Services Microsoft Azure Google Cloud Platform	Container labels, pod labels, service labels, deployment labels
IP management systems	Nokia VitalQIP Infoblox	IP addresses, FQDNs
User identity systems	Microsoft Active Directory RADIUS	Username attributes, group
Threat analytics systems	Open source feeds	IP reputation scores Threat scores

The use of labels/tags is probably the most common method to determine policy.

Who Maintains the External Metadata?

It should be obvious by now that the accuracy of the metadata sources is paramount in highly automated systems. Without accurate, up-to-date authoritative databases of metadata, the metadata-driven automation systems will instead become launch pads that dynamically roll out imprecise/incorrect policies!

So, who is responsible for maintaining the accuracy of the metadata? Unfortunately, it is usually not the network security team. In large enterprises, various infrastructure and application development teams have the (shared/overlapping) responsibility to maintain the metadata of their workloads and applications. For example, a server administration team may add/update/delete tags associated with VMs on its VM management system (like VMware vCenter or Microsoft System Center), and perhaps even manage container labels on the container management systems (like Docker Swarm or Kubernetes). But in the DevOps model, developers are increasingly given permission to tag/label containers and VMs they instantiate.

To recap, the network security team typically does not control the accuracy of the metadata used for policy automation. This needs to be addressed if GBP policy automation is to function safely and accurately.

Policy Controller

So far, the authors have discussed the concepts of groups, and metadata-driven group membership. Next, the authors will discuss the Policy Controller where decisions regarding which policies are applied to which group are made. The authors will first need to explain the basic concepts of policy rules that need to be considered by automation solutions.

Policy Rule Derivation in Different Contexts

In theory, network security policy rules are representations of higher level policies. A higher level policy could spawn a number of lower level "rules". For instance, a higher level policy that calls for securing database servers could result in one set of lower level firewall rules for MS-SQL database servers and another set of firewall rules for Oracle database servers.

Table 3 uses natural language to describe each constituent rule; but in practice, each rule will be written in a vendor-specific syntax. The purpose of the table is to show how a higher level policy can yield more than one lower level ruleset. Also notice that "MS-SQL DB servers", "Oracle DB servers" and "internal users" are in effect groups.

Even when dealing with the same group, different rulesets may be used depending on where they are to be enforced. In the above example, both rulesets for MS-SQL and Oracle are intended to be enforced on internal data center firewalls. The same higher level policy of securing databases may be translated as blocking all database traffic to/from external users (Table 4). (Actual translations to lower level rules are made by humans; and higher level policies typically are open to interpretation.)

Extending the concept further, the same higher level policy can be expressed in terms of implementation rules on different devices. In this example, rules can be implemented on firewalls and Intrusion Detection System/Intrusion Prevention System (IDS/IPS) devices.

This point will not be belabored any longer. The takeaway is that the same higher level policy can be implemented in terms of multiple lower level rulesets, depending on the context. This leads to the next point.

Policy Computation and Maintenance

Up to this point, it was simply stated that each policy group gets a policy ruleset that represents higher level policies. But the authors have not talked about who translated the higher level policy into various sets of lower level rulesets, and assigned them to appropriate groups. Nor have the authors talked about how accurate/effective those rules are, who monitors them, who updates them, etc.

Table 3. Sample rules for internal firewalls

Rule	Ruleset for MS-SQL Databases	Ruleset for Oracle Databases
Rule 1	Block all traffic initiated by the MS-SQL DB servers	Block all traffic initiated by the Oracle DB servers
Rule 2	Permit MS-SQL application traffic originated from "internal users" destined to TCP port number 1433	Permit Oracle-DB application traffic originated from "internal users" destined to TCP port number 1521
Rule 3	Block all traffic to MS-SQL DB servers	Block all traffic to Oracle DB servers

Table 4. Sample rules for external firewalls

Rule	Ruleset for External Firewalls
Rule 1	Block all database traffic in both directions

Most policy automation solutions today possess little or no policy computation capabilities. They rely on human admins to manually craft implementation-level rulesets, which ideally represent some higher level policies. But human-crafted rules are far too fallible, and may not remain accurate after a period in any case. Emerging security policy computation solutions are trying to address the problem by using artificial intelligence (AI), machine learning (ML) and Big Data techniques to compute policies as well as monitor their efficacy to keep the rules up-to-date. Those solutions come with what is generically called the "policy controller" that attempts to dynamically compute, monitor and update policies.

But as of this writing, dynamic policy computation is a still developing area. In most policy automation solutions, the policy controller is simply the management console where admins manually develop, deploy and manage rulesets for devices from one vendor. There are also network security policy managers (NSPMs), which serve as a common management platform for multiple products and vendors (Hils & Rajpreet, 2015). Though many automation platforms can now draw in a plethora of data from several sources, humans still ultimately write out rules.

Policy Prioritization

A key aspect of policy computation is determining the priority of the rules. The reason is that network security rules are traversed from top to bottom until a set of conditions are matched, in which case the specified action (e.g., permit, deny, redirect, etc.) is taken, and no rules below are examined. This is not a problem if the ruleset does not contain any overlaps in terms of groups. But when overlapping rules exist, the lower ranked rule or rules are "shadowed" to the extent of the overlap, and will not be examined. This may or may not be a problem. Sometimes, shadowing is there by design. Many times, it is not.

Let us use a simplified example depicted in Table 5.

In this case, Rule 60 is being shadowed by Rule 50; Rule 60 will never be examined so long as Rule 50 exists. Even if Rule 50 is there as intended, the presence of Rule 60 is unnecessary and potentially dangerous. What if a new higher level policy calls for revoking SSH traffic to Group-Y? If firewall admins remove only Rule 50, Rule 60 will now come into the fore, and allow SSH traffic from Group-X to Group-Y. In such cases, security loopholes are literally lurking in the shadows.

It was already a serious problem even when a single team controlled what went into the ruleset. It is not uncommon for network security teams to fail to check for overlapping rules. But what happens when network security admins no longer control all aspects of ruleset management? Remember, in the ethos of DevOps and metadata-driven automation, it is now the owners of metadata that ultimately control what policies are attached to applications and workloads! When multiple parties control what goes into the ruleset, chances of overlapping rules are suddenly far higher.

Table 5. Policy prioritization example

Rule	Ruleset
...	
Rule 50	Permit SSH traffic to Group-Y
...	
Rule 60	Permit SSH traffic from Group-X to Group-Y
...	

There are no simple fixes. One obvious step is to ensure that application/workload owners are authorized to place only their assigned labels/tags only on their applications/workloads. Security admins may also limit the rights of application teams so that app-team-generated rules cannot supersede infrastructure-wide rules.

In sum, policy prioritization, and constant monitoring and elimination of overlapping rules are critical functions of network security teams. Policy automation solutions need to handle them.

Policy Enforcers

The fourth component of GBP is the policy enforcer. The enforcer can be dedicated network security equipment like firewalls, proxies, and cloud access security brokers (CASBs) but can also be another network device with packet inspection and filtering capabilities like routers, switches, load balancers, Wi-Fi controllers, etc. Let us now review the main points about policy enforcers with regard to policy automation.

Right Place, Right Time, Right Enforcer

The first point is obvious: policy enforcers must be deployed in the right place in order to enforce policies. It does not matter how quickly policy rules can be generated if the right (capable) enforcers are not in the right place to inspect the traffic and take action. So much for automation!

Traditionally, enforcers are physically placed in the network path by connecting them with cables to other network devices, and traffic is then made to go through the enforcers through traditional switching and routing. Such methods are no longer sufficient in the age of dynamic "elastic" workloads and applications. First, traditional policy enforcers (e.g., firewalls) cannot be cabled fast enough to handle VMs and containers that can come up and down within seconds or minutes. Besides, even when they are cabled up, because they are sitting outside the servers, they are totally blind to all the traffic flows among the VMs and/or containers on the servers themselves.

Though beyond the scope of this chapter, a variety of (emerging) solutions—some of which are categorized under the names of SDN (Software Defined Networking), NFV (Network Functions Virtualization) and SFC (Service Function Chaining)—aim to scale up and down policy enforcers on-demand, and transport packets right to/from the policy enforcers (often through the use of network tunnels), thereby removing the need to physically insert the enforcers in the path.

The next obvious point is that the policy enforcer must have the capability to enforce the required policy. A firewall cannot do all the functions of an IDS/IPS, and vice versa. For now, let us assume that the right policy enforcers have been deployed in the right place within an acceptable time period.

Chains and Networks of Enforcers

Policy automation is not just for a single enforcer. It needs to account for all the various types of enforcers as well as the topology and sequence of enforcers in the environment. The policy controller will have to deal with a chain of policy enforcers, which may consist of same or different enforcers, in order to enforce policy consistently in the environment.

For example, if external users accessing an application are required to go through an IDS/IPS, a firewall and a load balancer before getting to the application server, the policy controller will need to develop consistent policies for each device in the sequence. Likewise, the controller will need to develop consistent policies across the firewalls that separate a three-tier application's web, application and database servers. And so on.

Ideally, the policy controller computes policies for every policy enforcer in real time, and sends tailored policies to each enforcer. Advanced policy computation capabilities are not the main topic of this chapter although the topic will briefly be covered in the Future of Network Security Policy Automation section. For now, let us assume that accurate policies have been computed for each and every policy enforcer in the environment.

Sample Workflows

Now that the basics of GBP have been covered, let us go through a few sample workflows. The workflows are highly generalized but are specific enough to illustrate how policy automation works.

Overview

Step 1

The first step in this policy automation workflow, as referred to in Figure 2, is to define the policy rules that need to be enforced. As discussed, policy computation can be automated although today most of the policy rules are manually developed by humans. There are many factors in developing a policy ruleset (the background context, policy prioritization, which policy enforcers, etc.) In this example, let us assume that the policy rules have been developed—either through manual or automated means, on the Policy Controller; and the necessary policy enforcers have been deployed in the right place.

Figure 2. Generalized step-by-step workflow

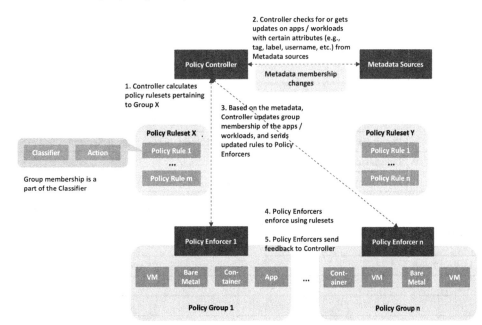

Also assume that the higher level policy is to secure the instances of App-X and the lower level policies are to permit only the App-X traffic destined to TCP port number 9999 on the App-X Servers, and block all other traffic to/from the App-X Servers (Table 6).

This simplified ruleset contains just a single explicitly defined group "App-X Servers". (In practice, a ruleset can contain several groups of servers, services and applications. But the authors will start with just one group for now.) The group "App-X Servers" is made up of containers with the label of "App-X".

Step 2

The Policy Controller now needs to figure out what those workloads with the tag "App-X" are. That information is held in the Container Manager (e.g., Kubernetes, Docker Swarm, etc.) The Policy Controller requests the Container Manager for a list of containers with the tag of "App-X". Here, the Controller is specifically looking for the IP addresses associated with those containers. Why? The Controller needs to convert higher level policies to lower level rules that Policy Enforcers can execute, and Policy Enforcers can only see those found in the actual packets such as IP addresses, protocols, ports, etc. In this case, the Policy Controller needs all corresponding IP addresses of containers with the label "App-X".

The Container Manager returns its current list, which in the example contains just two addresses (Table 7). (In practice, the Container Manager can return other attributes, which can be used for additional policy refinement.)

Step 3

The Policy Controller now updates the group membership, which updates the ruleset by placing the App-X related rules in the overall ruleset (Table 8).

Step 4

The Policy Controller now deploys the policy rulesets to the policy enforcer or enforcers. In the example, the Policy Controller deploys the ruleset to Policy Enforcer-1 and Policy Enforcer-2.

Table 6. Policy rules for App-X

Rule	Policy Rules for App-X
Rule 1	Permit App-X application traffic destined to TCP port 9999 on "App-X Servers"
Rule 2	Deny all traffic initiated by "App-X Servers"
Rule 3	Deny all traffic destined to "App-X Servers"

Table 7. Label information from Container Manager

Label	IP Address
App-X	10.1.1.11
App-X	10.1.1.12

Table 8. Ruleset for MS-SQL databases

Rule Order	Ruleset for MS-SQL Databases
...	
Rule 51	Permit App-X application traffic destined to {**10.1.1.11, 10.1.1.12**} on TCP port 9999
Rule 52	Deny all traffic initiated by {**10.1.1.11, 10.1.1.12**}
Rule 53	Deny all traffic destined to {**10.1.1.11, 10.1.1.12**}
...	

Step 5

The last step is feedback. Policy Enforcers can provide valuable feedback to the Policy Controller that can shape the next version of the policy rules. For example, both Policy Enforcers in the example may report they did not see any hits on Rule 51 for 10.1.1.12 in the last 90 days. This can be a trigger for network security admins to look into whether or not the workload with the IP address of 10.1.1.12, despite being tagged with App-X, truly is an App-X server, and if Rule 51 needs to be tightened to exclude 10.1.1.12.

In general, policy efficacy monitoring is an essential security practice. The metrics of unused and underused policies can be used to make deployed policies tighter (less permissive) and more accurate. Ideally, the process can be automated. This is discussed in the Future of Network Security Policy Automation section.

Now, let us go over the steps with the use cases mentioned earlier.

Dynamic Deployment and Removal of Applications

Assume two new App-X containers have just been instantiated, and one of the existing App-X containers decommissioned. How would the Policy Controller know about the changes? The Policy Controller can poll the Container Manager periodically for any membership changes. Or better yet, as in some setups, the Container Manager can at once send membership changes to the Policy Controller.

In this example, the Policy Controller polls the Container Manager every 10 seconds. Within 10 seconds, the Policy Manager learns from the Container Manager about its latest list of App-X instances. If the Container Manager is able to send the updates right away, the Policy Controller will learn of the changes more quickly on average. Anyway, Table 9 is the list provided by the Container Manager.

The Policy Controller compares the new list to its current list, and sees that 10.1.1.11 is gone, and 10.1.1.100 and 10.1.1.123 are new. It updates the App-X group membership, which is now three -strong. The membership change is reflected in any of the rules that have referenced the App-X group. In this example, rules 51 to 53 have referenced the group App-X, and the ruleset now looks (Table 10):

Table 9. Updated label membership from Container Manager

Label	Member IP Addresses
App-X	10.1.1.12
	10.1.1.100
	10.1.1.123

Table 10. Updated ruleset for App-X

Rule Order	Ruleset for App-X on Policy Enforcer 1
...	
Rule 51	Permit App-X application traffic destined to {**10.1.1.12, 10.1.1.100, 10.1.1.123**} on TCP port 9999
Rule 52	Deny all traffic initiated by {**10.1.1.12, 10.1.1.100, 10.1.1.123**}
Rule 53	Deny all traffic destined to {**10.1.1.12, 10.1.1.100, 10.1.1.123**}
...	

The Policy Controller sends updates to the required policy enforcers. In this workflow, the changes on the Container Manager are reflected in network security policy changes, almost instantaneously (10 seconds in this example.)

Since the Policy Controller continually polls the Container Manager for updates (or the Container Manager continually sends updates to the Policy Controller), the Policy Controller will know about the latest metadata membership at most within the polling interval, make the necessary updates, and propagate the updates to policy enforcers.

Dynamic Migration of Applications

Migration of applications from one host to another is really a combination of removing one application instance on one host, and instantiating one on another. The IP address of the migrating workload may or may not change. The task at hand is to ensure that the policies for App-X follow to the right Policy Enforcer(s).

Let us say that the App-X container instance of 10.1.1.100 is being moved to Host 2, and that Host 2 is protected by Policy Enforcer 2. And both Policy Enforcer 1 and Policy Enforcer 2 are already programmed with the required policies for App-X (Table 11).

If the IP address of the migrated App-X instance remains the same on Host 2, there is no need to change any policies on Policy Enforcer 2.

But what if the IP address of the container instance on Host 2 has changed to 10.2.2.200? This case is the same as the new deployment discussed in the last section. The Policy Controller will have learned that 10.1.1.12 is gone, and 10.2.2.200 has joined (Table 12).

Table 11. Rulesets for App-X on Policy Enforcers 1 and 2

Ordered Rules for App-X on Policy Enforcer 1	Ordered Rules for App-X on Policy Enforcer 2
...	...
Permit App-X application traffic destined to {10.1.1.12, 10.1.1.100, 10.1.1.123} on TCP port 9999	Permit App-X application traffic destined to {10.1.1.12, 10.1.1.100, 10.1.1.123} on TCP port 9999
Deny all traffic initiated by {10.1.1.12, 10.1.1.100, 10.1.1.123}	Deny all traffic initiated by {10.1.1.12, 10.1.1.100, 10.1.1.123}
Deny all traffic destined to {10.1.1.12, 10.1.1.100, 10.1.1.123}	Deny all traffic destined to {10.1.1.12, 10.1.1.100, 10.1.1.123}
...	...

Table 12. Updated label membership from Container Manager

Label	IP Address
App-X	10.1.1.100
	10.1.1.123
	10.2.2.200 (new!)

The Policy Controller will update the membership of App-X, and updates will be reflected on all policy enforcers with rules that reference App-X—i.e., both Policy Enforcer 1 and Policy Enforcer 2 (Table 13).

Dynamic Changes in Application Ownership

Now, let us switch gears a bit and deal with user identity-related use cases. As detailed in Use Case 4, user identity is a common metric to manage access to network and applications.

Continuing with the App-X example, the ruleset has been updated (Table 14) to include a new group, "App-X Users". The sample policy now requires to permit only those clients that belong to the group "App-X Users" to access "App-X Servers" on TCP:9999.

The Policy Controller now needs to update the membership of both "App-X Users" and "App-X Servers". But the membership of "App-X Users" is determined by user identity. This means the Policy Controller will need to consult with the Identity and Access Manager (IAM) to determine the membership of "App-X Users", in addition to checking in with the Container Manager for the membership of "App-X Servers".

The Policy Controller asks the IAM for its latest username accounts with the tag "App-X-User", and their currently known IP addresses (Table 15). (The assumption is that the IAM has already authenti-

Table 13. Ordered rules for App-X

Ordered Rules for App-X on Policy Enforcer 1	Ordered Rules for App-X on Policy Enforcer 2
…	…
Permit App-X application traffic destined to {10.1.1.100, 10.1.1.123, 10.2.2.200} on TCP port 9999	Permit App-X application traffic destined to {10.1.1.100, 10.1.1.123, 10.2.2.200} on TCP port 9999
Deny all traffic initiated by {10.1.1.100, 10.1.1.123, 10.2.2.200}	Deny all traffic initiated by {10.1.1.100, 10.1.1.123, 10.2.2.200}
Deny all traffic destined to {10.1.1.100, 10.1.1.123, 10.2.2.200}	Deny all traffic destined to {10.1.1.100, 10.1.1.123, 10.2.2.200}
…	…

Table 14. User-identity-based policy rules for App-X

Rule	Policy Rules for App-X
Rule 1	Permit App-X application traffic **by "App-X Users"** destined to "App-X Servers" on TCP port 9999
Rule 2	Deny all traffic initiated by "App-X Servers"
Rule 3	Deny all traffic destined to "App-X Servers"

cated the usernames, and checked their privileges to ensure that the accounts should be classified with the tag "App-X Users".)

As before, the Controller checks with the Container Manager for its list of containers with the label "App-X" (Table 16).

The Controller now updates the group memberships, which are reflected in the rulesets on policy enforcers (Table 17).

The Policy Controller will be regularly checking in with the metadata sources, and/or be receiving updates from those sources.

Context-Aware Policies

Though an additional variable has been added, the same group-based approach still automates the deployed policies. Now, let us increase the level of complexity. What if the policy requires that only the App-X users located in the internal network may access the App-X servers? This means a user dialing in from a non-internal network (e.g., from home) is not permitted to access the App-X servers.

No problem. The same approach can be extended to support the use case. The policy example now looks (Table 18):

Table 15. Membership information from IAM

Label	IP Address
App-X-Users	192.168.1.11 192.168.2.22

Table 16. Membership information from Container Manager

Label	IP Address
App-X	10.1.1.100 10.1.1.123 10.2.2.200

Table 17. Rules for App-X

Ordered Rules for App-X on Policy Enforcer 1	Ordered Rules for App-X on Policy Enforcer 2
…	…
Permit App-X application traffic **from {192.168.1.11, 192.168.2.22}** destined **to {10.1.1.100, 10.1.1.123, 10.2.2.200}** on TCP port 9999	Permit App-X application traffic **from {192.168.1.11, 192.168.2.22}** destined **to {10.1.1.100, 10.1.1.123, 10.2.2.200}** on TCP port 9999
Deny all traffic initiated by {10.1.1.100, 10.1.1.123, 10.2.2.200}	Deny all traffic initiated by {10.1.1.100, 10.1.1.123, 10.2.2.200}
Deny all traffic destined to {10.1.1.100, 10.1.1.123, 10.2.2.200}	Deny all traffic destined to {10.1.1.100, 10.1.1.123, 10.2.2.200}
…	…

Table 18. User- and network-aware policies for App-X

Rule	Policy Rules for App-X
Rule 1	Permit App-X application traffic by "App-X Users" located in "Internal Networks" destined to "App-X Servers" on TCP port 9999
Rule 2	Deny all traffic initiated by "App-X Servers"
Rule 3	Deny all traffic destined to "App-X Servers"

Note that three groups are now defined: "App-X Servers", "App-X Users" and "Internal Networks". And the source group is actually a *logical AND* of the groups "App-X Users" and "Internal Networks".

The Policy Controller will need to check with three sources: (1) the Container Manager for "App-X Servers"; (2) the Identity and Access Manager for "App-X Users", and; (3) the Network Manager (e.g., an IPAM) for "Internal Networks". (Note that in practice, the Policy Controller does not need to check in with the IPAM every 10 seconds if you know that your Internal Networks do not change often.)

Let us say that the Policy Controller gets the following (Table 19):

The Controller updates the group memberships (Table 20).

The net result of the logical AND operation is simply {192.168.1.11, 192.168.2.22}. Depending on the implementation, the Policy Controller may send the net group {192.168.1.11, 192.168.2.22} to the Policy Enforcers, or the Policy Enforcers themselves may compute the net result.

Table 19. Membership information from metadata sources

Source	Label	IP Address
Identity and Access Manager	App-X-Users	192.168.1.11 192.168.2.22 202.2.2.2
Container Manager	App-X Servers	10.1.1.100 10.1.1.123
IP Address Manager	Internal Networks	192.168.0.0/16 172.16.0.0/12 10.0.0.0/8

Table 20. Resultant rules for App-X

Ordered Rules for App-X on Policy Enforcer 1	Ordered Rules for App-X on Policy Enforcer 2
...	...
Permit App-X application traffic **from ({192.168.1.11, 192.168.2.22, 202.2.2.2} AND {10.0.0.0/8, 172.16.0.0/12, 192.168.0.0/16})** destined to {10.1.1.100, 10.1.1.123, 10.2.2.200} on TCP port 9999	Permit App-X application traffic **from ({192.168.1.11, 192.168.2.22, 202.2.2.2} AND {10.0.0.0/8, 172.16.0.0/12, 192.168.0.0/16})** destined to {10.1.1.100, 10.1.1.123, 10.2.2.200} on TCP port 9999
Deny all traffic initiated by {10.1.1.100, 10.1.1.123, 10.2.2.200}	Deny all traffic initiated by {10.1.1.100, 10.1.1.123, 10.2.2.200}
Deny all traffic destined to {10.1.1.100, 10.1.1.123, 10.2.2.200}	Deny all traffic destined to {10.1.1.100, 10.1.1.123, 10.2.2.200}
...	...

As in the previous examples, the Policy Controller will be polling various metadata sources for the updates, and/or be receiving membership changes from those sources. If there are any changes with any of group memberships, it will make the necessary updates for Policy Enforcers. Rinse, repeat.

Recap

The group-based approach can support multiple policy automation use cases. Indeed, network security policy automation is not just for policies securing workloads and applications; the same automation techniques can be applied to policies securing the network infrastructure. Furthermore, although the examples have been highly simplified to illustrate the ideas more clearly, many variations of the approach can be implemented to suit various deployment scenarios.

A few things to keep in mind are:

- Policy controllers can be traditional management stations (e.g., firewall managers), multi-vendor management stations, or more advanced orchestration engines.
- Metadata sources need not be vendor-specific management servers; they can be any data sources.
- Policy enforcers need not be just firewalls. Network security rules do not have to be just firewall-style access control rules.
- The groups used in the policy rulesets do not have to be just IP address groups. They can be any group types that policy rulesets support—such as groups of services, applications, etc.

The key requirements for policy automation to work properly in enterprise environments are:

- Having documented clear authoritative policies is a fundamental requirement if those policies are to be automated. In fact, it is a best practice to formally document all approved IT policies, and disseminate updated policies throughout the IT organization on a regular basis.
- Need up-to-date accurate authoritative metadata sources. Without them, group-based policy automation will not work properly, and can result in inaccurate policies.
- The component systems should be equipped with APIs (Application Programmable Interfaces).
- Policy monitoring is essential to ensure that policies are working as intended.
- In large enterprise environments, functionality alone is not sufficient. The system components need to be able to handle the load. The automation system needs to be able to handle component failures, and recover within a reasonable timeframe.

FUTURE OF NETWORK SECURITY POLICY AUTOMATION

This section looks at some of the emerging trends with regard to network security policy automation. Specifically, it covers: (1) use of infrastructure feedback; (2) dynamic security service insertion; (3) dynamic policy computation, and; (4) public and hybrid clouds. The overarching theme across the trends is the use of advances in Big Data and machine learning (ML)/artificial intelligence (AI) techniques.

Infrastructure Feedback Loop

Policy automation does not end with the initial policy deployment. It is critical to continually monitor the efficacy of deployed policies, and make continual adjustments to the policies. But as long as human admins are responsible for monitoring what is happening, and deciding what to do, the process will be inherently slow and error prone. Policies will not get updated as frequently and as accurately as they should be.

An important continuing development is the use of the infrastructure's feedback to increase the accuracy of policies. Think of it as a feedback loop: Just as metadata from authoritative sources can be used to automate policy enforcement, observed content and metrics ("facts on the ground") can be used to improve/enrich various metadata sources, which in turn yield more accurate policies. In general, observed facts on the ground include contents of the traffic as well as overall behavioral patterns in the environment.

Content Inspection

Examination of packet contents to make policy decisions is as old as networking itself. Yet, many network security devices are still configured to inspect only the outermost parts of data packets—typically to the network and transport layers even when they can inspect higher layer contents. The main reason used to be that deep packet inspection (DPI) was (and is) computationally expensive, and required specialized hardware to be performant. Increasingly, the reason is the encrypted nature of payloads. (Decryption is not just a technical issue but also a privacy one.) Enterprises, which need to gain insight into encrypted payloads of (some or all) applications, typically deploy specialized security devices (e.g., email security gateways, web-proxies, application delivery controllers, IPS/IDS, CASBs, etc.) in critical junctures of the network to decrypt the packets and glean certain information out of the contents.

Today, the gleaned information is typically not shared with the larger IT ecosystem. The idea then is to make the content information available to other systems. That is, the policy controller can collect content-specific information from some special policy enforcers (e.g., Web proxies, Application Delivery Controllers (ADCs)), and send the information to appropriate metadata sources. The enriched metadata may then be used to derive more accurate policies throughout the network.

For instance, assume that a firm has a mix of legacy network layer firewalls and application layer firewalls. If an application layer firewall observes that a given workload's traffic running on UDP port number 53 is not DNS, it will block the traffic, and inform the policy controller. The policy controller in turn tells the VM Manager to tag the workload as "Quarantine", which will dynamically update all the policies that use the group "Quarantine" throughout the network. Now, even the network layer firewalls will block the traffic from the workload although they lack application layer visibility. The overall network security posture has improved.

Behavioral Patterns

Any observed behavioral patterns in the network—not just packet contents—can be used to refine (add, modify, delete) existing network security policies. The behaviors can be anything deemed anomalous. They might include, for example, a workload/application that has not generated any traffic for the last 90 days; workloads with daily traffic volumes 50% above their 30-day average; application instances with different traffic patterns from other like application instances; etc. The tasks for automation solutions are to: (1) dynamically detect such anomalies, and; (2) take corrective actions—ideally with minimal user intervention.

Policy automation solutions are tackling both parts head-on. First, to detect anomalous behaviors, many solutions collect large amounts of telemetry data from various sources (network security devices, workload managers, threat intelligence sources, etc.), and use Big Data and AI/ML techniques to establish "normal" baseline behaviors for all the application relationships, network flow patterns and traffic volumes in the environment. They can continue to adjust the baseline over time, based on the new data. By dynamically discovering and adjusting baseline behaviors, AI/ML can point out even non-obvious anomalies that most admins simply do not have time or resources to discover on their own. For example, AI/ML can identify a SQL server that is generating traffic patterns markedly different from those of other SQL servers—even if the aberrant server's traffic patterns are still within the current policies defined by admins.

This is not to say that user input is no longer necessary. On the contrary, user guidance/supervision can speed up the machine learning process. Regular user reviews and adjustments can progressively improve the accuracy of ML analytics algorithms, and reduce the number of false positives.

This leads us to the second part: automation of actions. Most solutions already allow users to send alerts to the monitoring systems of their choice when anomalous conditions are met. But the alerts still require human admins to look into the matters. Some solutions have begun allowing users to specify the actions the systems can take by themselves. For example, a policy controller may be empowered to automatically remove applications or workloads that have not generated any traffic, or responded to any ARP requests in the last 90 days; or to instruct the VM Manager to reboot a particular VM with the standard image if the Controller observes anomalous network traffic from the VM; etc.

Actions that can be automated are endless. But practically speaking, admins are cautious about automating actions that could result in wide-scale service degradations/outages—especially since the triggering conditions can be based on false positives. It is one thing to automatically remove a seemingly idle workload; it is another to automatically switch to stricter DDoS (Distributed Denial of Service) prevention policies across all the policy enforcers. The scope and scale of service outages will continue to factor hugely.

In sum, Big Data and AI/ML are increasingly needed to keep up with all the dynamic behavioral patterns in the environment. Regular user feedback and nurturing of baseline behaviors will improve the accuracy of anomalous behavior identification. This will in turn boost the confidence of admins, who then may increase the types and scope of automated actions.

Dynamic Security Service Insertion

Now, let us tackle one of the previous assumptions in the chapter: That the right policy enforcers had been deployed in the right place within an acceptable period. The assumption was necessary to focus on policy automation workflows themselves. But the reader should see that there will not be any policy automation until the necessary Policy Enforcers are deployed in the right places!

Dynamic security service insertion has long been recognized as a critical automation requirement. It is a major component of Network Functions Virtualization (NFV) efforts in the standards community (SDX Central, 2018). It is available in various commercial (proprietary) orchestration solutions. Most of the solutions can be summed up as follows: dynamically instantiate security services (policy enforcers in this case) on workloads (VMs, containers), and use a traffic redirection method (e.g., over network overlays, service function chaining, routing table manipulations, etc.) to transport traffic flows to/from the security services, thereby removing the need to physically insert the services in the network path. (Note: with some solutions, policy enforcers may also be deployed on hypervisors, or as agents on workloads themselves.)

The promise is that policy enforcers can be rolled out with the same speed as new applications and servers, and policy automation can proceed. Many challenges remain. The complexity of setting up/maintaining network overlays is one. The performance/throughput of such virtual security services is another.

Dynamic Policy Computation

Let us deal with another earlier assumption: That someone has already created the policies for the policy controller to disseminate. The assumption allowed us to focus on the mechanics of populating policy groups with the right members. But in real life, those sets of policy rules that reference the policy groups need to have been created first.

It turns out that developing accurate policies is an extremely difficult problem. The reason is not just with translating of higher level IT policies into vendor-specific lower level rules—which is a multi-layered problem (Network Heresy, 2014). The chief reason often is admins not knowing what is really happening in their networks. (Admins are wary of blindly implementing policies that could cause service outages!) The problem is most acute in the internal networks. Because organizations tend to have few (or no) firewalls or monitoring systems looking at their intra-data center "East-West" flows, admins may not be aware of the happenings in the environment. (Organizations tend to have a (slightly) better grasp of "North-South" flows since they typically have to maintain firewall rules between their internal and external networks.)

Thus many policy computation solutions are starting with providing visibility into the flows! The idea is that if admins can view what is happening, then they will be in a better position to decide what policies to apply to which applications/workloads/flows. Such solutions collect traffic flows right from the network or workloads, and/or other data sources such as security information and event managers (SIEMs). They then can leverage Big Data and ML techniques to clean up, de-duplicate, aggregate and categorize several thousands of applications, workloads, and flows. The goal is to make it easy for admins to view applications, workloads and flows in some logical order of groupings, and allow them to make additional classifications as needed.

Even then, admins might still not know what policies to apply to. Many solutions now offer a set of built-in policy templates—typically, for common applications. A policy template for Microsoft Exchange, an email application, for example, may include a set of policies that Microsoft says an Exchange server should adhere to. Many solutions also offer users the ability to create their own templates. The benefits of using templates are as follows:

- Templates give users a reasonable starting point for the kinds of policies they might want to apply to. In the example, users may accept Microsoft's suggested policies for their Exchange servers, or tailor the policies to suit their requirements.
- Templates generate a consistent set of rules every time, differing only in the input variable(s). For example, if an App-X policy template takes in a container label as input, the set of rules it generates for the input label "DC1-App-X-Servers" and those it generates for the input label "DC2-

App-X-Servers" will be the same except for the server groups. This ensures consistency as well as accuracy.

A related development is the use of natural language to construct policies. Users may write a policy in a natural language syntax like: "Apply MS-Exchange-Policies to MS-Exchange-Servers in HQ." The policy controller will figure out what the MS-Exchange-Policies are (which presumably are codified in a policy template), what the MS-Exchange-Servers in HQ are (by checking appropriate metadata sources), and generate a set of policy rules. Note that natural language policy construction and policy templates are complementary. Policy templates can be constructed using a natural language syntax.

Another development is the ability to test the impact of candidate policy rules prior to their deployment. This feature, also known as pre-flight validation, allows users to simulate how their candidate rules would behave: e.g., would they shadow other rules or be shadowed by others; would they permit/block which historical/synthetic traffic flows; etc. This way, users are able to identify issues prior to actual deployment, which increases the confidence that the candidate rules would not cause a service outage when deployed. This impact simulation capability has become a key feature of policy computation engines.

Finally, policy computation is not just for one policy enforcer, or one type of enforcers. It must account for various types of enforcers as well as the topology and sequence of enforcers in the environment. That is, the policy controller will compute policies for policy enforcers in real time, and send tailored policies to each Enforcer. Some solutions, notably Network Security Policy Managers (NSPMs), have started to marry the ability to perform (more dynamic) policy computation with the ability to manage multiple types of network security devices in different topologies (Hils & Rajpreet, 2015). The trend will only continue to get stronger.

Policy Automation in the Cloud

The ability to manage consistent dynamic policies across on-premises and public cloud environments (or "hybrid" clouds) has become a key requirement as more organizations move a portion of their IT resources to the cloud.

Network security policy automation in the cloud is still nascent. While cloud providers have greatly reduced the time to deploy policies, they have done so largely by eliminating the planning, review and implementation processes common in enterprises. Developers can now dynamically implement network security policies on their workloads by using a simple firewall (called "security groups" or variations thereof) offered by their cloud provider. But in terms of functionality, most, if not all, of the security groups are quite basic: they are tied to a network or a workload's (virtual) network interface, and cannot filter beyond the transport layer (Layer 4). This basic functionality is probably by design—to be the lowest common denominator for all customers. But it also means that it is not possible to automate more advanced (e.g., application and user identity-based) policies using the security groups.

Increasingly, more organizations need more than what the cloud security groups have to offer. The primary driver is the rise of the hybrid cloud where applications and workloads can be instantiated (or moved) across on-prem and cloud networks. IT organizations need to ensure that the right policies are dynamically applied to applications and workloads, wherever applications/workloads may be located. (In addition, IT security organizations do not want to rely on application owners to be writing network security policy rules on their own.)

The good news is that the group-based policy approaches outlined in this chapter can be used to implement policy automation in hybrid environments. The policy controller (or a federation of controllers) will communicate with the pertinent metadata sources across on-premises and cloud environments to get metadata memberships; and update group-based policies on relevant policy enforcers across environments.

Third party vendors and cloud providers are responding. Many third party cloud firewalls already offer application layer filtering capabilities, and support more advanced metadata-based methods. Some cloud providers are beginning to add more capabilities (such as support for "tags" in security groups) that make GBP-style policy automations possible. To be sure, a number of challenges remain. For example, different metadata sources across environments will need to be managed, not a trivial task. And cloud versions of third party firewalls typically are not as capable as their on-premises cousins. Despite the challenges, the drive towards greater network security policy automation across hybrid networks will continue because the overall automation revolution requires it.

CONCLUSION

Network security policy automation is now a fundamental capability of modern infrastructure automation solutions. Effective policy automation enables the network security team to keep pace with increasingly dynamic changes in both on-premises and cloud infrastructures. It can greatly improve application security, and allow IT security teams to focus on more value-added tasks.

But oversight is still needed. Automation removes several traditional oversight processes that used to greatly delay application deployment. Without any guardrails, application owners may apply no or lax policies that could lower security to their applications and potentially beyond. But DevOps does not have to mean no oversight or lowered state of security. IT security teams must ensure that application owners can manipulate only their authorized applications and metadata, and that the metadata are tied to the right policy rules. They also need to continually monitor and review the efficacy of deployed policies across their dynamic on-premises and cloud environments.

Fortunately, more help is on the way for the overworked security admin. A new crop of emerging solutions, leveraging Big Data and AI/ML technologies, aim to automate various functions for which security teams traditionally have not been adequately resourced to perform. Such tasks include establishing and tracking baseline behaviors associated with the network, servers and applications; discovering application contents and behavioral patterns that can be used to update/enrich metadata sources, and make policy computation more accurate; intelligently detecting anomalies in granular contexts; taking actions on those anomalies with little or no human interaction; etc.

In all, several opportunities and challenges still exist for further network security policy automation. As an integral part of the overall automation trend, network security policy automation will have to continue developing to meet the needs of the overall automation drive in enterprise and cloud environments.

REFERENCES

Bastien, G., & Degu, C. (2003). CCSP SECUR Exam Certification Guide. Cisco Press.

CentralS. D. X. (2018). *NFV*. Retrieved from https://www.sdxcentral.com/nfv/

EU GDPR. (n.d.). *The Regulation*. Retrieved June 4, 2018 from https://www.eugdpr.org/the-regulation.html

Hils, A., & Rajpreet, K. (2015). *Network Security Policy Management Solutions Have Evolved*. Retrieved June 4, 2018 from https://www.gartner.com/doc/3159925/network-security-policy-management-solutions

Huttermann, M. (2012). *DevOps for Developers*. Apress. doi:10.1007/978-1-4302-4570-4

Kim, D., & Solomon, M. (2016). *Fundamentals of Information Systems Security*. Jones & Bartlett Learning.

Kubernetes.io Pods. (2018). Retrieved June 4, 2018 from https://kubernetes.io/docs/concepts/workloads/pods/pod/

Network Heresy. (2014). *On Policy in the Data Center: The Policy Problem*. Retrieved June 4, 2018 from https://networkheresy.com/2014/04/22/on-policy-in-the-data-center-the-policy-problem/

OpenStack. (2018). *Group-Based Policy for OpenStack*. Retrieved June 4, 2018 from https://wiki.openstack.org/w/images/a/aa/Group-BasedPolicyWhitePaper_v3.pdf

PCI Security Standards Council. (2016). *PCI DSS*. Retrieved June 4, 2018 from https://www.pcisecuritystandards.org/document_library?category=pcidss&document=pci_dss

451. Research. (2010). *The Rise of DevOps*. Retrieved June 4, 2018 from https://451research.com/report-long?icid=1304

SANS. (2018). *Information Security Policy Templates*. Retrieved June 4, 2018 from https://www.sans.org/security-resources/policies

Wikipedia. (2018). *Information Security*. Retrieved June 4, 2018 from .

KEY TERMS AND DEFINITIONS

DevOps: Practices and technologies that promote tighter coupling of software development (Dev) and operations (Ops)—typically marked by more automation, continuous monitoring, shorter development cycles and higher deployment frequencies. A key driver for security policy automation. DevSecOps is a related term that refers to practices and technologies that aim to embed security in DevOps practices.

Dynamic Security Service Insertion: Automated deployment of security services such as firewalls. Often enabled by network functions virtualization (NFV) and service function chaining (SFC) technologies. A key enabler of security policy automation.

Group-Based Policy: A security policy automation methodology that uses the metadata associated with entities such as applications and workloads to determine the policies that the entities need to be subject to.

Network Security Policy: A formal set of rules, principles, procedures, and guidelines to prevent unauthorized access to resources on the network. Areas of concern include access control, intrusion detection and protection, encryption, network infrastructure equipment security, and wireless security.

Network Security Policy Automation: Automation of implementation of codified network security policies in a dynamic manner. May cover the entire or a portion of the security policy lifecycle (e.g., planning, review, deployment, monitoring, updates, decommissioning) across different geographic regions, business units, on-premises networks, public clouds, etc.

Network Security Policy Computation: Determination of appropriate network security policies for a given entity or group of entities, based on various requirements including higher level IT policies and business requirements. Dynamic policy computation (e.g., by leveraging big data and machine learning techniques) is an emerging area.

Policy: A broad term that could refer to high level IT policies that support business objectives, detailed technical and procedural requirements for specific areas of IT, or anything in between.

Chapter 10
Automatic Address Scheduling and Management for Broadband IP Networks

Jun Bi
Tsinghua University, China

Chongfeng Xie
China Telecom, China

Chen Li
China Telecom, China

Qiong Sun
China Telecom, China

ABSTRACT

The increase in number, diversity, and complexity of modern network devices and services creates unprecedented challenges for the currently prevailing approach of manual IP address management. Manually maintaining IP addresses could always be sub-optimal for IP resource utilization. Besides, it requires heavy human effort from network operators. To achieve high utilization and flexible scheduling of IP network addresses, it is necessary to automate the address scheduling process in the Internet of the future. Based on analysis of the gap between existing address management methods and emerging requirements of the IP network, this chapter illustrates CASM, a new approach for IP address scheduling, including its background, use cases, requirements, general framework, system architecture, interface, and workflow. A prototype system is developed and evaluated based on data from real-world networks and users in two Chinese provinces. Experimental results demonstrate that our system can largely improve the address utilization efficiency and reduce the workload of network resource maintenance.

DOI: 10.4018/978-1-5225-7146-9.ch010

INTRODUCTION

As a typical large-scale information network system, broadband IP networks contain and maintain various resources such as IP addresses, link bandwidths, forwarding capacities, caches, sessions, and so on, that work as basic elements to provide broadband services. Resource management is then one of the key processes in network operations. Timely allocating resources to meet the needs of different categories of customers, and at the same time achieving the globally optimal efficiency with those limited resources, have always been the goals of network resource management. Meanwhile, network operators are devoting increasing attention to IP address management, since IP addresses are the primary resource to provide connectivity and other services on the broadband Internet. In this chapter, based on real-world Internet Service Provider (ISP) requirements for IP networks, the authors abandon the traditional manual and distributed configuration method of IP addresses, exploit the benefit of centralized control with SDN as discussed by McKeown et al. (2008), and propose CASM (Coordinated Address Space Management), a centralized IP resource pooling and intelligent management system, to automatically allocate and revoke addresses.

BACKGROUND

Currently (2018), in most cases, IP address management systems lack an automated control mechanism. For instance, the address system integrated in Broadband Remote Access Servers (BRASes) is configured by the OAM team via CLI, and the management of IP addresses is purely artificial. Network operators manually allocate IP addresses when they are exhausted on a BRAS. Some users may have to wait until new IP blocks are assigned to the BRAS. Therefore, the timeliness of address allocation cannot be guaranteed.

Moreover, the increase in number, diversity and complexity of modern network devices and services brings new challenges for address management in IP networks:

- The efficiency of manual assignment is often sub-optimal. Real-world addresses are often managed across multiple, partly disconnected systems. These different systems lack timely interactions about address usage, leading to the situation where one network segment falls short of IP addresses while another experiences redundancy. Manual resource management could cause untimely scheduling and reduced utilization efficiency.
- The burden of address configuration on network operators with network elements could be non-trivial and heavy. IP addresses for various network systems need to be adjusted quickly due to frequent user and traffic dynamics. Besides, IPv6 transition techniques produce the need for controlling and sharing addresses among entities. Addresses of different network slices should be configured on each transition instance for High Availability (HA) purposes. Therefore, resource utilization of network systems may change very quickly. However, the current IP address management system depends on manual administration and configuration, and lacks an open, programmable interface for automatic IP resource management. This leads to a heavy maintenance burden and untimely response to dynamics.

- Inefficient and trivial manual management leads to serious fragmentation of IP address space. Networks no longer consist of large blocks of consecutive addresses, but randomly scattered sets of many small blocks or even independent individual addresses. The granularity of IPv4 address distribution is often, in some networks, as trivial as /23 or /24. Such fragmentation further decreases resource utilization efficiency and complicates manual management. Without open programmable interfaces and automated control, the clustering of small blocks or single IP addresses is difficult to achieve.

The problems with manual monitoring and management of networks have been recognized by industry. Huawei Technologies Co. Ltd. has proposed the SDN-based refined O&M to achieve nanosecond level service quality for detection in data centers. Li, Huang and Liu (2014) have proposed a communication method, communication system, resource pool management system, switch device and control device to better utilize SDN flow tables and controller resources. However, no previous effort has addressed the challenges of IP address monitoring and management.

To improve the utilization efficiency of IP resources and reduce overall Operating Expenditure (OPEX) and Capital Expenditure (CAPEX) at the same time, operators have been looking for a more intelligent, agile and flexible approach to control and manage IP addresses. Assignment of such resources should work across multiple services, support flexible allocation, reclaiming and reallocation, support various network elements such as BRAS, vBRAS (virtual BRAS), Carrier Grade NAT (CGN) and firewalls and support different types of networks and addresses including public and private IPv4 addresses and IPv6 addresses.

Another pioneer work that should be mentioned here is IPAM (IPAM Worldwide, n.d.), which stands for Internet Protocol Address Management. It is a network management discipline applied to IP address allocation and planning for IPv4 and IPv6 dynamic address assignment via Dynamic Host Configuration Protocol (DHCP) services and name-to-address lookups via Domain Name System (DNS) services. As shown in Figure 1, IPAM entails its application to three inter-related core IP network functions:

- **IP Address Inventory:** The allocation, tracking and maintenance of IPv4 and IPv6 address spaces, from public or private blocks, allocated hierarchically down through the subnet level to individual assignments. An effective practice of the IP address inventory assures hierarchical block allocations, managed overlapping allocations, and unique address assignments.
- **DHCP:** Among addresses assigned from subnets, some may be assigned by DHCP servers, which are configured with corresponding IP address pools and associated client configuration information. DHCP management involves appropriate pool sizing and option value assignment to enable the DHCP server to assign IP addresses and configuration parameters to laptops, IP phones and wireless devices, among others.
- **DNS:** DNS performs the name lookup function, which provides the resolution of a domain name into IP addresses.

These three foundational IPAM cornerstones are tightly inter-related. A DHCP address pool must align with a provisioned subnet from the IP address plan, and a DNS name must map to the correct IP address as defined in the IP address plan and DHCP server. The practice of IPAM then requires cohesive management of these three IP network functions.

Figure 1. The architecture of IPAM

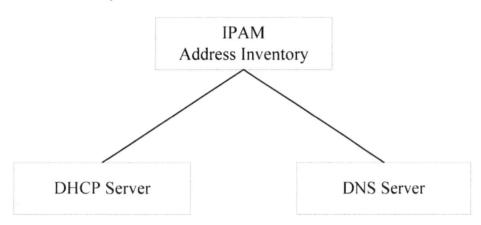

IPAM functions are crucial to the user experience in an IP network - if the DHCP doesn't provide a given device with an IP address, the user cannot connect it. If the DNS doesn't resolve the address of a given website, no one will reach it; and users rely on these functions every day to connect to the web or intranet applications.

IPAM has been successful in the market, and commercial products have been provided by several vendors. Nevertheless, the use cases for IPAM is limited: It has mainly been used for enterprise scenarios to provide address management services for enterprise customers, and does not consider the requirements of other use cases, such as metro area networks which are generally larger than enterprise networks. Another use case is related to the emerging cloud-based networks which introduce new techniques such as SDN and Network Function Virtualization (NFV).

In this chapter, CASM is the acronym of "Coordinated Address Space Management", it migrates traditional manual IP resource management to centralized, programmable and automated scheduling to increase the flexibility of address allocation. It maintains a centralized address pool and monitors the IP resource utilization of each network element, from which it dynamically allocates or revokes addresses to achieve optimal resource scheduling.

This chapter is organized as follow:

- The authors first introduce scenarios for address management in ISP networks and identify design requirements for IP resource pooling and management system to guide the system design.
- Then, the authors propose CASM, an SDN-based Centralized IP Address Pooling and Intelligent Management system to address the design requirements by providing flexible, automated, and optimal management of IP resources.
- Last, the authors evaluated CASM with extensive experiments based on data from real ISP networks and customers provided by China Telecom. The results show that CASM can improve the utilization efficiency of IP resources to a large extent while automating address management and reducing manual work.

SCENARIOS AND DESIGN REQUIREMENTS

Scenarios

Some common scenarios for IP address management in ISP networks are listed below:

- **Address Allocation for BRAS/vBRAS:** The BRAS/vBRAS devices requires pre-configured IPv4 and IPv6 prefixes to be allocated to users by means of DHCP or Point-to-Point Protocol over Ethernet (PPPoE) at the edge of IP networks. Generally, to meet the needs of different types of services and customers, each BRAS/vBRAS would have multiple local address pools and require a timely allocation of IP addresses in order to address user dynamics.
- **IPv6 Transition:** In order to meet the needs of different transition scenarios, networks often deploy more than one transition technology as well as keeping redundant backups. The need to make sure that new customers who will be assigned an IPv6 Prefix only can still access any Internet content (including IPv4-only content) can be addressed by mechanisms (e.g., DS-Lite (Hankins & Mrugalski, 2011), Lw4over6 (Cui, Sun, Boucadair, Tsou, Lee, & Farrer, 2015), etc.) that requires the configuration of global IPv4 address pools. A centralized address management entity should be provided among different transition instances.
- **Address Allocation for Third Party Systems:** Systems such as OSS and OpenStack (Sefraoui, Aissaoui, & Eleuldj, 2016) should be able to acquire IP addresses from the allocation system through RESTful APIs to allocate addresses to hosts under their management. Besides, some management systems (e.g., OpenStack) also require addresses from the allocation system in a RESTful manner. Therefore, the system should be able to provision such services in cooperation with DNS or DHCP servers.

Automatic IP address management approach can also be used in some other scenarios, such as IoT and connected cars, where massive amount of devices need to be dynamically configured with IP addresses before they are fully connected to the Internet. In some of these scenarios, connectivity is not required to be 24/7 online so efficient IP address management is important and the IP address release can be beneficial.

Requirements

Based on the above use cases, the authors illustrate their insights on the design requirements of the IP address pooling and management system.

In order to obtain the optimal efficiency of address allocation, an integrated and centralized IP address management solution is needed; such solution offers an aggregated comprehensive view on all stages of the IP resource life cycle, from selection and allocation to reclaiming.

As address consumption in each device is changing fast over time due to changes in users, services, traffic or session volumes, the management system should automatically gather resource utilization from the devices and react dynamically.

Address management policies should adapt to a broad variety of usage scenarios and multiple types of network entities, both physical and virtual, including BRASes, vBRASes, Broadband Network Gateways (BNGs), vBNGs (virtual BNGs), CGN, firewalls, Radio Access Networks (RANs) (V.EG, 2013), etc.

In order to build CASM, there is a clear need for documenting a set of requirements that must be the basis for defining the architecture framework for CASM. The requirements should be able to meet the various use cases identified in this chapter.

The following sub-sections identify the set of requirements that must be addressed by the CASM system.

General Operational Requirements

Some requirements are not specific to any particular functionality of CASM but applicable to all aspects of the CASM system.

- **Multi-Tenancy:** All interfaces exposed by the CASM system must be multi-tenant capable. This is highly desirable for cloud-based network management solutions. It may also be applicable to a service provider environment with different managed services.
- **Authentication and Authorization:** All interfaces exposed by the CASM system must support an authentication scheme. It is also highly desirable to support operational restrictions on certain resources based on identity for security reasons.
- **Audit Logging:** All the CASM activities must be logged for auditing or debugging purposes. The system must provide an interface to access these records.
- **Error Notification:** All the interfaces exposed by the CASM system must support error handling and a user-defined error notification mechanism such as alert or email.

Interface Modeling Requirements

The interface to an external user must be metadata driven as much as possible to meet a wider set of use-cases. For example, instead of requesting an explicit IPv4 address, the user should specify an address request based on its requirements.

The following requirements should be considered for address pool management purposes:

- **Interface Definition:** The attributes should be related to the requester which could be a physical device, a virtual machine, a container or other entities present in the network;
- **Functional Attributes:** Switches, routers, firewalls, servers end-points;
- **Form Factor Attributes:** Physical/virtual operational attributes such as the management plane, control plane, data plane;
- **Network Segment Identifiers:** VLAN, VxLAN, or any user-defined values;
- **Network Segment Types:** Point-to-point, multi-point, etc.;
- **Addressing Scope Attributes:** Private, public, Virtual Private Networking (VPN), unicast, multicast;
- **Extensible User-Defined Attributes**.

Functional Requirements

A CASM system should all the management of different kinds of address pools. The following pools should be considered for implementation. This is not mandatory or exhaustive by any means but listed here anyway as they are most commonly used in networks. The CASM system should allow user-defined pools with any address objects.

There should be a rich set of functionalities for the operations in a given pool, such as query, add, modify, delete, etc. In order to build a complete address management system, it is important that the CASM should be able to integrate with other address-related services, such as DHCP, DNS, or some address-management functions in the legacy network management system. This shall provide a complete solution to network operators without requiring any manual or proprietary workflow.

The address management system needs to handle IPv4 and IPv6 resources, networks including subnetting and prefixes with any valid configurable prefix lengths. All well-defined and standardized address types should be administrable.

IP address management shall meet additional requirements including high reliability, availability, security and performance, according to best practices for mission critical infrastructure.

GENERAL FRAMEWORK

Nowadays in providers' environments, address management is implemented at various levels, from centrally aggregated spreadsheets to application-specific databases/software (IPAM). Many IPAM software packages implement RESTful APIs so that organizations employing modern operational methods like DevOps can use and expand IPAM for their needs, while at the same time establishing a centralized database to administer their IP addresses. Often such systems need to be integrated with provisioning systems for domain name resolution features.

However, organizations use the IPAM system to manage their IP address space, often with proprietary databases and interfaces. One of the biggest challenges with IPAM systems is the lack of standardized interfaces for allocation, storing and retrieving information. So there is a pressing need to define a new address management system that meets this diverse set of requirements. Such a system must be built with well-defined interfaces so users can easily migrate from one vendor to another without rewriting their network management systems. CASM is a general architecture to meet the requirements of automatic address/pool management and allocation in a wide variety of scenarios. Hopefully, it can help reduce the workload of existing manual configuration approaches, and also use addresses more efficiently. Figure 2 shows the general architecture of CASM.

Each component of CASM is introduced in sub-sections.

CASM Application

The CASM Application is a functional entity which usually has the requirements of centralized address management to realize its specific upper-layer functions. In order to achieve this goal, it needs to manage, operate and maintain the CASM Coordinator. For example, an operator or external user can manage the address pool in the CASM Coordinator and access log, address allocation records, etc.

Figure 2. The architecture of CASM

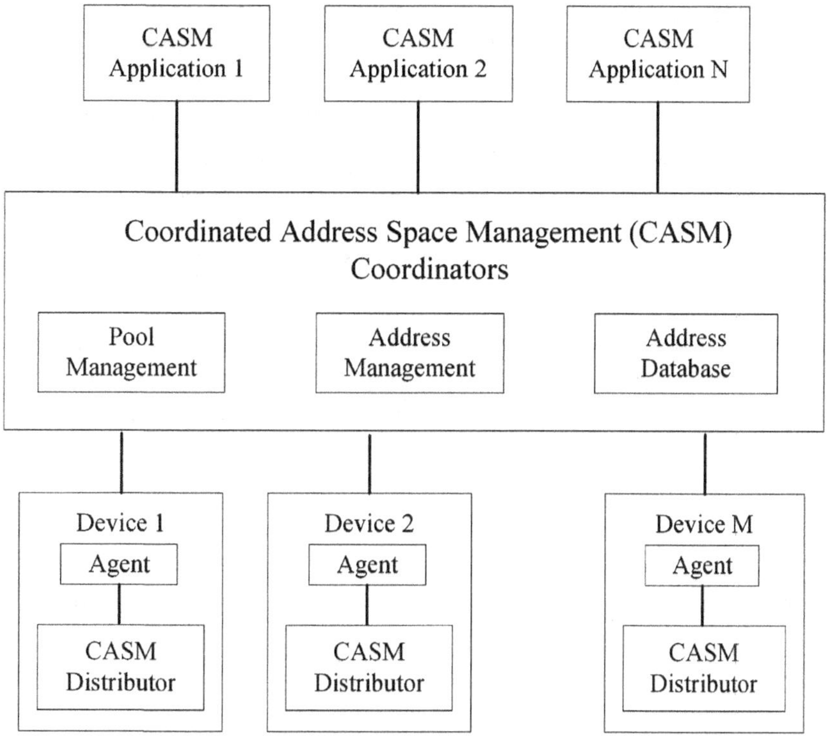

CASM Coordinator

The CASM Coordinator is a centralized address management coordinator for the CASM Application to maintain overall address pools, addresses, address properties, etc. It maintains an address database including the overall address pools (OAP) and the address pool status (APS). CASM Applications can maintain their remaining address pools in the OAP. They can also reserve some address pools for special purposes. The address pool status is to reflect the current usage of address pools for different devices. The CASM Coordinator also has the capability to maintain the address pools to different devices dynamically.

CASM Device

A CASM Device is responsible for distributing or allocating addresses from local address pools received from the CASM Coordinator.

The Device Agent (DA) is a component residing in a CASM Device through which the device can contact with the CASM Coordinator. On behalf of the device, the agent initiates the address pool allocation requests, passes the address pools to local instances, detect the availability of address pools or report the status of local address pool usage and update the address pool requests, etc. For some devices, e.g. IPv6 transition and VPN, additional routing modules are needed to update the routing table accordingly.

The CASM Distributor is another component in a CASM device. The DHCP server is a typical distributor that can assign IP addresses to client hosts, and the DHCP protocol is usually used for this task. The address assignment procedure between the CASM Distributor and the client host is out of the scope of this chapter.

The device determines whether the usage status of the IP address pool in that device satisfies the condition. The address pool is a sharable resource; when the resource in the device is insufficient or excessive, it sends an address pool request to the CASM Coordinator and receives a response with address pools allocated for it. It can then use these address pools to assign more addresses to end users.

Typical CASM Devices include BNGs, BRASes, CGNs, DHCP Servers, NATs, IPv6 Transitions, DNS Servers, etc.

The form of devices is diverse, it can be physical or virtual, and it can be box-integrated with a control plane and a user plane, or a separated control plane remote from the box, where one or more devices share the centralized control plane. In the latter case, the control plane will manage multiple user plane devices. A number of devices that are subordinate to the control plane will jointly share the address pools to make address utilization much higher.

The overall procedure is as follows:

- Operators configure remaining address pools centrally in the CASM Coordinator. There are multiple address pools which can be configured centrally. The CASM Coordinator server then divides the address pools into addressing units (AUs) which would be allocated to device agents by default.
- The agent will initiate an AddressPool request to the CASM Coordinator. It can carry its desired size of address pool with the request, or just use a default value. The address pool size in the request is only used as a hint. The actual size of the address pool is totally determined by the CASM Coordinator. It would also carry the DA's identification and the type of the address pool.
- The CASM Coordinator looks up remaining address pools in its local database, and then allocates a set of address pools to the DA. Each address pool has a lifetime.
- The DA receives the AddressPool reply and uses it for its purpose.
- If the lifetime of the address pool is going to expire, the DA should issue an AddressPoolRenew request to extend it, including IPv4, IPv6, port numbers, etc.
- The AddressPoolReport module keeps monitoring and reports the usage of all current address pools for each transition mechanism. If it is running out of address pools, it can renew the AddressPoolRequest for a newly allocated one. It can also release and recycle an existing address pool if that address pool has not been used for a specific and configurable time.
- When the connection of the CASM Coordinator is lost or it needs the status information of certain applications, it may pre-actively query the DA for its status information.

CASM Application to Broadband IP Networks

Following the CASM model, the authors design and implementation a system that primarily serves the devices on network edges.

The system includes three major components: (1) A centralized network resource pool manager that automatically performs IP address allocation and reclaiming according to network dynamics; (2) A centralized controller that communicates with underlying network devices by means of protocols such as NETCONF specified by Enns et al. (2011), and; (3) Network elements enhanced with an Address Management Agent (AMA) that monitors local resource usage and communicates with the centralized controller. Besides, the authors also designed an IP address management policy data model based on NETCONF / YANG (Bjorklund, 2016) model so that the controller can instantiate address management policies and gather resource utilization status.

The authors also consider deploying the system in NFV environment (NFV, 2013). The NFV Orchestrator (NFVO) is responsible for the overall management of virtual network elements such as vBRAS or vBNG in the underlying infrastructure, which is a pool of CPU, memory, storage, and other resources. The Virtualized Network Function Manager (VNFM) is responsible for lifecycle and performance management of vBRAS devices, such as element instantiation, expansion, shrinking, and other functions. The Element Management System (EMS) is responsible for performing the functions of the network element management tasks in virtual environment. In the virtualization environment, operators can dynamically create network elements in order to meet the requirements of increasing business and destroy them when the business requirements decrease. Taking vBRAS as an example, compared with the BRAS, it can be created or destroyed dynamically according to the business requirements to get more flexibility. It is challengeable to meet the IP address pool configuration requirements manually. Therefore, CASM provides a fast and agile IP address pool configuration approach for vBRAS.

The whole architecture of the system is shown in Figure 3. The function of each component is elaborated in the following sections.

Network Resource Pool Manager

Network resource pool manager (later referred as "Resource Manager") maintains a global IP address pool in a database, and the online information of all network elements in the vBRAS Management

Figure 3. The CASM implementation for Broadband Metro-Area Networks

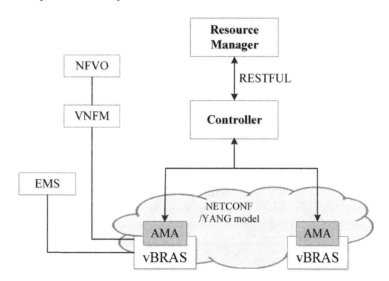

Module. As shown in Figure 4, to achieve intelligent scheduling of resources, it gathers the information of device deployment, IP address consumption of each network element in a centralized manner in the Address Inquiry Module, dynamically decides address allocation or reclaiming strategies in the Address Allocation Module according to device address usage ratio, and communicates the policies to the controller through the Controller Management Module. The User Interfaces (UIs) is designed for the Resource Manager to display address utilization status and statistical information to the administrator. Besides, in order to expose the capability of address allocation for third party systems including Operations Support System (OSS) and OpenStack, the Resource Manager expose the address management capabilities through RESTful interfaces. Finally, south-bound interfaces are also needed through which the Resource Manager communicates with the controller to issue policies, acquire address usage, and timely allocate or reclaim address blocks.

Centralized Controller

The centralized controller collects address utilization status of network elements through south-bound interfaces, after which it regulates different interface protocols into a standard format and reports the information to the Resource Manager through north-bound interfaces. Besides, the controller is responsible for distributing address-related policies to each network element and converging reports from each device in order to reduce the volume of information processed by the Resource Manager. The controller is implemented based on ONOS (ONOS, n.d.), a widely-used Open-Source controller with some functional extensions including network element address utilization status gathering and regulating, address policies distribution, and its support for various south-bound interfaces. As shown in Figure

Figure 4. The architecture of Resource Manager and Controller

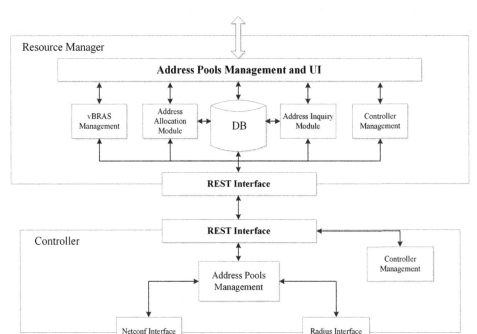

3, the authors implemented two types of south-bound interfaces including NETCONF for virtualized network elements, and RADIUS for hardware network elements.

Enhanced Network Elements

Enhanced network elements refer to all the equipment at the edge of network, such as vBRAS, which are under the management of CASM. Each network element is extended with an Address Management Agent (AMA) module that corresponds to the address pooling resources management functions. AMA is the combination of agent and distributor in each devices of Figure 2. The AMA module receives the address allocation or reclaiming policies, collects local address utilization status and reports the statistics to the controller regularly according to prior configurations through south-bound interfaces.

WORKFLOW OF CENTRALIZED ADDRESS RESOURCE SCHEDULING

CASM provides a centralized and automated scheduling to enhance the flexibility of address resource allocation. This section illustrates the workflow of the address pool management mechanism. The workflow is depicted in Figure 5. There are three major stages in the system as elaborated below.

Figure 5. The workflow of centralized address resource pooling and scheduling system

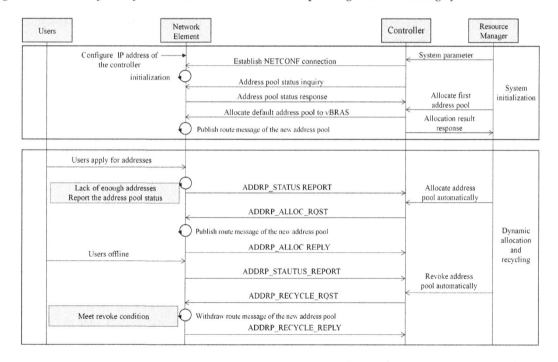

Network Element Initialization

The IP address of the controller is pre-configured to network elements. When a device gets online, it establishes a NETCONF connection with the controller and applies for the initial allocation of address pool resources, in the form of IP address blocks, from the Resource Manager. Then the device can allocate IP addresses to end users and broadcast the appropriate routing information. Meanwhile, the Resource Manager marks the allocated address block as occupied to avoid reallocating of the same resources.

Address Resource Allocation

Network elements, such as BRAS or vBRAS, calculate the utilization ratio of their own address pools, based on the proportion of the number of addresses these network elements have allocated to the total number of address resources, and reports to the controller regularly. If there is a rapid increase in the number of online users, the utilization ratio of the address pool resources will reach the pre-configured alarm threshold in address database of the coordinator. Under detection of such report or receipt of the corresponding notification sent by the network elements, the Resource Manager triggers a new address allocation process.

First, the Resource Manager selects appropriate IP blocks from the central resource pool that can satisfy the device's requirements and allocates them to the controller with the symbol of identification and domain name of the network element. The selection process can be based on many factors, such as the length of the prefix, the IP address consumption history of the given network element. Second, the controller sends the new address resources to the specified device according to the Resource Manager's instructions. Finally, the network element that became short of IP addresses will be able to timely obtain new IP addresses and allocate them to additional users.

Free Address Reclaiming

In situations such as a rapid decrease in the number of online users, the utilization ratio of address pool resources will reach the reclaiming bottom threshold. The Resource Manager will start its resource reclaiming process of free address blocks. First, the Resource Manager sends the identification of the reclaimed address resources and identification of the relevant network element to the controller. Second, the controller notifies the particular device to reclaim the address resources and withdraws the related routing information. Finally, a successful reclaiming is reported to the Resource Manager by the controller so that the status of the reclaimed address changes to "idle". Thus, the address resources can be recycled, which improves overall resource utilization efficiency across network elements even in different areas.

The management of IPv6 address pool is essentially the same as that of IPv4. That is, depending on the utilization ratio of IPv6 address pool resources, the Resource Manager decides whether to allocate more IPv6 prefixes/addresses or reclaim free IPv6 prefixes/addresses. However, since IPv6 has a huge address space, larger IPv6 address block can be allocated to a device and expect that the IP address requirements can be satisfied for a long time. Therefore, the frequency of allocation and reclaiming for address blocks is lower than that of IPv4. In such case, the CASM is more used to centrally manage and monitor the utilization ratio of IPv6 addresses.

Figure 6. The decision tree of the Resource Manager

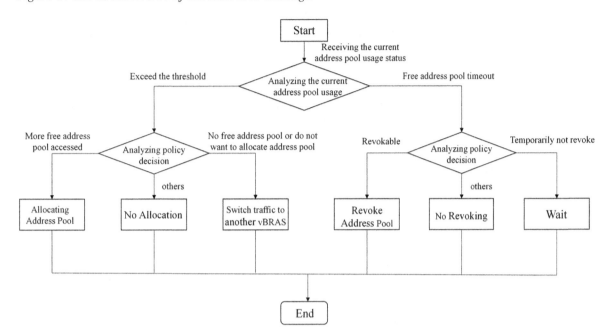

Decision Tree of the Resource Manager

In order to automatically manage IP address resources and obtain optimal utilization of address resource allocation, the decision tree of the Resource Manager plays a core role in the whole system. The policy decision tree in consideration of all kinds of situations is summarized in Figure 6.

South-Bound Interface Models

The design of address resource pooling and intelligent scheduling system can accommodate both NFV virtual network elements and legacy hardware network elements by developing a unified south-bound interface set. The major messages exchanged between the controller and underlying network elements include: regular report of IP resource utilization, IPv4/IPv6 address allocation and free address reclaiming. The authors developed a NETCONF YANG model (Bjorklund, 2016) to represent IP resource usage.

IP Resource Utilization Report Model

```
module: ietf-address-pool-status
+--rw address-pool-status
|  +--rw address-pool* [address-pool-name]
|     +--rw address-pool-name                          string
|     +--rw address-pool-id                            string
|     +--rw domain-name                             string
|     +--rw status                               enumeration
```

```
|     +--rw address-pool-entries
|       +--rw ipv4-addresss-block* [ipv4-adress-block-name]
|       |   +--rw ipv4-adress-block-name              string
|       |   +--rw address-pool-id                     string
|       |   +--rw peak-address-usage-ratio              uint32
|       |   +--rw average-address-usage-ratio           uint32
|       +--rw ipv6-addresss-block* [ipv6-adress-block-name]
|       |   +--rw ipv6-adress-block-name              string
|       |   +--rw address-pool-id                      string
|       |   +--rw peak-address-usage-ratio              uint32
|           +--rw average-address-usage-ratio     uint32
```

This model describes how IP address resources are used by network elements. The "address-pool-name" field describes the name of the address pool. The "status" field describes the status of the address pool (active or idle), the "peak-address-usage-ratio" describes the peak usage rate of the address block. The "average-address-usage-ratio" field indicates the average usage rate of the address block.

IPv4 Address Allocation Model

```
module: ietf-address-pools
  +--rw address-pools
  |   +--rw device-id                          int
  |   +--rw time                               double
  |   +--rw address-pool* [address-pool-name]
  |       +--rw address-pool-name                    string
  |       +--rw address-pool-id                      string
  |       +--rw domain-name                           string
  |       +--rw address-pool-entries
  |       | +--rw ipv4-adress-block* [ipv4-address-block-name]
  |       | | +--rw ipv4-address-block-name          string
  |       | | +--rw ipv4-address-block-id      int
  |       | | +--rw ipv4-prefix                       string
  |       | | +--rw ipv4-prefix-length?            int
  |       | | +--rw user-gateway          inet:ipv4-address-no-zone
  |       | | +--rw gw-netmask            yang:dotted-quad
  |       | | +--rw type                 address-pool-type
  |       | | +--rw lifetime              yang:date-and-time
  |       | | +--rw primary-dns              dns-primary
  |       | | +--rw secondary-dns            dns-secondary
```

This model is used for IP address allocation to the network elements. The "device-id" field describes the ID of the device that applied for address resource allocation. The "address-pool-name" field describes the name of address pool. The "ipv4-address-block-name" field describes the name of the IPv4 address block which is allocated to the device. The "lifetime" field describes the lifetime for the allocated address block, over which the device should renew its application for this address block.

Free IPv4 Address Reclaiming Model

```
module: ietf-address-pools
| +--rw address-pools
|    +--rw device-id                                      int
|    +--rw address-pool [address-pool-name]
|    +--rw address-pool-name                          string
|    +--rw address-pool-id                                int
|    +--rw address-pool-entries
|    |  +--rw ipv4-address-block* [ipv4-address-block-name]
|    |  | +--rw ipv4-address-block-name              string
|    |  | +--rw ipv4-address-block-id                  string
|       +--rw leasing-time                               int
```

This model describes the interface information of the reclaiming process. The "device-id" field describes the ID of device which releases address resources. The "address-pool-name" field describes the name of address pool. The "ipv4-address-block-name" field describes the name of IPv4 address block to be reclaimed. The "leasing-time" field describes the leasing time of the re-claimed address block.

IMPLEMENTATION AND EVALUATION

The authors have implemented the Resource Manager and the controller of CASM based on the ONOS controller (Xie, Bi, Yu, Li, Sun, & Liu, 2017), and extended the AMA module of a private software implementation of vBRAS. Based on the Apache Karaf Open Service Gateway Initiative (OSGI) framework adopted by ONOS, the authors implemented the Resource Manager and the controller of CASM as sub-system bundles and loaded them into ONOS as dynamic modules (9.2K LoC). The extended controller bundle can be further divided into three modules, including the north-bound interface module, the core control module, and the south-bound interface module. The north-bound interface implementation separates underlying device information from the Resource Manager. Therefore, under the situation where device failure occurs, the Resource Manager will not be affected. The core control module transforms message types between south-bound and north-bound formats. The south-bound interface implementation communicates with network elements including vBRAS or BRAS through NETCONF or RADIUS protocols.

For the vBRAS extension (2K LoC), based on the IETF YANG model (Bjorklund, 2016), the authors designed and implemented the south-bound interface extension to their original developed vBRAS software. The entire south-bound interfaces comply with RFC 6241 (Enns, Bjorklund, Schoenwaelder, & Bierman, 2011).

The authors deployed the system in two Chinese provinces where China Telecom is present. They also evaluated system performance with real network users.

Performance and CAPEX of VBRAS vs. BRAS

CASM considers NFV as an important use case for IP address management. Therefore, the authors implement CASM in NFV environment in a metro-area Network with vBRAS deployment. To provide equally high bandwidth (20Gbps) and support as many users (16,000) as BRAS, vBRAS needs a X86-based hardware server with 16 CPU cores. Currently vBRAS has no advantage in CAPEX compared with a physical BRAS with equal performance.

However, vBRAS provides a much higher flexibility and lower CAPEX when there is a need to upgrade network functions or support new network functions. For some scenarios where ISPs implement a dedicated BRAS for sparse value-added services in local networks that require NAT capabilities, the BRAS should be enhanced with such NAT functions. In this situation, the CAPEX of vBRAS suffers a dramatic increase of in CAPEX due to the additional NAT cards. Therefore, the CAPEX of vBRAS is much lower than traditional hardware BRAS. Moreover, virtualized implementation could dramatically decrease to a large extent the time for new network functions to come to the market. To enhance hardware BRAS with NAT capabilities, network operators should deploy additional hardware devices, adjust link resources, load bandwidth, etc. while virtualized implementation could be deployed with simple software upgrades.

Therefore, from the ISP's point of view, NFV could still reduce the overall CAPEX and the time for new network functions to come to the market.

OPEX of CASM vs. Traditional Manual Configuration

It is common agreed that there are hundreds of BRAS devices that can be deployed in a metro region. Manual IP address configuration of such a large number of devices will cost lots of human work and affect OPEX. During each address allocation process, the network operator has to configure many fields into the BRAS device including the IP address block name, the gateway, the address range, the DNS server for this address block and the domain name. Besides, the operator has to manually configure related routing information about this address block. All manual configurations of ONE address block for ONE device could cost minutes, and the configuration of the entire BRAS pool of metro region would affect OPEX budgets. However, in CASM, through central IP address pooling and automated configuration, the controller online registration process, the vBRAS devices' online registration process, device status report process and address allocation process could each be implemented in 60 milliseconds, as shown in Figure 7, which could save lots of human efforts and thus reduce OPEX.

In the situation where the IP resources for one device are exhausted, because all IP addresses have been allocated to other devices, the operator has to manually log into each device to check if there exists a free address block, withdraw related address information and routing information, and then re-allocate the reclaimed address block to the exhausted device. However, in CASM, a BRAS device can report its IP utilization status is in 60 ms. The centralized Resource Manager could analyze the resource utilization of each device according to its regular report and reclaim free addresses to the resource pool in 40 milliseconds. Thus, CASM could offer timely reaction for IP address exhaustion situations in seconds. This could not only reduce OPEX, but also provide better service experience for network tenants.

Figure 7. Time consumption of each stage in CASM

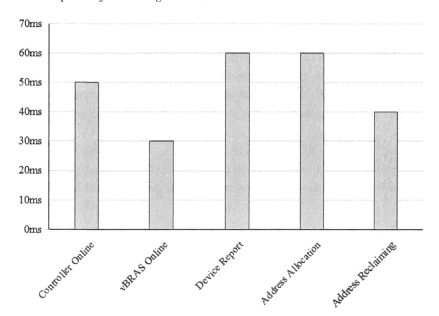

Address Utilization Efficiency of CASM vs. Manual Configuration

IP addresses used to be manually configured on network elements. IP addresses are dedicated to related devices. The device will not release the IP address blocks even if they are entirely free. However, when the IP address resources in one device are exhausted, the operator of traditional BRAS may have two options.

First, the operator could allocate a new address block to the device. However, if the address block of another device is entirely free, the overall resource utilization efficiency is degraded.

Second, the operator could "randomly borrow" IP addresses from a second device by migrating the entire or a subset of an address block from one device to the other. The size of the borrowed address block depends on how many addresses are free in the selected device. In some extreme cases, the operator has to fetch one IP address to fuel the exhausted device, which could lead to address block fragmentation at the cost of degrading the routing efficiency, let alone the address usage efficiency.

On the other hand, CASM manages a centralized shared IP address pool for all devices. The free address blocks reported by each device could be timely reclaimed, assuring timely re-allocation for devices with few IP address resources. Thus, IP address blocks are less likely to be partitioned, and the resource fragmentation situation could be alleviated.

CASM Scalability

The authors built an ONOS cluster comprised of three controller instances, and measured the maximum network elements that can be supported by the cluster. Evaluation results demonstrate that the cluster could maintain 3000 sessions with the same quantity of network elements, which could cover a metro-area network. CASM could support more network elements through extending the cluster size.

CONCLUSION AND FUTURE WORK

In this chapter, the authors proposed CASM, a centralized IP address resource pooling and intelligent management system based on SDN to satisfy real demands from ISPs. The authors introduced the system architecture, general requirement, workflow, address resource scheduling algorithm, and interface design of this system. Experimental results demonstrate that this solution can not only improve the utilization of IP network address resources immensely, but also reduce the address resource configuration burden of network managers.

For the future work, the authors will deploy CASM on large-scale networks to validate the feasibility and performance. Besides, the authors will try to apply the centralized management approach to other network resources, such as forwarding capacity, cache and so on, to achieve higher utilization.

ACKNOWLEDGMENT

This research was supported by National Key R&D Program of China (2017YFB0801701) and Beijing National Research Center for Information Science and Technology (BNRist).

REFERENCES

Bjorklund, M. (2016). *YANG-A data modeling language for the Network Configuration Protocol (NET-CONF)*. IETF RFC 7950.

Cui, Y., Sun, Q., Boucadair, M., Tsou, T., Lee, Y., & Farrer, I. (2015). *Lightweight 4over6: An Extension to the Dual-Stack Lite Architecture*. IETF RFC7596.

Enns, R., Bjorklund, M., Schoenwaelder, J., & Bierman, A. (2011). *NETCONF Configuration Protocol*. IETF RFC 6241.

ETSI. (2013). *Network Function Virtualisation (NFV): Use Cases*. Retrieved February 12, 2017, from http://www.etsi.org/deliver/etsi_gs/nfv/001_099/001/01.01.01_60/gs_nfv001v010101p.pdf

Hankins, DW, Mrugalski, T. (2011). *Dynamic Host Configuration Protocol for IPv6 (DHCPv6) Options for Dual-Stack Lite*. IETF RFC 6334.

IPAM Worldwide. (n.d.). Retrieved from the IPAM Worldwide: http://www.ipamworldwide.com/ipam/

Li, C., Huang, L., & Liu, Z. (2014). *Communication method, communication system, resource pool management system, switch device and control device*. U.S. Patent App. 15/122,323.

McKeown, N., Anderson, T., Balakrishnan, H., Parulkar, G., Peterson, L., Rexford, J., ... Turner, J. (2008). OpenFlow: Enabling innovation in campus networks. *Computer Communication Review*, *38*(2), 69–74. doi:10.1145/1355734.1355746

ONOS. (n.d.). Retrieved February 12, 2017, from http://onosproject.org/

Sefraoui, O., Aissaoui, M., & Eleuldj, M. (2012). Openstack: Toward an open-source solution for cloud computing. *International Journal of Computers and Applications*, *55*(3), 38–42. doi:10.5120/8738-2991

Xie, C., Bi, J., Yu, H., Li, C., Sun, C., Liu, Q., ... Liu, S. (2017). ARPIM: IP address resource pooling and intelligent management system for broadband ip networks. *IEEE Communications Magazine*, *55*(6), 55–61. doi:10.1109/MCOM.2017.1601001

KEY TERMS AND DEFINITIONS

CAPEX: The budget a company spends to buy, maintain, or improve its fixed assets, such as buildings, vehicles, equipment, or land.

Coordinator: A person or functional entity whose job is to organize activities and to negotiate with others in order to ensure they work together effectively.

DevOps: A software engineering practice that aims at unifying software development (Dev) and software operation (Ops).

IPAM: A means of planning, tracking, and managing the IP address space used in a network. IPAM integrates DNS and DHCP so that each is aware of changes in the other (for instance, DNS knowing of the IP address assigned to a client via DHCP, and updating itself accordingly).

NFV: A network architecture concept that uses the technologies of IT virtualization to virtualize entire classes of network node functions into building blocks that may connect, or chain together, to create communication services.

OPEX: An ongoing cost for running a product, business, or system.

YANG: A data modeling language used to model configuration and state data manipulated by the NETCONF protocol, NETCONF remote procedure calls, and NETCONF notifications. The YANG language was developed by the IETF NETCONF Data Modeling Language Working Group (NETMOD), and is defined in RFC 7950.

Chapter 11

A Perspective on the Standardization of Autonomic Detection of Service Level Agreement Violations

Jéferson Campos Nobre
University of Vale do Rio dos Sinos, Brazil

Lisandro Zambenedetti Granville
Federal University of Rio Grande do Sul, Brazil

ABSTRACT

Service level agreements (SLAs) allow networked services established between providers and their customers to operate according to the conditions defined in the SLA. Measurement mechanisms can be used to support SLA monitoring. However, these mechanisms are expensive in terms of resource consumption. In addition, if the number of SLA violations at any given time is greater than the available measurement sessions, some violations will likely be missed. The current best practice is to observe just a subset of network destinations based upon the expertise of a few human administrators. Such observation mode is error prone, reactive, and scales poorly. Such practice can lead to SLA violations being missed, which hampers the reliability of the SLA monitoring process. In this context, the use of autonomic network features can improve such processes, especially when these features are deployed in a decentralized manner. The use of these autonomic features is described in RFC 8316. The authors expect that such a document can lead to better SLA monitoring tools and methods.

INTRODUCTION

Communication requirements of distributed services running on top of an IP-based infrastructure have become increasingly demanding. Some examples are HealthCare applications (eHealth) and data-intensive science applications (eScience). The provisioning of such services with the adequate level of quality, as typically documented in the Service Level Specification (SLS) that pertains to the Service Level Agree-

DOI: 10.4018/978-1-5225-7146-9.ch011

ment (SLA), is conditioned by the accommodation of requirements that are usually expressed in terms of metrics, such as inter-packet delay variation, packet loss or latency. Such requirements usually lead to the definition of Service Level Objectives (SLOs) that must be met. Those SLOs are part of SLAs that define a contract between the provider and the consumer of the service.

Performance requirements can be employed effectively by both service providers and customers. In this context, SLOs reflect a service-level guarantee that the consumer of the service can expect to receive. Likewise, the provider of a service needs to ensure that the service-level guarantee and associated SLOs are met. When such SLOs are not met, SLAs usually include financial or other penalties, possibly with the risk of cancelling the deal. Besides, an adequate support of SLAs also improves the commercial reputation of the service provider, considering prospective customers.

The detection of SLA violations is based on the idea of identifying deviations from the contracted SLOs. In order to identify these deviations by using active measurements, it is necessary to have measurement sessions activated on key end-to-end network destinations. However, such activation is expensive in terms of resource consumption (both human and computational), let alone the amount of monitoring traffic that may jeopardize the performance of network devices and network bandwidth. Since a better monitoring coverage requires more active sessions, it increases the amount of consumed resources. On the other hand, enabling the observation of just a subset of all network flows decreases the resource consumption, but it can lead to insufficient coverage.

The decision about how to place measurement sessions is an important management issue, since it impacts the SLA monitoring coverage. The goal is to obtain the maximum coverage with a limited amount of measurement overhead. Specifically, the goal is to maximize the number of SLA violations that are detected with a limited number of resources. In this context, a feasible approach would be to add up the service levels observed across different path segments. This allows the decomposition of a large set of end-to-end measurements into a much smaller set of segment measurements. However, some end-to-end service levels cannot be determined by an additive approach. Some examples of metrics that are inadequate for additive approaches are end-to-end jitter and mean opinion scores, thus they must be measured end-to-end (Nobre, Granville, Clemm, & Prieto, 2018a).

Often, the current best practice for activating measurement sessions within a provider's network consists in relying on the network administrator's expertise to determine which destinations to select to activate the corresponding monitoring sessions. This practice has major shortcomings. Indeed, such practice assumes high dynamics and increases the complexity of network environments and delivered services. In order to provide solutions that better suit such dynamics and complexity, network-wide management solutions can be employed. A network-wide control of network devices can improve their abilities to accomplish management tasks. For example, a distributed network management algorithm can be used to allow that some devices provide additional resources for the execution of management tasks by other devices. This can be useful when either the computational load is not equally distributed among the network devices or there is heterogeneity in the computational resources of network devices. In this context, the global capability of the devices in a network can be greater than the sum of the capabilities of each device.

There is no standard solution for a distributed and autonomic detection of SLA violations. Current solutions are restricted to ad hoc scripts running on each node to automate some administrator actions. Network management researchers have investigated how to overcome analogous shortcomings considering different scenarios and management tasks. There are some proposals for passive probe activation - e.g., DECON (Di Pietro, Huici, Costantini, & Niccolini, 2010) and cSamp (Sekar, Reiter, Willinger,

Zhang, Kompella, & Andersen, 2008) - but these do not focus on autonomic features. In this context, RFC8316 (Nobre, Granville, Clemm, & Prieto, 2018a) describes a use case for the autonomic detection of SLA violations considering the use of Peer-to-Peer (P2P) techniques. The present chapter presents an overview of RFC8316, including the network management context which yielded its publication.

This chapter is organized as follows: In the Background Section, the authors present the fundamental concepts considering network measurements and P2P techniques in network management. In RFC8316 Section, the authors detail the context and the perspective of this document. In the Future Research Directions Section, the authors present what future holds for autonomic detection of SLA violations. Finally, concluding remarks are provided in the Conclusion.

BACKGROUND

Network Measurements

Several mechanisms can be used to enable network measurements, e.g., in-band/in-situ (Operations, administration and management) OAM (Norton, 2016). In general, these mechanisms are classified according to the injection of measurement traffic by the mechanisms themselves. This usually leads to two types of network measurement mechanisms: passive and active measurement mechanisms. Passive measurement is realized, for example, inside network devices through the use of packet sniffers. On the other hand, active measurement is deployed by means of active probes hosted along the network which inject synthetic (i.e., artificially generated) traffic and compute the current network performance. In addition, there are mechanisms that cannot be classified according to these two categories, and they are usually called hybrid mechanisms. In this subsection, the authors first cover some background on passive, active, and hybrid mechanisms.

Passive Measurement Mechanisms

In passive measurement, network conditions are said to be checked in a non-intrusive way, because no monitoring traffic is created by the measurement process itself. Passive measurement data can be used for a variety of purposes. Passive measurement is realized, for example, inside network devices when they observe the traffic flows that cross the device. In the context of IP Flow Information Export (IP-FIX), several documents were produced to define how to export data associated with flow records, i.e., data that is collected as part of passive measurement mechanisms, generally applied against flows of production traffic (e.g., (Claise, Trammell, & Aitken, 2013). In addition, it is possible to collect real data traffic (not just summarized flow records) with time-stamped packets, possibly sampled (e.g., (Duffield, Chiou, Claise, Greenberg, Grossglauser, & Rexford, 2009), as a means of measuring and also inferring service levels.

Flows can be defined as unidirectional sequences of packets that pass through a network device which are grouped according to some common properties. These properties can consider several packets fields, such as source/destination IP address and source/destination port number, layer 3 protocol identifier, Type of Service (ToS), and size (aggregated number of bytes). In addition, other information, such as source/destination Autonomous System (AS), and input/output interfaces can also be used to define flows. Representation of flow data must be uniform/homogeneous, as well as communication means to exchange such data between the network and the collection points (Claise, 2008). There are several protocols used to enable flow data production and exchange.

The IETF IP Flow Information eXport (IPFIX) Working Group has released several documents describing a protocol, based on the version 9 of NetFlow (Claise, 2008). Some enhancements in different domains (e.g., congestion-aware transport protocol and built-in security) were incorporated in the IPFIX protocol. Furthermore, IPFIX adopts an improved use of record templates through more precisely defined record items and measurable values. Unlike NetFlow, IPFIX requires Stream Control Transport Protocol (SCTP) (Dreibholz, Rathgeb, Rungeler, Seggelmann, Tuxen, & Stewart, 2011) to transport data. The use of SCTP provides a reliable transport and prevents congestion. Figure 1 shows the IPFIX logical model (which is based on the NetFlow logical model) as an example of a passive measurement model. In such model, metering exporters hosted in network elements (e.g., routers and switches) gather flow data and export IPFIX records to configured receivers, i.e., collectors (or collecting points).

Active Measurement Mechanisms

Active measurement mechanisms can be used to monitor SLOs and the health of a network as a whole. Such mechanisms inject synthetic traffic into specific network paths to measure the network performance in terms of, for example, delay, loss, jitter, and packet/frame loss. A well-defined injection of such traffic is usually called a measurement session. Active measurement mechanisms can be employed in different contexts, such as pre-deployment service validation and live network-wide SLA monitoring.

The generation of synthetic traffic and its computation to provide measurements results accordingly is usually performed according to an architecture that is comprised of two hosts with specific roles, a sender and a responder, also collectively known as (active) measurement probes. The exchange of packets between probes is usually defined by two inter-related protocols: a control protocol, used to initiate and control measurement sessions and to fetch their results, and a test protocol, used to send single measurement packets along the network path under test. Measurement support at the responder end may be limited to a simple echo function. There are several protocols used to enable active measurement.

Cisco Systems defines the SLA protocol (also known as IPSLA) which is described in an IETF informational RFC (Chiba et al., 2013). This widely deployed protocol measures service levels related to data link and network layers and it also emulates characteristics of different applications, both considering one-way and two-way metrics. The IPSLA logical model consists essentially of a sender and a responder, i.e., measurement probes. The protocol consists of two distinct phases: the control phase and the measurement phase. The control phase forms the base protocol, which establishes the identity of

Figure 1. Passive Measurement Model (IP Flow Information eXport)
Source: Claise, 2008

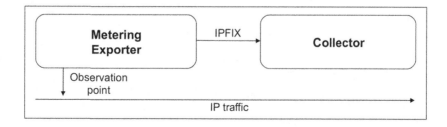

the sender and provides information for the measurement phase. The measurement phase is comprised of a sequence of measurement-request and measurement-response messages (test messages). Figure 2 shows the logical model used by IPSLA.

The IETF IP Performance Metrics (IPPM) Working Group has proposed open active measurement mechanisms that allow the exchange of packets to produce one-way and two-way metrics. These mechanisms are called One-Way Active Measurement Protocol (OWAMP, RFC4656) (Shalunov, 2006) and Two-Way Active Measurement Protocol (TWAMP, RFC5357) (Hedayat, 2008), respectively. The O/TWAMP mechanisms consist of two inter-related protocols: a control protocol, used to initiate and control measurement sessions and fetch their results, and a test protocol, used to send single measurement packets along the Internet path under test. Control protocol is performed by the control-client (requests, starts, and ends test sessions) and server (manages test sessions); and the test control is then executed by the sender (sending endpoint) and session-receiver/reflector (receiving endpoint).

Hybrid Measurement Mechanisms

The notions of active and passive measurement mechanisms are well-established. On the contrary, hybrid measurement mechanisms, which combine active and passive techniques, are fuzzier, and their definition varies depending on the standardization body. These hybrid mechanisms aim at providing some of the benefits of both active and passive mechanisms without embarking their disadvantages. In this context, the metrics produced by hybrid measurement usually have distinct properties, and they consume different amounts of resources for delivering the results. For example, in terms of delay, hybrid methods could provide results with better accuracy than passive methods, but without the network cost of active methods.

The IETF IPPM WG proposed a categorization for hybrid measurement mechanisms (Morton, 2016). The first type, Hybrid Type I, is based either on the augmentation or modification of the stream of interest, or the use of methods that modify the treatment of such stream. The second type denoted as Hybrid Type II, defines the use of mechanisms that use two or more different streams of interest with some degree of mutual coordination to collect both active and passive metrics and enable additional joint analysis. Some use of hybrid measurement mechanisms is also defined as spatial metrics and methods (Morton, 2016).

The IPv6 Option Header for Performance and Diagnostic Measurements (PDM) Internet-Draft (Elkins & Hamilton, 2017) proposes the addition of fields dedicated to the measurement of user streams. The measured stream has unknown characteristics until it is processed to add the PDM Option header. The use of PDM intends to have a minor effect on the measured stream and other streams in the network when it is added to network interfaces. Considering the IPPM classification, this is a Hybrid Type I method, having at least one characteristic of both active and passive mechanisms for a single stream of interest. The

Figure 2. Active Measurement Model (Cisco Service Level Assurance protocol)
Source: Chiba, Clemm, Medley, Salowey, Thombare, & Yedavalli, 2013

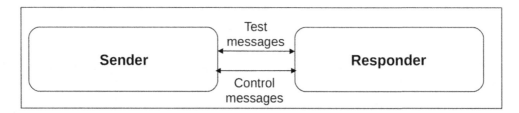

Alternate-Marking Method for Passive and Hybrid Performance Monitoring (Chen, Castaldelli, Mirsky, Mizrahi, Fioccola, Capello, & Cociglio, 2018) is a Hybrid Type I method as well. In this method, the stream is measured and time-stamped during that process to deliver network metrics. Thus, data packets are marked by different blocks of markers that change one or more bits of packets without altering either the normal processing in the network or adding delimiting packets regarding the measurement traffic.

This subsection only discusses the passive, active and hybrid measurements mechanisms. Readers may want to look at the survey performed by Nobre et al. (2018a) for more details.

P2P-Based Network Management

There is substantial research on models that addresses the structure of interactions required to execute network management tasks (dos Santos, Famaey, Schönwälder, Granville, Pras, & De Turck, 2016). In these models, various forms of decentralization (i.e., distribution) are used to produce, access, and store management data. In the traditional centralized model, a single management station typically controls the whole managed infrastructure. Scalability issues of the centralized model motivated intense research on Distributed Network Management (DNM) alternatives. Some management literature classifies the various flavors of DNM solutions (dos Santos, Famaey, Schönwälder, Granville, Pras, & De Turck, 2016). A possible approach to decentralize the execution of management tasks is to employ P2P techniques. Such techniques have proven to be adequate for different kinds of applications. Therefore, P2P techniques may also be successfully used for DNM. Figure 3 presents a general view of the P2P-Based Network Management (P2PBNM) model.

Figure 3. P2P-Based Network Management Model
Source: Nobre, Granville, Clemm, & Prieto, 2012

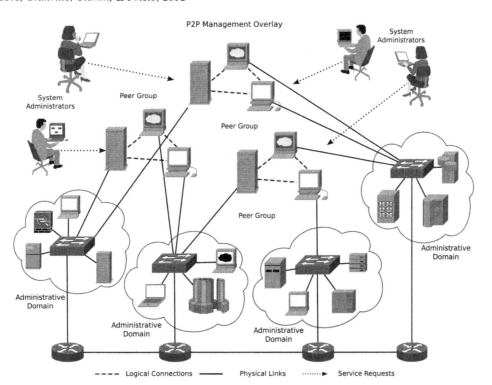

Figure 3 presents a P2P overlay in which shared computational resources are used to perform management tasks. The choice of protocols used to build a P2P management overlay differs significantly among P2PBNM research initiatives and prototypes. Some initiatives reuse well-established P2P protocols in order to reuse the properties of these protocols, which were already described in the literature. For example, the *Cyclon* protocol (Voulgaris, Gavidia, & Van Steen, 2005) is used for deploying management overlays. In addition, the reuse of P2P protocols eases the development of a P2PBNM system since the focus can remain on the management tasks (and not in building new P2P protocols). On the other hand, some initiatives built a P2P protocol from the scratch focusing only on the required features/properties to make the management overlay operational. A P2P protocol designed specifically for DNM does not add "compulsory" overheads needed to address requirements of general purpose P2P systems. Therefore, the P2PBNM system efficiency can be increased.

The approach to distribute management tasks also varies, depending on the nature of the P2PBNM approach. One possibility is to use Service-Oriented Architecture (SOA, Jones, 2005). When using SOA, management peers perform management tasks through management services. In this context, the result of these services is the execution of a management task. In general, these services are requested by system administrators (as shown in Figure 3) or automation procedures (which can be hosted either inside the peers themselves or even in a centralized entity). The software portion that is responsible for delivering management services is usually known as a management component. The spectrum of the technology used by these components is very broad, e.g., from simple monitoring probes to complex autonomic policies interpreters.

P2P techniques may also be a valuable tool to enable inter-domain management (Fiorese, Simões, & Boavida, 2009). P2PBNM systems typically use Application Layer Routing (ALR, RFC5693) (Burger & Seedorf, 2009) as their main message passing resource and ALR adapts more easily to administrative domain boundaries. In this context, logical connections among the peers are mapped into physical links. Figure 3 illustrates a scenario where participating peers (of peer groups) spread over different administrative domains; logical connections among peers are represented by dashed lines. Management entities in traditional management rely on the IP routing to communicate with one another. Thus, the definition of new routes is rigidly produced by current routing protocols. Furthermore, boundary boxes (e.g., application proxies, packet filters) break the end-to-end IP forwarding paradigm. The use of ALR can overcome network layer connectivity issues or, at least, optimize connectivity using information from the network layer (Burger & Seedorf, 2009).

RFC8316

RFC8316 (Nobre, Granville, Clemm, & Prieto, 2018a) depicts the use case of a service provider that needs to monitor the network it operates to detect SLA violations by using active measurements mechanisms, while limiting human intervention. The goal is to conduct the measurements in an effective manner to maximize the percentage of detected SLA violations with resource restrictions. This section describes RFC8316 and its context.

Background

There is a minimum set of properties which define an Autonomic System: automatic, i.e., it can "self-control its internal functions and operations"; adaptive, i.e., it can change its "configuration, state and functions"; and aware, i.e., it can "monitor its operational context". In addition, various definitions of an Autonomic System have been given, such as self-CHOP and MAPE-K. The application of autonomic systems to the complete network lifecycle (e.g., installation, commissioning, operating) is usually called Autonomic Networking (AN).

There has been substantial research on autonomic features related to network management solutions. The application of Autonomic Computing (AC) principles in network management, referred to as Autonomic Network Management (ANM), has been proposed as a means to address some issues faced by traditional network management, such as controlling highly dynamic environments as in ad hoc networks.

There were several antecedents to AN, for example, the use of artificial intelligence in network management, Self-Organising Networks, Declarative Policies, etc. Using the term "AN", Strassner (2004) presented a tutorial during a Network Operations and Management Symposium (NOMS) conference. This was one of the first traceable academic mentions of AN. Since 2004, some initiatives have been publicized, and they discussing different attributes of AN (e.g., Mortier & Kiciman, 2006; Agoulmine, Balasubramaniam, Botvich, Strassner, Lehtihet, & Donnelly, 2006).

AN was the focus of several research projects over the last decade. Some examples of such projects are AN Architecture (ANA) (Bouabene, Jelger, Tschudin, Schmid, Keller, & May, 2010), Generic ANA (GANA) (Chaparadza, 2009), etc. In this context, AN is usually addressed by several publications which have been presented over the years in the Network Management conferences (e.g., IM, NOMS, and CNSM). In the meantime, other networking technologies gained momentum, such as Software-Defined Networking (SDN) and Network Functions Virtualization (NFV). Finally, some new notions have been developed, and they somewhat overlap with AN, such as cognitive networking and intelligence-driven networking. However, there is a lack of successful deployment cases and standardization regarding AN.

The Network Management Research Group (NMRG) from the Internet Research Task Force (IRTF) also started to discuss AN. The first AN-related discussions were held during workshops, called "Autonomics for Network Management @ NMRG". There were also related efforts conducted by other IETF WGs and IRTF RGs, such as Simplified Use of Policy Abstractions (SUPA), Home Networking (HOMENET), Software Defined Networking Research Group (SDNRG), Network Functions Virtualization Research Group (NFVRG), Interface to the Routing System (I2RS), among others. In addition, some new groups have been proposed, such as Network Machine Learning Research Group (NMLRG) and Intelligent Defined Networking (IDN).

Some important outcomes of NMRG meetings (and its work in general) are related to autonomic networking. First, 2 RFCs were produced in this context, RFC7575 and RFC7576. The first document defines a common language and outlines design goals for autonomic functions (Behringer, Bjarnason, Jiang, Carpenter, Pritikin, Ciavaglia, & Clemm, 2015). The second document details a problem statement and a general gap analysis for an IP-based Autonomic Network that mainly relies upon distributed network devices (Jiang, Carpenter, & Behringer, 2015). Finally, there was the Use Cases for Autonomic Networking (UCAN) Bird of Feathers (BoF) session held during the IETF 90 meeting, and which attracted a large audience.

The UCAN BoF led to the creation of the ANIMA (Autonomic Networking Integrated Model and Approach) WG. With a focus on professionally-managed networks, the main goal of ANIMA is to produce the specification of a minimum set of reusable infrastructure components to support autonomic interactions and use cases. In this context, the definition of autonomic networking by ANIMA is "a system of autonomic functions that carry out the intentions of the network operator without the need for detailed low-level management of individual devices" (refer to Chapter 4 *"ANIMA: Secure Autonomic Network*

Infrastructure"). However, some of the Internet-Drafts presented during the UCAN BoF session have not been hosted by ANIMA as WG items, and the corresponding discussion was therefore progressed within NMRG. The Autonomic Networking Use Case for Distributed Detection of Service Level Agreement (SLA) Violations Internet-Draft was one of such "left aside" Internet-Drafts.

Use Case Description

The use case and the solution described in RFC8316 address an important practical issue, the detection of SLA violations. They are intended to provide a basis for further experimentation that can lead to solutions for wider deployment. Solutions that allow the service provider to monitor and troubleshoot the underlying communication infrastructure are crucial. In the RFC8316, the authors considered that this provider has a restricted resource budget with regard to SLA monitoring coverage, specifically in terms of the number of measurements that can be conducted concurrently and possibly the total amount of measurement traffic that is forwarded across the network.

The activation of measurement sessions is done through several steps. First, it is necessary to collect traffic information in order to grasp the traffic matrix. Then, the administrator uses this information to infer the best destinations to activate measurement sessions (i.e., the ones most prone to have SLA violations). After that, the administrator activates sessions on the chosen subset of destinations, taking the available resources into account. This practice has major shortcomings. It does not scale well and usually covers only a fraction of the network flows that should be observed. Network management researchers have investigated how to overcome similar shortcomings considering different scenarios and management tasks (Samaan & Karmouch, 2009). In order to provide solutions that better suit these scenarios, network-wide management solutions can be employed.

A network-wide control of network devices can improve their ability to accomplish management tasks. For example, a distributed network management algorithm can be used to allow some devices to provide additional resources for the execution of management tasks by other devices. This can be useful when either the computational load is not equally distributed among the network devices or there is heterogeneity in the computational resources of network devices. In this context, the global capability of the devices in a network can be greater than the sum of the capabilities of each device. In addition, the solution needs to be dynamic, being able to cope with network conditions that may change over time, and embeddable, considering network devices that control the deployment of measurement mechanisms.

The goal of an autonomic solution in the present use case is to conduct the measurements in a smart manner that ensures that the network destinations are broadly covered and that the probability of detecting SLA violations is improved. Clearly, static (i.e., defined a priori) solutions will have severe limitations. While at any given time, the number of measurements in progress is limited, it is possible for a device to change the destinations to measure over time. Thus, an autonomic solution is needed so that network measurements are automatically orchestrated and dynamically reconfigured from within the network. This can be exploited to achieve a balance of eventually covering all possible destinations using a reasonable amount of "sampling" (i.e., coverage versus resource consumption) where measurement coverage of a destination cannot be continuous.

A solution for the detection of SLA violation should focus on the use of measurement resources on destinations that are more likely to incur a violation (Nobre, Granville, Clemm, & Prieto, 2012). In any case, the solution still needs to spend (possibly) fewer resources on destinations that are more likely to be respecting SLOs. However, when a probe first comes online, it has no information about which measurements are more critical than others. At the same time, human administrators should not be in the loop for continuous dynamic reconfigurations of measurement probes. In the absence of information about past measurements, it may start with an initial set of measurement sessions, possibly randomly seeding a set of starter measurements.

The Use of P2P Techniques

Several authors (for a discussion on this, see (Samaan & Karmouch, 2009) claim that some level of decentralization plays an important role to perform autonomic actions in a more adequate manner. Different technologies could be employed as an infrastructure of a decentralized ANM system. P2P technology can provide the foundations for increasing the intelligence applied to the control of measurement mechanisms through sophisticated distributed network management algorithms. Network devices could benefit from a network-wide and distributed control of such mechanisms since it is feasible that measurement decisions (e.g., activation of active measurement sessions) are better made by considering the sharing of computational resources and management information. Thus, such decisions may take into account local and remote information as well as consider resources just from the device itself and from remote devices. In addition, the interfaces for the full control of active measurement mechanisms are usually provided only locally on the devices, which also hampers the use of centralized and hierarchical approaches.

The authors advocate for embedding P2P techniques within network devices in order to use autonomic control loops to make decisions about measurement sessions. A pragmatic approach to deploy such techniques in the control of the activation of active measurement sessions is to define principles to guide this deployment (Nobre, & Granville, 2017). Specifically, the authors advocate for: (1) network devices to implement an autonomic function that monitors service levels for violations of SLOs and that determines which measurement sessions to set up at any given time based on current and past observations of the node's service levels and of other peer nodes; (2) autonomic functions to provision the measurement overlay, since the provisioning of the such overlay should be transparent for the network administrator and should facilitate the exchange of data between different nodes to share measurement results so that each node can refine its measurement strategy not just based on its own observations, but also on observations from its peers, and; (3) remote measurements to optimize resource consumption, since they allow nodes to coordinate their measurements to obtain the best possible test coverage. Nodes may utilize observations that are made by their measurement peers in order to conclude which measurement targets may be more critical than others and to ensure that proper overall measurement coverage is obtained. Put simply, the above principles try to capture the common sense used by network administrators when using active measurement mechanisms to detect SLA violations.

The utilization of past service level measurement results can be exploited to detect whether a destination is likely to disrespect SLOs or not. To do so, descriptive statistical metrics can be used to measure how close past service level measurement results are regarding the SLO for a given destination. If the past measurements results for a given destination are close to a SLO, then the probability of activating a measurement session for this destination should increase. This is done by local logic, i.e., an application that runs locally on the network devices. By performing these functions locally and autonomously on the device itself, the measurements to conduct can be modified quickly, based on local observations while taking local resource availability into account. This enables more robust and more reactive solutions so that they can rapidly change service levels compared to central coordination designs. For example, a node could decide to adjust the amount of synthetic test traffic being sent during the measurement itself, depending on results observed so far on this node, and depending on other concurrent measurement sessions.

A distributed autonomic solution also allows nodes to coordinate their probing decisions to collectively achieve the best possible measurement coverage. Service level measurement results are produced by active measurement mechanisms around the network infrastructure. This information can speed up the detection of SLA violations and improve the number of detected SLA violations. In this context, human administrators can usually predict if SLA violations are likely to happen in a specific region of the network, by using information from measurements of other regions of the network. This is possible because administrators can use their experience and knowledge to infer the relation among the links within the network infrastructure. Because the number of resources available for SLA monitoring is limited, a node may be interested in identifying other nodes whose observations are similar to its own. This helps a node prioritize and decide which other nodes to coordinate and exchange data with.

P2P techniques can be used to capture one of the behaviors commonly adopted by human administrators to detect SLA violations: the sharing of measurement results. For example, if one device detects that a remote destination is about to violate an SLO, other devices may conduct additional measurements to the same destination or other destinations in its proximity. However, it is important to define which network devices are prone to share measurement results. For any given network device, the exchange of data may be more important with some devices than with others. Defining the network devices that exchange measurement data creates a new topology. Different approaches could be used to define this topology (e.g., correlated peers, Nobre, Granville, Clemm, & Prieto, 2012). Using the P2P overlay, measurements can be coordinated among different network devices to avoid hitting the same destination at the same time and to share results that may be useful for future probe placement.

Implementation Considerations

Network devices have increased substantially their level of programmability. Thus, management software can be embedded to control the activation of active measurement mechanisms. Embedded management peers can have direct access to the internal API of the active measurement mechanism, which could foster the configuration of measurement sessions. Since activating measurement sessions should be a dynamic process in modern network infrastructures, such fostering can improve measurement efficiency (e.g., in terms of monitoring coverage). Considering the ANIMA Autonomic Networking Infrastructure (ANI), Autonomic Service Agents (ASAs) can be implemented on nodes in the network, by using the devices' programmability interfaces (such as Juniper's Junos API or Cisco's Embedded Event Manager). Finally, it should be noted that there are multiple deployment scenarios, including scenarios that involve physical devices virtualized infrastructures hosting autonomic functions.

Embedded P2PBNM systems also make the growth of management resources more "organic" since they can grow without requiring a fork-lift upgrade (i.e., new devices can host by default new management peers). In this context, these systems could grow as new devices are added, bundled with embedded management peers. In order to bootstrap peer selection, each node should use its known neighbors (e.g., based upon the entries maintained by its FIB and RIB tables) as initial seeds to identify possible peers. In addition, an autonomic solution will be useful if topology information and network discovery functions are provided by the underlying ANI. The Autonomic Control Plane defined by the ANIMA ANI (Autonomic Network Infrastructure) provides an ideal candidate for the embedded P2P overlay to run on.

Each device needs to have self-knowledge about the local SLA monitoring. Thus, it is necessary to access and store historical measurement data and SLOs. In addition, measurement data and SLOs can be complemented with passive measurements such as flow data (to identify network destinations that are currently popular and critical). Since interoperability in a heterogeneous network monitoring environment is necessary, only a minimum set of features found on different active measurement mechanisms (e.g., OWAMP, TWAMP, and Cisco's Service Level Assurance Protocol) is required. In addition, the devices would run algorithms that can decide which probes should be activated at any given time. The choice of the algorithm for a specific situation would be made by means of autonomic networking. In this context, nodes would have a repository of algorithms (and correlation functions) that could fit given network conditions.

The autonomic solution for detecting SLA violations should assume that a typical infrastructure will have multiple network segments, ASs, and a reasonably large number of network devices with the capacity of performing measurement sessions. Such solution should also consider that multiple SLOs need to be achieved at any given time. In addition, the autonomic solution should make possible for nodes (or more specifically, the ASAs that are supported by these nodes) to autonomously set up measurement sessions without having to rely on a central management system or controller to perform configuration operations associated with configuring measurement probes and responders.

Use Case Limitations

Despite the several benefits an autonomic solution for the distributed detection of SLA violations provides, some limitations can be described considering the use case presented in RFC8316. This section describes such limitations.

Full autonomic solutions minimize human intervention in the distributed detection of SLA violations. In this context, practical autonomic features can, at least, minimize such intervention. However, there are some processes that still require a human administrator. The policies regarding how closely to monitor the network for SLA violations and the resource budget that is assigned to network devices for measurement operations may be set by a human administrator. With that budget, the number of SLO violations that are detected can be improved by the autonomic solution.

The use case considers features commonly supported by widely known active measurement mechanisms, such as TWAMP and IPSLA. In this context, the chosen mechanism for SLA monitoring does not need any modification to be controlled by the approach described in this use case. Furthermore, it is assumed that there is an open interface for the activation of measurement sessions in the network devices which support the measurement mechanism themselves.

Security issues are considered orthogonal to the present use case. However, the authors are aware that these use case has security implications and the authors regard options to overcome these implications as future work. In any case, the security of the autonomic detection of SLA violations hinges on the security of the network underlay, which is the Autonomic Control Plane in the case of an ANIMA ANI. If the Autonomic Control Plane were to be compromised, an attacker could undermine the effectiveness of measurement coordination by reporting fraudulent measurement results to peers. This would cause measurement probes to be deployed in an ineffective manner that would increase the likelihood that violations of SLOs go undetected.

FUTURE RESEARCH DIRECTIONS

The present use case is intended to be an initial step towards autonomic detection of SLA violations. It is also important to investigate how coordination features can enable composite measurement tasks. In addition, refinements in the definition of correlated peers can be included to allow a more selective peering. For example, throttling of overlay traffic can be introduced for "popular" peers. Furthermore, the information about correlated peers can have another usage, e.g., allow inferences about the underlying (physical) topology (i.e., the discovery of the topology of the network substrate).

The security of the autonomic detection of SLA violation hinges on the security of the deployment of such mechanism for autonomic functions and the ANI. In this use case, if the autonomic function that conducts the service-level measurements is hijacked by an attacker, such attacker could try to exhaust or exceed the resources that should be spent on autonomic measurements in order to deplete network resources. This could include network bandwidth due to higher-than-necessary volumes of synthetic test traffic generated by measurement probes. Furthermore, this could also lead to the report of misleading results, thereby resulting in a suboptimal selection of measurement targets. This could increase the likelihood that service-level violations go undetected. Finally, the (ANIMA) ANI could also be attacked, for example through the denial of service regarding the Autonomic Control Plane (ACP) availability and impersonating an autonomic node to participate in the ACP.

Future research and future standards on autonomic networking must consider highly virtualized and programmable infrastructures. In this context, it is necessary to investigate deployment issues in conjunction with Virtual Network Functions (VNFs). In addition, the deployment of new network technologies is typically a time-consuming and labor-intensive task. Thus, SDN techniques may help deploy solutions for an autonomic detection of SLA violations. The NMRG-conducted work on AN with the publication of RFC7575 (Behringer, Bjarnason, Jiang, Carpenter, Pritikin, Ciavaglia, & Clemm, 2015) and RFC7576 (Jiang, Carpenter, & Behringer, 2015) primarily focused on node-level aspects. In this context, the standardization of several ANI required elements and technologies remains an open question since the current standards are limited to specific ANI mechanisms. For example, it is still necessary new initiatives on (Policy) Intent, Use Cases, ASAs, etc., considering the ANI operation.

CONCLUSION

Violations of SLOs can be associated with significant financial loss in several network infrastructures. Such loss can be divided into two categories. First, there is the loss that can be incurred by the user of a service when the agreed service levels are not met. Second, there is the loss that is incurred by the provider of a service who is unable to achieve contractually defined SLOs. Those losses can take several forms, such as penalties for violating the service level agreement and even loss of future revenue due to a reduced customer satisfaction. Hence, SLOs are a key concern for the service provider. In order to ensure that SLOs are not being violated, service levels need to be continuously monitored in order to know, for example, when mitigation actions need to be taken. To that end, service-level measurements must take place. However, the deployment and operation of these measurements is a demanding task for human administrators.

The problem to be solved by AN in the present use case is how to steer the process of measurement session activation by a solution that sets all necessary parameters for this activation to operate efficiently, reliably, and securely, with no required human intervention other than setting global policies. The authors advocate the use of P2P techniques to increase the potential number of detected SLA violations by means of active measurement mechanisms. This use leads to the introduction of key concepts to support a self-organizing, embedded P2P measurement overlay that uses the capabilities of the network devices to control session activation. In practice, these factors combine to maximize the likelihood of SLA violations being detected while operating within a given resource budget, allowing a continuous measurement strategy. The solution takes into account past measurement results, observations of other measurements such as link utilization or flow data, measurement results shared between network devices, and future measurement activities coordinated among nodes. As a result, the proposed P2P-based solution could decrease the time to detect SLA violations and help reduce the workload of human administrators.

ACKNOWLEDGMENT

The initial presentation of the Internet-Draft that led to RFC8316 was supported by the Internet Society [Fellowship to the Internet Engineering Task Force (IETF)]. This presentation was made during the IETF Meeting 90 (2014), Toronto, Canada.

REFERENCES

Agoulmine, N., Balasubramaniam, S., Botvich, D., Strassner, J., Lehtihet, E., & Donnelly, W. (2006). Challenges for autonomic network management. In *Proceedings of the IEEE International Workshop on Modeling Autonomic Communications Environment (MACE)*. IEEE

Behringer, M., Bjarnason, S., Jiang, S., Carpenter, B., Pritikin, M., Ciavaglia, L., & Clemm, A. (2015). *Autonomic networking: Definitions and design goals. (RFC7575)*. Internet Engineering Task Force. doi:10.17487/RFC7575

Bouabene, G., Jelger, C., Tschudin, C., Schmid, S., Keller, A., & May, M. (2010). The autonomic network architecture (ANA). *IEEE Journal on Selected Areas in Communications, 28*(1), 4–14. doi:10.1109/JSAC.2010.100102

Burger, E. W., & Seedorf, J. (2009). *Application-layer traffic optimization (ALTO) problem statement (RFC5693)*. Internet Engineering Task Force.

Chaparadza, R., Papavassiliou, S., Kastrinogiannis, T., Vigoureux, M., Dotaro, E., Davy, A., & Wilson, M. (2009). *Creating a viable Evolution Path towards Self-Managing Future Internet via a Standardizable Reference Model for Autonomic Network Engineering*. In Future Internet Assembly.

Chen, M., Castaldelli, L., Mirsky, G., Mizrahi, T., Fioccola, G., Capello, A., & Cociglio, M. (2018). *Alternate-Marking Method for Passive and Hybrid Performance Monitoring (RFC8321)*. Internet Engineering Task Force.

Chiba, M., Clemm, A., Medley, S., Salowey, J., Thombare, S., & Yedavalli, E. (2013). *Cisco service-level assurance protocol (RFC6812)*. Internet Engineering Task Force.

Claise, B. (2008). *Specification of the IP flow information export (IPFIX) protocol for the exchange of IP traffic flow information (RFC5101)*. Internet Engineering Task Force.

Claise, B., Trammell, B., & Aitken, P. (2013). *Specification of the IP flow information export (IPFIX) protocol for the exchange of flow information (RFC7011)*. Internet Engineering Task Force.

Di Pietro, A., Huici, F., Costantini, D., & Niccolini, S. (2010). *Decon: Decentralized coordination for large-scale flow monitoring*. In *INFOCOM IEEE Conference on Computer Communications Workshops, 2010* (pp. 1-5). IEEE. 10.1109/INFCOMW.2010.5466642

Duffield, N., Chiou, D., Claise, B., Greenberg, A., Grossglauser, M., & Rexford, J. (2009). *A framework for packet selection and reporting (RFC5474)*. Internet Engineering Task Force.

Elkins, N., & Hamilton, R. (2017). *IPv6 Performance and Diagnostic Metrics (PDM) Destination Option (RFC8250)*. Internet Engineering Task Force. doi:10.17487/RFC8250

Fiorese, A., Simões, P., & Boavida, F. (2009). A P2P-based approach to cross-domain network and service management. In *IFIP International Conference on Autonomous Infrastructure, Management and Security* (pp. 179-182). Springer.

Hedayat, K., Krzanowski, R., Morton, A., Yum, K., & Babiarz, J. (2008). *A two-way active measurement protocol (TWAMP) (RFC5357)*. Internet Engineering Task Force.

Jiang, S., Carpenter, B., & Behringer, M. (2015). *General gap analysis for autonomic networking (RFC7576)*. Internet Engineering Task Force. doi:10.17487/RFC7576

Jones, S. (2005). Toward an acceptable definition of service service-oriented architecture. *IEEE Software. IEEE.*, *22*(3), 87–93. doi:10.1109/MS.2005.80

Mortier, R., & Kiciman, E. (2006, September). Autonomic network management: some pragmatic considerations. In *Proceedings of the 2006 SIGCOMM workshop on Internet network management* (pp. 89-93). ACM. 10.1145/1162638.1162653

Morton, A. (2016). *Active and Passive Metrics and Methods (with Hybrid Types In-Between) (RFC7799)*. Internet Engineering Task Force. doi:10.17487/RFC7799

Nobre, J., Granville, L., Clemm, A., & Prieto, A. G. (2018). *Autonomic Networking Use Case for Distributed Detection of Service Level Agreement (SLA) Violations (RFC8316)*. Internet Engineering Task Force. doi:10.17487/RFC8316

Nobre, J. C., & Granville, L. Z. (2017, May). Decentralized detection of violations of service level agreements using peer-to-peer technology. In *Integrated Network and Service Management (IM), 2017 IFIP/IEEE Symposium on* (pp. 835-840). IEEE.

Nobre, J. C., Granville, L. Z., Clemm, A., & Prieto, A. G. (2012). Decentralized detection of SLA violations using P2P technology. In *Proceedings of the 8th International Conference on Network and Service Management* (pp. 100-107). International Federation for Information Processing.

Nobre, J. C., Mozzaquatro, B. A., & Granville, L. Z. (2018). Network-Wide Initiatives to Control Measurement Mechanisms: A Survey. *IEEE Communications Surveys and Tutorials, 20*(2), 1475–1491. doi:10.1109/COMST.2018.2797170

Pras, A., Schonwalder, J., Burgess, M., Festor, O., Perez, G. M., Stadler, R., & Stiller, B. (2007). Key research challenges in network management. *IEEE Communications Magazine, 45*(10), 104–110. doi:10.1109/MCOM.2007.4342832

Samaan, N., & Karmouch, A. (2009). Towards autonomic network management: An analysis of current and future research directions. *IEEE Communications Surveys and Tutorials, 11*(3), 22–36. doi:10.1109/SURV.2009.090303

Sekar, V., Reiter, M. K., Willinger, W., Zhang, H., Kompella, R. R., & Andersen, D. G. (2008). cSamp: A System for Network-Wide Flow Monitoring. In NSDI (Vol. 8, pp. 233-246). Academic Press.

Shalunov, S., Teitelbaum, B., Karp, A., Boote, J., & Zekauskas, M. (2006). *A One-way Active Measurement Protocol (OWAMP) (RFC4656)*. Internet Engineering Task Force.

Strassner, J. (2004, April). Autonomic networking-theory and practice. In *Network Operations and Management Symposium, 2004. NOMS 2004. IEEE/IFIP* (Vol. 1, pp. 927-Vol). IEEE. 10.1109/NOMS.2004.1317811

Voulgaris, S., Gavidia, D., & Van Steen, M. (2005). Cyclon: Inexpensive membership management for unstructured P2P overlays. *Journal of Network and Systems Management, 13*(2), 197–217. doi:10.100710922-005-4441-x

ADDITIONAL READING

Bajpai, V., & Schönwälder, J. (2015). A survey on internet performance measurement platforms and related standardization efforts. *IEEE Communications Surveys and Tutorials, 17*(3), 1313–1341. doi:10.1109/COMST.2015.2418435

Boucadair, M., Jacquenet, C., & Wang, N. (2014). *IP Connectivity Provisioning Profile (CPP) (RFC7297)*. Internet Engineering Task Force.

Dobson, S., Denazis, S., Fernández, A., Gaïti, D., Gelenbe, E., Massacci, F., ... Zambonelli, F. (2006). A survey of autonomic communications. *ACM Transactions on Autonomous and Adaptive Systems, 1*(2), 223–259. doi:10.1145/1186778.1186782

dos Santos, C. R. P., Famaey, J., Schönwälder, J., Granville, L. Z., Pras, A., & De Turck, F. (2016). Taxonomy for the network and service management research field. *Journal of Network and Systems Management, 24*(3), 764–787. doi:10.100710922-015-9363-7

Dreibholz, T., Rathgeb, E. P., Rungeler, I., Seggelmann, R., Tuxen, M., & Stewart, R. R. (2011). Stream control transmission protocol: Past, current, and future standardization activities. *IEEE Communications Magazine, 49*(4), 82–88. doi:10.1109/MCOM.2011.5741151

Dressler, F., & Akan, O. B. (2010). A survey on bio-inspired networking. *Computer Networks*, *54*(6), 881–900. doi:10.1016/j.comnet.2009.10.024

Eardley, P., Morton, A., Bagnulo, M., Burbridge, T., Aitken, P., & Akhter, A. (2015). *A framework for Large-scale Measurement of Broadband Performance (LMAP) (RFC7594)*. Internet Engineering Task Force. doi:10.17487/RFC7594

Nobre, J. C. (2016). *Decentralized detection of violations of service level agreements using peer-to-peer technology*. Ph.D Thesis

Strassner, J., Agoulmine, N., & Lehtihet, E. (2006, April). *FOCALE–a novel autonomic computing architecture*. In *Proceedings of the 2006 Latin–American Autonomic Computing Symposium*.

KEY TERMS AND DEFINITIONS

Active Measurements: Techniques to measure service levels that involve generating and observing synthetic test traffic.

Autonomic Network: A network containing exclusively autonomic nodes, requiring no configuration, and deriving all required information through self-knowledge, discovery, or intent.

Autonomic Service Agent (ASA): An agent implemented on an autonomic node that implements an autonomic function, either in part (in the case of a distributed function, as in the context of this chapter) or whole.

Measurement Session: A communications association between a probe and a responder used to send and reflect synthetic test traffic for active measurements.

P2P: Peer-to-peer.

Passive Measurements: Techniques used to measure service levels based on observation of production traffic.

Probe: The source of synthetic test traffic in an active measurement.

Responder: The destination for synthetic test traffic in an active measurement.

SLA: Service level agreement.

SLO: Service level objective.

Chapter 12
The Open Source Community Choice:
Automate or Die!

Morgan Richomme
Orange Labs, France

ABSTRACT

Open source communities have had and continue to have a major influence on the evolution of the Internet. By their nature, such communities involve people with diverse coding cultures and skills. Automation has consequently been of major interest to open source software developers for a long time, and many open source tools have been developed to address code variability and sustainability challenges. This chapter discusses why open source communities must automate and the challenges they will face. Solutions and current examples of automation in open source projects are provided as a guide to what is achievable. OpenShift, OpenStack, and OPNFV communities are used to illustrate different approaches and best practices. Two recently initiated automation initiatives are detailed: "Cross Community Continuous Integration" (XCI) and "Cross Testing" (Xtesting). Finally, some recommendations are provided for new projects as a guide to ease adoption of appropriate tools and methods.

INTRODUCTION

Open Source communities have had a major influence on the evolution of the Internet with many projects initiated and developed in academia. Many key software projects are actually still distributed under associated permissive software licenses such as MIT license and BSD license with minimal restrictions about how the software can be redistributed.

Since mid-2000 the Open Source model has been widely adopted by many companies as a basis for commercial R&D activities. As a consequence the number of Open Source projects and contributors has increased dramatically, as shown in Figure 1. Many industry consortiums and foundations have also been created to support the increasing number of Open Source communities. Well-known foundations include the Linux Foundation, the Apache Foundation, OW2, and the Eclipse foundation.

DOI: 10.4018/978-1-5225-7146-9.ch012

This chapter deals with the global need for automation of most of the Open Source projects, which are now one of the catalysts of the Internet evolution (Web, relational and NOSQL databases, Big Data, Cloud, Artificial Intelligence and Machine Learning, etc.). It details the needs, the stakes, the tools, and a set of recommendations.

This chapter does not focus on the Open Source projects or communities working specifically on automation solutions especially for providers. For example, ETSI NFV (Gray & Nadeau, 2016) defined a full NFV Management and Orchestration stack (MANO) (NFV, 2018) aiming to allow the deployment of traditional complex provider' functions. Some early code implementations more or less close to the specification have been published such as open Source Mano (Dahmen-Lhuissier, n.d.), OpenBaton (Open Baton, n.d.), or Open Networking Automation Platform (ONAP) (ONAP, n.d.). The description of these solutions is out of scope of this chapter.

WHY AUTOMATE?: "L'ENFER C'EST LES AUTRES"

Changing the R&D approaches to rely heavily on Open Source code has introduced many challenges for developers. Firstly developers come from different companies with vastly different product technologies, software development standards, and code quality requirements.

"L'enfer c'est les autres" is a quote from "No Exit" (Sartre, 1955). An interpretation is that collaborative work is difficult, in part because others are needed to create your own identity. In order to magnify your own work however there is always the temptation to attribute the responsibility of the problems to "the others". This precisely captures a dilemma within Open Source communities but also hints at the possibility of a way out. By making collectively agreed rules for code that are checked automatically for instance, a developer will more readily accept refactoring his/her code. Feedback that is automatically given based on predefined rules, even though the rules are defined by consensus and programmed by humans, is a priori "fair" and is hence a key benefit gained from Open Source collaboration.

Figure 1. The number of Linux Foundation Open Source projects has rapidly increased since mid-2000 (Linux, n.d.)

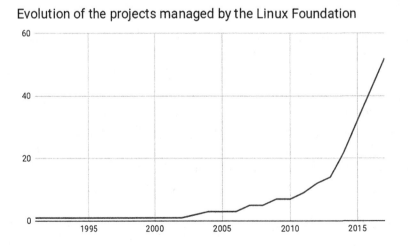

Evolution of the projects managed by the Linux Foundation

The number of contributors working on a particular Open Source project differs dramatically, from 2 to 10000, depending on the popularity of the community, as illustrated in Figure 2.

The explosion of Open Source projects has subsequently led to increasing dependency on other Open Source projects and hence ever increasing complex dependencies need to be managed. Open Source project dependencies usually arise from integrating libraries or plugins from other projects. Several communities have established a cadence of six months for major releases. This fast pace of evolution means that continuous code refactoring, is usually needed to maintain compatibility and feature parity. Table 1 shows the rate of change of some Open Source projects and illustrates the great variability of source code that has to be dealt with.

The variability of source code and the coding culture, the number and turnover of coders, and the entire project ecosystem in constant flux, impose a major challenge to ensure sustainability and quality of the software base.

Figure 2. Total contributions and contributions (April 2017 - April 2018) for a variety of Open Source projects (note that the y-axis scale is logarithmic)

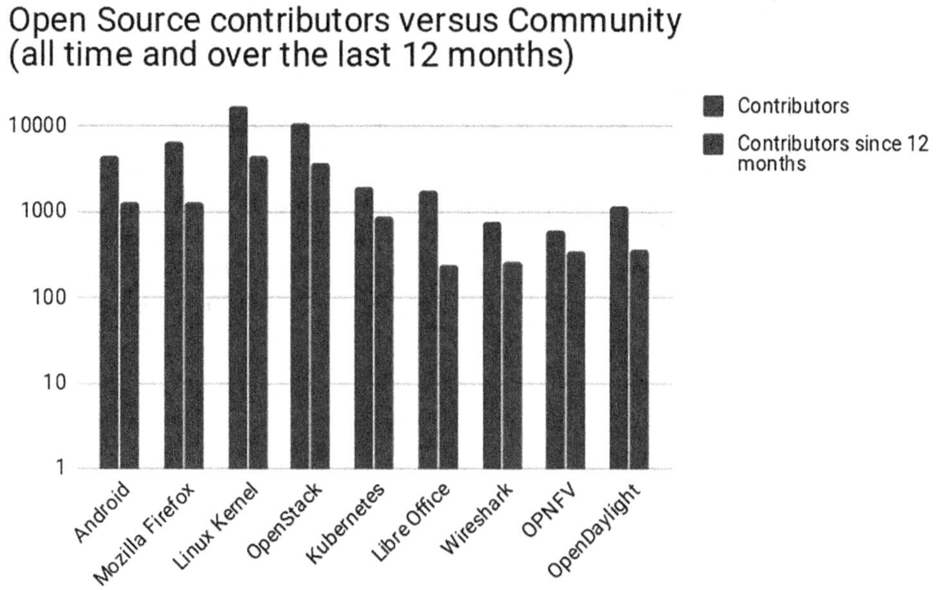

Table 1. Rate of change of code in some Open Source projects

Project	Change Rate (per month)
Linux Kernel	600/mo
OpenDaylight	2000/mo
OpenStack	5000/mo
OVS	200/mo
DPDK	200/mo

Source: openhub

An African proverb is often used to justify Open Source communities: *To go fast go alone, to go far go with many*. Collaborative work requires consistent behavior and rules that are as neutral as possible. Automation is a way to create such rules and forge a community identity beyond the simple notions of code quality.

Automation is also an obvious way to reduce risk of "big" projects by providing automatic builds, tests, and deployments. Integration tasks in big modular projects are not possible with automation. Indeed, a new code can be submitted at any time since developers usually work in all time zones on any module. Testing the module is obviously mandatory but does not guarantee side effects on the other modules. It is therefore necessary to test the module within an integrated system. Such systems may require resources that a developer does not own. Automation includes the need for de facto remote resources for testing. Even for smaller projects, automation can compensate for the lack of human resources and help to stabilize the code and result in more reliable releases with higher quality.

WHAT TO AUTOMATE?

Automation in the context of software development is usually synonymous with CI/CD (Continuous Integration/Continuous Delivery) and involves well-established methods and tools adopted by Open Source projects.

CI is sometimes called gating, the goal being to ensure the integration of a new code into the existing code base. CI is a development practice. CD, an extension of CI, is the ability to deliver a trusted fully functional code module to the end users by continuously testing the target release with end-to-end functional and performance tests. CD includes methods to maintain code in order to ensure the sustainability and stability for customers (Humble & Farley, 2010). The term CD can also be used when a software is automatically deployed into the target production environment. This process of integration, deployment, and testing creates a virtuous cycle of new features which improve therefore code quality. This process can be represented by the diagram shown in Figure 3.

Figure 3. CI/CD representation

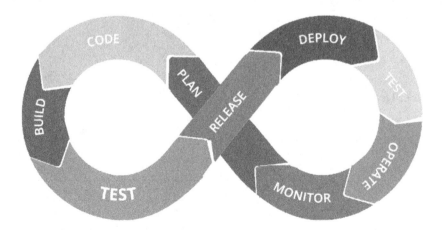

Builds and integration mostly happen on virtual machines due to the flexibility provided (e.g., make the process easy to manage). Less well established methods and tools can be used for deploying and testing integrated code in "real" environments (i.e., on bare-metal) after successfully building and testing at the component level.

The process can further be thought of as: Continuous Integration (Plan, Code, Build, Test) then Continuous Delivery (Release, Deploy, Test, Operate, Monitor). Testing is needed in both stages. These concepts are described in more details in the following section focusing on "gating" which is the process of successively providing feedback to the developer while simultaneously developing "trust" in quality of the code.

CONTINUOUS INTEGRATION (GATING)

Linting

The first level of a gating tool-chain allows contributors to receive fast feedback on the quality of the source code that they submit as a patch. This usually deals with checking coding conventions through linting software that analyses the source code. Linters exist for almost all programming languages (java, Python, C, etc.) as well as to check file formats (json, yaml, markdown, etc.). Once a developer submits a patch, he/she is notified (almost instantly) of any potential violations. This automatic check may also suggest refactoring to follow best practices or design patterns. Some tools may even score the quality of the patch. Depending on the project policy, the patch may be automatically rejected until the score reflects the minimum acceptable quality level. Such tools are quickly setup in big Open Source communities to enforce coding standards, which otherwise would result in code that is difficult to review, understand, and maintain.

Unit Tests

The second level of gating involves unit tests which are also highly recommended even when not mandatory in Open Source projects. Unit tests automatically run against each patch that is submitted. This includes the unit tests corresponding to new code (the patch) submitted and unit tests already provided for the existing code base. Automation of unit tests when submitting a patch helps provide a good level of trust for integration of new features. Test coverage may also be considered for gating and verification of test coverage criteria for unit tests can be automated. For example, if a patch decreases the overall unit test coverage the patch could be automatically rejected until the unit tests that cover the patch feature does not decrease the overall test coverage.

End-to-End Tests

A third level of gating is "end-to-end" tests. This kind of tests can be relatively complex to implement and take a long time to execute. In addition, end-to-end tests are often resource intensive and require CI/CD resources that a developer does not own. For example, realistic testing might require a bare-metal environment with multiple compute nodes and networks. Furthermore, in order to develop robust solutions, testing may need to be conducted in technically diverse environments, i.e., multiple similar, but not identical setups. The challenge, then, is to select suitable tests that are most representative in order to predict behavior in an unambiguous way.

While ideally full test suites including lint tests, unit tests and end-to-end tests should be run every time a patch is submitted this is rarely possible for practical reasons (for example, due to compute resource constraints and time constraints). Gating automates certain actions before promoting code as a candidate for review or attempting to merge code and therefore needs to provide feedback to the developer in a reasonable time. For this reason, long duration tests are excluded from the scope of gating as described above.

The chaining of the different stages (various linting checks, unit tests, end-to-end testing) is called the CI pipeline.

DOCUMENTATION

Documentation is a key artifact of successful Open Source projects. Open Source developers usually invest time to optimize the quality of the software they build, but the quality of the documentation is often forgotten. This is a very common criticism and one of the reasons many projects fail.

Static documentation is rarely current as the code evolves quickly. If the lack of documentation is a problem, the existence of deprecated and non-maintained documentation is just as problematic. The challenge consists of creating and maintaining documentation in sync with the code.

As developers like to optimize their code, one of the tricks to get better documentation is to treat documentation as code. Documentation is hosted under the versioning tool (git, svn, etc.) and is part of the source code of the project. Markdown (md) or reStructuredText (rst) are lightweight markup languages designed to be both "processable" by documentation-processing software and easily readable by human programmers. Additionally many programming languages now include built-in documentation capabilities.

Based on markup language, Sphinx ("Overview — Sphinx 1.8.0+ documentation," n.d.), a document generator written in Python and initially used by Python projects. It can transform "rst" files into html pages, LaTeX, pdf ePub, or plain text files; this format has been widely adopted by Open Source projects including the Linux Kernel.

Read the Docs ("Home | Read the Docs," n.d.) is another popular Open Source project dealing with documentation. The project simplifies software documentation by automating building, versioning, and hosting of the documentation in the Cloud. Lots of webhooks (git, subversion, etc.) are available to easily create CI/CD pipelines to keep documentation and code synchronized.

Big Open Source projects now systematically include a documentation project which focuses more on the automation of the documentation and templates rather than on documentation content which is the responsibility of the code contributors. Documentation is re-generated on each patch submission, which ensures the consistency between code and the documentation. Moreover automating documentation across all community projects or modules guarantees a coherent look and feel.

LONG DURATION TESTING

Long duration tests can be run daily or weekly and jobs are automatically triggered on certain configurations (e.g., git tag).

Adding new test cases or SUT (System Under Test) configurations can quickly result in adding hours, days, or even weeks to testing. This is not sustainable for use of the test resources. It is therefore usually desirable to create a "promotion" mechanism based on test criteria in order to save CI/CD resources so that not all tests run all the time. For example, long duration tests running over a number of days may be promoted to be run only once a week allowing time for other tests. If such tests fail, it will revert to daily jobs. This basic process of promotion can be useful whenever there are a number of candidates for long duration tests.

PERFORMANCE TESTING

Performance tests are important to qualify and validate a system. These tests always involve three functional parts:

1. Traffic Generator
2. Workload
3. Automation code or scripts

Traffic generators must be automatically installed and configured.

Pass/Fail criteria and threshold values may be difficult to define as they depend on the hardware, the configuration and the global environment. However, it is possible to compare results from one run to another especially if running the test regularly. The results collected through CI/CD chains can be post processed using machine learning algorithms. When the integration is complex, such algorithm can be useful to detect the influence of the different parameters on the performance test results. Such processing has been implemented in the OPNFV Yardstick project. Post processing based on R language has been used to evaluate the influence of integration, as well as the version and hardware on a given scenario. The tool processes the data to evaluate the explanatory power of the constituting factors (test context variables) regarding the key performance indicator (KPI) of the test as illustrated in the Figure 4 (each circle represents a CI run in a given configuration):

In this case, a CI/CD chain is very useful to evaluate the influence of one single parameter on the performance. In the example above, one test dealing with bandwidth management has been run daily on different hardware with different system configurations. Each black circle corresponds to one run. The quality of the model is directly linked to the ability to run the test frequently through CI/CD runs and get a representative statistical sample.

Figure 4. Influence of configuration parameters on a single OPNFV Performance test through machine learning post processing of the CI results

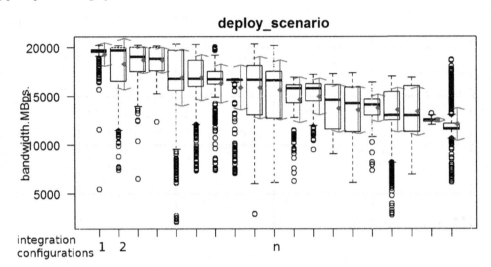

TEST AUTOMATION: THE THEORY AND THE PRACTICE

Software testing automation generates many articles and research papers. ISO/IEC/IEEE 29119 Software Testing (Ali & Yue, 2015) is an internationally agreed set of standards for software testing that can be used within any software development life cycle or organization (2013-2015 replacing previous standard dealing with test definition and unit testing). The topic is probably as old as software development, while there are still active discussions on the topic for complex equipment systems (Yin, Zhi-An, & Jiang-Ting-Ting, 2017), on cloud-based strategy (Pei, Yin, Xie, & Cai, 2017), and on the introduction of self-aware test automation (Eberhardinger, Habermaier, & Reif, 2017; (Pei, Yin, Xie, & Cai, 2017).

More generally the automation of acceptance tests has always been considered as a good way to increase the interoperability of systems. ISO/IEC 9646 was published in 1991 and the 1994 revision is still valid. This standard deals with the conformance testing methodology and framework of open systems Interconnection.

Table 2. Open Systems Interconnection, Conformance testing methodology and framework

Part	Description
1	General concepts
2	Abstract Test Suite specification
3	The Tree and Tabular Combined Notation (TTCN)
4	Test realization
5	Requirements on test laboratories and clients for the conformance assessment process
6	Protocol profile test specification
7	Implementation Conformance Statements

Source: ISO/IEC 9646-1:1994

Tests usually allow detecting a bug but cannot detect the absence of bugs, therefore increasing the number of tests written in different languages helps consolidate the quality of the code. It is therefore important that tests are created by different people and not only the code contributors.

The standardization of test languages such as Testing and Test Control Notation (TTCN) (Baumgarten & Giessler, 1994), Test Description Language (TDL) (Baumgarten & Giessler, 1994; "The ETSI Test Description Language TDL and its Application," 2014), associated with de facto standards provided by Open Source communities such as Robot Framework ("Robot Framework," n.d.), Cucumber (Limited, n.d.; "Robot Framework," n.d.), or more generally the rich Python testing ecosystem contribute to simplify the automation of the tests.

Robot Framework is a generic test automation framework widely adopted by the industry for acceptance testing and acceptance test-driven development (ATDD). Tests are easier to write and can be created by non-developers. As with many Open Source tools, Robot Framework has not been standardized but capitalizes on best practices inherited from standardization over the last 30 years. It is the result of a long Darwinian selection process.

Virtualization, especially the flexibility provided by containers (allowing the fast spawning of isolated, ephemeral and rich testing environments), big data, and deep learning technologies, has triggered a new interest in test automation.

ETSI TST ("Work Programme - Work Item Detailed Report," n.d.) aims to define a series of test cases using a machine readable language to describe the tests, such that they may be translated into executable code (Python, Ruby, or whatever).

TYPICAL PROBLEMS WITH AUTOMATION

Despite the many benefits, automation is not systematically used by most Open Source communities. This section details typical problems and key hurdles for adopting more automation.

Note that the Cloud Native Computing Foundation (CNCF) defined a Cloud Native trail map (Evans, 2018) which details the recommended steps to leverage Open Source cloud native technologies.

Ten steps have been defined, the first four key points are:

1. Containerization
2. CI/CD
3. Orchestration
4. Observability and Analysis

Problems typically involve dealing with physical resources, time and technical skills.

Some automation problems are similar to problems encountered for unit test adoption some decades ago. The benefits of test driven development (Ashbacher, 2003) have been theorized for a long time. Unit test frameworks have been improved continuously over time and are now common for all programming languages. Theory has been confirmed by academic studies "After a period of one year of utilizing automated unit testing practices on Version 2 of a product, the team realized a 20.9% decrease in test defects" (Williams, Kudrjavets, & Nagappan, 2009) . Despite this compelling evidence there are still projects, including some big projects, without a unit test strategy. When a software community focuses primarily on development, tests are often only considered a posteriori. If code is first implemented, unit tests may be considered as having little value since the code is already available. This is a short term view where the individual developer is central. For a mid-term view with a community centric approach, unit tests are mandatory and must be realized before system integration. Some Open Source communities impose rules for unit tests covering new code before any merge.

Another reason for not automating can be the relative complexity of the tools. Unit test frameworks are in fact now very easy to use and usually fully integrated with the most popular Integrated Development Environments (IDE). Such frameworks however remain closed to the developer coding ecosystem. Automation requires hardware resources, specific automation tools, policies, process and skills. Automation frameworks are also not static by design; they must be maintained and monitored. System or administrator skills are required in addition of developer skills.

Finally, even though it is now possible to externalize automation tool-chains using Cloud solutions, big projects may require a dedicated infrastructure. Setting up such dedicated infrastructure requires significant hardware investment (servers, switches, firewalls, etc.). In both cases automation will impact the project budget. Moreover, the success of an Open Source project is not predictable and up-front investment in automation is sometimes simply not planned.

KEY HURDLES FOR MORE AUTOMATION

The Mindset Question

The first hurdle is a question of mindset. Through the explosion of development frameworks, developers can quickly become an expert in one domain. Automation however requires new expertise that involves a wide scope of computer science skills (beyond a single framework). Development teams must therefore include these new types of skill-sets.

Some development frameworks now integrate automation features. Time is needed for developers to adopt these features and more generally adopt an automation driven development methodology. As for unit tests, we expect they will soon become a commodity and the need for specific skills will not be as high as it is today. Adopting automation methods can be synonymous with a major software development culture shift. Organization and workflows must be modified, which is usually not trivial. Such organizational change echoes the transformation policy announced by many companies to move from their traditional business to a more software-oriented business. The interaction with Open Source communities dramatically changed the development processes in the industry. After a long period of mistrust, lots of companies now consider Open Source as a virtuous model, however adoption of such model can be long and difficult. It is for instance sometimes difficult to impose a fully open peer review process. This is a prerequisite for the generalization of automation as most automation frameworks are Open Source and rely on the fact that code is submitted continuously and shared with community contributors and end users.

The Question of Resources

One of the key hurdles is the creation, maintenance, and management of the physical infrastructure supporting automation. This issue can be addressed by a dedicated project within the Open Source project. For example, the Open Platform for Network Function Virtualization (OPNFV) project initiated the

Pharos test infrastructure project which consists of a federation of distributed labs with resources that can be dynamically allocated for automation tasks ("Pharos - OPNFV," n.d.) and managed in the releng (release engineering) project.

Open Source projects must provision machines for CI/CD chains: for the gating operations and also for end-to-end tests or performance testing. Depending on the size of the project, the need for hardware may be critical. In lots of Open Source communities, such hardware is usually offered by companies involved in the projects. The project governance may also allocate budget for additional machines. OPNFV pharos labs are distributed all around the world and some of these labs are exclusively used for CI/CD chains.

Pharos federation was created at the beginning of the projects. As the project became more mature, new requirements were identified. For example, the multisite project reported the need for distributed configurations involving several remote labs. The automation of such tests is difficult because it requires a real time topology knowledge of the different nodes involved in the federation, troubleshooting is also complex and the current tooling is still not mature enough to provide such an environment.

The testing working group also identified the need for resources to automate very long duration tests. Automation of the chain deploying / testing prevents detection of insidious errors due to, for example, poor clean-up of resources used during the test for instance. Such errors can be detected only if the test can be repeated on the same system under test.

Test Promotion Mechanism

When running CI/CD chains, most of the tests must be stable. If the tests are stable, it is possible to imagine running them less frequently to save CI/CD resources and time. In this case, it is recommended to create a promotion mechanism. A daily test will be promoted according to the CI/CD policy after either N successful runs or when an associated trust indicator reaches the expected level of confidence. The trust indicator can be associated with a test case and set to 0 (no trust) on the first run, then this indicator will be increased or decreased according to the test policy. Once promoted, the test will run less frequently (e.g., weekly). The test may then be run once a week. If a test fails at some stage, the test frequency will revert back to daily and the trust indicator would be reduced.

Figure 5. OPNFV Pharos federation

Figure 6. Test Promotion Mechanism in Automation Loop

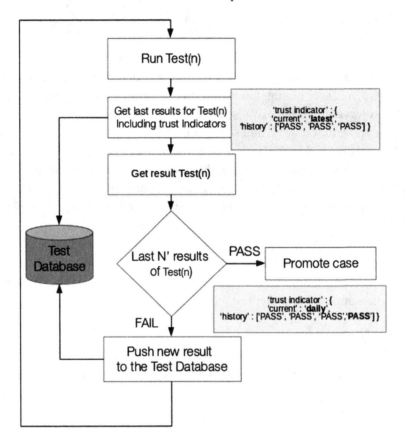

What Is a Good Test?

A good test is an automated, accurate, and unambiguous (i.e., can be easily interpreted).

When performing automated tests, the question of test accuracy must be continually considered. There are more and more test frameworks in all domains, with many languages to run any test suites. However, a day will always last 24 hours. Therefore, it is not workable to accumulate too many similar tests. That is why it is important to control the way test suites are added to CI/CD loops. Overlaps between test suites are sometimes hard to identify. Test projects must challenge the introduction of new tests in daily/weekly loops and plan a promotion mechanism. In Open Source projects, refactoring is frequent as shown in the monthly rate change of the projects (see Table 1), and test code follows the same rules.

What Is Good Feedback for Developers?

CI/CD chains must provide useful feedback to the community as well as developers. That is why it is also important to build a test result inventory and create result visualization adapted to different audiences. A developer may be satisfied with a simple feedback from the CI/CD pipeline (plain text/html page from CI/CD tooling). Release managers or end users may however expect a more consolidated and aggregated view. System administrators will be more interested in graphical views of the resources.

The volume of results may quickly overflow human capabilities. Middleware processing must therefore be done to extract the pertinent information. This means that specific development must be done to provide the optimal information in a way that is easy to access.

AUTOMATION TOOLING

Different categories of automation tools are relevant for Open Source projects. Tools should allow the completion of different processing chained tasks (also called pipeline) during gating phase as well as on a regular basis (daily/weekly/etc.). A comprehensive tool chain also includes a code versioning tool, code review capabilities, code test execution environment, results collection mechanism and a way to easily visualize history of what ran where, when and the detailed results.

Code repositories and version control softwares such as "svn", "git", or "git/gerrit" combine with automation tools to trigger jobs, check the code, launch unit tests, launch functional or performance tests, and report the results to humans.

In Table 3, a summary of some of the automation tools used by Open Source communities is provided.

Lots of rich Open Source back-ends have been created and can be used to provide accurate and visual feedback to the developers. Sometimes it is directly related to the tooling (Jenkins plugins, Robot visualization page).

The virtualization boosted the use and chaining of the different tools. The fast adoption of "docker" allows to setup complex complete chains very quickly whatever the size of the projects.

Jenkins

Jenkins ("Jenkins Handbook," n.d.) is a continuous integration server that can be considered as the Swiss army knife of CI/CD. Automation tooling has been developed over a long period. CruiseControl was one of the first tools addressing the question of continuous build (first release in 2001). Hudson became a better alternative in 2007 and was renamed Jenkins in 2011.

Jenkins includes a huge number of plugins (more than 1300) to integrate linting, statistics, and third party publications. Jenkins aims to automate the non-human part of the software development process by automatically launching some jobs on gating or periodically when target resources are available to execute the actions.

Jenkins is now very mature and provides Long Term Support (LTS) releases in addition of rolling releases.

Table 3. Automation tools

Versioning	Gating Tools	CI/CD Core Engine	Result Collection	Visualization
svn	Yamllint, markdown-lint, ansible-lint, ...	Jenkins, Zuul	influxDB	Grafana
Git, gerrit, gitlab, BitBucket	Pyyaml, pylint, pep8, SonarQube, ...	Gitlab-ci, Travis-ci, Spinnaker	Elasticsearch	Kibana
	Unittests	Bamboo, CircleCI, ...	Built-in databases	Built-in HTML pages

Gitlab-ci

The Gitlab ("Team Handbook," n.d.) Open Source project leverages "git" and its ecosystem. Since 2013, Gitlab has two versions: a community edition under MIT license and a proprietary community edition. The solution integrated a full built-in CI/CD feature in 2016.

Spinnaker

Spinnaker ("Spinnaker," n.d., "Team Handbook," n.d.) is the CI/CD solution developed and used by Netflix. It is tested in production daily. It is distributed through different modules. It is natively multi cloud and interoperable with "git" events, Travis CI, or Jenkins pipelines.

Chaos Monkey testing is a disruptive way of testing introduced in 2011. Netflix designed and implemented a testing framework to perform automatic resiliency testing on production servers. Netflix released the code of the tooling (Netflix, n.d.) under Apache 2 license and fully integrated it under its CI/CD tooling Spinnaker.

Travis CI

The Open Source project Travis CI ("Getting started - Travis CI," n.d.), allows a simple file to be used to link your repository to a CI/CD chain with integrated monitoring. It is free as an Open Source project. It is very popular for small projects. According to the Travis CI website, over 900 k open source projects and 600 k users are testing on Travis CI. It can be also an interesting solution for big projects that do not want to setup a dedicated infrastructure for their CI/CD chains.

A quick comparison of these solutions is provided in Table 4.

CircleCI, Skycap, Buddy, Semaphore, and Percy are other alternative solutions for continuous integration.

EXAMPLES OF AUTOMATION

Platform as a Service (PaaS): OpenShift

OpenShift ("Home | Red Hat OpenShift Documentation," n.d.) is a popular Open Source Platform as a Service (PaaS) solution. Web developers do not have to think about the network or the deployment

Table 4. Comparison of CI/CD integrated solutions

	First Release Date	Last Stable Release	Number of Contributors	Number of Lines of Code	Estimated Value	License
Jenkins	2004	14/2/2018	1894	929076	$13,954,780	MIT
Gitlab	2011	14/3/2018	1912	539985	$8,082,487	MIT
Spinnaker	2015	2018	406	430315	N.A	Apache v2
Travis-CI	2010	2018	826	185805	$2,623,661	MIT

Source: openhub

environment. They even do not have to care about load balancing and scalability, they can just focus on their application.

CI/CD contributed to OpenShift popularity as a Container Platform. OpenShift provides a certified Jenkins container for building CD pipelines and also scales the pipeline execution through on-demand provisioning of Jenkins slaves in containers. This is a classic CI/CD pipeline as shown in Figure 7.

The OpenShift CI/CD pipeline is classical. It includes a package build phase, code quality checks using SonarQube (unit tests and coverage), artifact creation integration tests and finally a deployment step.

Infrastructure as a Service (IaaS): OpenStack

OpenStack ("Open source software for creating private and public clouds," n.d.) is an Open Source software platform for cloud computing, widely deployed in production. The solution consists of lots of integrated modules providing virtual networking, compute and storage capabilities as well as many additional features (portals, container support, big data support, etc.). The "stackanalytics" website identifies more than 7800 developers from 404 companies working on 890 modules since the creation of the OpenStack project. OpenStack is now considered a reference for large Open Source projects.

Even if it is possible to install a basic OpenStack sandbox (e.g., devstack) on a laptop, most of the target environments require a large hardware configuration. The community developed a CI/CD strategy in order to guarantee the stability of the overall system and this involves several projects to ensure high quality gating with sophisticated end-to-end testing. Additionally, some features or performance requirements require specific hardware (e.g., smart NIC, specific I/O acceleration cards, specific network cards). Integration can therefore get very complex and resulting in numerous combinations of hardware and software configurations that need to be tested. That is why OpenStack requires a rich CI/CD environment.

Gating is controlled by the OpenStack Zuul project and sustainability issues are managed by Jenkins regular jobs. A new patch submitted to OpenStack will automatically trigger several robots. For each submitted patch, Zuul is triggered as well as several external CI chains from different vendors involved in the development of the solution. These chains run different tests: for instance Zuul runs openstack-tox-pep8 (code conformity), openstack-tox-py27 (unit tests in Python 2.7), tox-py35 (unit tests in python 3.5), and doc generation (sphinx). If one of the tests reports "-1" to the gate, then this patch is not be merged and requires corrective patches.

Figure 7. OpenShift CI/CD pipeline

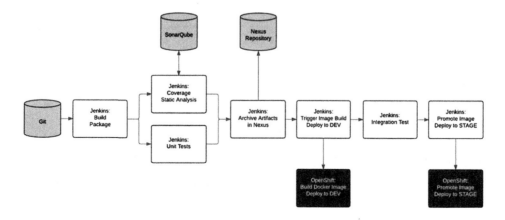

The OpenStack CI infrastructure is designed to be shared amongst other projects wanting a scalable cloud based CI system. It is therefore possible to connect a new node to the global CI/CD system ("Running your own CI infrastructure — OpenStack Project Infrastructure 2018.04.04 documentation," n.d.).

OpenStack documentation is also a reference for other large projects ("OpenStack Docs: Queens," n.d.). Due to the complexity and extreme modularity of OpenStack, documentation was very challenging. According to the OpenStack documentation project team, documentation is treated just like code and powered by the community in the same way as code. The documentation is very rich and includes user guides, installation guides, API guides, Operations and Maintenance guides, contributor guides, release notes, and lots of example code for each release (every 6 months). Release notes for each module are centralized. For the Queen release there were more than 250 release notes.

OPNFV CI/CD

OPNFV is an integration project and one of the founding LFN (Linux Foundation Networking Fund) projects. The other founding projects within LFN are FD.io, OpenDaylight, ONAP, PNDA, and SNAS.

Through system level integration, deployment and testing of Open Source projects of various sizes, OPNFV creates a reference NFV platform to accelerate the transformation of service provider networks to "telecommunication cloud". Several chains are available; some for development and project gating, some for deployment including deployment and test phases. Tests can be relatively complex and require many hours of dedicated CI resources. Management of these resources becomes critical to deliver timely and stable releases following planned release milestones.

OPNFV does not primarily develop new code but aims to integrated and validate how several upstream code bases work together. Experience from several releases showed that feedback from OPNFV activities to upstream projects was not resulting in consistently faster bugfix cycles. Each upstream project had its own CI/CD strategy and issues detected by OPNFV at integration time were not impacting upstream as was expected. As a result the release engineering project within OPNFV started a new initiative named XCI (Cross CommunityCI).

Figure 8. OPNFV CI/CD chain

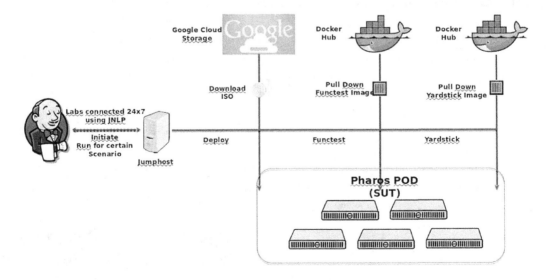

Cross CommunityCI (XCI)

The goal of the OPNFV XCI Initiative is to connect existing upstream CI chains by becoming part of upstream community testing resources in order to provide feedback to developers as quickly as possible.

Before XCI, an issue detected in OPNFV version N was reported manually to OPNFV project team who then worked to identify the upstream components impacted by the issue. The issue was subsequently reported upstream and a fix may or may not have been resolved in the next release of that upstream component. In other words issues were dealt with in an ad hoc and open loop process. The best case was if the upstream community made the fix quickly and if the release cycle happened to synchronize in a way that it would be integrated in OPNFV version N+1 (at least 6 months later). Often it wasn't until the next OPNFV release that developers even found out if the issue had been resolved in the new code base.

XCI eliminates the notion of a point release (in the case of OPNFV on a 6 month release cadence) and rather implements a rolling release. As a consequence a bug detected at integration time flags errors in XCI chains that are reported automatically and immediately (and continuously) to the upstream community. This motivates to fix the issue as soon as possible. Since error reporting is faster (automated though CI chains) the correction is also usually faster.

Cross-Community Testing (Xtesting)

Xtesting is an OPNFV project that evolved from the OPNFV Functest project, which was in charge of end-to-end functional testing of a Telco Cloud infrastructure (initially based on OpenStack). Several tiers of testing are included:

- The first "Healthcheck" tier deals with basic and quick tests checking the SUT connectivity, API conformity and possibly simple functional health. Usually the whole test suite lasts less than 5 minutes. "Healthcheck tier" is used systematically for gating patches.
- The second "smoke test" tier provides release gating, including mandatory tests that must pass. These tests are usually considerably more complex than the first tier and they may include tests of specific features. Tests usually last from minutes to a few hours. The test suite runs daily in the CI/CD chain and parts can eventually be used for gating production.

Figure 9. XCI (src: OPNFV XCI presentation)

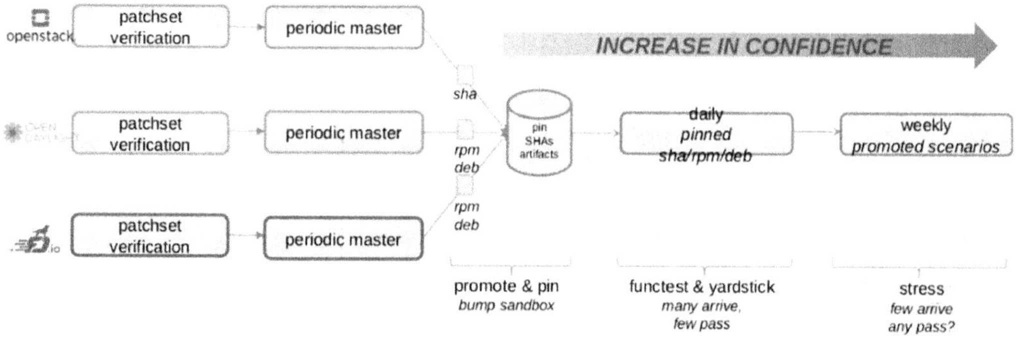

- The third and last tier deals with Virtual Network Function (VNF) testing, i.e., testing involves network applications running as VNFs on the platform. This is significantly more complex as it requires the start and the synchronization of several virtual machines. Tests may last many hours.

The OPNFV Functest framework aims to automate testing actions by:

1. Launching and controlling execution of the tests.
2. Collect test results.
3. Publish test results and make them easy to interpret and track over time.

The Functest framework is based on a docker container with each test tier corresponding to one container. These containers, based on alpines dockers ("Alpine Linux," n.d.), must be as small as possible to reduce the CI/CD processing duration. Heavy containers or large virtual machines will consume unnecessarily bandwidth and time so the choice of docker provides lots of flexibility to optimize testing. The framework is also partly agnostic to the nature of the tests by design, which means it is possible to run tests written in Python or in Bash (which opens the door to almost any type of test cases), robot framework (a popular test description language), or through a built-in VNF abstraction.

OPNFV projects initially dealt with only one type of VIM (Virtual Infrastructure Manager). Due to the evolution of projects new infrastructures have been integrated (e.g., Kubernetes). One solution would have been to duplicate the testing framework and associate one per infrastructure. It was decided, however, to build a testing framework that would be also agnostic to the infrastructure. As a consequence, the developer has to just focus on the test code, not on how or when it is launched and not on how the results are collected. The "dockerization" of the tests, as well as CI/CD integration and the publication of results is now natively provided by the Xtesting framework in OPNFV.

OpenCI: A Step Further?

OpenCI ("OpenCI," n.d.) is a community of CI/CD infrastructure practitioners across Open Source projects. It generalizes the XCI initiative and aims to harmonize automation processes as well as share

Figure 10. Results from Functest smoke tier CI (Euphrates version)
Source: https://build.opnfv.org/ci/view/functest

```
2018-03-30 15:37:08,395 - xtesting.ci.run_tests - INFO - Xtesting report:

+--------------------+---------------+---------------+---------------+---------------+---------------+
|     TEST CASE      |    PROJECT    |     TIER      |   DURATION    |    RESULT     |
+--------------------+---------------+---------------+---------------+---------------+---------------+
|      vping_ssh     |    functest   |     smoke     |     00:55     |     PASS      |
|    vping_userdata  |    functest   |     smoke     |     00:40     |     PASS      |
|  tempest_smoke_serial |  functest  |     smoke     |     15:18     |     PASS      |
|     rally_sanity   |    functest   |     smoke     |     28:18     |     PASS      |
|   refstack_defcore |    functest   |     smoke     |     04:28     |     PASS      |
|       patrole      |    functest   |     smoke     |     03:54     |     PASS      |
|     snaps_smoke    |    functest   |     smoke     |     50:37     |     PASS      |
|        odl         |    functest   |     smoke     |     00:00     |     SKIP      |
|     odl_netvirt    |    functest   |     smoke     |     00:00     |     SKIP      |
|    neutron_trunk   |    functest   |     smoke     |     00:00     |     SKIP      |
+--------------------+---------------+---------------+---------------+---------------+---------------+
```

Figure 11. Xtesting architecture

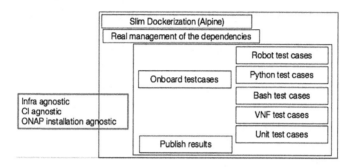

automation resources. This has resulted from the need of several companies contributing to multiple Open Source networking projects to build dedicated CI/CD infrastructure for each project. This was very costly in terms of both hardware and human resources. The recent reorganization of The Linux Foundation networking projects under LFN encouraged the optimization of resources that contributing companies invest. One of the key efforts initiated by OpenCI is to ensure the CI machines can communicate to each other using a standardized messaging protocol, an important step towards event driven CI ("Pipeline Messaging 0.1," n.d.).

To increase awareness in cross–community CI/CD, OPNFV initiated numerous presentations at Open Source community events including two keynote appearances (Open Source Summit Europe, OpenStack Summit Sydney). This has resulted in launching the OpenCI initiative in March 2018 with a cross-community Infra/CI/CD workshop arranged with 8 participating communities. The participants of OpenCI initiative are from OpenStack, CNCF, OpenDaylight, OPNFV, LFN, ONAP, Ansible, and FD.io. OpenCI reached out to other foundations such as Apache Foundation to increase the awareness, diversity and encourage participation.

Cross community testing is theoretically simple but practically complex. Resources owner may be reluctant to share resources for practical, connectivity, administrative or security reasons. The OpenDev summit organized in parallel of the OpenStack summit shall address this cross community topic.

RECOMMENDATIONS

Open Source projects must develop a CI/CD strategy, implement automation tools, and adopt suitable release engineering processes as early as possible. To help the community adopt an "automation culture", community leaders can play an important role by helping to understand the benefits, provide resources and support CI/CD evolution throughout the life of the project.

If the project is small and uses "github", solutions such as Travis-Ci may be appropriate. For bigger projects, however, it is recommended that dedicated projects be responsible for all automation tasks in the community: gating, daily jobs, artifact generation, etc. using Jenkins or Gitlab CI/CD pipelines. These "infrastructure" projects are essential for the success of large Open Source communities as they will determine the stability and the sustainability of the project. Automation activities touch every part of development and production lifecycles. The physical and human resources needed are usually underestimated.

The introduction of a gating solution such as Zuul v3 is highly recommended especially for complex modular projects, it would prevent from merging broken code and contribute to ensure the "trustability" of the integration.

For continuous delivery, the adoption of Spinnaker, a rich cloud native CD solution would help adopting most of the best practices of this domain. It abstracts the CD part to the developer, secures the promotion of a release candidate to production, and provides efficient rollback mechanisms even for complex rollouts.

Problems must not be hidden! The benefits of making everything easily visible at all times can include dramatically increased productivity and quality of release artifacts (this includes code and documentation). One of the best methods to attract developers and grow an Open Source community is to implement a transparent CI/CD tool-chain. Public visibility into all aspects of Open Source development including, contributions, testing, code maturity, and progress towards community objectives is a powerful motivators when part of an inclusive and supportive technical community. It means that visualization tools must be properly set to quickly identify and locate the errors.

Security aspects must also not be forgotten, and as most of software development aspects, security checks and audits must be automated and run regularly as soon as possible in the project life cycle. A posteriori security audits are always costly and painful for everybody. Integrating security into automation strategy can save lots of money. The audits may deal with different aspects: from standard legal considerations such as the respect of the code licensing to chaos monkey campaigns aiming to detect the weaknesses of a system in production.

REFERENCES

Ali, S., & Yue, T. (2015). Formalizing the ISO/IEC/IEEE 29119 Software Testing Standard. *2015 ACM/ IEEE 18th International Conference on Model Driven Engineering Languages and Systems (MODELS)*. 10.1109/models.2015.7338271

Alpine Linux. (n.d.). Retrieved April 5, 2018, from http://wiki.alpinelinux.org/wiki/Main_Page

Ashbacher, C. (2003). Test-Driven Development: By Example, by Kent Beck. *Journal of Object Technology*, 2(2), 203. doi:10.5381/jot.2003.2.2.r1

Baumgarten, B., & Giessler, A. (1994). *OSI Conformance Testing Methodology and TTCN*. North-Holland.

Dahmen-Lhuissier, S. (n.d.). *Open Source MANO*. Retrieved June 6, 2018, from http://www.etsi.org/ technologies-clusters/technologies/nfv/open-source-mano

Eberhardinger, B., Habermaier, A., & Reif, W. (2017). Toward Adaptive, Self-Aware Test Automation. *2017 IEEE/ACM 12th International Workshop on Automation of Software Testing (AST)*. 10.1109/ast.2017.1

Evans, K. (2018, March 8). *Introducing The Cloud Native Landscape 2.0 - Interactive Edition*. Cloud Native Computing Foundation. Retrieved April 5, 2018, from https://www.cncf.io/blog/2018/03/08/ introducing-the-cloud-native-landscape-2-0-interactive-edition/

Getting started - Travis CI. (n.d.). Retrieved April 5, 2018, from https://docs.travis-ci.com/user/getting-started/

Gray, K., & Nadeau, T. D. (2016). ETSI NFV ISG. In Network Function Virtualization (pp. 49–76). Academic Press.

Humble, J., & Farley, D. (2010). *Continuous Delivery: Reliable Software Releases through Build, Test, and Deployment Automation (Adobe Reader)*. Pearson Education.

Jenkins Handbook. (n.d.). Retrieved April 5, 2018, from https://jenkins.io/doc/book/index.html

Limited, C. (n.d.). *Cucumber*. Retrieved April 5, 2018, from https://cucumber.io/

Linux Foundation. (n.d.). *Projects - The Linux Foundation*. Retrieved June 4, 2018, from https://www.linuxfoundation.org/projects/

Netflix. (n.d.). *Netflix/chaosmonkey*. Retrieved April 5, 2018, from https://github.com/Netflix/chaos-monkey

Nfv, E. (2018). *Network Functions Virtualisation (NFV) Release 2; Management and Orchestration; Functional requirements specification* (No. RGS/NFV-IFA010ed241). ETSI.

ONAP. (n.d.). Retrieved June 6, 2018, from https://www.onap.org/

Open, C. I. (n.d.). Retrieved April 5, 2018, from https://openci.io/

Open Baton. (n.d.). *Open Baton: an open source reference implementation of the ETSI Network Function Virtualization MANO specification*. Retrieved June 6, 2018, from https://openbaton.github.io/

Open source software for creating private and public clouds. (n.d.). Retrieved April 5, 2018, from https://www.openstack.org/

OpenStack Docs Queens. (n.d.). Retrieved April 5, 2018, from https://docs.openstack.org/queens/

Overview — Sphinx 1.8.0+ documentation. (n.d.). Retrieved April 5, 2018, from http://www.sphinx-doc.org

Pei, H., Yin, B., Xie, M., & Cai, K.-Y. (2017). A cloud-based dynamic random software testing strategy. *2017 IEEE International Conference on Industrial Engineering and Engineering Management (IEEM)*. 10.1109/IEEM.2017.8289943

Pharos - OPNFV. (n.d.). Retrieved April 5, 2018, from https://www.opnfv.org/community/projects/pharos

Pipeline Messaging 0.1. (n.d.). Retrieved April 5, 2018, from https://docs.google.com/document/d/122 6nsoKtOJwghtohIyWqRettvxsPHjsNFKgfgeUlucc/edit?usp=embed_facebook

Read the Docs. (n.d.). Retrieved April 5, 2018, from https://readthedocs.org/

Red Hat OpenShift Documentation. (n.d.). Retrieved April 5, 2018, from https://docs.openshift.com/index.html

Robot Framework. (n.d.). Retrieved April 5, 2018, from http://robotframework.org/

Running your own CI infrastructure — OpenStack Project Infrastructure 2018.04.04 documentation. (n.d.). Retrieved April 5, 2018, from https://docs.openstack.org/infra/system-config/running-your-own.html

Sartre, J. P. (1955). *No exit, and three other plays*. Vintage.

Spinnaker. (n.d.). Retrieved April 5, 2018, from https://www.spinnaker.io/

Team Handbook. (n.d.). Retrieved April 5, 2018, from https://about.gitlab.com/handbook/

The ETSI Test Description Language TDL and its Application. (2014). *Proceedings of the 2nd International Conference on Model-Driven Engineering and Software Development*. doi:10.5220/0004708706010608

Williams, L., Kudrjavets, G., & Nagappan, N. (2009). On the Effectiveness of Unit Test Automation at Microsoft. *2009 20th International Symposium on Software Reliability Engineering*. 10.1109/ISSRE.2009.32

Work Programme - Work Item Detailed Report. (n.d.). Retrieved April 5, 2018, from https://portal.etsi.org/webapp/workProgram/Report_WorkItem.asp?wki_id=54031

Yin, L., Zhi-An, S., & Jiang, T-T. (2017). A Software Reliability Test Suite Generating Approach Based on Hybrid Model for Complex Equipment System. *2017 International Conference on Dependable Systems and Their Applications (DSA)*. 10.1109/DSA.2017.32

KEY TERMS AND DEFINITIONS

Cloud Native: Cloud native is a term used to qualify applications designed and implemented in and for the cloud. It goes beyond the virtualization of applications by integrating cloud concepts as defined in the cloud computing manifesto. It usually requires to fully redesign applications in order to split atomic functions into isolated virtual resources (micro-services).

Continuous Delivery: The continuous delivery (CD) concept, defined by Martin Fowler in 2013, is a software development discipline where software can be promoted from release candidate to production environment automatically. It has been largely enriched since 2010 thanks to the development and the adoption of cloud and virtualization technologies. CD is usually associated with the devops approach for the methodology and the "on demand" aspect for the business.

Continuous Integration: In software engineering, continuous integration (CI) is the practice of merging all developer code contributions to a shared mainline several times a day. The term was introduced in 1991 by Grady Booch, known for his work on oriented object programming concepts.

Gating: In software engineering, the gating consists in different check points triggered by an automation system, potentially in parallel, before merging any change to the reference source code. Gating aims to ensure the good quality of the code by running test suites and linting operations. It is part of the CI.

Linux Foundation: Founded in 2000, The Linux Foundation is dedicated to building sustainable ecosystems around open source projects to accelerate technology development and industry adoption. It is among the largest open source non-profit organization. It works to promote, protect, and advance Linux and collaborative development through different and unparalleled initiatives such as the Cloud Native Computing Foundation, OPENAPI initiative, OPEN CONTAINER initiative, OPNFV, or ONAP projects.

Open Source: The open source model is a decentralized software-development model that encourages open collaboration and imposes the use of an open source license for the source code. Open source licenses must guarantee that the source code, blueprint or design can be used, modified and/or shared under defined terms and conditions. Open source is sometimes considered as a more industry-oriented rephrasing of the free software model. The free software foundation created in 1985 considers the freedom as the cornerstone of the model. The open source initiative officially announced in 1998 puts the efficiency as the key point of the collaborative model.

Test-Driven Development: Test-driven development (TDD) is a software development approach consisting in writing the tests prior to the code. TDD ensures that the source code is thoroughly unit tested and leads to modularized, flexible and extensible code. It aims to simplify and clarify the software design as only the code necessary to pass tests has to be written.

Virtualization: In computing, virtualization refers to the act of creating virtual resources, including virtual computer hardware platforms, storage devices, and computer network resources. Virtualization is as old as computer science but became very popular with the hardware improvement in particular in chipset industry and the development of Linux. The different virtualization technologies are heavily used by the cloud computing industry. Virtualization is also a key driver for the development of the web technologies especially on distributed storage, big data, machine learning, and artificial intelligence.

Compilation of References

22261. g20. (n.d.).

3. GPP TR 28.801. (2017). *Study on management and orchestration of network slicing for next generation network* (Release 15).

3. GPP TS 23.501. (2017). *System Architecture for the 5G System.*

3. GPP. (2011). Self-configuring and self-optimizing network (SON) use cases and solutions. *Third Generation Partnership Project (3GPP) specification TR36902*, V9.

451. Research. (2010). *The Rise of DevOps.* Retrieved June 4, 2018 from https://451research.com/report-long?icid=1304

5. GEx. (2016). *5GEx Initial System Requirements and Architecture.* Deliverable 2.1.

5. GEx. (2017). *5GEx Final System Requirements and Architecture.* Deliverable 2.2.

5. GPPP Network Management & Quality of Service Working Group. (2017). *Cognitive Network Management for 5G.* Retrieved from https://5g-ppp.eu/wp-content/uploads/2017/03/NetworkManagement_WhitePaper_1.pdf

5G. PPP. (2015). *White papers on vertical industries.* Retrieved from https://5g-ppp.eu/white-papers/

5G. PPP. (2016). *5G empowering verticals.* Retrieved from https://5g-ppp.eu/wp-content/uploads/2016/02/BROCHURE_5PPP_BAT2_PL.pdf

5G. TRANSFORMER. (2018). *Definition of vertical service descriptors and SO NBI.* Deliverable 3.1.

Addis, B., Belabed, D., Bouet, M., & Secci, S. (2015). Virtual network functions placement and routing optimization. *2015 IEEE 4th International Conference on Cloud Networking (CloudNet)*, 171–177. 10.1109/CloudNet.2015.7335301

Agoulmine, N., Balasubramaniam, S., Botvich, D., Strassner, J., Lehtihet, E., & Donnelly, W. (2006). Challenges for autonomic network management. In *Proceedings of the IEEE International Workshop on Modeling Autonomic Communications Environment (MACE).* IEEE

Agrawal, A., Gans, J., & Goldfarb, A. (2018). *Prediction Machines: The Simple Economics of Artificial Intelligence.* Harvard Business Press.

Ali, S., & Yue, T. (2015). Formalizing the ISO/IEC/IEEE 29119 Software Testing Standard. *2015 ACM/IEEE 18th International Conference on Model Driven Engineering Languages and Systems (MODELS).* 10.1109/models.2015.7338271

Allybokus, Z., Perrot, N., Leguay, J., Maggi, L., & Gourdin, E. (2018). Virtual function placement for service chaining with partial orders and anti-affinity rules. *Networks*, *71*(2), 97–106. doi:10.1002/net.21768

Alpine Linux. (n.d.). Retrieved April 5, 2018, from http://wiki.alpinelinux.org/wiki/Main_Page

Amaldi, E., Coniglio, S., Koster, A. M., & Tieves, M. (2015). On the computational complexity of the virtual network embedding problem. In *International Network Optimization Conference (INOC)*. Warsaw, Poland: Elsevier.

Amaldi, E., Coniglio, S., Koster, A., & Tieves, M. (2016). On the computational complexity of the virtual network embedding problem. *Electronic Notes in Discrete Mathematics, 52*, 213–220. doi:10.1016/j.endm.2016.03.028

Amiri, A., & Pirkul, H. (1999). Routing and capacity assignment in backbone communication networks under time varying traffic conditions. *European Journal of Operational Research, 117*(1), 15–29. doi:10.1016/S0377-2217(98)00162-3

Analysys Manson. (2017). *Telefónica's UNICA architecture strategy for network virtualization*. Retrieved from http://www.analysysmason.com/telefonica-UNICA-architecture-strategy-for-network-virtualisation-report

ANIMA WG. (2018, March). Retrieved April 2018, from IETF: https://datatracker.ietf.org/wg/anima/about/

Ansible. (2018, June 1). Retrieved from Ansible: https://www.ansible.com

Antoniou, G., & Van Harmelen, F. (2009). Web ontology language: OWL. In *Handbook on ontologies* (pp. 91–110). Berlin: Springer. doi:10.1007/978-3-540-92673-3_4

An, X., Zhou, C., Trivisonno, R., Guerzoni, R., Kaloxylos, A., Soldani, D., & Hecker, A. (2016). On end to end network slicing for 5G communication systems. *Transactions on Emerging Telecommunications Technologies, 28*(4), e3058. doi:10.1002/ett.3058

Applegate, D., & Cohen, E. (2006). Making routing robust to changing traffic demands: Algorithms and evaluation. *IEEE/ACM Transactions on Networking, 14*(6), 1193–1206. doi:10.1109/TNET.2006.886296

Architecture and specification of data communication network. (2001). ITU-T Recommendation G.7712/Y.1703, International Telecommunication Union.

Architecture, 5GPPP. (2016). *View on 5G Architecture*. Retrieved from https://5g-ppp.eu/wp-content/uploads/2014/02/5G-PPP-5G-Architecture-WP-July-2016.pdf

Architecture, P. P. P., & Group, W. (2017). View on 5G Architecture (Version 2.0).

Ashbacher, C. (2003). Test-Driven Development: By Example, by Kent Beck. *Journal of Object Technology, 2*(2), 203. doi:10.5381/jot.2003.2.2.r1

Assem, H., & O'Sullivan, D. (2015). Towards Bridging the Gap between Machine Learning Researchers and Practitioners. *IEEE International Conference on Smart City/SocialCom/SustainCom (SmartCity)*. 10.1109/SmartCity.2015.151

Assem, H., Buda, T., & O'Sullivan, D. (2016). *Spatio-Temporal Clustering Approach for Detecting Functional Regions in Cities*. EEE ICTAI. doi:10.1109/ICTAI.2016.0063

Assem, H., Buda, T., & O'Sullivan, D. (2017). *RCMC: Recognizing Crowd Mobility Patterns in Cities based on Location Based Social Networks Data. ACM Transactions on Intelligent Systems and Technology*.

Autonomic Networking Configuration and Deployment Guide. (2017). Cisco IOS XE Everest 16.6. Retrieved from https://www.cisco.com/c/en/us/td/docs/ios-xml/ios/auto_net/configuration/xe-16-6/an-auto-cfg-deploy-16-6.html

Awduche, D., Berger, L., Gan, D., Li, T., Srinivasan, V., & Swallow, G. (2001). *RSVP-TE: Extensions to RSVP for LSP Tunnels*. RFC Editor.

Azar, Y., Cohen, E., Fiat, A., Kaplan, H., & Räcke, H. (2004). Optimal oblivious routing in polynomial time. *Journal of Computer and System Sciences, 69*(3), 383–394. doi:10.1016/j.jcss.2004.04.010

Barker, I. (2018, February). *Security service providers suffer from false positive alert overload.* Retrieved April 2018, from Beta news: https://betanews.com/2018/02/12/false-positive-alert-overload/

Barnhart, C., Hane, C. A., & Vance, P. H. (1997). Integer Multicommodity Flow Problems. *Network Optimization*, 17–31. doi:10.1007/978-3-642-59179-2_2

Bastien, G., & Degu, C. (2003). CCSP SECUR Exam Certification Guide. Cisco Press.

Bauguion, P.-O., Ben-Ameur, W., & Gourdin, E. (2015). Efficient algorithms for the maximum concurrent flow problem. *Networks*, *65*(1), 56–67. doi:10.1002/net.21572

Baumgarten, B., & Giessler, A. (1994). *OSI Conformance Testing Methodology and TTCN*. North-Holland.

BBF. (2018). *End-to-End Network Slicing*. SD-406 (work in progress).

Beasley, J. E., & Christofides, N. (1989). An algorithm for the resource constrained shortest path problem. *Networks*, *19*(4), 379–394. doi:10.1002/net.3230190402

Behringer, M., Bjarnason, S., Jiang, S., Carpenter, B., Pritikin, M., Ciavaglia, L., & Clemm, A. (2015). *Autonomic networking: Definitions and design goals* (RFC 7575).

Behringer, M., Carpenter, B., Eckert, T., Ciavaglia, L., & Nobre, J. (2018). *A Reference Model for Autonomic Networking*. IETF Internet draft.

Behringer, M., Carpenter, B., Eckert, T., Ciavaglia, L., & Nobre, J. (2018). *A Reference Model for Autonomic Networking*. Retrieved from https://tools.ietf.org/html/draft-ietf-anima-reference-model-06

Behringer, M., Pritikin, M., Bjarnason, S., Clemm, A., Carpenter, B., Jian, S., & Ciavaglia, L. (2015). *Autonomic Networking: Definitions and Design Goals. RFC7575*. Internet Research Task Force. doi:10.17487/RFC7575

Ben-Ameur, W. (2002). Multi-hour design of survivable classical IP networks. *International Journal of Communication Systems*, *15*(6), 553–572. doi:10.1002/dac.551

Ben-Ameur, W., & Gourdin, E. (2003). Internet routing and related topology issues. *SIAM Journal on Discrete Mathematics*, *17*(1), 18–49. doi:10.1137/S0895480100377428

Ben-Ameur, W., & Kerivin, H. (2005). Routing of Uncertain Traffic Demands. *Optimization and Engineering*, *6*(3), 283–313. doi:10.100711081-005-1741-7

Bendriss, J., & Grida, I. (2017). AI for SLA Management in Programmable Networks. *DRCN 2017-Design of Reliable Communication Networks; 13th International Conference; Proceedings of*, 1-8.

Bendriss, J., & Grida, I. (2017). Forecasting and anticipating SLO breaches in programmable networks. *20th Conference on Innovations in Clouds, Internet and Networks (ICIN)*, 127-134. 10.1109/ICIN.2017.7899402

Bennacer, L., Amirat, Y., Chibani, A., Mellouk, A., & Ciavaglia, L. (2015). Self-diagnosis technique for virtual private networks combining Bayesian networks and case-based reasoning. *IEEE Transactions on Automation Science and Engineering*, *12*(1), 354–366. doi:10.1109/TASE.2014.2321011

Bhatia, R., Hao, F., Kodialam, M., & Lakshman, T. V. (2015). Optimized network traffic engineering using segment routing. *Proceedings - IEEE INFOCOM*, *26*, 657–665. doi:10.1109/INFOCOM.2015.7218434

Bienstock, D., & Raskina, O. (2002). Asymptotic analysis of the flow deviation method for the maximum concurrent flow problem. *Ser. B*, *91*, 479–492. doi:10.1007101070100254

Bijnens, N., & Hausenblas, M. (2017). *Lamnda Architecture*. Retrieved from http://lambda-architecture.net/

Bilger, B. (2013, November 25). Auto Correct. *The New Yorker*.

Bjorklund, M. (2016). *The YANG 1.1 modeling language*. Internet Engineering Task Force, RFC7950. Retrieved from https://tools.ietf.org/html/rfc7950

Bjorklund, M. (2016). *The YANG 1.1 modeling Language*. Internet Engineering Task Force, RFC7950. Retrieved from https://tools.ietf.org/html/rfc7950

Bjorklund, M. (2016). *YANG – A data modeling language for the network configuration protocol (NETCONF)*. Internet Engineering Task Force, RFC6020. Retrieved from https://tools.ietf.org/html/rfc6020

Bjorklund, M. (2016). *YANG-A data modeling language for the Network Configuration Protocol (NETCONF)*. IETF RFC 7950.

Bley, A. (2008). Routing and capacity optimization for IP networks. *Operations Research Proceedings*, *2007*, 9–16. doi:10.1007/978-3-540-77903-2_2

Bley, A., Fortz, B., Gourdin, E., Holmberg, K., Klopfenstein, O., Pióro Michałand Tomaszewski, A., & Ümit, H. (2010). Optimization of OSPF Routing in IP Networks. In A. Koster & X. Muñoz (Eds.), *Graphs and Algorithms in Communication Networks: Studies in Broadband, Optical, Wireless and Ad Hoc Networks* (pp. 199–240). Berlin: Springer Berlin Heidelberg; doi:10.1007/978-3-642-02250-0_8

Bolla, R., Lombardo, C., Bruschi, R., & Mangialardi, S. (2014). *DROPv2: energy efficiency through network function virtualization*. IEEE Network.

Bonhomme, T. (2017, March/April). *Global Telecoms Business*.

Bormann, C., Carpenter, B., & Liu, B. (Eds.). (2017). *A Generic Autonomic Signaling Protocol (GRASP)*. Retrieved from https://tools.ietf.org/html/draft-ietf-anima-grasp-15

Botero, J. F., Hesselbach, X., Duelli, M., Schlosser, D., Fischer, A., & De Meer, H. (2012). Energy Efficient Virtual Network Embedding. *IEEE Communications Letters*, *16*(5), 756–759. doi:10.1109/LCOMM.2012.030912.120082

Bouabene, G., Jelger, C., Tschudin, C., Schmid, S., Keller, A., & May, M. (2010). The autonomic network architecture (ANA). *IEEE Journal on Selected Areas in Communications*, *28*(1), 4–14. doi:10.1109/JSAC.2010.100102

Boucadair, M., Lévis, P., Griffin, D., Wang, N., Howarth, M., Pavlou, G., ... García-Osma, M. L. (2007). A Framework for End-to-End Service Differentiation: Network Planes and Parallel Internets. *IEEE Communications Magazine*, *45*(9), 134–143. doi:10.1109/MCOM.2007.4342868

Boutin, E., Ekanayake, J., Lin, W., Shi, B., Zhou, J., Qian, Z., . . . Zhou, L. (2014). Apollo: scalable and coordinated scheduling for cloud-scale computing. In *USENIX Symp. on Operating Systems Design and Implementation, OSDI*. USENIX.

Bryskin, I., Liu, X., Guichard, J., Lee, Y., Contreras, L.M., Ceccarelli, D., & Tantsura, J. (2018). *Use Cases for SF Aware Topology Models*, draft-bryskin-teas-use-cases-sf-aware-topo-model-03 (work in progress).

Burger, E. W., & Seedorf, J. (2009). *Application-layer traffic optimization (ALTO) problem statement (RFC5693)*. Internet Engineering Task Force.

Burton, D., & Toint, P. L. (1992). On an instance of the inverse shortest paths problem. *Mathematical Programming*, *53*(1–3), 45–61. doi:10.1007/BF01585693

Caesar, M., Castro, M., Nightingale, E. B., O'Shea, G., & Rowstron, A. (2006). Virtual Ring Routing: Network Routing Inspired by DHTs. In *Proceedings of the 2006 Conference on Applications, Technologies, Architectures, and Protocols for Computer Communications* (pp. 351-362). New York, NY: ACM. 10.1145/1159913.1159954

CentralS. D. X. (2018). *NFV*. Retrieved from https://www.sdxcentral.com/nfv/

Chaparadza, R., Papavassiliou, S., Kastrinogiannis, T., Vigoureux, M., Dotaro, E., Davy, A., & Wilson, M. (2009). *Creating a viable Evolution Path towards Self-Managing Future Internet via a Standardizable Reference Model for Autonomic Network Engineering*. In Future Internet Assembly.

CHARISMA. (2016). *CHARISMA Project*. Retrieved from http://www.charisma5g.eu/index.php/overview/

Chef Docs. (2018). Retrieved April 2018, from https://docs.chef.io/chef_overview.html

Chekuri, C., Gupta, A., Kumar, A., Naor, J., Raz, D., & Kleinberg, J. (2002). *Building Edge-Failure Resilient Networks*. Academic Press.

Chen, M., Castaldelli, L., Mirsky, G., Mizrahi, T., Fioccola, G., Capello, A., & Cociglio, M. (2018). *Alternate-Marking Method for Passive and Hybrid Performance Monitoring (RFC8321)*. Internet Engineering Task Force.

Chen, Y., Qin, Y., Lambe, M., & Chu, W. (2015). Realizing network function virtualization management and orchestration with model based open architecture. *11th International Conference on Network and Service Management (CNSM)*. 10.1109/CNSM.2015.7367393

Chiba, M., Clemm, A., Medley, S., Salowey, J., Thombare, S., & Yedavalli, E. (2013). *Cisco service-level assurance protocol (RFC6812)*. Internet Engineering Task Force.

Cianfrani, A., Listanti, M., & Polverini, M. (2017). Incremental Deployment of Segment Routing into an ISP Network: A Traffic Engineering Perspective. *IEEE/ACM Transactions on Networking*, *25*(5), 3146–3160. doi:10.1109/TNET.2017.2731419

Ciavaglia, L., Ghamri-Doudane, S., Smirnov, M., Demestichas, P., Stavroulaki, V. A., Bantouna, A., & Sayrac, B. (2012). Unifying management of future networks with trust. *Bell Labs Technical Journal*, *17*(3), 193–212. doi:10.1002/bltj.21568

Cisco. (2016). *The zettabyte era - trends and analysis*. Retrieved from http://www.cisco.com/c/en/us/solutions/collateral/service-provider/visual-networking-index-vni/VNI_Hyperconnectivity_WP.htm

Claise, B. (2008). *Specification of the IP flow information export (IPFIX) protocol for the exchange of IP traffic flow information (RFC5101)*. Internet Engineering Task Force.

Claise, B., Trammell, B., & Aitken, P. (2013). *Specification of the IP flow information export (IPFIX) protocol for the exchange of flow information (RFC7011)*. Internet Engineering Task Force.

Clark, D. D., Partridge, C., Ramming, J. C., & Wroclawski, J. T. (2003). A knowledge plane for the internet. In *Proceedings of the 2003 conference on Applications, technologies, architectures, and protocols for computer communications* (pp. 3-10). ACM.

Clemm, A. E. (2108, May 31). *YANG Datastore Subscription*. Retrieved from IETF: https://datatracker.ietf.org/doc/draft-ietf-netconf-yang-push/

CogNet. (2017). *CogNet final requirements, scenarios and architecture*. Author.

Combes, R., Altman, Z., & Altman, E. (2013). Coordination of autonomic functionalities in communications networks. In *Modeling & Optimization in Mobile, Ad Hoc & Wireless Networks (WiOpt), 2013 11th International Symposium on* (pp. 364-371). IEEE.

Cominardi, L., Contreras, L. M., Bernardos, C. J., & Berberana, I. (2018). Understanding QoS applicability in 5G transport networks. *Proc. of the 13th IEEE International Symposium on Broadband Multimedia Systems and Broadcasting*.

Coniglio, S., Koster, A., & Tieves, M. (2016). Data Uncertainty in Virtual Network Embedding: Robust Optimization and Protection Levels. *Journal of Network and Systems Management*, 24(3), 681–710. doi:10.100710922-016-9376-x

Contreras, L. M., López, V., Vilalta, R., Casellas, R., Muñoz, R., Jiang, W., ... Toka, L. (2018). Network management and orchestration. In P. Marsch, Ö. Bulakci, O. Queseth, & M. Boldi (Eds.), 5G System Design: Architectural and Functional Considerations and Long Term Research. John Wiley & Sons. doi:10.1002/9781119425144.ch10

Contreras, L.M., Bernardos, C.J., López, D.R., Boucadair, M., & Iovanna, P. (2015). *Cooperating Layered Architecture for SDN*, draft-contreras-sdnrg-layered-sdn-04.

Contreras, L. M., Doolan, P., Lønsethagen, H., & López, D. R. (2015). Operation, organization and business challenges for network providers in the context of SDN and NFV. *Elsevier Computer Networks*, 92, 211–217. doi:10.1016/j.comnet.2015.07.016

Csoma, A., Sonkoly, B., Csikor, L., Németh, F., Gulyás, A., Jocha, D., ... Sahhaf, S. (2014). Multi-layered Service Orchestration in a Multi-domain Network Environment. *Third European Workshop on Software Defined Networks*. 10.1109/EWSDN.2014.32

Cui, Y., Sun, Q., Boucadair, M., Tsou, T., Lee, Y., & Farrer, I. (2015). *Lightweight 4over6: An Extension to the Dual-Stack Lite Architecture*. IETF RFC7596.

Curic, M., Carle, G., Despotovic, Z., Khalili, R., & Hecker, A. (2017). *SDN on ACIDs. In CAN '17 (CoNEXT)*. New York, NY: ACM.

D'oro, S., Galluccio, L., Mertikopoulos, P., Morabito, G., & Palazzo, S. (n.d.). *Auction-based Resource Allocation in OpenFlow Multi-Tenant Networks*. Retrieved from http://mescal.imag.fr/membres/panayotis.mertikopoulos/files/OpenFlowAuction.pdf

Dahmen-Lhuissier, S. (n.d.). *Open Source MANO*. Retrieved June 6, 2018, from http://www.etsi.org/technologies-clusters/technologies/nfv/open-source-mano

Dai, J. G., & Lin, W. (2008). Asymptotic Optimality of Maximum Pressure Policies in Stochastic Processing Networks. *Annals of Applied Probability*, 18(6), 2239–2299. doi:10.1214/08-AAP522

Damianou, N., Dulay, N., Lupu, E., & Sloman, M. (2001). *The ponder policy specification language. In Policies for Distributed Systems and Networks*. Springer Berlin Heidelberg.

Davoli, L., Veltri, L., Ventre, P.L., Siracusano, G., & Salsano, S. (2015). Traffic engineering with segment routing: SDN-based architectural design and open source implementation. *Ieeexplore.ieee.org*, 2015(1).

Davy, S., Jennings, B., & Strassner, J. (2007). The policy continuum–a formal model. In *Proceedings of the Second IEEE International Workshop on Modelling Autonomic Communications Environments* (pp. 65-79). IEEE.

Di Pietro, A., Huici, F., Costantini, D., & Niccolini, S. (2010). *Decon: Decentralized coordination for large-scale flow monitoring*. In *INFOCOM IEEE Conference on Computer Communications Workshops*, 2010 (pp. 1-5). IEEE. 10.1109/INFCOMW.2010.5466642

Diarrassouba, I., Mahjoub, M., Mahjoub, A., & Yaman, H. (2018). *k-node-disjoint hop-constrained survivable networks: Polyhedral analysis and branch and cut*. Academic Press. doi:10.100712243-017-0622-3

Dinitz, Y., Garg, N., & Goemans, M. X. (1999). On the single-source unsplittable flow problem. *Combinatorica*, 19(1), 17–41. doi:10.1007004930050043

Donadio, P., Fioccola, G. B., Canonico, R., & Ventre, G. (2014). A PCE-based architecture for the management of virtualized infrastructures. *IEEE 3rd International Conference on Cloud Networking (CloudNet).*

Donovan, P., Shepherd, F. B., Vetta, A., & Wilfong, G. (2007). *Degree-constrained network flows.* Academic Press.

Doverspike, R. D., Ramakrishnan, K. K., & Chase, C. (2010). Structural Overview of ISP Networks. In C. R. Kalmanek, S. Misra, & Y. R. Yang (Eds.), *Guide to Reliable Internet Services and Applications. Springer-Verlag.* doi:10.1007/978-1-84882-828-5_2

draft-geng-coms-problem-statement-01 - Problem Statement of Supervised Heterogeneous Network Slicing. (2017). Retrieved from https://tools.ietf.org/pdf/draft-geng-coms-problem-statement-01.pdf

Duffield, N. G., Goyal, P., Greenberg, A., Mishra, P., Ramakrishnan, K. K., & van der Merive, J. E. (1999). A flexible model for resource management in virtual private networks. *Computer Communication Review, 29*(4), 95–108. doi:10.1145/316194.316209

Duffield, N., Chiou, D., Claise, B., Greenberg, A., Grossglauser, M., & Rexford, J. (2009). *A framework for packet selection and reporting (RFC5474).* Internet Engineering Task Force.

Durham, D. (2000). *The COPS (Common Open Policy Service) Protocol.* Internet Engineering Task Force, RFC2748. Retrieved from https://tools.ietf.org/html/rfc2748

Durham, D. (2001). *COPS for Policy Provisioning (COPS-PR).* Internet Engineering Task Force, RFC3084. Retrieved from https://tools.ietf.org/html/rfc3084

Eberhardinger, B., Habermaier, A., & Reif, W. (2017). Toward Adaptive, Self-Aware Test Automation. *2017 IEEE/ACM 12th International Workshop on Automation of Software Testing (AST).* 10.1109/ast.2017.1

Eckert, T., Behringer, M., & Bjarnason, S. (2018). *An Autonomic Control Plane (ACP).* Retrieved from https://tools.ietf.org/html/draft-ietf-anima-autonomic-control-plane-13

Eckert, T., & Behringer, M. (2018). *Using Autonomic Control Plane for Stable Connectivity of Network OAM. RFC8368.* Internet Engineering Task Force.

Elkins, N., & Hamilton, R. (2017). *IPv6 Performance and Diagnostic Metrics (PDM) Destination Option (RFC8250).* Internet Engineering Task Force. doi:10.17487/RFC8250

Elwalid, A., Jin, C., Low, S., & Widjaja, I. (2001). MATE: MPLS adaptive traffic engineering. *Proceedings IEEE IN-FOCOM 2001. Conference on Computer Communications. Twentieth Annual Joint Conference of the IEEE Computer and Communications Society (Cat. No.01CH37213), 3,* 1300–1309. 10.1109/INFCOM.2001.916625

Enns, R., Bjorklund, M., Schoenwaelder, J., & Bierman, A. (2011). *NETCONF Configuration Protocol.* IETF RFC 6241.

Enns, R., Bjorklund, M., Schoenwaelder, J., & Bierman, A. (2011). *Network Configuration Protocol (NETCONF).* Internet Engineering Task Force, RFC6241. Retrieved from https://tools.ietf.org/html/rfc6241

ETSI GR NFV-EVE 012. (2017). *Report on Network Slicing Support with ETSI NFV Architecture Framework.* V3.1.1.

ETSI GR NFV-IFA 028. (2018). *Report on architecture options to support multiple administrative domains.* V3.1.1.

ETSI GS NFV 002 V1.2.1. (2014). *Network Functions Virtualisation (NFV); Architectural Framework.* Retrieved from http://www.etsi.org/deliver/etsi_gs/NFV/001_099/002/01.02.01_60/gs_NFV002v010201p.pdf

ETSI GS NFV-EVE 005. (2015). *Report on SDN Usage in NFV Architectural Framework.* V1.1.1.

ETSI GS NFV-IFA-014. (2018). *Management and Orchestration; Network Service Templates Specification.* V2.4.1.

ETSI NFV. (2012). Retrieved April 2018, from ETSI: http://www.etsi.org/technologies-clusters/technologies/nfv

ETSI. (2013). *Network Function Virtualisation (NFV): Use Cases*. Retrieved February 12, 2017, from http://www.etsi.org/deliver/etsi_gs/nfv/001_099/001/01.01.01_60/gs_nfv001v010101p.pdf

ETSI. (2014). *Network Functions Virtualisation (NFV); Management and Orchestration v1.1.1.* Retrieved from http://www.etsi.org/deliver/etsi_gs/NFV-MAN/001_099/001/01.01.01_60/gs_nfv-man001v010101p.pdf

ETSI-NFV. (2016). Retrieved from http://www.etsi.org/technologies-clusters/technologies/nfv

EU GDPR. (n.d.). *The Regulation*. Retrieved June 4, 2018 from https://www.eugdpr.org/the-regulation.html

Evans, K. (2018, March 8). *Introducing The Cloud Native Landscape 2.0 - Interactive Edition*. Cloud Native Computing Foundation. Retrieved April 5, 2018, from https://www.cncf.io/blog/2018/03/08/introducing-the-cloud-native-landscape-2-0-interactive-edition/

Event-driven programming. (2018, June 1). Retrieved from Wikipedia: https://en.wikipedia.org/wiki/Event-driven_programming

Eykholt, K. E. (2018, April 10). *Robust Physical-World Attacks on Deep Learning Models*. Retrieved April 2018, from arxiv: https://arxiv.org/abs/1707.08945

Feamster, N., Rexford, J., & Zegura, E. (2014). The Road to SDN: An Intellectual History of Programmable Networks. *ACM Sigcomm Computer Communication, 44*(2), 87–98. doi:10.1145/2602204.2602219

Figueiredo, G. B., da Fonseca, N. L. S., & Monteiro, J. A. S. (2004). A Minimum Interference Routing Algorithm. *IEEE International Conference on Communications, 4*(c), 1942–1947. 10.1109/ICC.2004.1312859

Filsfils, C., Nainar, N. K., Pignataro, C., Cardona, J. C., & Francois, P. (2015). The segment routing architecture. *2015 IEEE Global Communications Conference, GLOBECOM 2015*. 10.1109/GLOCOM.2015.7417124

Fiorese, A., Simões, P., & Boavida, F. (2009). A P2P-based approach to cross-domain network and service management. In *IFIP International Conference on Autonomous Infrastructure, Management and Security* (pp. 179-182). Springer.

Fischer, A., Beck, M. T., & De Meer, H. (2013). An Approach to Energy-efficient Virtual Network Embeddings. *Integrated Network Management (IM 2013), 2013 IFIP/IEEE International Symposium on*, 1142–1147.

Fischer, A., Felipe Botero, J., Till Beck, M., de Meer, H., & Hesselbach, X. (n.d.). *Virtual Network Embedding: A Survey*. Retrieved from http://www.fim.uni-passau.de/fileadmin/files/lehrstuhl/meer/publications/pdf/Fischer2013a.pdf

Fischer, A., Botero, J. F., Beck, M. T., de Meer, H., & Hesselbach, X. (2013). Virtual Network Embedding: A Survey. *IEEE Communications Surveys and Tutorials, 15*(4), 1888–1906. doi:10.1109/SURV.2013.013013.00155

Ford, M. (2015). *Rise of the Robots: Technology and the Threat of a Jobless Future*. Basic Books.

Fortz, B., & Thorup, M. (2000). Internet traffic engineering by optimizing OSPF weights. *Proceedings IEEE INFOCOM 2000. Conference on Computer Communications. Nineteenth Annual Joint Conference of the IEEE Computer and Communications Societies (Cat. No.00CH37064), 2*, 519–528. 10.1109/INFCOM.2000.832225

Galani, A., Tsagkaris, K., Demestichas, P., Nguengang, G., BenYahia, I. G., Stamatelatos, M., . . . Ciavaglia, L. (2012). Core functional and network empower mechanisms of an operator-driven, framework for unifying autonomic network and service management. In *Computer Aided Modeling and Design of Communication Links and Networks (CAMAD), 2012 IEEE 17th International Workshop on* (pp. 191-195). IEEE. 10.1109/CAMAD.2012.6335330

Galis, A., Abramowicz, H., Brunner, M., Raz, D., Chemouil, P., & Pras, A. (2009). Management and Service-aware Networking Architectures (MANA) for Future Internet - Position Paper: System Functions, Capabilities and Requirements. *IEEE 2009 Fourth International Conference on Communications and Networking in China –ChinaCom.*

Galis, A., Denazis, S., Brou, C., & Klein, C. (Eds.). (2004). *Programmable Networks for IP Service Deployment.* Artech House.

Garcia-Molina, H., Ullman, J., & Widom, J. (2008). *Database Systems: The Complete Book.* Upper Saddle River, NJ: Prentice Hall Press.

Geng, L., Qiang, L., Ordonez, J., Adamuz-Hinojosa, O., Ameigeiras, P., Lopez, D., Contreras, L.M. (2018). *COMS architecture,* draft-geng-coms-architecture-02 (work in progress).

Getting started - Travis CI. (n.d.). Retrieved April 5, 2018, from https://docs.travis-ci.com/user/getting-started/

Giannoulakis, I., Xylouris, G., Kafetzakis, E., Kourtis, A., Fajardo, J. O., Khodashenas, P. S., & Vassilakis, V. (2016). *System architecture and deployment scenarios for SESAME: Small cEllS coodinAtion for Multi-tenancy and Edge services. In IEEE NetSoft Conference and Workshops.* NetSoft.

Gil-herrera, J., Isolani, P. H., Neves, M. C., Zambenedetti, L., Botero, J. F., Barcellos, M. P., & Gaspary, L. P. (2017)... *Security of Networks and Services in an All-Connected World, 10356,* 62–76. doi:10.1007/978-3-319-60774-0_5

Giotis, K., Kryftis, Y., & Maglaris, V. (2015). Policy-based orchestration of NFV services in Software-Defined Networks. *1st IEEE Conference on Network Softwarization (NetSoft).* 10.1109/NETSOFT.2015.7116145

Gopi, D., Cheng, S., & Huck, R. (2017). Comparative analysis of SDN and conventional networks using routing protocols. *IEEE CITS 2017 - 2017 International Conference on Computer, Information and Telecommunication Systems,* 108–112. 10.1109/CITS.2017.8035305

GRASPY. (2018). Retrieved from https://github.com/becarpenter/graspy

Gray, K., & Nadeau, T. D. (2016). ETSI NFV ISG. In Network Function Virtualization (pp. 49–76). Academic Press.

Gray, J., & Reuter, A. (1992). *Transaction Processing: Concepts and Techniques.* San Francisco, CA: Morgan Kaufmann Publishers Inc.

Grötschel, M., Monma, C. L., & Stoer, M. (1995). Design of Survivable Networks. *Handbooks in Operations Research and Management Science, 7,* 617–672. doi:10.1016/S0927-0507(05)80127-6

GSMA. (2017). *An introduction to network slicing.* Retrieved from https://www.gsma.com/futurenetworks/wp-content/uploads/2017/11/GSMA-An-Introduction-to-Network-Slicing.pdf

Guerzoni, R., Trivisonno, R., Vaishnavi, I., Despotovic, Z., Hecker, A., Beker, S., & Soldani, D. (2014). *A novel approach to virtual networks embedding for SDN management and orchestration. NOMS.* Krakow, Poland: IEEE.

Guo, J., Liu, F., Lui, J. C. S., & Jin, H. (2016). Fair Network Bandwidth Allocation in IaaS Datacenters via a Cooperative Game Approach. *IEEE/ACM Transactions on Networking, 24*(2), 873–886. doi:10.1109/TNET.2015.2389270

Gupta, A., Jaumard, B., Tornatore, M., & Mukherjee, B. (2016). *Multiple Service Chain Placement and Routing in a Network-enabled Cloud.* Retrieved from http://arxiv.org/abs/1611.03197

Halpern, J., & Pignataro, C. (2015). *Service Function Chaining (SFC) Architecture. RFC 7665.* IETF. doi:10.17487/RFC7665

Hankins, DW, Mrugalski, T. (2011). *Dynamic Host Configuration Protocol for IPv6 (DHCPv6) Options for Dual-Stack Lite*. IETF RFC 6334.

Harrington, D., Presuhn, R., & Wijnen, B. (2002). *An architecture for describing simple network management protocol (snmp) management frameworks* (RFC 3411).

Hedayat, K., Krzanowski, R., Morton, A., Yum, K., & Babiarz, J. (2008). *A two-way active measurement protocol (TWAMP) (RFC5357)*. Internet Engineering Task Force.

Hewlett-Packard Enterprise. (2015). *Monasca, Monitoring tool*. Retrieved from http://monasca.io/

Hils, A., & Rajpreet, K. (2015). *Network Security Policy Management Solutions Have Evolved*. Retrieved June 4, 2018 from https://www.gartner.com/doc/3159925/network-security-policy-management-solutions

Hmaity, A., Savi, M., Musumeci, F., Tornatore, M., & Pattavina, A. (2016). Virtual Network Function placement for resilient Service Chain provisioning. *Proceedings of 2016 8th International Workshop on Resilient Networks Design and Modeling, RNDM 2016*, 245–252. 10.1109/RNDM.2016.7608294

Hock, D., Hartmann, M., Menth, M., Pióro, M., Tomaszewski, A., & Zukowski, C. (2013). Comparison of IP-based and explicit paths for one-to-one fast reroute in MPLS networks. *Telecommunication Systems*, *52*(2), 947–958. doi:10.100711235-011-9603-4

Houidi, I., Louati, W., Ben Ameur, W., & Zeghlache, D. (2011). Virtual network provisioning across multiple substrate networks. *Computer Networks*, *55*(4), 1011–1023. doi:10.1016/j.comnet.2010.12.011

Houidi, I., Louati, W., & Zeghlache, D. (2015). Exact multi-objective virtual network embedding in cloud environments. *The Computer Journal*, *58*(3), 403–415. doi:10.1093/comjnl/bxu154

Huin, N., Jaumard, B., & Giroire, F. (2017). Optimization of network service chain provisioning. *IEEE International Conference on Communications*. 10.1109/ICC.2017.7997198

Humble, J., & Farley, D. (2010). *Continuous Delivery: Reliable Software Releases through Build, Test, and Deployment Automation (Adobe Reader)*. Pearson Education.

Huttermann, M. (2012). *DevOps for Developers*. Apress. doi:10.1007/978-1-4302-4570-4

Iacoboaiea, O. C., Sayrac, B., Ben Jemaa, S., & Bianchi, P. (2014). SON conflict resolution using reinforcement learning with state aggregation. In *Proceedings of the 4th workshop on All things cellular: operations, applications, & challenges* (pp. 15-20). ACM. 10.1145/2627585.2627591

IBM Knowledge Center. (2018, June 1). *Rule-based event-driven solutions*. Retrieved from IBM: https://www.ibm.com/support/knowledgecenter/en/SSQP76_8.9.0/com.ibm.odm.itoa.overview/topics/con_how_to_develop_solution.html

IETF. (2002). *Policy Framework (policy)*. Retrieved from http://www.ietf.org/html.charters/policy-charter.html

IETF. (2016). *The Open vSwitch Database Management Protocol*. Retrieved from https://tools.ietf.org/html/rfc7047

IHS Markit. (2018). *Service Provider Capex, Opex, Revenue and Subscribers Database*. Author.

Inführ, J., & Raidl, G. R. (n.d.). *Introducing the Virtual Network Mapping Problem with Delay, Routing and Location Constraints*. Retrieved from https://rd.springer.com/content/pdf/10.1007%2F978-3-642-21527-8_14.pdf

Intanagonwiwat, C., Govindan, R., & Estrin, D. (2000). *Directed Diffusion: A scalable and robust communication paradigm for sensor networks*. ACM MOBICOM. doi:10.1145/345910.345920

International Telecommunication Union (ITU-T) (2007). *Enhanced Telecom Operations Map (eTOM) – The business process framework, ITU-T Recommendation M.3050.1.*

IPAM Worldwide. (n.d.). Retrieved from the IPAM Worldwide: http://www.ipamworldwide.com/ipam/

Irnich, S., & Desaulniers, G. (2005). Shortest Path Problems with Resource Constraints. In *Column Generation* (pp. 33–65). New York: Springer-Verlag; doi:10.1007/0-387-25486-2_2

ITU-R. (2015). *IMT Vision – Framework and overall objectives of the future development of IMT for 2020 and beyond.* Recommendation M.2083-0. Retrieved from https://www.itu.int/dms_pubrec/itu-r/rec/m/R-REC-M.2083-0-201509-I!!PDF-E.pdf

ITU-T. (2011). *Framework of network virtualization for future networks.* Recommendation Y.3011.

ITU-T. (2012). *Framework of Network Virtualization for Future Networks, Next Generation Network –future Networks.* Recommendation Y.3011.

ITU-T. (2014). *Framework of software-defined networking. 5G connectivity to meet demanding services: examples of connected cars and mobile health.* Retrieved from https://ec.europa.eu/digital-agenda/events/cf/ict2015/item-display.cfm?id=15141

James, M. (2017). *Scrum Reference Card.* Retrieved from https://www.collab.net/sites/default/files/uploads/CollabNet_scrumreferencecard.pdf

Jenkins Handbook. (n.d.). Retrieved April 5, 2018, from https://jenkins.io/doc/book/index.html

Jiang, S., Carpenter, B., & Behringer, M. (2015). *General gap analysis for autonomic networking* (RFC 7576).

Jiang, S., Du, Z., Carpenter, B., & Sun, Q. (2018). *Autonomic IPv6 Edge Prefix Management in Large-scale Networks.* Retrieved from https://www.ietf.org/id/draft-ietf-anima-prefix-management-07.txt

Jiang, S., Carpenter, B., & Behringer, M. (2015). *General Gap Analysis for Autonomic Networking. (2015). RFC7576.* Internet Research Task Force. doi:10.17487/RFC7576

Jin, X., Liu, H., Gandhi, R., Kandula, S., Mahajan, R., Zhang, M., & Wattenhofer, R. (2014). *Dynamic Scheduling of Network Updates. In SIGCOMM'14.* New York: ACM.

Johnson, D. S., Lenstra, J. K., & Kan, A. H. G. R. (1978). The complexity of the network design problem. *Networks, 8*(4), 279–285. doi:10.1002/net.3230080402

Jones, K. L., Lustig, I. J., Farvolden, J. M., & Powell, W. B. (1993). Multicommodity network flows: The impact of formulation on decomposition. *Mathematical Programming, 62*(1–3), 95–117. doi:10.1007/BF01585162

Jones, S. (2005). Toward an acceptable definition of service service-oriented architecture. *IEEE Software. IEEE., 22*(3), 87–93. doi:10.1109/MS.2005.80

Józsa, B. G., & Makai, M. (2003). On the solution of reroute sequence planning problem in MPLS networks. *Computer Networks, 42*(2), 199–210. doi:10.1016/S1389-1286(03)00189-0

Kaloxylos, A., Mannweiler, C., Zimmermann, G., Di Girolamo, M., Marsch, P., Belschner, J., . . . Nikaein, N. (2018). Network Slicing. In P. Marsch, Ö. Bulakci, O. Queseth, & M. Boldi (Eds.), 5G System Design: Architectural and Functional Considerations and Long Term Research. John Wiley & Sons. doi:10.1002/9781119425144.ch8

Kar, K., Kodialam, M., & Lakshman, T. V. (2000). Minimum interference routing of bandwidth guaranteed tunnels with MPLS traffic engineering applications. *IEEE Journal on Selected Areas in Communications, 18*(12), 2566–2579. doi:10.1109/49.898737

Karsten, C. V., Pisinger, D., Ropke, S., & Brouer, B. D. (2015). The time constrained multi-commodity network flow problem and its application to liner shipping network design. *Transportation Research Part E, Logistics and Transportation Review, 76*, 122–138. doi:10.1016/j.tre.2015.01.005

Kephart, J. (2003). *The vision of autonomic computing*. Academic Press.

Kephart, J., & Chess, D. (2003). The Vision of Autonomic Computing. *IEEE Computer, 36*(1), 41–50. doi:10.1109/MC.2003.1160055

Kephart, J., & Walsh, W. (2004). An artificial intelligence perspective on autonomic computing policies. *Proceedings 5th IEEE Workshop on Policies for Distributed Systems and Networks (Policy 2004)*, 3–12. 10.1109/POLICY.2004.1309145

Kerivin, H., & Mahjoub, A. R. (2005). Design of Survivable Networks: A survey. *Networks, 46*(1), 1–21. doi:10.1002/net.20072

Kim, D., & Solomon, M. (2016). *Fundamentals of Information Systems Security*. Jones & Bartlett Learning.

Klopfenstein, O. (2008). Rerouting tunnels for MPLS network resource optimization. *European Journal of Operational Research, 188*(1), 293–312. doi:10.1016/j.ejor.2007.04.016

Kodialam, M., & Lakshman, T. V. (n.d.). Minimum Interference Routing with Applications to MPLS. *Traffic Engineering.*

Kohalmi, S. (2018, April). *AINet 2018, Day 3*. Retrieved April 2018, from Upperside Conferences: https://www.upsideconferences.com/ainet/ainet_2018_agenda_day_3.html

Koley, B. (2016). *Twelfth International Conference on Network and Servce Management*. Montreal: IFIP; https://edas.info/web/cnsm2016/index.html

Koutsouris, N., Tsagkaris, K., Demestichas, P., Altman, Z., Combes, R., Peloso, P., . . . Galis, A. (2013). Conflict free coordination of SON functions in a unified management framework: Demonstration of a proof of concept prototyping platform. In *Integrated Network Management (IM 2013), 2013 IFIP/IEEE International Symposium on* (pp. 1092-1093). IEEE.

Krarup, J., & Pruzan, P. M. (1983). The simple plant location problem: Survey and synthesis. *European Journal of Operational Research, 12*(1), 36–81. doi:10.1016/0377-2217(83)90181-9

Kreutz, D., Ramos, F., Veríssimo, P.E., Rothenberg, C. E., Azodolmolky, S., & Uhlig, S. (2015). *Software-Defined Networking: A Comprehensive Survey*. Academic Press. doi:10.1109/JPROC.2014.2371999

Kubernetes.io Pods. (2018). Retrieved June 4, 2018 fromhttps://kubernetes.io/docs/concepts/workloads/pods/pod/

Kulkarni, S. G., Zhang, W., Hwang, J., Rajagopalan, S., Ramakrishnan, K., Wood, T., & Fu, X. (2017). *NFVnice: Dynamic Backpressure and Scheduling for NFV Service Chains. Sigcomm*. Los Angeles, CA: ACM. doi:10.1145/3098822.3098828

Li, C., Huang, L., & Liu, Z. (2014). *Communication method, communication system, resource pool management system, switch device and control device*. U.S. Patent App. 15/122,323.

LIBEST. (2018). Retrieved from https://github.com/cisco/libest

Limited, C. (n.d.). *Cucumber*. Retrieved April 5, 2018, from https://cucumber.io/

Linux Foundation. (n.d.). *Projects - The Linux Foundation*. Retrieved June 4, 2018, from https://www.linuxfoundation. org/projects/

Lobo, J., Bhathia, R., & Naqvi, S. (1999). A policy description language. *Proceedings 16th National Conference on Artificial Intelligence (AAAI-99)*, 291-298.

López, J. A. L., Muñoz, J. M. G., & Morilla, J. (2007). A Telco Approach to Autonomic Infrastructure Management. In *Advanced Autonomic Networking and Communication* (pp. 27–42). Birkhäuser Basel. doi:10.1007/978-3-7643-8569-9_2

López, V., Dios, O. G., Fuentes, B., Yannuzzi, M., Fernández-Palacios, J. P., & López, D. (2014). *Towards a network operating system. Optical Fiber Communications Conference and Exhibition*. OFC.

Luizelli, M. C., Bays, L. R., Buriol, L. S., Barcellos, M. P., & Gaspary, L. P. (2015). Piecing together the NFV provisioning puzzle: Efficient placement and chaining of virtual network functions. *Proceedings of the 2015 IFIP/IEEE International Symposium on Integrated Network Management, IM 2015*, 98–106. 10.1109/INM.2015.7140281

Luo, W., Zeng, J., Su, X., Li, J., & Xiao, L. (2012). A mathematical model for joint optimization of coverage and capacity in self-organizing network in centralized manner. In *Communications and Networking in China (CHINACOM), 2012 7th International ICST Conference on* (pp. 622-626). IEEE.

Madhyastha, H. V., Isdal, T., Piatek, M., Dixon, C., Anderson, T., Krishnamurthy, A., & Venkataramani, A. (2006). iPlane: An information plane for distributed services. In *Proceedings of the 7th symposium on Operating systems design and implementation* (pp. 367-380). USENIX Association.

Magnanti, T. L., & Raghavan, S. (2005). Strong formulations for network design problems with connectivity requirements. *Networks, 45*(2), 61–79. doi:10.1002/net.20046

Marotta, A., Kassler, A., & Zola, E. (n.d.). On the energy cost of robustness for green virtual network function placement in 5G virtualized On the Energy Cost of Robustness for Green Virtual Network Function Placement in 5G Virtualized Infrastructures. *Computer Networks, 125*, 64–75. doi:10.1016/j.comnet.2017.04.045

Maymounkov, P., & Mazieres, D. (2002). Kademlia: A peer-to-peer information system based on the xor metric. *International Workshop on Peer-to-Peer Systems*, 53-65. 10.1007/3-540-45748-8_5

McKeown, N., Anderson, T., Balakrishnan, H., Parulkar, G., Peterson, L., Rexford, J., ... Turner, J. (2008). OpenFlow: Enabling innovation in campus networks. *Computer Communication Review, 38*(2), 69–74. doi:10.1145/1355734.1355746

Mechtri, M., Ghribi, C., & Zeghlache, D. (2016). A scalable algorithm for the placement of service function chains Djamal Zeghlache. A scalable algorithm for the placement of service function chains. *IEEE eTransactions on Network and Service Management, 13*(3), 1–14. doi:10.1109/TNSM.2016.2598068

Mestres, A., Rodriguez-Natal, A., Carner, J., Barlet-Ros, P., Alarcón, E., Solé, M., ... Estrada, G. (2017). Knowledge-defined networking. *Computer Communication Review, 47*(3), 2–10. doi:10.1145/3138808.3138810

Mia, J., He, G., Pei, X., Martiny, K., Klotz, M., Khan, A., ... Lopez, D. (2017). *Zero-touch Network and Service Management – Introductory White Paper*. Retrieved from https://portal.etsi.org/TBSiteMap/ZSM/OperatorWhitePaper

Mijumbi, R., Serrat, J., Gorricho, J.-L., & Boutaba, R. (2015). A Path Generation Approach to Embedding of Virtual Networks. *IEEE eTransactions on Network and Service Management, 12*(3), 334–348. doi:10.1109/TNSM.2015.2459073

Minoux, M. (2008). *Programmation Mathématique. Théorie et Algorithmes*. Lavoisier.

Mohammadkhan, A., Ghapani, S., Liu, G., Zhang, W., Ramakrishnan, K. K., & Wood, T. (2015). Virtual function placement and traffic steering in flexible and dynamic software defined networks. *IEEE Workshop on Local and Metropolitan Area Networks*. 10.1109/LANMAN.2015.7114738

Moore, B., Ellesson, E., Strassner, J., & Westerinen, A. (2001). *Policy core information model – version 1 specification.*

Mortier, R., & Kiciman, E. (2006, September). Autonomic network management: some pragmatic considerations. In *Proceedings of the 2006 SIGCOMM workshop on Internet network management* (pp. 89-93). ACM. 10.1145/1162638.1162653

Morton, A. (2016). *Active and Passive Metrics and Methods (with Hybrid Types In-Between) (RFC7799)*. Internet Engineering Task Force. doi:10.17487/RFC7799

Mosharaf, N. M., Chowdhury, K., Boutaba, R., & Cheriton, D. R. (2008). *A Survey of Network Virtualization*. Retrieved from https://cs.uwaterloo.ca/research/tr/2008/CS-2008-25.pdf

Mosharaf, N. M., Chowdhury, K., Rahman, M. R., & Boutaba, R. (2009). Virtual network embedding with coordinated node and link mapping. *Proceedings - IEEE INFOCOM*, 783–791. doi:10.1109/INFCOM.2009.5061987

Moy, J. (1998). *OSPF Version 2*. IETF. Retrieved from http://www.rfc-editor.org/rfc/rfc2328.txt

Nakano, T., & Suda, T. (2005). Self-Organizing Network Services and Evolutionary Adaptation. *IEEE Transactions on Neural Networks*, 6(5), 1269–1278. doi:10.1109/TNN.2005.853421 PMID:16252832

Neely, M. J. (2009). Delay Analysis for Maximal Scheduling With Flow Control in Wireless Networks with Bursty Traffic. *IEEE/ACM Transactions on Networking, 17*(4), 1146-1159.

Netflix. (n.d.). *Netflix/chaosmonkey*. Retrieved April 5, 2018, from https://github.com/Netflix/chaosmonkey

Network Heresy. (2014). *On Policy in the Data Center: The Policy Problem*. Retrieved June 4, 2018 from https://networkheresy.com/2014/04/22/on-policy-in-the-data-center-the-policy-problem/

Neves, P., Cale, R., Costa, M. R., Parada, C., Parreira, B., Calero, J. M., & Barros, M. J. (2016). *The SELFNET Approach for Autonomic Management in an NFV/SDN Networking Paradigm*. IJDSN.

Nfv, E. (2018). *Network Functions Virtualisation (NFV) Release 2; Management and Orchestration; Functional requirements specification* (No. RGS/NFV-IFA010ed241). ETSI.

NGMN (2016). *Description of Network Slicing Concept*. NGMN.

NGMN Alliance. (2015). *NGMN 5G White Paper*. Retrieved from https://www.ngmn.org/uploads/media/NGMN_5G_White_Paper_V1_0_01.pdf

NGMN. (2015). *5G White Paper*. Retrieved from https://www.ngmn.org/uploads/media/NGMN_5G_White_Paper_V1_0.pdf

Nicklish, J. (1999). *A rule language for network policies*. Policy.

NMRG. (2018, April). Retrieved April 2018, from IRTF: https://datatracker.ietf.org/rg/nmrg/about/

Nobre, J. C., & Granville, L. Z. (2017, May). Decentralized detection of violations of service level agreements using peer-to-peer technology. In *Integrated Network and Service Management (IM), 2017 IFIP/IEEE Symposium on* (pp. 835-840). IEEE.

Nobre, J. C., Granville, L. Z., Clemm, A., & Prieto, A. G. (2012). Decentralized detection of SLA violations using P2P technology. In *Proceedings of the 8th International Conference on Network and Service Management* (pp. 100-107). International Federation for Information Processing.

Nobre, J. C., Mozzaquatro, B. A., & Granville, L. Z. (2018). Network-Wide Initiatives to Control Measurement Mechanisms: A Survey. *IEEE Communications Surveys and Tutorials*, 20(2), 1475–1491. doi:10.1109/COMST.2018.2797170

Nobre, J., Granville, L., Clemm, A., & Prieto, A. G. (2018). *Autonomic Networking Use Case for Distributed Detection of Service Level Agreement (SLA) Violations (RFC8316)*. Internet Engineering Task Force. doi:10.17487/RFC8316

NORMA. (2015). *5G NORMA Deliverable D3.1 Functional Network Architecture and Security Requirements*. Retrieved from https://5gnorma.5g-ppp.eu/wp-content/uploads/2016/01/5G_NORMA_D3.1.pdf

OASIS Topology & the Orchestration Specification for Cloud Applications Technical Committee. (2016). *TOSCA Simple Profile in YAML Version 1.1*. Retrieved from http://docs.oasis-open.org/tosca/TOSCA-Simple-Profile-YAML/v1.1/os/TOSCA-Simple-Profile-YAML-v1.1-os.html

OASIS. (2005). *Extensible access control markup language (xacml) version 2.0. 2011-09-24*. Retrieved from http://docs oasisopen org/xacml/2.0/access_control-xacml-2.0-core-spec-os. pdf

Odini, M.-P. (2017). *SDN and NFV Evolution Towards 5G*. IEEE Softwarization. Retrieved from https://sdn.ieee.org/newsletter/september-2017/sdn-and-nfv-evolution-towards-5g

OIF (2017). *Flexible Ethernet Implementation agreement*. OIF-FLEXE-01.1.

ONAP. (n.d.). Retrieved June 6, 2018, from https://www.onap.org/

ONOS. (n.d.). Retrieved February 12, 2017, from http://onosproject.org/

Onus, M., Richa, A. W., & Scheideler, C. (2007). Linearization: Locally Self-Stabilizing Sorting in Graphs. *ALENEX*, 7, 99–108.

Open Baton. (n.d.). *Open Baton: an open source reference implementation of the ETSI Network Function Virtualization MANO specification*. Retrieved June 6, 2018, from https://openbaton.github.io/

Open Networking Foundation. (2016). *Intent NBI – Definition and Principles. ONF TR523*. Paolo Alto.

Open source software for creating private and public clouds. (n.d.). Retrieved April 5, 2018, from https://www.openstack.org/

Open, C. I. (n.d.). Retrieved April 5, 2018, from https://openci.io/

OpenConfig Community. (2018). *Public release models VLAN*. Retrieved from https://github.com/openconfig/public/blob/master/release/models/vlan/openconfig-vlan.yang

OpenFlow. (2017). *OpenFlow Home Page*. Retrieved from https://www.opennetworking.org/sdn-resources/openflow

Opensource tool. (n.d.). *SIPp, test tool / traffic generator for Session Initiation Protocol*. Retrieved from http://sipp-wip.readthedocs.io/en/latest/

OpenStack Docs Queens. (n.d.). Retrieved April 5, 2018, from https://docs.openstack.org/queens/

OpenStack. (2018). *Group-Based Policy for OpenStack*. Retrieved June 4, 2018 from https://wiki.openstack.org/w/images/a/aa/Group-BasedPolicyWhitePaper_v3.pdf

Ordonez-Lucena, J., Ameigeiras, P., López, D., Ramos-Munoz, J. J., Lorca, J., & Folgueira, J. (2017). Network slicing for 5G with SDN/NFV: Concepts, architectures, and challenges. *IEEE Communications Magazine*, 55(5), 80–87. doi:10.1109/MCOM.2017.1600935

Overview — Sphinx 1.8.0+ documentation. (n.d.). Retrieved April 5, 2018, from http://www.sphinx-doc.org

PCI Security Standards Council. (2016). *PCI DSS*. Retrieved June 4, 2018 fromhttps://www.pcisecuritystandards.org/document_library?category=pcidss&document=pci_dss

Pei, H., Yin, B., Xie, M., & Cai, K.-Y. (2017). A cloud-based dynamic random software testing strategy. *2017 IEEE International Conference on Industrial Engineering and Engineering Management (IEEM)*. 10.1109/IEEM.2017.8289943

Pharos - OPNFV. (n.d.). Retrieved April 5, 2018, from https://www.opnfv.org/community/projects/pharos

Pipeline Messaging 0.1. (n.d.). Retrieved April 5, 2018, from https://docs.google.com/document/d/1226nsoKtOJwghto hIyWqRettvxsPHjsNFKgfgeUlucc/edit?usp=embed_facebook

Pras, A., Schonwalder, J., Burgess, M., Festor, O., Perez, G. M., Stadler, R., & Stiller, B. (2007). Key research challenges in network management. *IEEE Communications Magazine*, *45*(10), 104–110. doi:10.1109/MCOM.2007.4342832

Pritikin, M., Richardson, M., Behringer, M., Bjarnason, S., & Watsen, K. (2018). *Bootstrapping Remote Secure Key Infrastructures (BRSKI)*. Retrieved from https://tools.ietf.org/html/draft-ietf-anima-bootstrapping-keyinfra-13

Pritikin, M., Yee, P., & Harkins, D. (2013). *Enrollment over Secure Transport. RFC7030*. Internet Engineering Task Force.

Puppet. (2018). Retrieved April 2018, from https://puppet.com

Räcke, H. (2002). Minimizing Congestion in General Networks. *Proceedings of the 43rd IEEE Symposium on Foundations of Computer Science*, 43–52.

Raz, Y. (1992). *The Principle of Commitment Ordering, or Guaranteeing Serializability in a Heterogeneous Environment of Multiple Autonomous Resource Mangers Using Atomic Commitment. In VLDB* (pp. 292–312). San Francisco, CA: Morgan Kaufmann Publishers.

Read the Docs. (n.d.). Retrieved April 5, 2018, from https://readthedocs.org/

Red Hat OpenShift Documentation. (n.d.). Retrieved April 5, 2018, from https://docs.openshift.com/index.html

Robot Framework. (n.d.). Retrieved April 5, 2018, from http://robotframework.org/

Rost, M., & Schmid, S. (2018). *NP-Completeness and Inapproximability of the Virtual Network Embedding Problem and Its Variants*. Retrieved from http://arxiv.org/abs/1801.03162

Running your own CI infrastructure — OpenStack Project Infrastructure 2018.04.04 documentation. (n.d.). Retrieved April 5, 2018, from https://docs.openstack.org/infra/system-config/running-your-own.html

Saad, W., & Han, Z. (n.d.). *Coalitional Game Theory for Communication Networks : A Tutorial*. Academic Press.

SAE International. (2016). *Taxonomy and definitions for terms related to driving automation systems for on-road motor vehicles*. Standard J3016.

Salehie, M. a. (2009). Self-adaptive Software: Landscape and Research Challenges. *ACM Trans. Auton. Adapt. Syst.*, *4*(2), 14:1–14:42.

SaltStack. (2018). Retrieved April 2018, from https://saltstack.com

Samaan, N., & Karmouch, A. (2009). Towards autonomic network management: An analysis of current and future research directions. *IEEE Communications Surveys and Tutorials*, *11*(3), 22–36. doi:10.1109/SURV.2009.090303

Samdanis, K., Costa-perez, X., & Sciancalepore, V. (2016). *From Network Sharing to Multi-Tenancy: The 5G Network Slice Broker*. Academic Press.

Sang, Y., Ji, B., Gupta, G. R., Du, X., & Ye, L. (2017). Provably efficient algorithms for joint placement and allocation of virtual network functions. *Proceedings - IEEE INFOCOM*. doi:10.1109/INFOCOM.2017.8057036

SANS. (2018). *Information Security Policy Templates*. Retrieved June 4, 2018 from https://www.sans.org/security-resources/policies

Sanvito, D., Filippini, I., Capone, A., Paris, S., & Leguay, J. (n.d.). *Adaptive Robust Traffic Engineering in Software Defined Networks*. Academic Press.

Sartre, J. P. (1955). *No exit, and three other plays*. Vintage.

Schiff, L., Schmid, S., & Kuznetsov, P. (2016). In-band synchronization for distributed sdn control planes. *Computer Communication Review*, *46*(1), 37–43. doi:10.1145/2875951.2875957

Schrijver, A. (2002). *Combinatorial Optimization: Polyhedra and Efficiency*. Springer Berlin Heidelberg.

Sciancalepore, V., Samdanis, K., Costa-Perez, X., Bega, D., Gramaglia, M., & Banchs, A. (2017). Mobile traffic forecasting for maximizing 5G network slicing resource utilization. In *IEEE INFOCOM 2017 - IEEE Conference on Computer Communications*. IEEE.

Script Kiddie. (2018). Retrieved from https://en.wikipedia.org/wiki/Script_kiddie

Sefraoui, O., Aissaoui, M., & Eleuldj, M. (2012). Openstack: Toward an open-source solution for cloud computing. *International Journal of Computers and Applications*, *55*(3), 38–42. doi:10.5120/8738-2991

Sekar, V., Reiter, M. K., Willinger, W., Zhang, H., Kompella, R. R., & Andersen, D. G. (2008). cSamp: A System for Network-Wide Flow Monitoring. In NSDI (Vol. 8, pp. 233-246). Academic Press.

Self-Organizing Networks. (2016, December 7). Retrieved April 2018, from Wikipedia: https://en.wikipedia.org/wiki/Self-organizing_network

Sgambelluri, A., Paolucci, F., Giorgetti, A., Cugini, F., & Castoldi, P. (2015). SDN and PCE implementations for segment routing. *2015 20th European Conference on Networks and Optical Communications, NOC 2015*, 1–4. 10.1109/NOC.2015.7238607

Shahrokhi, F., & Matula, D. W. (1987). On solving large maximum concurrent flow problems. In *Proceedings of the 15th Annual Conference on Computer Science, St. Louis, Missouri, USA, February 16-19, 1987* (pp. 205–209). ACM. 10.1145/322917.322949

Shahrokhi, F., & Matula, D. W. (1990). The Maximum Concurrent Flow Problem. *Journal of the Association for Computing Machinery*, *37*(2), 318–334. doi:10.1145/77600.77620

Shalunov, S., Teitelbaum, B., Karp, A., Boote, J., & Zekauskas, M. (2006). *A One-way Active Measurement Protocol (OWAMP) (RFC4656)*. Internet Engineering Task Force.

Shen, W., Yoshida, M., Minato, K., & Imajuku, W. (2015). vConductor: An enabler for achieving virtual network integration as a service. *IEEE Communications Magazine*, *53*(2), 116–124. doi:10.1109/MCOM.2015.7045399

SliceNet. (2018). *SliceNet Project*. Récupéré sur SliceNet Project: https://slicenet.eu/

SNBI. (2018). Retrieved from https://wiki.opendaylight.org/view/SNBI_Architecture_and_Design

Soares, J., Dias, M., Carapinha, J., Parreira, B., & Sargento, S. (2014). Cloud4NFV: A platform for Virtual Network Functions. *IEEE 3rd International Conference on Cloud Networking (CloudNet)*. 10.1109/CloudNet.2014.6969010

Soares, J., Gonçalves, C., Parreira, B., Tavares, P., Carapinha, J., Barraca, J. P., ... Sargento, S. (2015). Toward a telco cloud environment for service functions. *IEEE Communications Magazine*, *53*(2), 98–106. doi:10.1109/MCOM.2015.7045397

SOCRATES. (2011, February 22). Retrieved from fp7: http://www.fp7-socrates.eu

SONATA. (2016). *SONATA project*. Retrieved from https://sonata-project.org/

Spinnaker. (n.d.). Retrieved April 5, 2018, from https://www.spinnaker.io/

Stamatelatos, M., Yahia, I., Peloso, P., Fuentes, B., Tsagkaris, K., & Kaloxylos, A. (2013). Information model for managing autonomic functions in future networks. In *International Conference on Mobile Networks and Management* (pp. 259-272). Springer. 10.1007/978-3-319-04277-0_20

Stefanello, F., Buriol, L. S., Aggarwal, V., & Resende, M. G. C. (n.d.). *A New Linear Model for Placement of Virtual Machines across Geo-Separated Data Centers*. Academic Press.

Stoica, I., Morris, R., Karger, D., Kaashoek, M. F., & Balakrishnan, H. (2001). Chord: A scalable peer-to-peer lookup service for internet applications. *Computer Communication Review*, *31*(4), 149–160. doi:10.1145/964723.383071

Strassner, J. (2004, April). Autonomic networking-theory and practice. In *Network Operations and Management Symposium, 2004. NOMS 2004. IEEE/IFIP* (Vol. 1, pp. 927-Vol). IEEE. 10.1109/NOMS.2004.1317811

Strassner, J., & Schleimer, S. (1998). Policy framework definition language. Internet Engineering Task Force, Internet Draft draft-ietf-policy-framework-pfdl-OO. txt, vol 17.

Streaming telemetry. (2018, June 1). Retrieved from OpenConfig: http://openconfig.net/projects/telemetry/

Suresh, P. L., Canini, M., Schmid, S., & Feldmann, A. (2015). *CaC3: Cutting Tail Latency in Cloud Data Stores via Adaptive Replica Selection. In NSDI*. USENIX.

Sutton, R., & Barto, A. (1998). *Reinforcement Learning: An Introduction*. MIT Press.

Szabo, R., Kind, M., Westphal, F. J., Woesner, H., Jocha, D., & Csaszar, A. (2015). Elastic network functions: Opportunities and challenges. *IEEE Network*, *29*(3), 15–21. doi:10.1109/MNET.2015.7113220

Tastevin, N., Obadia, M., & Bouet, M. (2017). A graph approach to placement of Service Functions Chains. *Proceedings of the IM 2017 - 2017 IFIP/IEEE International Symposium on Integrated Network and Service Management*, 134–141. 10.23919/INM.2017.7987273

Team Handbook. (n.d.). Retrieved April 5, 2018, from https://about.gitlab.com/handbook/

Telemanagement Forum – TMF. (2018). *GB922 Information Framework R17.5*. Parsippany, NJ: SID.

The ETSI Test Description Language TDL and its Application. (2014). *Proceedings of the 2nd International Conference on Model-Driven Engineering and Software Development*. doi:10.5220/0004708706010608

TS23.501. (2017). *System Architecture for the 5G System*. 3GPP.

TS29.500. (2017). *5G System; Technical Realization of Service Based Architecture; Stage 3*. 3GPP.

Tsagkaris, K., Nguengang, G., Peloso, P., Fuentes, B., Mamatas, L., Georgoulas, S., . . . Smirnov, M. (2013). *Unified Management Framework (UMF) Specifications - Release 3 – UniverSelf Deliverable D2.4*. Retrieved from http://www.univerself-project.eu/tecnical-reports

Velasco, L., Castro, A., King, D., Gerstel, O., Casellas, R., & López, V. (2014). In-Operation Network Planning. *IEEE Communications Magazine*, *52*(1), 52–60. doi:10.1109/MCOM.2014.6710064

Verma, A., Pedrosa, L., Korupolu, M., Oppenheimer, D., Tune, E., & Wilkes, J. (2015). Large-scale cluster management at Google with Borg. *Proc. European Conf. on Computer Systems, EuroSys.* 10.1145/2741948.2741964

Vincenzi, M., Antonopoulos, A., Kartsakli, E., Vardakas, J., Alonso, L., & Verikoukis, C. (n.d.). *Multi-tenant slicing for spectrum management on the road to 5G.* Retrieved from https://upcommons.upc.edu/bitstream/handle/2117/111753/IEEE WCM Slicing 5G 2017.pdf

Voulgaris, S., Gavidia, D., & Van Steen, M. (2005). Cyclon: Inexpensive membership management for unstructured P2P overlays. *Journal of Network and Systems Management, 13*(2), 197–217. doi:10.100710922-005-4441-x

Wang, H., Xie, H., Qiu, L., & Yang, Y. (2006). COPE: Traffic engineering in dynamic networks. *ACM Sigcomm*, 99–110. doi:10.1145/1151659.1159926

Watsen, K. (2017, February). *RFC 8071.* Retrieved from IETF: https://tools.ietf.org/html/rfc8071

Watsen, K. (2018, March 5). *Zero Touch Provisioning for Networking Devices.* Retrieved from IETF: https://tools.ietf.org/html/draft-ietf-netconf-zerotouch-21

Watsen, K., Abrahamsson, M., & Farrer, I. (2018). *Zero Touch Provisioning for Networking Devices.* Retrieved from https://tools.ietf.org/html/draft-ietf-netconf-zerotouch-21

Watsen, K., Richardson, M., Pritikin, M., & Eckert, T. (2018). *Voucher for Bootstrapping Protocols. RFC8366.* Internet Engineering Task Force. doi:10.17487/RFC8366

Weikum, G., & Vossen, G. (2001). *Transactional Information Systems: Theory, Algorithms, and the Practice of Concurrency Control and Recovery.* San Francisco, CA: Morgan Kaufmann Publishers Inc.

Wikipedia. (2018). *Information Security.* Retrieved June 4, 2018 from .

Williams, L., Kudrjavets, G., & Nagappan, N. (2009). On the Effectiveness of Unit Test Automation at Microsoft. *2009 20th International Symposium on Software Reliability Engineering.* 10.1109/ISSRE.2009.32

Wojdak, W. (2003). *Rapid Spanning Tree Protocol: A new solution from an old technology.* Reprinted from CompactPCI Systems.

Work Programme - Work Item Detailed Report. (n.d.). Retrieved April 5, 2018, from https://portal.etsi.org/webapp/workProgram/Report_WorkItem.asp?wki_id=54031

Wu, Q., Liu, W., & Farrel, A. (2018). *Service Models Explained.* Internet Engineering Task Force, RFC8309. Retrieved from https://datatracker.ietf.org/doc/rfc8309/

Wu, Q., Litkowski, S., Tomotaki, S., & Ogaki, K. (2018). *YANG Data Model for L3VPN Service Delivery. RFC8299.* Internet Engineering Task Force. doi:10.17487/RFC8299

Xie, C., Bi, J., Yu, H., Li, C., Sun, C., Liu, Q., ... Liu, S. (2017). ARPIM: IP address resource pooling and intelligent management system for broadband ip networks. *IEEE Communications Magazine, 55*(6), 55–61. doi:10.1109/MCOM.2017.1601001

Xu, L. (2016). CogNet: Network Management Architecture Featuring Cognitive Capabilities. *European Conference on Networks and Communications (EUCNC 2016).* 10.1109/EuCNC.2016.7561056

Yin, L., Zhi-An, S., & Jiang, T-T. (2017). A Software Reliability Test Suite Generating Approach Based on Hybrid Model for Complex Equipment System. *2017 International Conference on Dependable Systems and Their Applications (DSA).* 10.1109/DSA.2017.32

Yoshida, M., Shen, W., Kawabata, T., Minato, K., & Imajuku, W. (2014). MORSA: A multi-objective resource scheduling algorithm for NFV infrastructure. *16th Asia-Pacific Network Operations and Management Symposium (APNOMS)*. 10.1109/APNOMS.2014.6996545

Yu, M., Yi, Y., Rexford, J., & Chiang, M. (2008). Rethinking virtual network embedding: Substrate support for path splitting and migration. *Computer Communication Review, 38*(2), 19–29. doi:10.1145/1355734.1355737

Zhang, Q., Xiao, Y., Liu, F., Lui, J. C. S., Guo, J., & Wang, T. (2017). Joint Optimization of Chain Placement and Request Scheduling for Network Function Virtualization. *Proceedings - International Conference on Distributed Computing Systems*, 731–741. 10.1109/ICDCS.2017.232

Zhang, X., Phillips, C., & Chen, X. (2011). An overlay mapping model for achieving enhanced QoS and resilience performance. *2011 3rd International Congress on Ultra Modern Telecommunications and Control Systems and Workshops (ICUMT)*, 1–7.

Zhu, Y., & Ammar, M. (2006). Algorithms for Assigning Substrate Network Resources to Virtual Network Components BT. *Infocom IEEE International Conference on Computer Communications*.

About the Contributors

Mohamed Boucadair is an IP Networking Strategist within "Strategies for IP Networking" team part of the Wireline Technical Strategy Directorate, which is part of Orange. In charge of novel IP techniques activity within "Strategies for IP Networking" team. Contributes to the definition of strategies for fixed networks, based upon the integration of IPv6, intra and inter-domain routing, Policy-based management, SDN (Softwire-Defined Networking), Network Automation, Service Function Chaining (SFC), Power-Aware Networking, Multipath TCP, Dynamic Service Negotiation & Provisioning, Performance-based Routing, Multicast, Denial of Service, transport protocols evolution, autonomous networking, multi-homing and traffic engineering techniques, including an active contribution to the IETF standardization (45 IETF RFCs) and patent deposits.

Christian Jacquenet graduated from the Ecole Nationale Supérieure de Physique de Marseille, a French school of engineers. He joined Orange in 1989, and he's currently the Referent Expert of the "Networks of the Future" Orange Expert community. Until March 2017, he was the Director of the Strategic Program Office for advanced IP networking within Orange Labs. He is also the head of Orange's IPv6 Program that aims at defining and driving the enforcement of the Group's IPv6 strategy. He conducts development activities in the areas of Software-Defined Networking (SDN), IP networking, automated service delivery procedures, including service function chaining techniques. He authored and co-authored several Internet standards in the areas of dynamic routing protocols and resource allocation techniques, as well as numerous papers and books in the areas of IP multicast, traffic engineering and automated IP service delivery techniques. He also holds several patents in the areas of advanced home and IP networking techniques.

* * *

Haytham Assem is the Chief Scientist & Technical Manager of the IBM Innovation Exchange in Dublin, Ireland. Haytham has several years of industrial experience with the first two years in Mentor Graphics and the latter years in IBM. His research interests include Machine Learning, Big Data, Urban Computing and Ubiquitous Computing. Currently, he is leading the Cognitive Computing Group (CCG) in Dublin, passionate about using Machine Learning & Cognitive Computing Technologies for solving problems in Urban Computing, Social and Telco domains. Haytham has several papers published in top tier conferences and more than 35 patents filed with IBM in different domains such as: Smart Cities, Machine Learning and, Social Network Analysis. In 2015, Haytham has been named as the youngest Master Inventor in IBM history. In addition, Haytham received 12 IBM Invention and Achievement awards and won the first announced Innovation Development Team (IDT) Award by IBM in 2015. Haytham's work has been covered in various media articles including: Daily Mail, Live24 news, Datetime, IBM. com, and others. Early in 2018, Forbes announced Haytham as one of the top 30 under 30 Innovators and disruptors across Europe in the Technology Sector.

Jaafar Bendriss is a PhD student at Orange Labs and Telecom SudParis. He obtained his MS+Eng degree at the University of Technology of Troyes in 2014. His main work revolves around Network Function Virtualization and their management using Machine Learning techniques.

Amal Benhamiche holds a PhD in Combinatorial Optimization from Paris-Dauphine University. She joined Orange Group in 2016 and is currently part of the Traffic and Resource Modelling department at Orange Labs (France) where she works on optimization problems for future networks.

Jun Bi received BS, MS, and Ph.D. degrees in computer science from Tsinghua University, China. He was a postdoctoral scholar and a research scientist at Bell Labs. Currently he is the Changjiang Scholar Distinguished Professor, Deputy Dean of Tsinghua University Institute of Network Science & Cyberspace and Director of its Network Architecture Research Division. His research interests include Internet architecture and protocols. He published over 200 papers and 4 Internet RFCs. He is the senior member of IEEE and ACM.

Teodora Sandra Buda is a Principal Investigator in machine learning and performance engineering within Innovation Exchange, IBM Ireland. She is also an Associate Faculty Lecturer at National College of Ireland, where she teaches Programming for Big Data for the Higher Diploma in Data Analytics. Prior to joining IBM, she worked as a Big Data Engineer on the High Performance Computing Cluster at LexisNexis, Ireland and has been involved in multiple EU and Irish research projects. Her main interests are machine learning, performance engineering, resource management, distributed processing and big data analytics. Sandra received her Bachelor in Computer Engineering from the "Politehnica" University of Timisoara, Romania in July 2010, studying one semester at Universidad "Politécnica" de Madrid, Spain with the Erasmus scholarship. Upon finishing her Bachelor, she worked in industry for one year through AIESEC at an SME in Brasilia, Brazil. Following that, Sandra completed her PhD in Computer Science with a scholarship from University College Dublin (UCD) and IBM in the Performance Engineering lab.

Yannick Carlinet received his Ph.D. in computer science from University of Rennes, France in 2010. He also received an engineering degree from the "Ecole Nationale Supérieure des Mines de Nancy" in 1999. He is a researcher at Orange since 2002 and his current topics of interest include traffic supervision, traffic modeling, Content Distribution Systems and Network Virtualization. He is a former guest researcher at NIST (in the Advanced Network Technologies Division). He is the owner of 7 patents in the network field.

Laurent Ciavaglia works at Nokia Bell Labs in Paris, France inventing new technologies for networks, turning concepts into real-life innovations. Recently, he is having fun (and some headaches) trying to combine network management and artificial intelligence. Laurent serves as co-chair of the IRTF Network Management Research Group (NRMG), and participates in standardization activities related to network and service automation in IETF and ETSI. Laurent serves as Editor-in-Chief of the IEEE

SDN initiative Softwarization newsletter, vice-chair of the IEEE CNOM, and Standards Liaison Officer of the IEEE Emerging Technologies Initiative on Network Intelligence, and regularly in the technical committees of IEEE, ACM and IFIP conferences and journals in the field of network management and network Softwarization. Laurent has co-authored more than 80 publications and holds 35 patents in the field of communication systems.

Luis Miguel Contreras Murillo earned a Telecom Engineer degree at the Universidad Politécnica of Madrid (1997), and holds an M. Sc. on Telematics from the Universidad Carlos III of Madrid (2010). Since August 2011 he is part of Telefónica I+D Telefónica Global CTO unit, working on SDN, virtualization, transport networks and their interaction with cloud and distributed services, as well as on interconnection topics. He is part-time lecturer at the Universidad Carlos III of Madrid. Before the position in Telefónica he worked in Alcatel Spain and Orange Spain. He is actively involved in research and innovation activities, with 40+ papers published in relevant journals, magazines and conferences, being regular speaker at reputed academic and industrial events. He has participated on the projects funded by the EU GEYSERS (FP7) and XIFI (FI-PPP), and the ESA funded project CloudSat. Currently he is working on the EU H2020 projects 5G-Crosshaul and 5GEx, where he leads the architectural work package On the standardization arena, he is active contributor to IETF (authoring two RFCs), ETSI and ONF, where he organized and coordinated the first-ever proof-of-concept on the application of SDN to wireless transport networks, hold in October 2015 on 5TONIC premises.

Maja Curic is a PhD student at Technische Universität München. She received her M.Sc in electrical engineering from University of Sarajevo, Bosnia and Herzegovina. Currently she works as a researcher in Huawei Research Center in Munich, Germany. Her research interests include programmable networks and services.

Zoran Despotovic received his M.Sc from University of Belgrade, Serbia and his PhD in Computer and Communication Systems from École Polytechnique Fédérale de Lausanne (EPFL), Switzerland. The main areas of interest during his doctoral studies were Peer-to-Peer systems. After his graduation he worked for NTT DOCOMO until September 2011, first as a senior researcher and then as a manager. The main topics of interest during that time were peer-to-peer systems, mobile network architectures, cloud computing and network virtualization. In 2011 he joined Huawei European Research Center in Munich, where he still works as a principal engineer. His main topics of interest are QoE for mobile broadband networks and future network architectures, including Software Defined Networking. He published around forty scientific papers.

Toerless Eckert is a Distinguished Engineer at Huawei USA working on future network architecture and standards. He is a generalist for networks and distributed systems technologies and an SME on IP multicast, network and applications integration and network automation. Toerless has more than 30 years experience working for both research organizations and commercial vendors. This includes planning, building and operating networks with new technologies, supporting customers around the globe to do these same, researching, developing, standardizing and building network products, protocol and services and developing advanced, network integrated multimedia applications.

Eric Gourdin obtained his Ph.D. in 1994 from Ecole Polytechnique de Montréal. He worked on a TMR Grant from 1996 to 1998 at ULB (Université Libre de Bruxelles) on traffic management problems. He joined Orange (former France Telecom) in 1998 where he has been working on various network optimization problems, with a special focus on IP networks. He has been in charge of OR (Operation Research) for several years and has lead various optimization oriented projects at Orange Labs. He has co-authored many scientific papers and contributed to several books. His latest interest lies in routing problems, Content Delivery architectures and virtual networks. Since nov 2016, he is in charge of the department TRM (Traffic Resource Management).

Lisandro Zambenedetti Granville is Associate Professor at the Federal University of Rio Grande do Sul (UFRGS). He served as TPC Co-Chair of IEEE ICC 2018, IEEE NetSoft 2018, IFIP/IEEE DSOM 2007 and IFIP/IEEE NOMS 2010, and as General Co-Chair of IFIP/IEEE CNSM 2014. Lisandro served as Chair of the IEEE ComSocs Committee on Network Operations and Management (CNOM), and is currently Co-Chair of the IRTFs Network Management Research Group (NMRG), and President of the Brazilian Computer Society. His interests include network management, software-defined networking (SDN), and network functions virtualization (NFV).

Imen Grida Ben Yahia is currently with Orange Labs, France, as a Research Project Leader on Autonomic & Cognitive Management and Expert in Future Networks. She received her PhD degree in Telecommunication Networks from Pierre et Marie Curie University in conjunction with Télécom Sud-Paris in 2008. Her current research interests are autonomic and cognitive management for software and programmable networks that include artificial intelligence for SLA and fault management, knowledge and abstraction for management operations, intent- and policy-based management. She contributed to several European research projects like Servery, FP7 UniverSelf, the H2020 CogNet and currently the 5G SliceNet. Imen authored several scientific conference and journal papers in those research domains. She gave speeches and talks in different conferences on the topic of Network Intelligence.

Artur Hecker (MSc Universität Karlsruhe and PhD ENST, Paris) is Director of Future Network Technologies at the Munich Research Center of Huawei Technologies. From 2006 to 2013, Artur was Associate Professor at Télécom ParisTech, where he was leading Security and Networking research. Overall, Artur looks back at more than 15 years of entrepreneurial, academic and industry experience in networks, systems and system security.

Ramin Khalili is a senior researcher at Huawei Research Center in Munich, working in area related to performance evaluation and optimization, machine learning, and the design of (wireless) networking systems. He has received his doctorate from Universite Pierre et Marie Curie in France, and worked as a researcher at various places, including UMASS-Amherst, EPFL, and TLabs, before joining Huawei. He has earned various awards, including ACM CoNEXT 2012 best paper award, ACM e-Energy 2011 best paper award, and special prize for exceptional performance from the dean of computer and communication department at EPFL in 2011.

Kireeti Kompella, currently SVP and CTO of Juniper Engineering at Juniper Networks, was formerly CTO at Contrail Systems. Dr. Kompella has deep experience in Packet Transport, large-scale MPLS, VPNs, VPLS, and Layer 1 to Layer 3 networking, and has been very active in the IETF, as past chair of the CCAMP Working Group and as author of several Internet Drafts and RFCs across several WGs (including CCAMP, IS-IS, L2VPN, MPLS, NVO3, OSPF, and TE). His focus now is on Self-Driving Networks and the application of Machine Learning to networking. Prior to Juniper, Dr. Kompella worked on file systems at NetApp, SGI, and ACSC (acquired by Veritas). Dr. Kompella received his BS EE and MS CS at IIT, Kanpur, and his PhD in Computer Science at USC, specializing in Number Theory and cryptography.

Chen Li is a senior engineer of IP & Future Network Research Center, China Telecom Corporation Limited Beijing Research Institute. His research fields include next generation network, software-defined networking and network function virtualization. He led or participated in several projects which were supported by the government.

Patrick N. Moore is presently the Director of Network Automation Strategy at Itential LLC, where he has responsibility for managing the delivery of services to implement network automation for clients leveraging Itential products, custom solutions, and 3rd party controllers and orchestrators. With more than 25 years' experience in the implementation and management of networks, including membership in the Society of Cable Telecommunications Engineers, North American Network Operators Group and Open Networking Foundation, regularly speaks at conferences and has been published multiple times on the topic of network automation. He holds a BS in Mathematics from Jacksonville State University.

Jéferson Campos Nobre is an assistant professor at Polytechnic School of the University of Vale do Rio dos Sinos (UNISINOS). His is an Electrical Engineer (2003), Master (2010) and Doctor (2015) in Computer Science at Federal University of Rio Grande do Sul (UFRGS). Between 2011 e 2012, Jéferson performed Ph.D studentship at Cisco Systems in USA, performing research tasks about Network Management in the Network Operating Systems Technology Group (NOSTG). Besides that,Jéferson was a post-doctoral researcher at Federal University of Pará (UFPA) during 2016. Jéferson is also a invited professor for undergraduate and graduate courses from several universities. Previously, Jéferson was a telecom engineer in different mobile network operators in Brazil. His main research topics include Autonomic Networking, Network Management and Security, Measurement Mechanisms, and Delay/ Disruption Tolerant Networking (DTN).

Pierre Peloso is a research scientist at Nokia Bell Labs in Paris Saclay area. His initial research was related to the physics and architecture of optical and IP networks. He then focused on autonomic networking and network management research. He performed his work through his involvement in different external collaborations and the achievement of their prototypes. He noticeably held the role of lead architect for the FP7-UniverSelf project. Since then, he has been involved in standardization for autonomic networking inside IETF working group ANIMA. Nowadays, he pursues work on network management considering also the context of home and enterprise networks. He has been recognized as a Distinguished Member of the Technical Staff of Bell Labs in 2010.

Nancy Perrot received her Ph.D. degree in Applied Mathematics with a specialization in Operations Research from the University of Bordeaux1 in 2005. She joined the Orange Group in 2005, first as a post doc on optical networks optimization. Then she has been working as a researcher on various network optimization problems, the most recent of which relate to software-defined networks and network virtualization as well as end-to-end security in heterogeneous systems. She has co-authored many scientific publications and she has supervised several M.Sc. and Ph.D. students. She is currently leading the Operations Research activities inside Orange.

Morgan Richomme is a NFV senior architect in Orange. Primarily involved in VoIP and IMS (IP Multimedia Subsystem) deployment for Orange affiliates, he has more than 10 years' experience in managing open source solutions. Morgan was instrumental in the setup, launch and run of the international Emerginov project, an open source PHP PaaS targeting education and co-innovation within Africa. He organized and animated several hackathons in both Africa and Europe. He was the project Team Leader of the OPNFV functest project dealing with functional testing of open source Telco Cloud solutions as defined in OPNFV. He has been elected as TSC member by his pair in 2016 and is still an OPNFV ambassador. He is currently involved in ONAP project, an open source project aiming to manage the lifecycle of Virtual Network function (VNF). Morgan Richomme is an open source evangelist of the Orange core network division and part of the Orange networking expert community.

Qiong Sun is SDN Technology R&D Center Director of China Telecom Beijing Research Inst. She is also the Board member of LFN. She has been engaged in IP/IPv6 network design, next generation network architecture (CTNet2025) design for China Telecom for over 8 years. Currently she is leading the next generation operation system design for China Telecom.

Yi Sun is a founding member and chief architect at vArmour. He has more than 20 years of software development and management experience in networking, security, SDN, real time computing and mobile domains. He was a senior software architect and engineering manager at various networking and security firms such as Juniper Networks, Netscreen and Lynx Software. He is a cofounder of Android-X86.org, an open source project. He holds multiple US patents in networking and cyber security.

Xun Xiao is now a researcher with Huawei Munich Research Center (MRC) in Germany since Dec. 2014. Before joining Huawei MRC, from Dec. 2012 to Nov. 2014, he was a postdoctoral researcher in Max Planck Institute of Molecular Cell Biology and Genetics (MPI-CBG) in Dresden Germany. He earned his Bachelor and Master Degrees both in computer science at South-Central University for Nationalities in Wuhan China, in 2006 and 2009 respectively. He earned his Ph.D. degree in computer science at City University of Hong Kong in 2012. His main research interests focus on applying optimization and game theory in networking resource allocation. In addition, he is also interested in system engineering.

Chongfeng Xie received Ph.D. degree in electronic engineering from Tsinghua University, China. He was a visiting scholar in University of California, Los Angeles (UCLA), in 2009. Now he works in IP and Future Network Research Center at China Telecom Beijing Research Institute (CTBRI). His research interests include network architecture and protocols, IPv6, SDN, NFV, etc. He published more than 20 papers and 10 Internet RFCs or drafts.

Meng Xu is a founding engineer and chief architect at vArmour Networks, where he has led the team in building a series of data center micro-segmentation solutions as well as application security and policy computation products. Meng has over 20 years of experience in networking, security, data center and cloud developments, and has served in various architect and engineering leadership roles. Meng holds several patents in security, virtualization and data center technologies.

Myo Zarny is a technologist with over 20 years of experience in enterprise networking and network security engineering. He is Director of Product Management at vArmour, responsible for developing the firm's application security, analytics and policy products. Prior, he spent most of his career at Goldman Sachs where he was a senior network architect and VP of network security engineering. He is a coauthor of RFC-8192 and RFC-8300, and holds a patent on microsegmentation.

Index

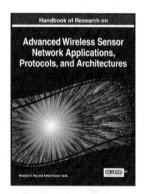

Ensure Quality Research is Introduced to the Academic Community

Become an IGI Global Reviewer for Authored Book Projects

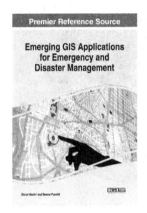
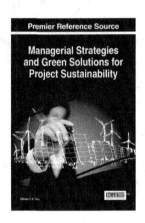

The overall success of an authored book project is dependent on quality and timely reviews.

In this competitive age of scholarly publishing, constructive and timely feedback significantly expedites the turnaround time of manuscripts from submission to acceptance, allowing the publication and discovery of forward-thinking research at a much more expeditious rate. Several IGI Global authored book projects are currently seeking highly qualified experts in the field to fill vacancies on their respective editorial review boards:

Applications may be sent to:
development@igi-global.com

Applicants must have a doctorate (or an equivalent degree) as well as publishing and reviewing experience. Reviewers are asked to write reviews in a timely, collegial, and constructive manner. All reviewers will begin their role on an ad-hoc basis for a period of one year, and upon successful completion of this term can be considered for full editorial review board status, with the potential for a subsequent promotion to Associate Editor.

If you have a colleague that may be interested in this opportunity, we encourage you to share this information with them.

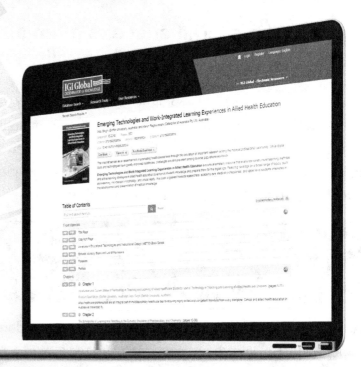

Printed in the United States
By Bookmasters